Casebook and Study Guide

Abnormal Psychology
Second Edition

Rosenhan and Seligman

CHRISTOPHER PETERSON
University of Michigan

with Lisa M. Bossio

W • W • NORTON & COMPANY • NEW YORK • LONDON

Grateful acknowledgment is extended to the holders of copyright for granting permission to reprint excerpts on the following pages: *p. 12*: Foucault, M. *Madness and civilization: A history of insanity in the Age of Reason*, translated by Richard Howard. Copyright © 1973 Pantheon Books, A Division of Random House, Inc. Reprinted by permission. *p. 19*: Steinmann, A. The psychopharmacological treatment of Anna O. In M. Rosenbaum & M. Muroff (Eds.), *Anna O.: Fourteen contemporary reinterpretations*. Copyright © 1984 Free Press. Reprinted by permission. *p. 39*: Burgess, A.W., & Holmstrom, L.L. *Rape: Victims of crisis*. Copyright © 1974 Robert J. Brady Publishers. Reprinted by permission. *p. 40*: Brownmiller, S. *Against our will: Men, women and rape*. Copyright © 1975 Simon & Schuster, Inc. Reprinted by permission of Simon & Schuster, Inc. *pp. 57–58*: Alexander, F. *Psychosomatic medicine: Its principles and applications*. Copyright © 1987, 1950 by W.W. Norton & Company, Inc. Reprinted by permission. *p. 63*: Cousins, N. *Anatomy of an illness as perceived by the patient*. Copyright © 1979 by W.W. Norton & Company, Inc. Reprinted by permission. *pp. 77 and 79*: Bernheim, K.F., & Lewine, R.R.J. *Schizophrenia: Symptoms, causes, and treatments*. Copyright © 1979 by Kayla F. Bernheim and Richard R.J. Lewine. Reprinted by permission of W.W. Norton & Company, Inc. *p. 88*: Laing, R.D. *The divided self: An existential study in sanity and madness*. Copyright © 1965 Tavistock Publishers. Reprinted by permission. *p. 109*: Gravitz, H.L., & Bowden, J.D. *Recovery: A guide for adult children of alcoholics*. Copyright © 1985 Simon & Schuster, Inc. Reprinted by permission of Simon & Schuster, Inc. *p. 117*: Goldstein, W. *An introduction to the borderline conditions*. Copyright © 1985 Jason Aronson Inc. Reprinted by permission. *p. 120*: Spitz, R.A. Anaclitic depression: An inquiry into the genesis of psychiatric conditions in early childhood, II. *The Psychoanalytic Study of the Child, 2,* 313–357. Copyright © 1946 by Ruth S. Eissler, M.D. Reprinted by permission of Ruth S. Eissler, M.D.

Cover illustration: *Composition: "City People"* by Abraham Rattner. Collection of Charles E. Curry. Photograph courtesy of Kennedy Galleries, Inc., New York.

The text of this book is composed in Times Roman. Composition by Roberta Flechner.

ISBN 0-393-95698-9

W. W. Norton & Company, Inc., 500 Fifth Avenue, New York, N.Y. 10110
W. W. Norton & Company Ltd., 10 Coptic Street, London WC1A 1PU

5 6 7 8 9 0

CONTENTS FOR THE CASEBOOK

CONTENTS FOR THE STUDY GUIDE

TO THE STUDENT

This casebook and study guide is intended to help you understand the material presented in the second edition of *Abnormal Psychology* by David Rosenhan and Martin Seligman. The material here is a substitute neither for the textbook nor for your time and energy. However, it should help make *Abnormal Psychology* familiar and comfortable. The cases and the study guide sections correspond to chapters in the textbook, and you should read and study them in conjunction with the relevant material in *Abnormal Psychology*.

Casebook

The casebook was prepared with the assistance of Lisa M. Bossio. We greatly appreciated the suggestions of Donald Fusting, David Rosenhan, and Martin Seligman.

Each case amplifies or exemplifies a major idea in the text. We envision the cases sparking discussion, in and out of class. Cases are deliberately brief, so they can best serve as starting points. We tried to choose cases that raise central issues, and in each instance, we follow the case with questions that direct you to some of these issues. But don't be constrained by our questions.

Study Guide

Each chapter in the study guide has several sections: "Chapter Overview," "Essential Terms," "Sample Exam," (multiple-choice questions), "Self-Test (fill-in questions), "Tying It Together," "Further Readings," "Term-Paper Topics," and "Exercises." These sections serve several purposes: (a) aiding you in acquiring the important ideas in each chapter; (b) preparing you for course examinations; (c) helping you to see the big picture presented in *Abnormal Psychology*; and (d) directing you toward further activity: reading, writing, and doing. Let me comment briefly on the sections contained in each chapter of this study guide.

Chapter Overview

The chapter overviews describe the purpose of the chapter and its major topics so that you will know what to expect as you read the textbook. You may find it useful to read the chapter overview before you read the chapter itself. The study guide's overviews have been written independently of the textbook's summaries, so that you will have two points of view about each chapter's important ideas.

Essential Terms

Students are often overwhelmed by the vocabulary of psychology. Some of these terms seem familiar; we use them in everyday conversation. Other terms seem esoteric; we must write them down to remember their meanings and even how to spell them. And yet other terms may seem downright contrary. But the terminology of abnormal psychology is not just jargon. It is the way in which the understanding provided by psychology is expressed; in a sense, it *is* the understanding. Imagine watching a baseball game and not knowing what strikes or balls are, or what an infield fly, a balk, or a designated hitter is. You are not watching the same game as an individual who has mastered baseball terminology. The same is true of psychology. When its terminology is mastered, psychology looks different—richer, more coherent, and more interesting.

For this reason I have extracted from each chapter the important terms and provided a brief definition of each. In most cases, I have tried to use the phrasing of the textbook in explaining a term. However, the best way for you to learn terms is to express them, in your own words. As you read the textbook, you may wish to compile your own list of definitions. Another good way to master terms is to think of your own example for each one. If you think of *positive reinforcement* as an environmental event that increases the frequency of an operant, you understand this term on an abstract level. If you also think of *positive reinforcement* as exemplified by the Hershey bar (with almonds) you buy after studying in the library for three hours, you will have an additional understanding of this term.

Sample Exam (Multiple-Choice Questions)

For each chapter there are multiple-choice questions that cover the textbook material. They follow the order of the textbook chapter. In almost all cases there is one best answer, but for a handful of questions there are several "best" answers.

Multiple-choice questions like these are often used in examinations because they employ a common format with which to assess several different aspects of what you have learned: (a) factual information; (b) distinction among concepts; (c) similarity among concepts; (d) application of concepts; and (e) integration of concepts. Most of the questions cover material presented in the textbook, but some of the questions deal with material that was not presented. Abnormal psychology is a growing and changing field, and in some areas, knowledge is incomplete. The textbook authors have been careful to distinguish what is known from what is not known, and I have tried to help you make the same distinction by asking you in some questions about what is *not* the case.

How should you make use of these multiple-choice questions? Read the chapter carefully. Then answer the questions. They touch upon most of the important concepts in a chapter, so you should try to see the point of each. If possible, try to answer a question before you look at the alternatives. When you do look at the choices, do more than select the best answer. Reflect on why your answer strikes you as being the best, and, just as important, reflect on why the other alternatives do not seem as good. When you take a multiple-choice examination in a course, you will probably employ strategies of answering, such as eliminating obviously wrong alternatives and making educated "guesses" from among those left. You can practice such strategies

here, but I urge you also to understand why any given strategy does or does not work.

Correct answers and the page numbers on which the answer can be found in the text are provided at the end of each sample exam. Don't peek!

Self-Test (Fill-In Questions)

There are fill-in questions for each chapter. Like multiple-choice questions, they are also frequently used in examinations, where they do a good job of assessing your knowledge of terminology and your understanding of concepts. Unlike multiple-choice questions, fill-ins ask you to produce answers rather than just recognize them. The questions, which follow the order of the textbook chapter, ask you to provide the missing word or phrase. Use these questions as you use the multiple-choice questions: answer them correctly, but also know why your answers are good ones.

Again, correct answers are provided at the end of each self-test.

Tying It Together

In this section I briefly describe some of the ways in which the chapter pertains to other chapters—those already read as well as those yet to be read. Abnormal psychology is a coherent discipline, but students encountering the field for the first time may see it as more fragmented than it really is. The textbook covers topics ranging from brain chemistry to historical change, from unconscious desires to political persecution. In particular, the disorders described in the textbook are extremely varied, representing the range of human experience.

What I have tried to do is to direct you toward the forest that may be hidden by the trees of abnormal psychology. The "big picture" that emerges will be your own, but I hope that this aspect of the study guide starts you on your way toward seeing it.

It may be a good idea to read "Tying It Together" before as well as after studying each chapter. There is nothing in these sections to memorize. Rather, they contain food for thought. Psychologists have long investigated learning and memory, and what has emerged from this research is that individuals usually do not learn material verbatim. Rather, they learn the gist of material; they abstract its major points. Details are not "stored" in memory so much as they are "reconstructed" from the structure created by the individual when material is learned. To the degree that you are successful in creating your own "big picture" to serve as this structure, the material in *Abnormal Psychology* will be yours long after your psychology course is completed.

Further Readings

Almost all topics in abnormal psychology are interesting, but the textbook cannot go into as much detail as you may like for all topics. What I have tried to do in this section of the study guide is to suggest some readings pertinent to the textbook chapter. Some of these are from technical sources, while others are from popular sources. You should be able to find most of them in your college library or in your campus bookstore.

Term-Paper Topics

Your instructor may ask you to write a paper as part of the course. This section contains possible topics for such papers. Each suggestion asks you to take a stance on some issue and then to defend it as best you can. In my opinion the key to a good paper is knowing, before you start, just what you are trying to convey to the reader. Once you have this knowledge, you also have answers to question that may otherwise seem quite puzzling to you: "How should it start?" "How should it end?" "How many pages should it be?" "How many references should it have?"

P.S. Type your papers! In the last twelve years, I have read and graded thousands of student papers. Please believe me, typed papers are better for all concerned.

Exercises

Abnormal psychology is not a discipline that lends itself to an undergraduate laboratory course. Unlike the classic studies in physics, chemistry, or general psychology, the classic investigations of abnormal psychology are not easily replicated. Considerations of time, money, and ethics preclude replication attempts. However, learning is well served by active doing, and for this reason I have tried to come up with exercises that take off from the chapter material. These are not the same thing as laboratory experiments, but they serve the same purpose: providing you with hands-on experience with concepts important to the field.

In each case the exercises bring important ideas down to earth. Some pose thought problems for you to solve. Others ask you to see a movie or read a book. And still others ask you to talk to people. These latter exercises must be approached carefully because they may infringe on people's right not to be talked to about certain matters. It would be wise to follow the ethical guidelines employed by psychologists in their research. Prior to the exercise, (a) tell the persons what you will require of them and obtain their permission to conduct the exercise (informed consent); (b) inform the persons that they can cease their interaction with you at any time (right to withdraw); and (c) let them know that you will answer any questions about the exercise to the best of your ability when it is finished (debriefing). If you have any doubts or questions about the appropriateness of an exercise, please consult with your instructor!

Christopher Peterson
Ann Arbor, MI
July 1988

The Damm Family:
Homeless in America

What is abnormal? Rosenhan and Seligman argue that abnormality involves a social judgment based on fuzzy criteria. There is no line, rigidly drawn, that separates the normal from the abnormal. If we try to draw such a line, many of us would be straddling it. A good example of the fuzziness of abnormality has to do with the homeless in America—a growing problem.

You may have seen homeless individuals in cities large and small: people carrying around their possessions in bags and satchels, people who look tired and dirty, people without anything to do except stay alive. Your reaction might be curiosity. It might be repulsion. And it might be the judgment that these people are crazy. Why would someone live like that unless they were abnormal? The purpose of this case is to examine this last reaction to the homeless in light of Rosenhan and Seligman's criteria of abnormality.

First, let us give you some background about homelessness. Accurate estimates of its prevalence are difficult to nail down, but there might be as many as 2 to 3 million individuals in our country without homes. (The total population in the United States is about 300 million.) One-third of the homeless are families with children.

These numbers may seem too vast to comprehend. So, we'll reduce the scope and concentrate just on the city of New York. Contemplate these more specific statistics provided by Kozol (1988):

- In 1978, on any given night, 900 homeless families were provided shelter by city authorities; by 1987, this figure had grown to 5,000 families.
- By 1990, more than 400,000 people in New York will be homeless, out of a total population of 7 million.
- In 1983, there were 500,000 legal actions for eviction; half of these were against people on welfare.
- In 1987, the city spent $274 million to provide emergency shelter for the homeless, yet this figure doesn't begin to come close to providing the needs of everyone without a home.

It's difficult to understand homelessness just by reading statistics. Let's take an even closer look, and focus on a particular case of a homeless family. We take the details from a picture essay in *Life* magazine (Fadiman, 1987). You may want to read the essay itself, because it is accompanied by a series of gripping photographs.

Keep several things in mind when you read about this homeless family. First, why might one be tempted to regard these people as abnormal? Second, why might this be a hasty conclusion? Taken together, your answers to these two questions illustrate the important idea that judgments of abnormality are complex and reflect a host of social biases.

THE DAMM FAMILY

Any homeless family has one overriding complaint: no home. But other problems entwine themselves with this central complaint. They may be causes or consequences of homelessness. Regardless, homeless people experience difficulties in bunches.

Indeed. The Damm family as described in *Life* has their share of problems. To introduce the family, there is mother Linda (age twenty-seven), father Dean (age thirty-three), daughter Crissy (age six), and son Jesse (age four). And then there is the family dog Runtley (who bears an ironic resemblance to Spuds McKenzie of beer advertisement fame), as well as their 1971 Buick Skylark, which provides them not only with transportation but with shelter. Don't read past this phrase without understanding what it means: the Damm family lives in their car.

Originally from Colorado Springs, the family moved to the Los Angeles area after Linda and Dean were unsuccessful in finding jobs for two years. Linda had worked as a nursing-home aide, and Dean as a truck driver. They heard that work was more plentiful in California than Colorado. Further, California welfare allotments are the highest in the nation.

Once in California, they did not find work. And since the family arrived with an empty gas tank and less than ten cents, their life became a constant struggle to find money to buy necessities. They sold parts of their car. They pawned their wedding rings. Dean regularly sold blood plasma. Not only was he given $10 for each visit, but a meal as well. He remarked that the blood center is one of the few clean places he ever visited.

The Damms were homeless, broke, and unemployed. Even more problems followed. They found a federally subsidized shelter in which to stay, but they were evicted because they had children. The federal grant for homeless families has expired. If they were childless, they could have continued to stay. Then they applied for welfare, and faced a number of bureaucratic hassles. A check was mysteriously delayed. An-

other check was made out for too much money, and the family had to
return it instantly or risk further problems. In one incident, Dean lost
his temper at the guard in the welfare office. "I'm sick of your goddamn
system . . . you're jerking my family around! You're treating us like
garbage! *We are not garbage!*"

Naturally, homelessness took a toll on the children. The little girl became hyperactive whenever she saw her parents pack up their belong-
ings to move, which of course was frequently. She was enrolled in a
school, and Linda and Dean worried about how she would be treated
by classmates and teachers. Crissy's clothes, from charitable organizations, didn't fit. She had no food to bring for lunch. In one poignant
scene, the Damm family dropped her off at school in the morning,
along with other parents doing the same. The car behind them was a
Porsche.

Jesse reacted to the stress of homelessness by becoming timid and
overly obedient. He was too young for school, and the family was unable to find subsidized child-care for him. So he accompanied Linda
and Dean on their rounds: to the welfare office, to look for inexpensive
apartments, to the trade schools that his parents attended.

They constantly searched for a place to live. Although it is illegal to
discriminate against individuals on welfare, this was apparently a common practice among landlords. Even if someone was willing to rent to
such individuals, the typical demand for a damage deposit, plus first
month's rent, and last month's rent, was simply too much for the family
to provide up front. Another problem resulted because they had no
telephone: no landlord could ever call them back about an apartment.
The little money they did have went into pay telephones, twenty-five
cents at a time.

Are you surprised that Dean and Linda sometimes fought? Are you
surprised that they had feuds with their relatives in the Los Angeles
area? We could detail other problems that the Damm family encountered, but we think by now you have a sense of their lot in life.

ABNORMALITY AND NORMALITY

Remember the elements of abnormality that Rosenhan and Seligman
present. How many of these apply to the Damm family? First there is
suffering. Certainly, on this score, the family qualifies as abnormal.
Their situation is difficult, physically and mentally. They must go without food. They must suffer the scorn of others, perhaps even their own
scorn at times.

Second there is *maladaptiveness*. Again, aspects of the Damms' existence strike us a maladaptive. They are unable to find work. They have
trouble providing a roof over their heads. They cannot raise their children in the way we suspect would be optimal.

At the same time, Linda and Dean do things that show intelligence and industry. Each is enrolled in technical classes, Linda to learn emergency medical care and Dean to learn telephone installation. Each is the best student in their respective class. If they complete a twenty-six-week program, they quite possibly will find skilled work. Here Linda and Dean are acting in an extremely adaptive fashion, and don't seem at all abnormal.

Next there are *irrationality and incomprehensibility*. These are more difficult criteria to apply. On the face of it, the existence of the Damm family is irrational. Why would anyone live in a car? But when we learn something about their history, it is not difficult to understand them. We can make sense of what they are all about. If anything, society as a whole may strike us as irrational and incomprehensible. Consider all of the Catch-22s inherent in the welfare system, in the shelter system, and in the work force.

What about *unpredictability and loss of control*? By the account we've presented, the Damm family does not exemplify this criterion of abnormality. Dean loses his temper, but only occasionally. The rest of the family is extremely disciplined in their behavior.

Are these people *vivid and unconventional*? Yes, certainly, at least to those of us with middle-class sensibilities. The pictures in *Life* magazine that accompany the story of the Damms are haunting. Their car is missing the hood and windows on the driver's side. The upholstery is torn. They have ninth-hand clothing. It is difficult for them to keep themselves clean. Linda owns no underwear.

The Damms elicit *observer discomfort* in those who are in contact with them. The whole concept of homelessness in America makes us uncomfortable, for various reasons. It contradicts what we have been taught to believe, that the United States is the land of hope and plenty. It makes us feel just a trifle guilty, doesn't it, that people can live such a barren existence while we worry about the details of our material worlds? Oh dear, what brand of CD player should we buy this week? What color telephone? Which pair of pants?

Indeed, one worrisome sign of observer discomfort is the growing outrage people feel about the homeless. Here we mean not outrage against the social and political situation that makes homelessness possible but against the homeless individuals themselves. Kozol (1988) details striking instances of backlash, including random violence against homeless individuals. Sleeping individuals have been set afire, or stabbed to death, or chased with dogs. He quotes an internal memo from a train station that denies the homeless shelter within. "Can't we get rid of this trash?" When grocers or restaurant owners put waste food in their dumpsters, they may adulterate it—i.e., poison it—so that the homeless will not forage through it. Is observer discomfort behind this? We would think so.

This leads us to the next criterion: *violation of moral and ideal standards*. The homeless are at odds with what we think is right. People ought not to behave as they do. They ought not to make us feel guilty. They ought to have a home, a career, and a well-scrubbed family.

Philosophers use the term "naturalistic fallacy" to refer to the confusion between what is and what ought to be. The naturalistic fallacy is often implicit in rationalizations of the status quo: we have always lived this way, and therefore it is natural and good that we continue to live this way. A variant of the naturalistic fallacy may come into play with our reactions to the Damm family and others in their situation. They live this way, therefore they ought to live this way, and they must—indeed—be condemned if they do. Psychologists call this "blaming the victim."

So, the Damm family qualifies as abnormal by several of the criteria specified by Rosenhan and Seligman. But they don't qualify as abnormal by other criteria. And even the criteria that stamp them as abnormal are not all that clear-cut.

The magazine story ended on an upbeat note. The Damms found an apartment they could afford, and they moved in. Linda walked by a barrel that day, with a sign saying "Help the Homeless." She dropped in a handful of pennies.

DISCUSSION QUESTIONS

1. In cases of unambiguous abnormality, many of which you will read in this casebook, psychologists are interested in *etiology*: the causes of a problem. Even in ambiguous cases like that of the Damm family we can wonder about the factors that lead to homelessness. What might some of these be? Are your explanations consistent with the fact that homelessness is greatly increasing in our country?

2. Psychologists are also interested in the *prognosis* of a case: what will happen to someone's problem as time passes. How do you think the Damm family will be doing in five years or ten years? What can their children expect? More generally, what is the prognosis for the general problem of homelessness in America?

3. Often, an important part of a case is the description of a *preferred treatment* for a particular problem. So, what concretely could be done to help the Damm family? What concretely could be done to "treat" the problem of homelessness? What concretely could be done to prevent homelessness in the first place?

4. Consider the plight of the homeless mentally ill, people without a home who are unambiguously abnormal. The Damm family is most definitely not in this group, although there are large numbers of homeless individuals who have profound problems: anxiety, depression, substance abuse, schizophrenia, and so on. How are your answers to questions 1, 2, and 3 changed when we focus on the homeless who are mentally ill?

REFERENCES

Fadiman, A. (1987). A week in the life of a homeless family. *Life,* December 10, pp. 30–38.

Kozol, J. (1988). *Rachel and her children: Homeless families in America.* New York: Crown Publishers.

Wolf Madness

The text observes that abnormality is recognized in all times and places, although the particular thoughts, feelings, and actions that are judged abnormal may show considerable variation. This is an important idea at several levels. One reading of the relativity of abnormality conjures up a host of possible worlds. In each world, people act much the same. In some worlds, a particular behavior is considered abnormal, and in other worlds, the same behavior is considered normal.

An example here comes from the realm of delinquency. When an adolescent from the lower class steals a hubcap, this is a crime (i.e., abnormal). But if the thief is from the upper class, then the theft of a hubcap is a prank (i.e., normal). Another example is the so-called double standard of sexual conduct. Females and males who engage in the identical style of sexual behavior are regarded quite differently.

There is another level, however, to the relativity of abnormality. Consider possible worlds in which people act very differently. It is not just the judgments of abnormality versus normality that change as we move from one world to another, but the behaviors to which these judgments apply as well. Striking examples of this second level of the relativity of abnormality come from historical and cultural studies that reveal problems elsewhere that have no clear counterpart in our own world.

One instance of this is mentioned briefly by Rosenhan and Seligman: *lycanthropy*, or wolf madness, the topic of this case. This form of abnormality, present in Europe from about 300 A.D. to 1700 A.D. involved a person's belief that he or she was indeed a wolf. Someone who was so afflicted acted out this belief:

> He will goe out of the house in the night like a wolfe, hunting about the graves of the dead with great howling, and plucke the dead mens bones out of the sepulchers, carrying them about the streetes, to the great feare and astonishment of all them that meete him . . . Melancholike persons of this kinde, have pale faces, soaked and hollow eies, with a weake sight, never shedding one teare to the view of the worlde, a drie toong, extreme thirst, and they want spittle and moisture exceedingly . . . . (Tommaso Garzoni, 1600, quoted by Jackson, 1986, pp. 346–347).

EXPLANATIONS OF WOLF MADNESS

Since wolf madness occurred during the animistic era, you might think that people afflicted with this disorder were thought to be werewolves; that is, people who turn into wolves when there was a full moon. This is a reasonable guess, but it's an oversimplification. Although people in the Middle Ages indeed believed in werewolves, those with wolf madness were carefully distinguished from those who were werewolves. So, a werewolf was someone who became a literal wolf, whereas a person with wolf madness became a wolf only in his or her own mind. The first instance was obvious enchantment, and the latter instance was obvious madness.

Animistic explanations were nonetheless applied to wolf madness. Let us give you some background. Thousands of years ago, people used elaborate classification systems to explain the world. Specifically, they used the same number of pigeonholes, over and over. (Nowadays we call these approaches numerology, and classify them with astrology and the like.) Great significance was placed on these particular numbers, and to this day some of them survive as "lucky" numbers, for example, seven, or eleven, etc.

At any rate, one popular system emphasized the number four. Groupings of four mapped onto each other, with any single explanation also being many explanations, because groupings were nested. There were four elements of the universe: earth, fire, water, and air. There were four seasons. There were four ages of man. There were also four humours or bodily fluids: blood, yellow bile, black bile, and phlegm. Hippocrates, the Greek physician who gave us the Hippocratic Oath that physicians still swear, based much of his system of medicine on the notion of the four humours. Good health was marked by a balance among the fluids. Indeed, the expression "to be in good humor" still refers to happiness and health. Poor health followed an imbalance among the humours. Depending on which humour predominated, illness took various forms. Thus, too much black bile created melancholy, a state usually marked by excessive sadness. Today we call such states depression, and we explain them in various scientific ways. But in the Middle Ages, explanations were phrased in terms of the four humours, with wolf madness considered by most as a variation of melancholia.

Is this an animistic explanation? It certainly is not what we would call a scientific account. The way in which black bile produced melancholia was by wandering about the body, finding no exit, and lodging itself in the soul. The soul then took on the character of black bile, causing distress for the person and reflecting all other parts of the universe with which this humour was aligned.

So, wolf madness was understood as a metaphor for excess black bile, which in turn was a metaphor for many other notions. Remember from the descriptions we quoted that individuals with wolf madness were always thirsty. This makes perfect sense because black bile corresponds with the element of earth. As the earth absorbs water, so too does the person with wolf madness.

One of the interesting things about melancholia in bygone times is that it was characterized by gastric symptoms, as befitting a problem produced by excess black bile. Diagnosis of melancholia could be made by looking at the color of someone's vomit. Black vomit meant melancholia. Today, however, gastric upset and vomiting have little or nothing to do with depression, as you can see by reading Chapter 11 of the textbook. Thus, not only do explanations of disorders change, but so too does the complex of symptoms that make up the disorder. In many ways, melancholia of the Middle Ages and depression of the twentieth century are continuous, but in other ways they are not. This suggests to us that our explanations play some role in shaping the phenomena to which they are applied.

So what puts the humours out of balance? There were various possibilities, including improper diet and excessive indulgence. Wolf madness was thought to be more likely in February, implying the influence of the stars. Rabies was another possible cause, one very much consistent with an animistic view of the world. Rabies is transmitted through the bite of a mad animal. Once bitten, you were thought to take on the character of that animal. Direct intervention by divine powers could also be responsible. Do you remember King Nebuchadnezzar as described in the Bible? Because of his sins, he went mad. His symptoms seem like wolf madness: "He was driven from among men, and ate grass like an ox, and his body was wet with the dew of heaven till his hair grew as long as eagles' feathers, and his nails were like birds' claws" (Daniel 4:33).

Nebuchadnezzar was rescued from his madness when he learned to praise and honor God. What happened to other individuals with wolf madness? According to available accounts, some got better by themselves, others wasted away, and still others suffered a violent death. When treatment was possible, it followed two strategies. First, the amount of black bile was decreased through moistening with broths, syrups, and baths. Second, the other humours were strengthened through purging and bloodletting. Also thought to be helpful in restoring one's humours to good balance were soothing music and poetry!

DISCUSSION QUESTIONS

1. Lycanthropy is not the only disorder to pass in and out of history. Consider hysteria or catatonic schizophrenia on the one hand as instances of abnormality that are rarely encountered today, and depression or anorexia on the other hand as instances of abnormality that are much more common now than ever before. What factors are responsible for the waxing and waning of disorders across history?

2. There have been no cases of wolf madness reported since the 1700s. Specifically, why did it go away?

3. What problems in contemporary life might our descendants one thousand years in the future find as exotic as we find wolf madness today?

4. Granted that someone believes he or she is an animal, why was a wolf so frequently chosen in the Middle Ages? Other "popular" choices were dogs. Why not butterflies? Why do some people judged to be abnormal today believe themselves to be machines?

5. From your reading or traveling, do you know any examples of psychological problems in different cultures that have no counterpart in our own? How are these explained in their native cultures? How would we explain them?

6. Granted that problems often change across time and place, what significance can we attach to the handful of psychological difficulties that stay much the same? (We won't tell you what these are, so why don't you speculate about what they might be.) Are we justified in arguing that these must have a biological basis?

REFERENCE

Jackson, S. W. (1986). *Melancholia and depression from Hippocratic times to modern times.* New Haven, CT: Yale University Press.

Tracking Down the
Ship of Fools

In Chapter 2 of the text, the authors mention *narrenschiffe,* so-called ships of fools. Not so long ago, textbooks of abnormal psychology, when recounting the history of abnormality, included mention of these ships as a common "treatment" of abnormality during the Middle Ages. Here are some representative descriptions from three different texts (quoted by Maher & Maher, 1982, p. 758):

> Ships filled with disturbed and disturbing people were sent from port to port in Europe. At dockside the "ship of fools" would be displayed to the public for a fee (Price & Lynn).

> [The mad] . . . were often separated from the rest of society by being set adrift on "ships of fools" on the rationale that they must have come, not from solid land, but the ceaseless unrest of the sea, to which they should return (Altrocchi).

> Another interesting practice common in the fourteenth and fifteenth centuries was to relinquish the insane to a boatman who would often deposit them in another city (Rosen, Fox, & Gregory).

Rosenhan and Seligman go on to note, however, that the "ship of fools" is now believed to be a myth. They cite an article by Winifred and Brendan Maher (1982), who tracked down the original story and found it to have no basis in reality. In this case, we'd like to describe their scholarship and share with you their conclusions about why these nonexistent ships became very real when the history of abnormality was retold.

MICHEL FOUCAULT'S *MADNESS AND CIVILIZATION*

In the 1960s, an influential book by French psychologist Michel Foucault was translated into English. Foucault presented a provocative history of insanity. He also introduced the ship of fools. Subsequent writers cited Foucault's *Madness and Civilization* when they wanted to document these ships because Foucault argued strongly for their reality and indeed their popularity.

> . . . the *Narrenschiff* . . . had a real existence . . . these boats that conveyed their insane cargo from town to town. Madmen then led an easy wandering existence. The towns drove them outside their limits; they were allowed to wander in the open countryside, when not entrusted to a group of merchants or pilgrims. The custom was especially frequent in Germany . . . It is not easy to discover the exact meaning of this custom. One might suppose it was a general means of extradition by which municipalities sent wandering madmen out of their own jurisdiction . . . [but this] hypothesis will not in itself account for the facts, since certain madmen, even before special houses were built for them, were admitted to hospitals and cared for (Foucault, 1973, pp. 8–9).

Foucault concluded that the practice stemmed from the belief that water might purify the souls of the mad. Regardless, as told by Foucault, the story of the ship of fools was a compelling one, and it became a part of the generally accepted history of abnormality.

MAHER AND MAHER'S DETECTIVE WORK

Skepticism concerning ships of fools is not hard to generate once it is appreciated that sea vessels of the fourteenth and fifteenth century were small and costly. Maher and Maher (1982) raised a very reasonable question: Would the masters of these ships sacrifice their precious cargo space to carry the insane? Further, would they entrust their ships to mad navigators? Something here isn't plausible. Consider the late twentieth century. Would we place the insane on jumbo jetliners? Hardly. If we put them anywhere, it would be on AMTRAK or Greyhound. In the Middle Ages, the equivalent would be carts and certainly not ships.

So, Maher and Maher began a search, writing to various libraries and museums in Europe that specialized in maritime history. Was there any record of departures, arrivals, taxes, or duties that described such ships or those who sailed upon them? Were there diaries or logs from those who sailed on ships of fools or encountered them in their travels? Did any of these ships survive? How about artifacts from them? Did any of these ships have a name? To all their inquiries, the answer was no.

They did gather ample evidence that the *idea* of a ship of fools existed in the Middle Ages. In literature, it was a metaphor for the human condition, used to emphasize that all people are fools who live without destinations. (And in that era, the interpretation of this metaphor was clearly religious.) But the metaphor had nothing to do with literal ships. And it certainly did not apply in particular to the insane.

Maher and Maher also learned that "ships of fools" appeared in medieval carnivals as what we would nowadays call floats. A ship on wheels was pulled by men in a procession. The ship was decorated to represent the medieval vision of hell, and on its mast was someone costumed as a devil . . . or a fool. At the end of the procession, the boat was burned. Again, the idea here is important, but it has nothing to do with real boats or real insane people.

CONCLUSIONS

Where does this leave the ship of fools? Maher and Maher conclude that Foucault appropriated the idea from medieval accounts without appreciating the metaphorical nature of the *narrenschiffe*. Subsequent authors appropriated Foucault's account, again not appreciating that they were treating a metaphor as a historical fact.

Two questions arise. First, why was the metaphor of the ship of fools so compelling that respected scholars confused it with facts? Second, what difference does it make to our present understanding of abnormality? Maher and Maher suggest that the answers to these two questions are closely related.

The ship of fools, or any metaphor for that matter, is compelling to the degree that it fits with one's pre-existing beliefs about the world. As Rosenhan and Seligman point out, the metaphor conveys strongly the idea that society at large rejects abnormality. This is not simply an idle notion, but rather a strong belief that reflects political and moral ideology. If you are captivated by the metaphor of the ship of fools, you probably believe that society at large is not always kind, that it may scapegoat the unfortunate, that it creates problems like madness but then takes no responsibility for solving them. This ideology is alive and well today. In fact, many psychologists would ascribe to it, including us. Read between the lines of Case 1 and see our outrage that homelessness exists in today's world.

So, historical accuracy is important simply because our ideologies may lead us to make the "facts" more compelling than they really are. Indeed, Maher and Maher show that Foucault's account of the ship of fools grew like Pinocchio's nose as retold by subsequent writers, who embellished it with their own details.

Historical accuracy keeps us honest as psychologists. As you will see in the text, there is more than enough difference of opinion about how to explain the facts concerning abnormality. We need as little controversy as possible concerning what the facts themselves actually are.

DISCUSSION QUESTIONS

1. The image of the fool is a popular one in Western culture. Think of Don Quixote as described by Cervantes or Falstaff as described by Shakespeare. (And if you're not so literate, think of The Three Stooges, Pee Wee Herman, the Beastie Boys, or any of the movie characters played by Jerry Lewis!) Further, the image of the fool is frequently merged with that of the madman. What do they share in common? How do they differ? What is the relevance of these traditional images to our modern conception of abnormality?

2. Maher and Maher (1982) chide psychologists for not always being careful with their historical homework. They suggest as an example of careful scholarship an article by Spanos (1978) on witchcraft and abnormality. Read this article, and then discuss the text's treatment of witchcraft in light of the points Spanos makes.

3. Let's not be too hard on psychologists. It is a human tendency to go beyond the facts, to tell better stories than what really happened. Two books we've greatly enjoyed reading are by Jan Harold Brunvand (1981, 1984). He recounts what he calls urban legends. These are stories that everyone has heard from someone who heard it from someone else who heard it from their cousin. We're sure you know about the person who found a rat in a soft drink bottle and was given a huge settlement to keep quiet about it, or the stupid babysitter who mistakenly put a child in the microwave oven to dry its hair, or the hospital patient who had the wrong leg amputated, and so on. According to Brunvand, the people in these tales are sailing somewhere on the ship of fools, because there is really no evidence for any of these legends. Nevertheless, the stories persist. Your task: explain why we find such stories so compelling. What do urban legends share in common? (And where is Elvis Presley really living?)

4. If you haven't read too far in the Rosenhan and Seligman text, this is a good opportunity to examine beliefs you have about abnormality that may or may not be based on reality. What do you know about electroconvulsive shock treatments? What do you know about lobotomies? Is there such a thing as seasonal affective disorder? What is the relationship between schizophrenia and creativity? How common is multiple personality disorder? How successful is the insanity plea? Keep your opinions in mind when you get to the pertinent chapters in the text.

REFERENCES

Brunvand, J. H. (1981). *The vanishing hitchhiker: American urban legends and their meanings.* New York: Norton.

Brunvand, J. H. (1984). *The choking doberman and other "new" urban legends.* New York: Norton.

Foucault, M. (1973). *Madness and civilization: A history of insanity in the Age of Reason.* New York: Vintage.

Maher, W. B., & Maher, B. (1982). The ship of fools: *Stultifera Navis* or *Ignis Fatuus? American Psychologist, 37,* 756–761.

Spanos, N. (1978). Witchcraft in histories of psychiatry: A critical analysis and an alternative conceptualization. *Psychological Bulletin, 85,* 417–439.

Anna O. from
Different Perspectives

In the field of abnormal psychology, different theoretical approaches compete in explaining particular instances of abnormality. The text calls these approaches models. Each model consists of a set of related assumptions about human nature, about the nature of abnormality, and about the treatment of abnormality.

First, the *psychodynamic model* regards people as energy systems, striving for quiescence. Problems are cast in energy terms as well. Symptoms represent a bad investment, so to speak, of someone's finite psychological energy. The energy devoted to symptoms is not available for more productive use elsewhere. Treatment from the psychodynamic perspective attempts to free the energy tied up in symptoms, leading to a "thanks, I needed that" reaction from the person with the problem.

Second, the *biomedical model* regards people as physical systems, striving for equilibrium. When problems develop, they are seen as due to physical damage, breakdown, or malfunction. Solutions to problems are similarly physical. The biomedically oriented therapist tries to undo or correct the presumed physical breakdown, relying on drugs, operations, and related interventions.

Third, the *environmentalist model* proposes that people are thinking hedonists (or hedonistic thinkers, if you prefer). We try to maximize rewards and minimize punishments, and our cognitive abilities are brought into service to achieve this aim. When we have problems, the environmentalist model looks either to the situation or to the way that we make sense of the situation. Perhaps the environment encourages us to act in abnormal ways. Perhaps we lack the skills, behavioral and/or cognitive, to thrive in a particular environment. The solution? Change the world, or change the person, depending on the nature of the particular problem.

Each model has its own domain, a set of problems and treatments that it does a particularly good job of explaining. At the same time, appreciate that a specific model can never fully capture everything important about abnormality. A model represents a deliberate narrowing of perspective, in the hope that only the unimportant aspects of a phenomena are lost. The text warns that this hope is not always met. Sometimes models put blinders on psychologists.

In this case, we'd like to illustrate how different models can profitably be applied to the same instance of abnormality. Each thereby achieves its own insights. Our inspiration for this case is a book that examines one of history's most famous patients—Anna O.—from fourteen contemporary perspectives (Rosenbaum & Muroff, 1984). We won't describe fourteen models for you, just the three featured in your text. Appreciate, however, that these three models do not exhaust the theoretical possibilities.

THE CASE OF ANNA O.

Anna O. is the name given to the *first* psychoanalytic case, a woman seen in therapy not by Sigmund Freud but by his early collaborator Josef Breuer. Anna O. was an intelligent young woman who showed a variety of puzzling symptoms (Breuer & Freud, 1895). At various times, she lost the ability to move her right arm, her legs, and her head. She was unable to feed herself. She had a chronic cough. She had trouble seeing, and thus could not read or write. Sometimes she spoke in broken sentences, complaining that snakes were in the room with her. She often did not hear what people said to her. She was weak, yet she refused food that was offered to her. At times she was suicidal.

At the time she saw Breuer, Anna O. was given the diagnosis of hysteria, which means that she experienced loss of bodily functions, yet these losses could not be traced to an underlying physical cause. Breuer followed a common procedure for treating hysteria by hypnotizing Anna O. and suggesting that she give up her symptoms. It soon became clear, however, that it was not necessary to hypnotize her in order to relieve her various symptoms. Instead, she merely needed to talk about the symptoms and about when they had first appeared. This would bring her dramatic relief.

Some writers speculate that the patient rather than the doctor should be credited with inventing this new technique. At any rate, Anna O. called this talking about her symptoms and their history "chimney-sweeping." Psychology has come to know it by the more formal name of *catharsis*. The specific technique of saying whatever comes to mind, without censoring, is now called *free association*. Freud developed free association into the principle technique of psychoanalytic therapy, regarding it as a way of unearthing unconscious material and freeing the psychological energy that kept this material hidden.

There is more to the case than what we've described so far. Although Breuer successfully treated her symptoms, Anna O. did not make an immediate recovery. Indeed, after Breuer ended therapy with her, Anna O. experienced a bizarre state in which she mistakenly yet vividly believed she was giving birth to a child, and that the child was Breuer's!

This phantom pregnancy shook Breuer greatly, but Freud saw it as compelling proof that the relationship between client and therapist could be highly entwined with unconscious desires and wishes.

The real name of Anna O. was Bertha Pappenheim, and she was an extremely important person in her own right. In her later life, Pappenheim was an active feminist and a pioneer in developing the field of social work in Germany. She was a leader in the Jewish community. She was a champion of women and children and the mentally retarded. When she died in 1936 at the age of seventy-seven, Bertha Pappenheim was an honored and respected citizen of the world.

THE PSYCHODYNAMIC MODEL

How is the case of Anna O. interpreted from the perspective of the psychodynamic model? First, her problems are seen as a tying up of psychological energy into symptoms. Second, the impetus for the symptoms are seen in her unconscious motives. Breuer and Freud felt that Anna O. had experienced an unacknowledged sexual attraction for her father. Because this attraction was threatening to her conscious mind, it was actively repressed. Because her energy had no healthy outlet, it was converted into unhealthy symptoms. Third, the particular symptoms she experienced bore a symbolic relationship to her underlying motives. By this view, the snakes she hallucinated were phallic symbols, representing her hidden desires for her father. Fourth, she became attracted to Breuer because he stood for her father. Her false pregnancy seemed a rather blatant representation of her unconscious wishes.

Therapy proceeded by freeing up psychological energy. Remember how this was done. Anna O. talked about the circumstances in which particular symptoms had first developed. In the course of her associations, she would come up with the heretofore unconscious motive that the symptom represented. Once brought into open air, the motive no longer produced the symptom.

THE BIOMEDICAL MODEL

Does the psychodynamic model provide the only way to interpret the case of Anna O.? Not at all. Martorano (1984) described how a biologically oriented psychiatrist would proceed. The initial treatment would be with drugs. Successive medications would be tried, and the pattern of her responses would aid in the diagnosis. Martorano observed that on the face of it, Anna O. seemed to qualify for the diagnosis of hysteria neurosis. This problem is believed to have excessive anxiety at its base, and so the first medication to be tried would be a so-called minor tranquilizer, probably diazepam (trade name: Valium).

Some of Anna O.'s symptoms suggested that she might be depressed: loss of appetite, weight loss, sluggishness, and so on. If tranquilizing medication did not bring relief to her symptoms, then Martorano would prescribe antidepressants, and see their effect. Here patience is required, because it takes at least several weeks for antidepressants to have an effect on the symptoms of depression.

One more possibility is that Anna O. suffered neither from hysteria nor from depression, but from schizophrenia. Again, some of her symptoms were consistent with this diagnosis: hallucinations, delusions, and neglect of self-care. So, medication appropriate to this problem would be tried, one of the so-called major tranquilizers (like Thorazine or Haldol). What effects would these medications have on Anna?

Let us comment on the strategy of treatment that Martorano outlined. It may seem a trial-and-error process, but this is not inherent in the biomedical model. Rather, Breuer did not describe the symptoms of Anna O. in a way that makes it simple to choose among competing diagnoses. One of the contemporary benefits of careful diagnosis is that it provides the therapist with a good clue about how to proceed with treatment. Different problems are best treated with different interventions, in this case, various medications.

In Breuer's era, precise diagnosis did not pay this dividend, since the pharmacological treatment of abnormality was very much in its infancy. If Anna O. were to walk into Dr. Martorano's office today, he would undertake a thorough diagnostic interview, with the hope of clarifying her specific diagnosis. Then he would be able to prescribe a specific drug known to have a beneficial effect in such cases.

THE ENVIRONMENTALIST MODEL

One more perspective on the case of Anna O. comes from the environmentalist model. Proponents of this view of abnormality would start by locating the woman in her environment. Let us do so first in broad terms:

> [She was] . . . a young woman of the last part of the nineteenth century. Although Anna O.'s formal education had ended at age sixteen, she was a quick and avid learner and continued to educate herself. No matter how closeted she was by the religious orthodoxy of her family, she could not have helped by absorb the intellectual ferment of her time. Like a true Viennese, she must have visited the coffee houses, enjoyed the theater and music, read the journals and books of her day. . . . Certainly her achieving self was fostered by the excitement of what was occurring in the world around her . . . (Steinmann, 1984, p. 119).

Now let us sketch the more immediate environment of this intelligent young woman living in a fascinating city in a fascinating era. Anna O. spent her days nursing her dying father. Despite the possibilities that beckoned her, Anna O.'s day-to-day life was narrow and boring.

According to the environmentalist model, anyone in Anna O.'s circumstances would respond by doing something to create change. The major option available to Anna O. was to act physically ill. Perhaps her symptoms represented a way to escape an intolerable situation. Indeed, her symptoms put her in a position to collaborate with an influential physician in developing an intriguing therapy technique. The relief of her symptoms may have been due to the reinforcement she gained by letting each symptom go, one at a time, and thereby pleasing Breuer. Her distress when Breuer terminated therapy, and hence their relationship, was understandable.

A contemporary therapist working from the vantage of the environmentalist model would pay great attention to the details of Anna O.'s situation in life. The therapist might encourage Anna O. to continue her education, to find friends and activities outside her immediate family, to articulate her desires and find ways to satisfy them. That Bertha Pappenheim eventually lived a distinguished life should not obscure the fact that her accomplishments might well have been possible in a more direct and satisfying fashion.

DISCUSSION QUESTIONS

1. Which of the three explanations of the case of Anna O. do you find most compelling? Which is the least compelling? Explain your reasons.

2. The three models of abnormality need not contradict each other. How might the psychodynamic, biomedical, and environmentalist approaches be combined to explain the problems of Anna O. and how to treat them?

3. If you know anything about sociobiology, speculate about how the case of Anna O. might be conceptualized from an evolutionary viewpoint. How is hysteria adaptive? How did this syndrome evolve? Are there analogues or equivalents of this disorder among animals?

4. Place Anna O. in her cultural and historical setting. How would a feminist explain her case?

5. According to the approach to abnormality known as family systems, all problems are best conceived and treated as problems of the family. By this view, Anna O. would simply be the member of her family with the blatant symptom. How would a family systems therapist treat the Pappenheim family?

6. The case of Little Hans is another important psychoanalytic study

(Freud, 1909). It is described in Chapter 8 of the text. How might this case be interpreted from the perspective of the biomedical model? From the perspective of the environmentalist model?

7. Analogously, the case of Little Albert plays an important role in the environmentalist model (Watson & Rayner, 1920). Read the description of this case in Chapter 8 of your text. How might this case be interpreted from the perspective of the biomedical model? From the perspective of the psychodynamic model?

8. What would a unified model of abnormality look like? Does so-called eclectic therapy exemplify a unified approach?

REFERENCES

Breuer, J., & Freud, S. (1895). Studies on hysteria. In J. Strachey (Ed. and Trans.), *The complete psychological works* (Vol. 2). New York: Norton, 1976.

Freud, S. (1909). Analysis of a phobia in a five-year-old boy. In J. Strachey (Ed. and Trans.), *The complete psychological works* (Vol. 10). New York: Norton, 1976.

Martorano, J. T. (1984). The psychopharmacological treatment of Anna O. In M. Rosenbaum & M. Muroff (Eds.), *Anna O.: Fourteen contemporary reinterpretations*. New York: Free Press.

Rosenbaum, M., & Muroff, M. (Eds.) (1984). *Anna O.: Fourteen contemporary reinterpretations*. New York: Free Press.

Steinmann, A. (1984). Anna O.: Female, 1880–1882; Bertha Pappenheim: Female, 1980–1982. In M. Rosenbaum & M. Muroff (Eds.), *Anna O.: Fourteen contemporary reinterpretations*. New York: Free Press.

Watson, J. B., & Rayner, R. (1920). Conditioned emotional reactions. *Journal of Experimental Psychology, 3*, 1–14.

Causal Explanations and Depression: Research As a Woven Fabric

Chapter 6 in your text describes a variety of research methods, all useful in learning about the causes and treatments of abnormality. Several important points are made:

- Methods are tools, not ends in themselves.
- Because the purposes to which methods are put vary, there is no single best method for all purposes.
- Each method has its own inherent strengths and weaknesses.
- These strengths and weaknesses differ across methods.
- The best research strategy may be one that simultaneously uses a variety of methods.

Presumably, multi-method investigations use strategies that complement each other. The weaknesses in one method are offset by the strengths of the others, and vice versa. Findings from such investigations represent a "woven fabric" of results more substantial and convincing than any particular strand.

This is fine advice in the abstract, but it is seldom put into concrete practice. There are several reasons for this. First, not all questions in psychology admit to different methods. Sometimes it is all a researcher can do to devise one way of investigating a topic of interest to her. Second, particular research methods can be difficult to master or implement. A given psychologist may not have the time or skill or resources to mount a multi-method investigation. A good experimentalist may be all thumbs, so to speak, when carrying out a case study. Third, sometimes the results from studies using different methods are not as substantial as a researcher would hope. Instead of a woven fabric, what results is a heap of thread, or worse.

Many findings in psychology are method-bound, which means that some procedures reliably produce the results, but other procedures don't. On a theoretical level, this is a considerable bother and embarrassment, since it implies that a theory has been pitched at the wrong level of abstraction. On a practical level, researchers may be dissuaded from attempting a multi-method investigation in the first place. Suppose you use three different research strategies to attack the same topic and end up with three different results. What then do you do?

These ideas help explain the relative scarcity of multi-method research in psychology. They don't detract, however, from the occasional lines of research that do correspond to the ideal of a woven fabric. In this case, we'd like to describe one example of converging results from different research methods. You'll encounter these findings elsewhere in the text (in Chapter 11 on depression, to be specific). Here let us focus less on abnormality and more on research per se. The example comes from work done in collaboration with Martin Seligman, one of the authors of your text. We intentionally carried out simultaneous investigations of the same hypothesis using disparate strategies of investigation (Peterson & Seligman, 1984). We hoped that results would converge. They did.

THE HYPOTHESIS

Our general prediction stemmed from a cognitive perspective on depression. According to this view, certain ways of thinking put an individual at risk for depression when bad events occur. Other ways of thinking protect someone from the depressing effect of unfortunate occurrences. Specifically, here is our hypothesis: people who explain bad events with causes that point to something about themselves ("it's me") that is long-lasting ("it's the way I am") and pervasive ("it's going to mess up everything") are apt to become depressed in the wake of bad events. The opposite way of explaining bad events, with causes external to the self that are transient and circumscribed, allows people to encounter bad events yet shrug off their psychological effects.

Suppose two people get in an automobile accident. Standing around waiting for the police to show up, the first person shakes his head and says to the second, "I knew this was going to happen. Bad things always happen to me. I'm such a loser. I'm such a careless person. I'm going to die old and lonely, if I live that long, which I doubt. I saw the accident starting to happen, but I froze. I always freeze when the situation calls for action." The second person also shakes her head, but in responding to the first person, she says something quite different. "Oh well, accidents are just one of those things. I don't have much experience with them, and I never expect to have another one. Did you know I was on my way to a job interview? When I reschedule it, I bet I get an offer. I usually make an impression on people." Which person do you think is more likely to be depressed following the accident?

In real life, sometimes there are unambiguous causes of events. When someone explains these events, they say nothing that is psychologically meaningful. Our prediction is not meant to apply in these instances, but rather it is meant to apply when there is legitimate uncertainty about what causes what. Then a person's causal explanations reveal something about his or her psychological makeup. All other things being equal, we predict that one style of explaining bad events makes depression more likely, whereas the opposite style makes depression less likely.

RESEARCH STRATEGIES

Here are thumbnail sketches of the various ways we tested this prediction. We developed a questionnaire that measured how people explained hypothetical bad events, and then we administered this questionnaire in a *correlational study* along with a measure of the degree to which someone experienced common depressive symptoms, like sleep disturbance, loss of weight, and thoughts of death. Consistent with our prediction, the way people explained bad events indeed related to the extent of their reported depression. A *meta-analysis* of one hundred different correlational studies testing our prediction showed it to be generally supported (Sweeney, Anderson, & Bailey, 1986).

Such correlational studies show a link between the two variables, explanatory style and depression, but they fail to address the direction of the relationship. Perhaps depression affects the way someone explains events, which exactly reverses our prediction. Accordingly, we thought a *longitudinal study* was needed, one in which causal explanations were measured prior to depression. Again, several such studies supported our hypothesis.

We also conducted several *experiments of nature*, measuring the way people explain bad events prior to some disaster in their lives. Specifically, we studied one group of individuals who did poorly on a midterm examination and another group of individuals who were sent to prison. (Of course, these events differ, but from the respective viewpoints of those experiencing them, they are both negative.) By the prediction, only people with a pessimistic explanatory style should become depressed following failure or imprisonment. This is exactly what we found.

Laboratory models were also part of our research strategy. We manipulated in the lab success and failure at tasks, and the way that people explained these. Then we measured their mood. Were some subjects more depressed than others? Note here that depressed mood is regarded as analogous to a full-blown depression, a simplifying assumption like those made in all laboratory models. And as we predicted, pessimistic causal explanations coupled with failure led to a depressed mood. Other causal explanations and/or success did not.

Finally, we conducted several *case studies* by devising a way of measuring causal explanations from written material. Specifically, we would read such material until we found a bad event that the person explained. We then coded this explanation along the dimensions of theoretical concern. Did our codes relate to other things we knew about the person?

One study looked at transcriptions of therapy sessions with a patient, Mr. Q, notable for his rapid mood shifts, in and out of depression (Peterson, Luborsky, & Seligman, 1983). Did particular causal explanations foreshadow his mood shifts as our hypothesis suggests? By comparing causal explanations before the different types of mood shifts, we were able to answer this question once more in the affirmative.

In a second study, we used a similar procedure with a much better-known subject, Lyndon Baines Johnson (Zullow, Oettingen, Peterson, & Seligman, 1988). We coded causal explanations from his press conferences and found that "depressive" explanations were followed by passive foreign policy decisions, whereas "nondepressive" explanations were followed by active decisions, specifically escalation of the Vietnam War. What an interesting study, if we do say so ourselves.

Taken together, results from these different lines of research converge to support our prediction, and thus they exemplify the woven fabric that Rosenhan and Seligman recommend. In passing, let us note that another way to weave a fabric strongly is to obtain the same results with different samples of research subjects: children, adolescents, college students, adults, psychiatric patients, workers, the elderly, and so on.

DISCUSSION QUESTIONS

1. In our presentation, we refrained from detailing the strengths and weaknesses of the particular research strategies. Using the ideas from Chapter 6, do so for each of the research strategies used in this case.

2. Chapter 10 in your book describes another multi-method research strategy, this time investigating the hypothesis that "depressive" explanations, as described here, put an individual at risk for illness and death. First, anticipate the sorts of studies that might be done to test this hypothesis. Second, describe how studies might be undertaken to determine who becomes depressed versus who falls ill, granted the same style of explaining bad events. (These latter studies have yet to be conducted by anyone, so you will be treading on new ground.)

3. Here are some hypotheses about psychopathology and psychotherapy:

   - Poverty is a risk factor for schizophrenia.
   - Unhappiness leads a person to abuse alcohol.
   - Therapist warmth is a necessary ingredient for successful therapy.
   - The client's expectation of benefit makes therapy successful.

How would you pursue these hypotheses with a multi-method research strategy?

4. Some psychology students are bored with the "research" part of abnormal psychology. Explain this attitude. Is it a reasonable one? Without research, just what does the field of abnormal psychology become?

5. Compare the way psychologists do research with the way other social scientists (like sociologists, historians, anthropologists, or economists) conduct their studies. Also compare it with the way that natural scientists (like biologists, chemists, or physicists) do their research. What generalizations can you offer about psychological research? Are psychologists obsessed with methods as some critics have charged?

REFERENCES

Peterson, C., Luborsky, L., & Seligman, M. E. P. (1983). Attributions and depressive mood shifts. *Journal of Abnormal Psychology, 92,* 96–103.

Peterson, C., & Seligman, M. E. P. (1984). Causal explanations as a risk factor for depression: Theory and evidence. *Psychological Review, 91,* 347–374.

Sweeney, P. D., Anderson, K., & Bailey, S. (1986). Attributional style in depression: A meta-analytic review. *Journal of Personality and Social Psychology, 50,* 974–991.

Zullow, H., Oettingen, G., Peterson, C., & Seligman, M. E. P. (1988). Explanatory style and pessimism in the historical record; CAVing LBJ, presidential candidates, and East versus West Berlin. *American Psychologist, 43,* 673–682.

Projective Test Protocols

To diagnose particular forms of abnormality, a psychologist requires a variety of information. He will talk to the individual, conducting what is called a mental status exam, the psychological equivalent of the physical exam that a physician carries out. He will observe how the individual behaves. He will ascertain the individual's psychological history, again paralleling the physical history in which a physician is interested. He will talk to friends and family members. Finally, he will make use of the results of psychological tests.

In arriving at a final diagnosis, and along with it a treatment recommendation and a likely prognosis, a psychologist integrates all of the information available to him. As you know, the judgment of abnormality is inherently fuzzy, and the making of particular diagnoses is far from foolproof. There are no sure signs that given problems are present or not. Don't forget these cautions when reading the present case, where we present actual responses to two common projective tests, the Rorschach Inkblot Test (Rorschach, 1942) and the Thematic Apperception Test (Morgan & Murray, 1935).

As you read these protocols, we encourage you to make inferences about the individuals who produced the responses. Appreciate, however, that actual diagnosticians do not work from such protocols alone. They have available a wealth of other information about the person. The purpose of this case is not to illustrate the whole process of diagnosis but simply to let you see some of the raw ingredients involved.

RORSCHACH PROTOCOL

As the text describes in Chapter 7, the Rorschach test consists of a series of ten symmetric inkblots printed individually on heavy card stock. These are shown to an individual one at a time. First the person is asked to say what the blot looks like. He gives as many or as few answers as possible. Then the person is asked specific questions about each of his perceptions. Where does it occur in the blot? What makes it look like whatever it looks like?

The popular conception of how the Rorschach is scored focuses simply on the contents of the perception. Although these are important, less obvious characteristics matter just as much. For instance, does the individual locate a perception in part or all of the blot? Although of course the blot is ambiguous, some perceptions nevertheless "fit" better with the actual stimulus than do others. What proportion of responses show a good versus poor fit? Does the individual respond quickly or slowly when cards are first presented? And so on.

Here are the actual responses given to the ten Rorschach cards by someone tested about eight years ago. This subject was unusually productive, giving many more than the typical number of responses to each card. The actual inkblots are not shown, since psychologists try not to make these images widely available. Nevertheless, do your best to make sense of the responses. What commonalities do you find?

Card #1

1. a bug or beetle about to fly
2. two monks
3. a shark
4. the ocean crashing on rocks
5. African mask used in initiation rite
6. a person's face in profile
7. two dogs
8. a map: the coast of Maine
9. a bell
10. the face of a rhinoceros

Card #2

1. two roosters doing a dance
2. film negative of a face
3. inside of a shell
4. two elephants reaching for God knows what
5. two rabbits
6. a tern
7. bust of Beethoven
8. flower
9. dancers in the Nutcracker ballet
10. a top

Card #3

1. two guys sitting around a fire
2. two waiters pulling on something
3. seagulls

4. seedpod
5. a bowl with an elaborate top
6. panda bear climbing a tree
7. woman with big boobs laughing
8. a pancreas
9. Chinese urn
10. monkey making a gesture
11. ice shaker

Card #4

1. Chinese dragon
2. seaweed
3. iris
4. a dead duck—really, I mean it!
5. nodes on the inside of a violin

Card #5

1. bat
2. butterfly
3. guy's face

Card #6

1. dragonfly
2. a boar on its back

Card #7

1. garden statues . . . in poor taste
2. hourglass
3. top of a castle
4. bedpost

Card #8

1. flower, kind of an orchid but not exactly
2. uterus
3. an animal crawling around on rocks
4. biology textbook page

Card # 9

1. the wizard in the Wizard of Oz
2. a baby's head
3. guy playing saxophone

Card #10

1. fantastic-looking flowers
2. all sorts of flowers
3. snapdragons surrounded by dragonflies
4. caricatures of two boys bickering
5. poodle
6. waterfall

THEMATIC APPERCEPTION TEST PROTOCOL

The Thematic Apperception Test, or TAT, also presents subjects with ambiguous stimuli printed on heavy card stock, although in this case the images carry more meaning in themselves than do inkblots. Many TAT pictures contain people. What are they doing? Ah, that's for the respondent to say.

There are thirty different TAT cards, but not all are shown to the same individual. Some are intended for children; others for adults. Some are for females; others for males. So, a subset of the cards are shown. In each case, the person is asked to tell a story about what is going on in the picture. No constraints are placed on the story, except that it must have a beginning, middle, and end. A TAT protocol therefore consists of a description of the scene, what led up to it, and what will follow from it.

Protocols from adults are usually 300 words in length. What follow here are edited stories from someone tested in 1980. These stories are shorter than the actual ones told. As you did for the Rorschach protocol, try to get some sense of the person telling these stories. What themes recur? What fears are evident? What defenses abound?

Card #1

The young boy here is attempting to envision what the future will hold for himself. He has been playing his violin with great passion, and he has stopped to wonder if he might be able to have a career as a musician. He envisions a ballet for which he has composed the music. He plays first violin for the orchestra at the opening. The scene is very exciting and grand, but it is difficult for him to hold it in focus.

Card #2

The woman in the left of the picture is a college student, back home for a brief time with her family. The family is a farm family, and their life is hard, simple, and satisfying. The young woman is wondering if she is making the right decision in going to college and following such a different direction. Her mother is again pregnant, and the thought confuses the young woman. She cannot reconcile her belief that women should pursue professions with her mother's obvious happiness about being pregnant.

Card #4

These characters look like they're out of a 1940s movie billboard. He is an adventurer, a reckless do-gooder who takes far greater chances than common sense would dictate. But he always succeeds. After all, this is Hollywood. He has curly black hair and intense blue eyes. The woman is a nurse, in a hospital where our hero has been recovering from a bullet wound to his shoulder. She has fallen in love with him, and is trying to discourage him from leaving the hospital to search for the men who shot him. They are greasy and immoral bandits, and our hero intends to rid the country of them.

Card #5

She has opened the door because she has heard a loud crash. It seems as if a large potted plant, hanging from the ceiling, has fallen to the floor, scattering dirt all over the carpet. She is relieved that the noise signified nothing more serious, but she is also annoyed because she must now clean up the mess.

DISCUSSION QUESTIONS

1. What are your inferences about the person who produced the Rorschach protocol? Is this a male or female? What age? What kind of personality does this person have? What issues are important to this person? What problems does he or she have?

2. Make the same inferences about the person who produced the TAT protocol. And have you considered whether this person is the same as the one who responded to the Rorschach?

3. Compare your impressions with those of your classmates. Do you agree or disagree? What do you conclude about the reliability and validity of projective tests?

4. Take a step back from the controversy that surrounds the usefulness of projective tests in diagnosis. Why would a clinical psychologist favor these tests? Why would another clinical psychologist find them of no value? Does the model of abnormality to which a psychologist ascribes have anything to do with his or her reaction to projective tests?

5. Go back to your inferences. What other information would you need to know to evaluate whether these are good or bad judgments? How would you gather this information?

REFERENCES

Morgan, C. D., & Murray, H. A. (1935). A method for investigating fantasies. *Archives of Neurology and Psychiatry, 34,* 289–306.

Rorschach, H. (1942). *Psychodiagnostics: A diagnostic test based on perception.* Berne: Huber.

Dread of Church Steeples: Simple Phobia

A phobia is a fear of some object or situation that is greatly out of proportion to the danger actually posed. The text describes several common types of phobias. Let us provide one more example, drawing on Morton Prince's (1914) case of a forty-year-old woman with a strong fear of church steeples and towers. This is an interesting case because it seems to demand a psychoanalytic interpretation. Steeples and towers are clearly phallic symbols, and so this woman's phobia at first glance involves a conflict over sexuality. Let us see how well this interpretation stands up to further scrutiny.

THE CASE

Here is how Prince (1914, pp. 389–390) presents the symptoms of his patient:

> The patient . . . dreaded and tried in consequence to avoid the sight of [church steeples and towers of any kind]. . . . When she passed by such a tower she was very strongly affected emotionally, experiencing always a feeling of terror or anguish accompanied by the usual marked physical symptoms. Sometimes even speaking of a tower would at once awaken this emotional complex which expressed itself outwardly in her face. . . . Considering the frequency with which church and schoolhouse towers are met with in everyday life, one can easily imagine the discomfort arising from such a phobia. . . . She was unable to give any explanation of the origin or meaning of this phobia and could not connect it with any episode in her life, or even state how far back in her life it had existed. Vaguely she thought it existed when she was about fifteen years of age and that it might have existed before that. Now it should be noted that an idea of a tower with bells had in her mind no meaning whatsoever that explained the fear.

These symptoms along with others that Prince presented make the DSM-III-R diagnosis of a *simple phobia* quite straightforward.

First, the woman feared a circumscribed stimulus (steeples and towers). Second, exposure to this stimulus provoked an anxiety response. Third, she avoided the stimulus whenever possible. Fourth, her fear and avoidance interfered with her everyday life. Fifth, the patient appreciated that her fear was inappropriate.

What else should we note about this fear? Although the particular stimulus is somewhat unusual, in other ways this fear is typical of a simple phobia. The patient is a female. The phobia seems to date from her adolescence. And it shows remarkable endurance.

HISTORY

As noted earlier, fear of church steeples looks like a phobia that conforms well to a psychoanalytic explanation. This possibility occurred to Prince as well, and so he used Freud's method of free association with the patient to uncover the thoughts and feelings she linked to steeples. This failed to reveal any associations. Then he used hypnosis, again failing to find any deeper meaning to the phobia. Finally, he again hypnotized the woman and put a pencil in her hand. While talking about another subject altogether, the woman "automatically" began to write as follows (p. 391):

> G_____ M_____ church and my father took my mother to Bi_____ where she died and we went to Br____ and they cut my mother. I prayed and cried all the time that she would live and the church bells were always ringing and I hated them.

Here then was a clue about the etiology of the phobia. Prince proceeded to question the patient concerning the events that surrounded the death of her mother.

When the patient was about fifteen years of age, her mother was taken to a famous surgeon in another town for an operation needed to save her life. While her mother was in the hospital, the patient went twice a day to a nearby church to pray for her recovery. The church bells chimed while she prayed. Further, the church was close to the hotel where the patient and her father were staying. Every fifteen minutes she heard the bells chime. And so the bells came to be strongly associated with the fear that the patient experienced about her mother's possible death.

Her mother indeed died. It had so happened that on one occasion, the patient had neglected her prayers. At that time, the thought occurred to her that her lapse might be the cause of her mother's death. And so the bells also came to be strongly associated with the guilt that the patient subsequently experienced.

The etiology of the phobia was now revealed. Church bells were linked with fear and guilt. The patient thus avoided bells to avoid these associations. She stayed away from church steeples because these were the only places where church bells were to be found. And because these memories were painful, she pushed them out of her awareness, leaving only the overt fear and avoidance of steeples and towers.

EXPLANATION

This is an interesting case. The etiology sketched by Prince is compelling, but it is somewhat difficult to fit into just one of our popular models of abnormality. On the one hand, there are components of a behavioral account. That is, associations between negative emotions and a particular stimulus were forged through classical conditioning. Had the patient prayed for her mother's recovery in a silent church, it seems likely that the phobia would not have developed. These associations then generalized from church bells to include church steeples. The woman avoided steeples, and thus she never extinguished her fear.

On the other hand, this case also has psychodynamic components. Although the steeples did not signify sexuality, the symbolic significance of the bells was great indeed. They stood for the patient's guilt, and she was not aware of this symbolism until it was revealed in the course of treatment. Why? Because the self-reproach of the patient was too threatening to her. She blamed herself for her mother's death.

Let us give you some more background from the case. When the patient was thirteen years old, i.e., two years before her mother's death, the family was abroad, and the girl fell ill. The family subsequently delayed its return home. The patient believed that had the family returned home sooner, her mother's illness would have been diagnosed sooner, with a happier outcome. So, the neglected prayer was not the only thing about which the patient felt guilty. Had she not fallen ill, then her mother would not have died.

This network of meanings, most of which existed below the level of awareness, are not at all accommodated by classical conditioning. We need an explanation with "depth" to it, like that provided by psychodynamic accounts, to fully explain the patient's fear of church steeples.

TREATMENT

Were this woman to visit a psychologist today with her fear of church steeples, the treatment would be straightforward and in all likelihood quite successful. One of the behavioral strategies would be followed, for instance, systematic desensitization. The woman would be instructed in how to relax. A hierarchy of steeples with bells would be constructed, ranging from those that aroused little anxiety to those that traumatized her. She would relax and then imagine the different steeples, working her way up the hierarchy until she could think without anxiety of the church where she had prayed for her mother's recovery.

Morton Prince did not have these techniques available. Here is how he proceeded. He focused on her self-reproach. Was it really the case that the family delayed its return home because the young girl was ill? Upon examination, this belief seemed to have no basis whatsoever. Relying on the patient's own memories for his arguments, Prince convinced her that she was not particularly ill. After all, she was not taken to doctors or hospitals. She was not housebound. After all, the family traveled extensively. Her mother and father were not worried about her health. After all, they had a wonderful time.

Apparently, the girl's "illness" was just an excuse for the family to continue its vacation. Had the unfortunate death of her mother not followed on the heels of this vacation, the patient would have probably forgotten about her own illness, or perhaps have remembered it for the minor incident that it was. But because of the way that events unfolded, her illness took on great meaning and provided the foundation of her phobia. As these ideas were made clear, the patient remarked to Prince (p. 410):

> Why, of course, I see it now! My mother did not stay in Europe on account of my health but because she enjoyed it, and might have returned if she wanted to. I never thought of that before! It was not my fault at all!

With this realization, the phobia was gone.

DISCUSSION QUESTIONS

1. Do you have any fears or anxieties that are analogous to this woman's fear of church steeples—emotions linked to particular objects because of the *meaning* these objects have? Note that the behavioral account of phobias says nothing about meaning, just associations. Does this limit the range of fears to which classical conditioning applies?

2. One theory of phobias that we did not mention in this case is the notion of prepared learning. Does this provide an explanation for the woman's fear of church steeples?

3. How would a psychoanalyst explain Prince's successful treatment of the phobia? How would a behavior therapist? How would a cognitive therapist?

4. Consider someone with a phobia of traveling by plane. How might such a fear arise in the first place? How could it be treated?

5. Why are women more likely to have simple phobias than men?

REFERENCE

Prince, M. (1914). *The unconscious: The fundamentals of human personality normal and abnormal.* New York: Macmillan.

Rape Trauma Syndrome: Post-Traumatic Stress Disorder

Post-traumatic stress disorder (PTSD) follows an event outside typical human experience: combat, assault, kidnapping, auto accidents, severe burns, concentration camp internment, torture, and so on. Although all people who experience these events show a short-term reaction, some additionally show a long-term effect marked by reliving the event, anxiety, and numbness to the external world. This is PTSD.

Psychologists increasingly recognize that one route to PTSD lies through sexual assault. Indeed, the term *rape trauma syndrome* describes a typical reaction to rape. It is a good example of PTSD. The purpose of the present case is to describe the syndrome and show how it illustrates PTSD. In so doing, we draw on cases presented by Burgess and Holmstrom (1974) in their book *Rape: Victims of Crisis*, and by Brownmiller (1975) in her book *Against Our Will: Men, Women, and Rape*. What follows is not the account of a single victim of rape but rather a composite drawn from the numerous instances detailed by these authors.

RAPE TRAUMA SYNDROME

The rape trauma syndrome consists of two phases. In the immediate or acute phase, right after the rape, the victim's life is disrupted and disorganized by the crisis that the rape represents. In the long-term phase, the victim must deal with this disorganization, trying to reconstruct her life-style (Burgess & Holmstrom, 1979). Technically speaking, it is in the long-term phase of the rape trauma syndrome that we find PTSD, but let us describe both phases so you can fully appreciate the impact of rape on a victim.

Immediate phase. Women show a variety of reactions immediately following rape. Some may be overwhelmed by anger or fear or anxiety:

> When he finally finished raping me, he told me to turn over. I was so scared. I didn't know what he was going to do . . . I just got hysterical after he left. I'm usually pretty cool and level headed, but I just went to pieces. I ran out into the street. It's a main street, but no one stopped, and I was running around (Burgess & Holmstrom, 1974, p. 3).

Other victims may be subdued. Either type of reaction makes sense following an extremely frightening experience, since fear can be expressed as either extreme activity or extreme passivity.

Immediately following the assault, the rape victim experiences physical disruption. She has trouble falling asleep or even staying asleep. She often has no appetite, and experiences stomach aches or nausea. Her body hurts, or itches, or burns.

What is the primary emotion that a rape victim feels immediately after the attack? Popular stereotypes may suggest shame or guilt, but Burgess and Holmstrom (1974) dismiss these stereotypes. Overwhelmingly, they report, the major emotion is fear—of injury, mutilation, or death. Other emotions may occur, but fear predominates:

> Sometimes I am nervous inside. A book falls at work and I jump. On Monday and Tuesday I was really jumpy. . . . I want to calm myself down. . . . I can feel the tension building up (Burgess & Holmstrom, 1974, p. 39).

As Chapter 8 of your text explains, fear is marked by characteristic thoughts, specifically expectations of danger, and these are part of the immediate phase of the rape trauma syndrome. A victim may expect to encounter the rapist again. She may believe that other attacks are likely. The rape itself haunts her, occurring over and over in her mind. She tries to figure out how she might have handled the situation differently.

Long-term phase. According to Burgess and Holmstrom (1974, 1979), the immediate reaction to a rape lasts from a few days to a few weeks. No firm line marks the transition to the long-term phase of the rape trauma syndrome, but it is easily recognized once it is there. First, the victim changes her normal routine of life. She goes to work or to school, but curtails all other activities. Or she stays home altogether, going out only when accompanied by someone. Victims often turn to their families, visiting them or even moving back home to their parents. Particularly if the rape occurred where the victim lived, she is apt to change her residence. She removes her name from her mailbox. She changes her telephone number, often requesting an unlisted one.

Her sleep disturbance remains. Dreams and nightmares are common. Sometimes the dreams resemble the actual attack. The victim tries to escape and fails. Sometimes the dream represents mastery over the situation. The victim triumphs over her attacker. Burgess and Holmstrom (1974) regard this as a sign that the victim is coming to grips with the attack and the psychological damage it has done to her.

Part of the long-term reaction is the development of specific phobias: of crowds, of being alone, of being in situations like the one where the attack occurred. Particular characteristics of the rapist, when seen in other men, may produce fear and avoidance. Sometimes the victim of rape becomes afraid of men in general.

POST-TRAUMATIC STRESS DISORDER

You should now have a sense of how rape may affect its victims. Let's examine the rape trauma syndrome as an instance of PTSD. Remember the DSM-III-R criteria for this disorder. First, there is a traumatic event markedly distressing to anyone who would experience it. Obviously, rape qualifies. Second, some time after the original trauma, the victim persistently reexperiences the event. We've already mentioned that nightmares about the rape are common in the long-term phase of the rape trauma syndrome. So too is the expectation that the rape will occur again:

> I keep thinking I saw him—on the street, in the elevator at work, on the bus. I was convinced that he was still after me, and he'd get me for reporting it, that he'd come back to finish me off. Whenever the phone rang and the person hung up, I was sure it was him. I moved and got an unlisted number (Brownmiller, 1975, p. 405).

When reminders of the rape are encountered, the victim is distressed, and reexperiencing it is even more likely.

Third, in PTSD, individuals avoid stimuli associated with the original trauma. We saw several examples of this in the description of the long-term phase of the rape trauma syndrome. Accompanying this avoidance is a general turning away from the ongoing world: loss of interest in activities, estrangement from others, restriction of feelings:

> What it affected was my career. I stopped taking chances, that's what it was. I wouldn't say that my experience caused my career problems, but it certainly aggravated them. It hits you where you're most vulnerable. Even though I had been very strong during my encounter, I felt more vulnerable in every way (Brownmiller, 1975, p. 407).

Rape victims may feel distant from their friends and family members, including their husbands. As you might imagine, the subsequent sexual activity of victims may be adversely affected by the trauma.

And fourth, PTSD is characterized by signs of increased arousal, like insomnia, difficulty concentrating, irritability, and hypervigilance. Again, these characteristics mark the long-term phase of the rape trauma syndrome. In fact, all the criteria of post-traumatic stress are met by the long-term phase of the rape trauma syndrome.

Burgess and Holmstrom (1974) recommend that counseling for rape victims should take into account the two phases of the syndrome. In the short term, attention should be directed to the disorganization that the rape creates. In the long term, counseling should help the person put her life back together. Eventually, many victims of rape—but certainly not all—put the psychological consequences of the trauma behind them.

DISCUSSION QUESTIONS

1. Why does PTSD occur? There is no generally accepted answer to this question, but sketch how the different models of abnormality might grapple with it. Do you find one account more compelling than the others?

2. Drawing on the material presented in the text, how might the rape trauma syndrome among victims be prevented? How might it be treated?

3. We've discussed the rape trauma syndrome as a particular instance of PTSD. But rape and its aftermath also have unique characteristics, since rape is embedded in a host of societal beliefs, many of which have no basis in fact (see Brownmiller, 1975). Contrast the rape trauma syndrome and other types of PTSD. How might these differences affect the particular course of the rape trauma syndrome? To what should a clinical psychologist helping a rape victim be sensitive?

4. Why is rape as prevalent as it is? Granted that it is so prevalent, why are there so many false beliefs about rape?

REFERENCES

Brownmiller, S. (1975). *Against our will: Men, women, and rape.* New York: Bantam.

Burgess, A. W., & Holmstrom, L. L. (1974). *Rape: Victims of crisis.* Bowie, MD: Brady.

Burgess, A. W., & Holmstrom, L. L. (1979). Adaptive strategies and recovery from rape. *American Journal of Psychiatry, 136,* 1278–1282.

The Insistent Ideas of Miss M.: Obsessive-Compulsive Disorder

In contrast to disorders like phobia, where fear and anxiety can readily be observed, other disorders have these emotional states beneath the surface. The psychologist must infer their presence. One example is obsessive-compulsive disorder. Here the individual experiences recurrent thoughts (obsessions) and intentions to behave (compulsions) that are intrusive and unpleasant. When obsessions or compulsions are interrupted, the individual experiences great anxiety. When allowed to continue, anxiety does not occur. The purpose of this case is to illustrate this disorder. We use as an example a patient, Miss M., originally described by Edward Cowles (1888) a century ago.

THE CASE

When Cowles first met the patient, she was twenty-eight years old. Here is a description of her:

> She was of a good family . . . both the parents were then living, and over seventy years of age. She was the youngest of ten children. . . . The patient had a good physique, was a little above the average in stature, and in good bodily health in all particulars. She [was] . . . a person of more than ordinary intelligence and good sense . . . usually amiable, pleasing, and dignified in manner; though reticent, she was not unsocial. She was disposed, however, to dress very plainly and to be negligent in this regard. . . . She was well-informed, read good books, chose the most intelligent persons as companions, . . . was keen of insight and quick at repartee. . . . In brief, she was in many respects an interesting person (pp. 230–231).

So what was the problem that brought Miss M. to the mental hospital where Dr. Cowles first met her?

She was depressed and suicidal, but these were secondary to a host of other difficulties that she herself referred to as a "monomania" and that DSM-III-R would unambiguously classify as an obsessive-compulsive disorder. Specifically, she believed that ordinary acts she might commit would bring harm to a close female friend. Although Miss M. recognized that her beliefs were absurd, that there could be no actual connection between her acts and anything that would befall her friend, she nonetheless could not rid her mind of them. These beliefs caused her great distress, and she despaired of ever ridding herself of them.

Her obsession dated to adolescence and revolved around a close friend, Miss C., by all accounts a lovely, charming young woman. Although Miss M. cared deeply for Miss C., she at the time was jealous of the attention paid to her friend because of her beauty. Miss M. began to have fleeting thoughts of doing harm to her friend, and she severely reprimanded herself for these thoughts. Still, they continued. Miss M. experienced great anxiety in connection with them, not so much remorse over the possible injury to her friend but over the guilt she—Miss M.—would experience if something harmful did occur.

Miss M. discovered a way of allaying some of her anxiety. When she started to think of something bad happening to Miss C., she substituted another person in her mind, letting that person take the brunt of the injury.

> This worked well for a while, but soon began to be refined upon. It became necessary to choose for the substituted person someone with many opposite characteristics to C.; for example, there had to be a difference in age, sometimes of sex, initials of name, color of eyes and hair, stature, distance as to residence from C., and at last peculiar requirements as to time, place, etc., etc., to an endless extent. Next it became necessary to have ready in mind a number of chosen persons, two, or three, or four of whom, as the case might be, must be thought of in a certain order, etc. After a while, thinking of these persons ceased to give mental relief and another set had to be chosen, to wear out in turn (p. 241).

Her growing obsession was accompanied by compulsions as well. She began to fear that particular things she would do might bring harm to Miss C.

> It affected the taking of certain articles of food, or going to certain places; interdicted certain things, or permitted them on certain days and not on others. Colors, pictures, and ornaments were banished from her room. She was fond of dress, but certain materials and many colors could not be worn, although she most liked them. Certain days were tabooed for shopping . . . and certain shops could not be entered (pp. 244–245).

Although Cowles provides many more details concerning Miss M.'s thoughts and actions, those just discussed clearly show that she experienced obsessions and compulsions.

Other criteria for a DSM-III-R diagnosis were met as well. Her obsessions and compulsions caused Miss M. great distress, took a great deal of time, and interfered with her ordinary life. Indeed, her rituals became her life. Although she had been an outstanding student, she left school, unable to study. She had trouble reading, because what she read frequently triggered her obsessions, which triggered her compulsions. She gave up many of her friends. To compound her difficulties even more, Miss M. did not discuss her problems with anyone. She kept her mental and behavioral routines a secret. Immediately prior to her hospitalization, Miss M. attempted suicide. Her motive was not to die but to have herself taken to a hospital, which was what happened. It was then that she confided in the attending physician.

HISTORY

According to Cowles, the first hint of Miss M.'s disorder appeared as early as age ten or twelve, when she was occasionally depressed and had worries about death. During early adolescence, she experienced several severe illnesses, during which her fears increased. At this time, she found herself repeating acts several times because her initial performance didn't quite seem "right" and might thereby bring harm to her. As her illnesses resolved, so too did these tendencies. With puberty, however, Miss M. again began to repeat her actions, particularly those associated with dressing or undressing. She felt insecure about her own attractiveness, and she became quite jealous of other young women, notably the lovely Miss C.

An important event occurred when Miss M. was twenty years old. She spent several months living in the home of Miss C. This exacerbated her obsessions and compulsions. On one occasion, Miss M. actually took a razor in her hand and made a threatening swipe at Miss C.'s throat. It was passed off as a joke, but now Miss M. had not only her imagined sins to worry about but an actual one as well.

Also important was the fact that as years passed, and the number of "substitute" victims increased, some number of them died. This only added to Miss M.'s anxieties, because she had wished that they would die. Her fears of her own thoughts were thereby intensified, since she had evidence for their power.

Miss M. did not improve much during her hospitalization, and she devised her own solution to her problems. Perhaps if she herself suffered physically, she would no longer suffer mentally. On a walk away from the hospital, she obtained a pistol and shot herself in the shoulder and hip, hoping to damage her joints and cripple herself. The wounds she inflicted were only superficial, though, and quickly healed. Miss M. was left with her obsessive-compulsive disorder. Cowles closes by saying that he was unaware of her subsequent history. Granted what we know about the prognosis of these disorders, though, we can assume that Miss M. probably continued to suffer.

DISCUSSION QUESTIONS

1. How typical is Miss M.'s obsessive-compulsive disorder? In other words, describe what this case shares with other cases described in Chapter 9 as well as how it is different. Consider age and circumstances surrounding onset, course of the disorder, content of the obsessions, and so on.

2. Explain Miss M.'s disorder from the viewpoint of psychoanalytic theory. How would treatment proceed?

3. Explain Miss M.'s disorder from the viewpoint of cognitive-behavioral theory. How would treatment proceed?

4. Integrate your answers to questions 2 and 3 to give a full account of this case of obsessive-compulsive disorder. Why did Miss M.'s particular obsessions and compulsions escalate?

REFERENCE

Cowles, E. (1888). Insistent and fixed ideas. *American Journal of Psychology, 1,* 222–270.

George's Bullet Therapy: Obsessive-Compulsive Disorder

Remember in Case 9, that of Miss M., that she attempted to get rid of her obsessive-compulsive disorder by shooting herself. She hoped that by turning herself into a cripple, her physical anguish would outweigh her mental anguish. The strategy failed.

One hundred years later, an ironic postscript to this case was widely reported in the popular press (e.g., *San Francisco Chronicle,* 1988). George, a man with a severe obsessive-compulsive disorder, shot himself in the head with a .22 caliber bullet. His motive was not as complex as that of Miss M. He merely wanted to die, so distressed was he by his symptoms. But George survived the suicide attempt. Further, his obsessive-compulsive disorder was gone. Whatever damage the bullet did to his brain had the effect of eradicating his problem. Further, he showed no negative effects in his general intellectual functioning. He returned to school, finished high school, and started college.

George was nineteen years old when he tried to kill himself. His disorder had revolved around fear of germs. He had obsessed about contamination. He had washed his hands hundreds of times per day, and he had taken frequent showers. He could not attend school or hold a job. When the stories about George appeared, it had been five years since his suicide attempt. His disorder had not returned, although it is reported that George washes his dishes much more thoroughly than most people. George lives alone. Apparently, he is a somewhat isolated individual.

DISCUSSION QUESTIONS

1. The case of George really happened, so we don't have to speculate if a bullet through the head could really "cure" obsessive-compulsive disorders. We know that it can. But we don't know why this

happened. The immediate possibility is that the bullet removed some part of the brain responsible for his disorder. Based on what the text says about the biological basis of obsessive-compulsive disorders, what neurological effects did the bullet have?

2. Is it possible that surgery will ever be used to treat obsessive-compulsive disorders, or does this case just show a one-in-a-million coincidence?

3. Might there be a psychological reason why George's suicide attempt led to a cessation of his symptoms? Sketch a rationale based on psychoanalytic theory. Sketch one based on cognitive theory.

REFERENCE

Bullet in the brain cures man's mental problem. *San Francisco Chronicle*, February 23, 1988, pp. 1+.

Mr. P.'s Travels: Psychogenic Fugue

Pierre Janet, the French psychiatrist who figures prominently in the history of abnormality as described in Chapter 2 of your text, visited Harvard University in the early part of this century to give a series of lectures. He presented a number of cases, including the one we'll describe here, that of Mr. P., who experienced psychogenic fugue. As you know, fugue is a variant of amnesia. An individual suffers partial or total loss of memory, travels from his or her customary residence, and establishes a new identity. Like the other disorders covered in Chapter 9, fugue is caused by anxiety. Although anxiety is not overt, it is under the surface. Keep the hypothesized role of anxiety in mind while you read this case.

THE CASE

Let us quote directly from Janet (1920) to provide the background of Mr. P.'s fugue:

> The subject is a man, P., thirty years old, employed in a railway station in a town in the east of France. Although an active and clever fellow, he was a little eccentric, and had already led a somewhat adventurous life. In his youth he had had frequent fits of somnambulism, sometimes in the day, but mostly at night. Moreover, the tendency to somnambulism is to be found in his family. . . . This man, P., was also very affected, predisposed to fixed ideas. One day, in the notary's office where he worked, he was slightly suspected, though not accused of stealing a trifle. He fell ill, and was very distressed. Night and day he discussed that suspicion, and, although everybody tried to prove to him how trifling it was, he could not remain in that office. Moreover, he had a tendency to exaggerated fears. He had left Lorraine after its annexation to Germany, and during many years he was haunted by the fear of the German police, whom he always believed to be running after him . . .

At the age of twenty, he got a situation in a railway company, and was soon in easy circumstances. He married, and had a child he dearly loved. His wife was again pregnant when the following incident took place. Although he led a quiet and rather happy life, he was uneasy in his mind, and gave himself up to intellectual labours too hard for a man who had no great acquirements. To his work in the railway office he added bookkeeping . . . He was made uneasy in his mind by family quarrels: his brother, who was jealous of him, had just quarrelled with him and had charged him with shameful and dishonest acts. The charge was groundless, and nobody around him troubled about it, but we know how easily upset, how susceptible he was in that quarter . . .

It is in these conditions that we come to the third of February, 1895. He was alone . . . he went to a coffee-house where he was well known. During the afternoon, a part of which he spent with some friends at this coffee-house in playing billiards, he drank a cup of coffee, two glasses of beer, and a small glass of vermouth . . . He told us himself all these circumstances, which he remembers quite well. . . . He left that coffee-house about five . . . but a few yards off, while crossing the Stanislas bridge over the railway line, just as he got to the middle (that also he perfectly remembers), he felt a violent pain in his head, as if he had been struck . . . immediately after that something must have changed in the mental state of our patient, as he entirely lost the memory of all that happened afterwards on that Sunday, the third of February, 1895 (pp. 45–48).

Somnambulism is sleepwalking, in case you didn't see this from the context. And appreciate that the "violent pain" that Mr. P. experienced was not due to a physical blow. Amnesia or fugue may be brought about by a physical injury, but in these cases, they take a different form.

At any rate, when Mr. P.'s recollections returned, he found himself not in France but in Belgium, near Brussels. He was lying in a snow-covered field. It was nine days since he had lost his memory while crossing the bridge. He had no recollection of what had ensued during this period.

Mr. P. sought assistance. He was taken to Paris and then to the Salpetrière, where he came under the care of Dr. Janet. Although Janet skips over just how he helped Mr. P. recapture his lost memories, here is what was discovered about the lost nine days:

- On the Stanislas Bridge, Mr. P. became overwhelmed with fear over the accusations by his brother.
- He went home, continuing to worry about the charges, and became even more anxious.
- He wandered the streets, wondering how to escape the consequences of the accusations.
- He returned home for money and then checked into a hotel to spend the night.
- The next morning, he went to a railway station (not the one where

he worked) and traveled to another city.

- He got off the train and walked to a nearby town, all the time hiding from the police he supposed were pursuing him.
- He took another train to yet another city, then another city, then still another city.
- The idea occurred to him that he should eventually seek refuge in a distant country.
- He came to Brussels and set out to find a job, in order to save money for his long journey.
- He was unsuccessful in finding work.
- His finances dwindled, and he sought help in a shelter; a man there took pity on him and wrote for him a letter of introduction to a local charity.
- Mr. P. attempted to enlist for service in the Dutch Indies but was turned down.
- Exhausted, broke, and thwarted, he stretched out in a field of snow to die.

As Mr. P. prepared himself for death, he thought of his family. (He had not thought of his family for the previous nine days.) He was jarred, since his memories struck him as so vague. He read the letter of introduction that was still in his pocket, which recounted part of his story, and his memory returned, except for what had transpired during the last nine days. You know the rest.

ANALYSIS

This case well conforms to the DSM-III-R depiction of psychogenic fugue. Consider the formal diagnostic criteria. First, the individual suddenly travels away from home, and is unable to recall his past. This is exactly what Mr. P. did. Second, a new identity is assumed, which may be partial or complete. In the case of Mr. P., the new identity was but a partial one, with some links to his past. Third, there is no physical basis to the disorder. Remember, the pain in his head that marked the beginning of the fugue state was purely psychological.

Something that is hard to grasp about fugue is what the person is thinking about when he is "in" the fugue state. The answer is simple but perhaps not obvious. The person thinks about ongoing business. In the case of Mr. P., he had his travel arrangements in mind, his search for a job, his plans for the Dutch Indies, and so on. Think of your own state of mind when you embark on a project. Do you think about your first-grade teacher, or the pennant race of 1987, or your mother's birthday? Probably not. The difference between you and the person with amnesia is that you *could* bring these topics to mind. They are not threatening to you, unless of course you forgot to send your mother a birthday card this year!

Those in a fugue state are not able to bring back personal memories on demand, since these memories cohere around threatening events. Nonetheless, their conscious minds are coherent, and they are unaware that their personal history has missing parts. Janet (1920) describes the present awareness of such individuals as dissociated—separated from the rest of their mental life:

> . . . a system of images which has separated from the totality of consciousness and has an independent development. It brings about two things: a blank in the general consciousness, which is represented by an amnesia, and an exaggerated and independent development of the emancipated idea. . . . The feeling that arises from the fear of an ignominious charge, the feeling of curiosity for distant countries, the feeling of love and jealousy toward a lover . . . these are systems of thoughts . . . not always easy to express in words . . . but they nonetheless possess a mental unity (pp. 64–65).

DISCUSSION QUESTIONS

1. How would a psychoanalytic theorist explain Mr. P.'s fugue? What would an advocate of the environmentalist model wish to add to this explanation?

2. Is sleepwalking an example of a dissociative disorder?

3. How do you think Dr. Janet helped the patient regain his memories? Would you do anything differently nowadays?

4. Why is fugue such a rare disorder? Why is it most prevalent during wartime or in the wake of a natural disaster?

5. According to the text, once a patient's memories return, a psychologist should help that individual resolve the problems and conflicts to which amnesia was a reaction. Imagine you are Mr. P.'s therapist. (Brush up on your high school French.) What treatment plan would you propose? In other words, specify your goals for therapy and what you would do to achieve them. What model of abnormality does your proposed treatment exemplify?

REFERENCE

Janet, P. (1920). *The major symptoms of hysteria.* New York: Macmillan.

Two Cases of Multiple Personality Disorder

One of the most fascinating of the problems in which anxiety presumably lurks under the surface is multiple personality disorder. Within the same person, we find several distinct personalities, each with characteristic traits, feelings, habits, and memories. Barriers of amnesia may exist between these different selves, which is why multiple personality is classified with amnesia and fugue as a dissociative disorder.

At one time in the recent past, multiple personality disorder was thought to be extinct. From this conclusion followed the conclusion that the disorder never existed—that reports were fanciful exercises in imagination. As Chapter 9 of your text explains, however, multiple personality disorder was "rediscovered" in the 1980s. Although rare, these disorders certainly exist, and they are now a topic of much research and theorizing.

Because of this current concern, we see renewed interest in some of the classic cases of multiple personality disorder. One of these is the case of Miss Beauchamp, described in much detail by Morton Prince (1905, 1914, 1921, 1929). The other is the case of Felida, described by Pierre Janet (1920). Let us present some of the interesting aspects of these two cases. Compare them to the more contemporary cases the authors describe in the text.

THE CASE OF MISS BEAUCHAMP

This woman had three different personalities that alternated with one another. Here are Prince's (1929) characterizations of each of these three selves. Personality "B I" (also known as the "Saint") was a woman of great piety. She was highly religious and moral, and was consistently meek, mild, and unassertive. B I never expressed anger or resentment. "B IV" (also known as the "Realist") was quite different; she was strong, resolute, and argumentative. The third personality, "Sally," was very much a child; she was mischievous and playful, free of responsibility and care. Sally was psychologically the most interesting personality, since she possessed what Prince termed "coconsciousness." In other words, although she took her turn alternating with the other two personalities as the major self, she was also always present. So, when B I or B IV was manifest in Miss Beauchamp, so too was Sally. At these times, there literally were two I's in existence.

Prince conducted a series of studies on Miss Beauchamp's three personalities and found that each possessed characteristic emotions, sentiments, and intellectual skills. For instance, although B I and B IV were educated individuals, Sally was not. These other personalities spoke foreign languages, but Sally could not. They could take shorthand and work mathematical problems, but again Sally could not.

Prince (1929) attempted to understand the origin of these different personalities, and some of his theorizing foreshadowed the more contemporary hypotheses of Eugene Bliss (1980), as described in your text. So, he reported that Miss Beauchamp had been a sensitive, highly idealistic, and introspective child. She grew up in an unsympathetic atmosphere, perhaps spurring her to dwell very much in her fantasy life. While still a child, she fashioned for herself the identity of a saint. At the same time, though, the little girl in her survived as the coconscious self called Sally.

The saintly role in which Miss Beauchamp cast herself was not always possible to maintain, however, and as she grew older, she was not able to remain consistent. She found herself doing things that horrified herself. A brief sexual encounter occasioned the splitting off of B I. Miss Beauchamp found herself feeling both aroused and repulsed (by her arousal). Unable to reconcile this contradiction, she became the Saint and thereby blocked the sexual episode from her conscious memory. Some years later, she was reminded of the earlier sexual encounter and suffered great agitation, which was resolved by the emergence of the Realist.

These three personalities alternated in Miss Beauchamp for years. Eventually, though, B IV displaced B I altogether, and became integrated with Sally. What resulted was "a complete, united, and normal personality" (Prince, 1929, p. 208). Indeed, Prince concludes the case of Miss Beauchamp by saying that she lived happily ever after.

THE CASE OF FELIDA

When she first came to the attention of Janet (1920), Felida was a fifteen-year-old adolescent female. She was described as a reserved, sad, and timid individual. She suffered from a variety of physical and mental complaints, and she probably warranted a diagnosis of conversion disorder. But there was more to her problems than this:

> There appeared from time to time . . . another very strange phenomenon. She seemed to faint away for a few minutes.

... Then she would wake up suddenly, become gay and active, and bustle about, without any anxiety or pain; she no longer had those painful sensations or those insensibilities which troubled her before, and she was in much better health than in the preceding period. . . . She preserved a very clear remembrance of all her former life, of all the sufferings she had undergone. . . . So everything went quite well; but this state of comfort lasted but a short time. After one to three hours . . . [she returned to] the preceding state, considered as normal . . . she resumed again all her infirmities, and the slow melancholy character which was her usual one. But there was now one phenomenon more: she had quite forgotten the few preceding hours filled by the State No. 2, or the lively state. All this period for her did not exist.

This caused no great inconvenience at that time, since the state called No. 2 occurred only from time to time and lasted an hour or two. But, little by little, this state developed singularly; it lasted for hours and days, and as the subject was now much more active, it was filled with all kinds of serious incidents (pp. 79–80).

For instance, in State No. 2, Felida made love to a man and became pregnant. Her original self had no memory of the incident and couldn't understand in the ensuing months why her abdomen was becoming larger. State No. 2 found the confusion of State No. 1 to be amusing, and laughingly apologized to the attending physician.

As Felida became older, she continued to alternate between her two selves. The second self eventually took over most of the time, however, since it had the advantage of total memory, which the first self did not. When in State No. 1, Felida was at a loss to account for gaps in her life. She feared she was going mad, and she would hide herself away until the second self emerged.

COMMENT

Multiple personality disorders are difficult to describe because the very language we have available for talking about people and personality presupposes the unity of self and consciousness. In the case of Felida, we see two selves in one body, with one self knowing about the second self but not vice versa. This is hard for us to grasp. In the case of Miss Beauchamp, we have an even more elusive state of affairs, the conscious self of Sally. Here we see not only alternation among selves, but sometimes their simultaneous presence.

We suspect that the renewed interest in multiple personality disorders stems not just from a fascination with the cases themselves nor just from a desire to help these individuals, but also from the realization on the part of psychologists that the existence of such disorders challenges the way we think about all people. Perhaps a more sophisticated conception of personality will emerge from the intense scrutiny of cases of multiple personality disorder.

DISCUSSION QUESTIONS

1. In what ways are people with multiple personalities similar to those of us with different aspects to our singular selves? In what ways are they different? Is multiple personality disorder a condition that is either present or absent, or is there something in between?

2. Describe the cases of Miss Beauchamp and Felida in terms of the etiological theory of Bliss.

3. Is there any significance to the fact that the three personalities of Miss Beauchamp seem to correspond to the psychoanalytic notions of id, ego, and superego?

4. Compare and contrast the cases of Miss Beauchamp and Felida with the modern cases of Eve and Sybil.

5. Recent research shows that the vast majority of individuals today with multiple personality disorder were sexually abused as children. Do you think this is true of cases in the last century? (Neither Prince nor Janet provide any information that suggests childhood sexual abuse in the cases under consideration.)

6. Granted that individuals with multiple personality disorder were abused as children, why is it that not all children who were abused develop this disorder?

7. Multiple personality disorder is more common among females than males. Why might this be so?

8. Using the ideas described in the text, design a program of therapy for Miss Beauchamp or for Felida. Why do you think their disorders resolved on their own?

REFERENCES

Bliss, E. L. (1980). Multiple personalities: Report of fourteen cases with implications for schizophrenia and hysteria. *Archives of General Psychiatry, 37,* 1388–1397.

Janet, P. (1920). *The major symptoms of hysteria.* New York: Macmillan.

Prince, M. (1905). *The dissociation of a personality.* New York: Longmans, Green, and Co.

Prince, M. (1914). *The unconscious.* New York: Macmillan.

Prince, M. (1921). *The unconscious.* 2nd ed. New York: Macmillan.

Prince, M. (1929). *Clinical and experimental studies of personality.* Cambridge, MA: Sci-Art.

Ulcer-Prone Personalities: Psychosomatic Disorder

The definition of a peptic ulcer is simple: erosion of the mucous membrane because of excess gastric secretions. Its explanation is more difficult. Chapter 10 describes research that implicates factors deemed important by all the popular models of abnormality: biomedical, psychodynamic, and environmentalist. In this case, we will describe a clinical study originally reported by Kapp, Rosenbaum, and Romano (1947) of twenty men with peptic ulcers. The goal of this research was to identify personality styles and conflicts that characterize individuals who develop ulcers. Keep in mind the three models of abnormality as you read about their results.

METHOD

Twenty men, with age ranging from seventeen to fifty-four, were selected for the study solely on the basis of an unambiguous diagnosis of ulcers. The hope was that they represented a range of ulcer patients. Most of the patients were white (n = 18), and the others were black (n = 2). Most had been hospitalized at one time because of their ulcer. Sixteen patients had a duodenal ulcer, one a gastric ulcer, one both types, and two had ulcers that could not be exactly located. Perforation of the ulcer had occurred in two cases, and bleeding in another seven.

Each subject was interviewed between three and eight times. Additional information was obtained from friends or family members. The researchers attempted to find common themes in these subjects' personalities and the conflicts they habitually experienced.

RESULTS

Rather than one pattern, the researchers found three distinct clusters of individuals. Here is a thumbnail sketch of each cluster, along with an illustrative case for each.

Cluster one (six patients). These individuals struck the researchers as outwardly independent and successful, but inwardly needy and dependent. Note that this characterization captures the psychosomatic picture of the ulcer-prone personality that Franz Alexander (1950) proposed, as described in the text. The following case represents the patients in this group:

> *Case 1.* The patient was a twenty-six-year-old, white, businessman who came to the hospital with a bleeding duodenal ulcer. His life story was illustrated in his own words. "I've always tried to make something of myself. I didn't want my children to go without what I have." The patient was an extremely ambitious, hard-working man who prided himself on his independence. His father died when he was only a year old, and although his mother remarried and had five more children, he remained her favorite. His childhood was characterized by severe and prolonged economic insecurity. At the age of eight he started working and always held at least two jobs at the same time since then. He married an emotionally immature girl on whom he felt dependent, but continued to aid in the support of his mother and half-siblings. He and his wife lived with her family despite the fact that he felt they did not appreciate him. Gastric symptoms were first noted when he encountered serious difficulty with his domineering and demanding mother-in-law; and his symptoms were accentuated by the births of each of his children. Several weeks before admission to the hospital the patient suffered several financial losses, and on the evening before hospitalization he had a dispute with his wife which ended when she told him to get out of the house. Shortly after this he developed a severe hemorrhage from a duodenal ulcer (p. 701).

Note how the symptoms of this patient follow on the heels of particular conflicts that activate his insecurities.

Cluster two (five patients). These individuals were outwardly timid and shy. Again, they seemed dependent, and in each case they were overtly dependent on their mother or a reasonable facsimile for support. Here is a representative patient in this group:

> *Case 2.* The patient was a seventeen-year-old, white school boy, admitted to the hospital with a perforated prepyloric peptic ulcer. He was born and raised in Tennessee, the fourth of five children and stated that his parents gave him everything he wanted. He always remained close to home and to mother, and was a model child. At school he was an excellent student and "teacher's pet." Epigastric distress first appeared when he entered high school and could no longer come home at noon for lunch. During a summer vacation he left home for the first time and came to Cincinnati to visit a married brother. Although homesick, he obtained a temporary job where he was well liked. His consumption of

food during this period increased manyfold. A week before his contemplated return home, the patient received a telegram stating that his mother was gravely ill. He asked his employer for his wages so he could immediately return home, but his boss refused to pay him until he had finished out the week. He met this decision of his boss without outward or even conscious appropriate feeling or behavior. However, fifteen minutes later the patient's ulcer perforated (pp. 701–702).

As in Case 1, note the timing between the possible loss of the patient's mother and the worsening of his symptoms.

Cluster three (nine patients). These individuals showed a disturbed character; the majority were chronic alcoholics. All were self-destructive, unable to hold a job, and acted out frequently via gambling or minor criminal activity. Consider the following example:

Case 5. The patient was a twenty-eight-year-old, white, chronic alcoholic and gambler, admitted to the hospital with a bleeding duodenal ulcer. His father had emigrated from Italy and had become financially successful in this country. The patient was told by his father, "You were breast-fed for a little too long because you were your mother's first born, and she like to indulge you." His childhood was happy, and his parents provided almost everything he wanted—even a pony. When the patient was thirteen years old his mother developed an agitated depression. Shortly afterwards he began drinking, gambling, whoring, and playing hooky. Father disapproved, but repeatedly forgave the patient and attempted to find him satisfactory jobs. He never held a job long and became known as the black sheep of the family. The patient married at the age of twenty-three, but continued to live in his father's home. Indigestion first appeared when his wife threatened to leave him. She divorced him after two years, and he soon remarried. His second wife had to go to work in order to support them. She finally became disgusted with his delinquent behavior, and threatened divorce. Two hours after the patient realized she was serious, his hematemesis occurred (p. 703).

Like the other two cases, we again see a close temporal relationship between threat and symptoms.

DISCUSSION QUESTIONS

1. Kapp, Rosenbaum, and Romano conclude that all three clusters of patients have conflict surrounding dependence versus independence. Do you agree with this in all cases, or do some better exemplify these conflicts than others?

2. In this research, the "data" reported come from unstructured interviews. Is there any reason to be skeptical about this information?

3. How would each of the models of abnormality apply to these ulcer patients? What factors would be emphasized as critical in each?

4. One of the difficulties in studying patients once their problems already exist is reconstructing their pasts to discover the correct sequence of events: the proverbial chicken-and-egg problem. Is it conceivable that gastric upset leads to dependency rather than vice versa? Discuss this for the three cases we've presented.

5. The text observes that Alexander's psychosomatic account of ulcers does not hold for women. How does the experience of women in our society differ from that of the three men described in the cases here? Do these differences explain why the psychodynamic formula does not apply to women who develop ulcers?

6. How would you treat each of these three patients? Presumably, you would start by prescribing cimetidine, but what psychological therapies might you undertake in each case?

REFERENCES

Alexander, F. (1950). *Psychosomatic medicine: Its principles and applications*. New York: Norton.

Kapp, F. T., Rosenbaum, M., & Romano (1947). Psychological factors in men with peptic ulcers. *American Journal of Psychiatry, 103*, 700–704.

Norman Cousins:
Anatomy of an Illness

Chapter 10 of your text describes the new field of psychoneuroim-munology, which investigates how psychological states influence the working of our body's immune system. Recent studies show that such characteristics as hopelessness, helplessness, and pessimism indeed foreshadow poor health and even early death. Appreciate that such cor-relations are impossible to accommodate within the medical theories that have prevailed throughout most of the twentieth century.

Modern medicine began in the 1800s with the formulation of the germ model of illness: i.e., germs are necessary and sufficient causes of disease. This model has been of inestimable value to science and soci-ety, because it points specifically to a convenient target for those who wish to intervene to prevent or treat illness. The germ model has been such a practical success that it has crowded out of the picture other theoretical perspectives, including those that propose that health and illness reflect psychological determinants as well as biological ones.

As a general statement about important factors that contribute to well-being or its absence, there is nothing wrong with the traditional germ theory of illness. In fact, there is so much right about it that it is easy to understand why other factors have been ignored. A problem nonetheless ensues when the traditional view is used to define the boundaries of admissible causes. Then there are obvious limitations. We know that a person can harbor germs without falling ill. We also know that there are environmental risk factors for disease that have nothing to do with germs. And we know that certain diseases like can-cer are extremely difficult to conceptualize using the traditional germ theory.

At the present time, psychoneuroimmunology is being accorded in-creasingly respectable status. Your text describes studies that have proved important in legitimizing the possibility that psychology has something to say about health and illness, but so too has the case that we're about to describe.

Norman Cousins is a well-known writer, and for years he was the ed-itor of *Saturday Review*. In 1964, he fell ill, and according to one specialist, he had only one chance in five hundred of surviving. Not a quitter, Cousins decided to muster his body's psychological resources to combat his illness. He succeeded. His subsequent account of his battle is presented in his book *Anatomy of an Illness*, which has become a well-known and often-cited example of the relationship between psychological factors and illness. We'll draw on his book for the details of the present case.

THE ILLNESS

Cousins returned from a trip abroad with a slight fever and a feeling of achiness. Rather than going away, these symptoms worsened, and within a week, he found it difficult to move his neck, his arms, or his legs. He sought out a physician, and medical tests revealed that he was suffering a massive infection. He was admitted to a hospital in critical condition.

A precise diagnosis proved elusive, although the examining physicians agreed that Cousins had a collagen illness: a disease of the connective tissue of the body. His symptoms worsened. He could barely turn over in his hospital bed. Nodules appeared all over his body. His jaws virtually locked together. It was believed that the tissue in his spine was disintegrating. Cousins was in bad shape, falling apart—literally. His physicians felt that he had little chance of surviving this illness.

THE POSSIBLE CAUSES

Many people might well have closed their eyes and passed away. Cousins instead asked about the possible causes of such a disease. One hypothesis was that it resulted from poisoning by heavy metals. How could this have happened?

Cousins thought back to his trip abroad. He had stayed in a hotel next to a housing project under round-the-clock construction. Diesel trucks drove past his window all night long, expelling their fumes. Cousins woke each morning slightly nauseated. And as he flew home, he caught the exhaust fume of a jet square in his face as it pivoted on the runway. Since exhaust fumes are loaded with heavy metals, it was conceivable that these experiences contributed to the illness from which he was now dying. But his wife had accompanied him on his trip, and had inhaled the same fumes without ill effect.

So an additional hypothesis was suggested to account for his condition: his immune system was depressed, because his adrenals were exhausted. Why? His trip had been a series of frustrations. On his last day, he was supposed to arrive someplace at 5:00 P.M., but when his chauffeur became lost, he was greatly delayed, not arriving until

9:00 P.M. He was embarrassed and thwarted. Then he flew home, falling ill, and within a week was dying.

These hypotheses can be combined into a diathesis-stress account. A weakened immune system (the diathesis) blasted by exhaust fumes (the stress) led to Cousins's illness. But what good does it do to know the etiology of an illness? A full understanding of a psychological disorder should give clues to possible treatments. This is no less true for physical disorders. Cousins set about undoing the factors that had led to his illness in the first place.

THE TREATMENT

The heavy metals were no longer an issue; they were gone. Cousins thus focused his attention on how to bolster his immune system. First, he thought about the medication he was taking, most of which had been prescribed to combat his considerable pain: e.g., aspirin, phenylbutazone, codeine, colchicine, and sleeping pills. Perhaps these drugs were further poisoning his system. He was given maximum doses, and his body was hypersensitive to everything else, so why not to the painkillers? So he stopped taking them. He also started to take massive doses of Vitamin C, based on several studies that found that people with collagen diseases were deficient in Vitamin C.

Second, believing that negative emotions can suppress one's immune functioning, he concluded that positive emotions might play a fortifying role. So, he set out to cultivate good feelings. You may be surprised at his initial step. He moved out of the hospital: "I had a fast-growing conviction that a hospital is no place for a person who is seriously ill" (Cousins, 1981, p. 29).

Permit us an interesting tangent. Florence Nightingale, the famous nurse from the Crimean War, owes much of her fame to her careful documentation of exactly this conclusion a century ago. Soldiers sent to hospitals for care were much more likely to die than those who were not sent to them (Kennedy, 1984)!

At any rate, Cousins felt that the familiar characteristics of hospitals, including too-frequent medical tests, lousy food, and the precedence of mindless routines over therapeutic needs (e.g., "wake up and take your sleeping pill"), were taking a toll on his already decimated immune system by making him unhappy. He checked into a plush hotel, which ended up costing only one-third of what his hospital room did.

The epitome of the positive emotions is probably laughter, and thus Cousins decided that laugh was exactly what he would do. He obtained comedy films and reruns of Candid Camera, and he watched them with great delight. "I made the joyous discovery that ten minutes of genuine belly laughter had an anesthetic effect and would give me at least two hours of pain-free sleep. When the pain-killing effect of the laughter wore off, we would switch on the motion-picture projector again, and, not infrequently, it would lead to another pain-free sleep interval" (pp. 39–40).

THE CURE

With repeated doses of Vitamin C and Candid Camera, Cousins's symptoms began to improve. His fever went down. His pulse slowed to normal. Inflammation began to go away, and he was able to move his thumbs without pain. But his symptoms did not all go away suddenly. For months and even years, some of his movements were restricted. But Cousins was able to return to his work full time. He presents the following conclusion about his experience:

> . . . the will to live is not a theoretical abstraction, but a physiologic reality with therapeutic characteristics. . . . I didn't accept the verdict, [and thus] I wasn't trapped in the cycle of fear, depression, and panic that frequently accompanies a supposedly incurable illness. . . . I have learned never to underestimate the capacity of the human mind and body to regenerate—even when the prospects seem most wretched. The life-force may be the least understood force on earth (pp. 44–48).

Psychoneuroimmunology attempts to grasp this life-force in scientific terms.

DISCUSSION QUESTIONS

1. As you know, case studies like that of Norman Cousins make it difficult to isolate critical causes. We've presented this case as if psychological factors were responsible for his recovery, but what other causes might have been operating here? Design a study that would distinguish these factors from psychological ones.

2. Psychological characteristics affect health and illness not just through the immune system but in other ways as well. Describe some of these.

3. Something we did not bring out in our brief presentation of the present case is that Cousins had an excellent working relationship with his personal physician, who supported and facilitated his unusual treatment. How important can a good "bedside manner" on the part of a physician be in treating illness?

4. Suppose you were asked to redesign hospitals so that they encouraged what Cousins calls the will to live. What changes would you make? What would you leave the same?

5. One intriguing implication of this case, and of the entire field of

psychoneuroimmunology, is that illness can be prevented in the first place by psychological interventions. Sketch the form that these might take.

6. We recently read a book by Leonard Sagan (1987) in which he examines the possible reasons for the dramatic increase in human longevity over the last few centuries. The conventional explanations for our increased life expectancy point to biological factors: decline of infectious disease, better nutrition, improved medical care, and so on. Sagan disagrees, arguing instead for psychological and social factors. According to him, we live longer today because we are more robust, and we are more robust because we experience less stress and greater efficacy than individuals during any other period in history. Examine this argument in light of the present case. And consider a dire prediction by Sagan: to the degree that personal happiness is being increasingly thwarted in the United States during the late twentieth century, we should expect illness and death to become more likely.

REFERENCES

Cousins, N. (1981). *Anatomy of an illness as perceived by the patient.* New York: Bantam.

Kennedy, G. (1984). The lady with the data. In *Invitation to statistics.* Oxford: Basil Blackwell.

Sagan, L. A. (1987). *The health of nations: True causes of sickness and well-being.* New York: Basic Books.

Cognitive Therapy for Mr. N.: Unipolar Depression

One of the notable developments in abnormal psychology during the past two decades is the growth of the cognitive perspective. Particularly with respect to unipolar depression, theories that link the origin and maintenance of symptoms to an individual's thoughts and beliefs have been widely accepted. One reason for the popularity of these theories is that they lead to specific forms of therapy that try to change our thoughts and beliefs (Beck, Rush, Shaw, & Emery, 1979). As an individual's way of thinking changes, so too does his or her depression. The text notes that the overall effectiveness of cognitive therapy matches that of antidepressant medication as a treatment. And obviously, cognitive therapy has no physical side effects like medication does. We can expect to see cognitive therapy become even more widely used in the years to come.

The present case describes the treatment of Mr. N., a depressed patient given cognitive therapy. One interesting aspect of this case is that Mr. N. suffered a relapse into depression shortly after therapy ended. This relapse is instructive with regard to cognitive therapy, so read our description of treatment carefully and see if you can detect what the psychologist did wrong the first time.

THE CASE

When first seen for therapy, Mr. N. was thirty-eight years old, a slim man with long hair. He was a Vietnam veteran, and had been admitted to a Veterans Administration hospital with complaints of various depressive symptoms. According to the notes taken by the therapist during his initial interview with Mr. N., these complaints included:

- extremely depressed mood
- feelings of hopelessness about the future, particularly with regard to finding employment
- difficulty sleeping
- loss of interest in his life-long hobby of tinkering with mechanical devices and gadgets
- no interest in sex
- difficulty concentrating
- recurrent thoughts of suicide

During Mr. N.'s initial interview, he reported neither a plan for suicide nor the intention to devise one. He just sat in a chair and did not move. He made no eye contact with the psychologist. Although Mr. N. answered all questions politely and coherently, he spoke very slowly, pausing frequently to sigh. He said nothing that was not a specific response to a question.

As you can see, Mr. N. unambiguously met the DSM-III-R criteria for a major depressive episode. This was apparently the first time he had warranted such a diagnosis, although years before, following his discharge from the army, he started to have serious problems with drinking. He lost several jobs because he was too hung over to go to work. He eventually lost his driver's license because of too many drunk driving convictions. This led him to seek help at an alcohol treatment program. His treatment went well, and Mr. N. had abstained from alcohol for the last two years.

When he was admitted to the hospital, he had been depressed for about one month, since the loss of his most recent job as a custodian. His employers apparently had decided to switch from full-time employees kept on the payroll year-round to part-time employees hired only when they were needed, which was not at this time of the year. Remember that Mr. N. did not have a driver's license, and the absence of public transportation in the small town where he lived made it difficult to find other work.

Before we discuss treatment, let's complete the full DSM-III-R description of Mr. N. by considering how he was evaluated on the other axes. You already know his Axis One diagnosis: major depressive episode. With regard to Axis Two, where personality disorders are described, there was a hint of a dependent style on his part (this style became pertinent during the treatment as you will see). On Axis Three, he was medially sound, according to an examining physician, except for a slight limp that dated to Vietnam. Again, remember this detail. On Axis Four, where environmental stressors are noted, Mr. N.'s recent circumstances were deemed relatively severe. He had lost his job, had little money and few prospects. Finally, using Axis Five, the psychologist described Mr. N.'s previous functioning as generally good since the time he had completed the alcohol treatment program, but not so good when a longer view was taken.

THE TREATMENT

Mr. N. believed that the alcohol treatment program he had successfully completed had been a godsend, allowing him to turn his life away from a highly destructive course. His wife, when she was interviewed by the psychologist, completely agreed. His abstinence had allowed him to find and hold a steady job, and let them lead a stable existence for the first time in their marriage. When he lost his custodian job, the most readily available one in their immediate neighborhood, they both felt that the rug had been pulled from beneath their feet.

The psychologist believed that the environmentalist model explained Mr. N.'s condition. The job loss was an uncontrollable event, and Mr. N. did not have the ability to cope with its aftermath. He was hopeless and helpless, and his pessimistic beliefs seemed largely responsible for the ensuing depression. It became clear in the course of treatment, however, that Mr. N.'s beliefs were not entirely at odds with the facts. So, although cognitive therapy was undertaken, more than his thoughts and beliefs needed to change. The world had to become easier for him to negotiate as well.

Cognitive therapy goes through a series of discrete steps. First, the patient is "socialized" into the appropriate client role and the therapist provides him or her with explanations of the basic tents of cognitive theory. Mr. N. was told how thoughts influence moods, and was encouraged to think of instances where his outlook indeed produced one feeling or another. He readily grasped the point.

Second, the patient is encouraged to capture and examine the particular thoughts that precede his actual depressed moods. What is the evidence for the automatic thoughts that make him depressed? If evidence is lacking, the patient is told to entertain more realistic beliefs. And if the facts seem to justify the depressing belief, then the patient is helped to change things so that this is no longer the case.

Mr. N. soon became adept at identifying his automatic thoughts. They fell into two groups. The first group was composed of general conclusions that he was a loser and a worthless person. These were combatted with contrary evidence. Mr. N. had several laudable strengths and accomplishments. Notable, he had served with distinction in a difficult and unpopular war. He had taken control of his runaway alcoholism and solved that problem. His wife was steadfast and supportive.

The other group of automatic thoughts were somewhat more specific beliefs about things going on in his life that were objectively bad. Mr. N. had no job. He had no money. He had no driver's license. And so on.

The psychologist enlisted the help of other professionals in the hospital to devise solutions to these particular problems. Mr. N. applied for a partial government pension because of his limp, which was demonstrable and clearly due to an injury suffered while serving in Vietnam.

The examiners told him to expect the pension, which would help alleviate his family's monetary problem.

Mr. N. also received vocational counseling. His name was placed on the register for civil service positions, where his status as a veteran would give him an advantage over non-veteran applicants.

Finally, Mr. N. reapplied for his driver's license. His psychologist wrote a letter to the Bureau of Licenses attesting to Mr. N.'s sobriety of several years. Because the state in which Mr. N. lived gave special consideration to individuals with suspended licenses who need to drive to get to work, he had cause to be optimistic.

In the course of his stay in the hospital, Mr. N.'s depression lifted entirely. He became cheerful and anxious to get on with his life. He was thus discharged from the hospital, and his psychologist continued to meet with him in outpatient therapy.

THE RELAPSE

Mr. N. did not live happily ever after, or at least not right away. A series of bad events occurred which led to another depressive episode. Let us explain. Some weeks after his discharge, Mr. N. was offered a civil service job near his home. He was told to show up for a physical exam prior to starting work. But he failed the physical because of the injury to his leg. Mr. N. just missed the cutoff. This perhaps would not have upset him in its own right, except that the very next day, he received a letter turning down his request for a pension. In this case, he didn't limp badly enough to warrant any support. He fell just short of the required cutoff. Different branches of the government used different values!

Then Mr. N.'s request to have his driver's license reinstated was turned down without an explanation. He became dismayed with his psychologist, reasoning that his therapist—as a government employee— ought to have been able to write a more persuasive letter to other government employees than he had obviously written. Mr. N. became depressed again.

Does this represent a failure of cognitive therapy? Not exactly. Mr. N.'s thoughts and beliefs were still linked to his moods. His relapse represented instead a failure to implement cognitive therapy as broadly as this case required. So, Mr. N.'s dependent style was never explicitly addressed in the initial therapy. Indeed, the practical help he received from the various professionals in the hospital—although well-intended —did nothing to make him feel more capable. What in effect happened was that a number of people did things that made his future prospects look more cheery. When all of these steps failed, Mr. N. became depressed. His own helplessness was underscored once again.

MORE TREATMENT

In attacking Mr. N.'s second depression, again with cognitive therapy, both the patient and the psychologist had learned something from the first treatment. This time, Mr. N. was encouraged to devise and implement his own solutions to the practical problems in his life. He did so by contacting local organizations that served as advocates for Vietnam veterans. He wrote his own letters. He arranged his own appointments. He cut his own red tape. Again, things began to look up for him. Again, his depression lifted. This time, when there were setbacks, as of course there always are, Mr. N. persevered rather than becoming depressed.

DISCUSSION QUESTIONS

1. The case of Mr. N. is presented from a cognitive perspective. But as Chapter 11 emphasizes, a variety of factors conspire to create depression. What would a biomedical theorist add to the cognitive account? What would a psychodynamic theorist wish to stress?

2. Describe Mr. N's depression in terms of the learned helplessness model. Speculate about the nature of his explanatory style.

3. Does the case of Mr. N. provide any hints about why unipolar depression is on a precipitous rise? In what ways is he representative of the common person in the United States in the late twentieth century?

4. Would Beck's cognitive therapy be more accurately described as a cognitive-behavioral therapy? Why or why not?

5. Is a hopeless outlook on the future (i.e., an expectation that outcomes will not depend on responses) a sufficient condition for depression, as the learned helplessness model implies? Is it possible to believe that outcomes are independent of one's responses and not be depressed? Rothbaum, Weisz, and Snyder (1982) propose this second possibility, suggesting that belief systems like those provided by religion serve to protect a person from the depressing effects of hopelessness. What do you think of this idea? Would Mr. N. have become depressed if he had had a strong religious commitment?

REFERENCES

Beck, A. T., Rush, A. J., Shaw, B. F., & Emery, G. (1979). *Cognitive therapy of depression.* New York: Guilford.

Rothbaum, F., Weisz, J. R., & Snyder, S. S. (1982). Changing the world and changing the self: A two-process model of perceived control. *Journal of Personality and Social Psychology, 42,* 3–37.

Moods and Great Men: "Bipolar Depression"

In bipolar depression, also known as manic-depression, depressive episodes alternate with manic episodes. The text mentions briefly that several famous men—Abraham Lincoln, Theodore Roosevelt, and Winston Churchill—are thought by some to have suffered from bipolar disorder.

In the present cases, we'll draw on details presented in a book by psychiatrist Ronald Fieve (1976) to examine the lives of these men in light of their supposed affective disorder. Let us emphasize that historical figures cannot really be given a diagnosis at a distance in the same way that a flesh-and-blood patient can be given a diagnosis when observed and questioned up close. Such interpretations can be informative but must be regarded as highly speculative, because there is no way to check them out. Although we agree with Fieve and others that some of these great men probably experienced bipolar depression, take the "diagnosis" that follows with a grain of salt.

These cases are interesting, though, because they illustrate the creative aspect of mania and thereby raise some hard questions about what we should consider to be abnormal. When individuals are extremely manic, their behavior is obviously dysfunctional. They cannot concentrate on tasks; they act recklessly; they offend and anger other people. But when individuals are slightly manic, their boundless energy and optimism may lead to impressive accomplishments.

Lincoln, Roosevelt, and Churchill were not great men simply because they had manic episodes. Rather, their intelligence, vision, and leadership abilities were independent of any affective abnormality they may have experienced. But a slightly manic state—when coupled with other skills and opportune circumstances—can pay dividends. Or at least that is what the present case implies. See if you agree.

ABRAHAM LINCOLN (1809–1865)

If you are like us, you have a cache of miscellaneous information about Honest Abe. Does what you recall from grade school include any of the following details that Fieve recounts?

Possible depressive episodes. The description of Lincoln as a depressive is straightforward, not at all controversial. His contemporaries and biographers alike uniformly commented on his bouts with melancholy. At age twenty-nine, for instance, following the death of Ann Rutledge, whom he greatly loved, he was profoundly depressed. His friends feared that he would kill himself, and they hid knives and razors from him. This episode lasted for many months, longer than one would expect if it were normal bereavement, and it was marked not only by sadness but fatigue, indecision, and self-doubt.

Another well-documented episode of depression occurred when Lincoln and Mary Todd were engaged to be married. He didn't show up at the wedding! Friends later found him wandering about—restless, desperate, and unhappy. Again, those around Lincoln believed that suicide was a distinct possibility, and they kept a close watch over him until the threat passed.

There is also frequent documentation of Lincoln's slowness, lack of energy, and indecision. As you know, these are typical manifestations of depression. Perhaps the worst episode in his later life occurred when his son Willie died. Although Lincoln was at that time President, and the Civil War was going on, he spent long periods of time sitting alone, doing nothing except mourning his son.

Possible manic episodes. Fieve acknowledges that one must read between the lines of the historical record to find any evidence that Lincoln was sometimes manic. Reportedly, as a young man, Lincoln went through a wild phase that might have been a manic episode. He was overtalkative and got involved in a series of fistfights. He was bombastic and insulting.

Once his political career began, Lincoln showed bursts of prodigious energy, which Fieve interprets as manic episodes. Obviously, we have to be careful not to let Fieve read so far between the lines that facts themselves are ignored. He may be guilty of this. At any rate, Fieve emphasizes that Lincoln often gave numerous speeches in a short period of time, and this was in the days when a speaker wrote his own lines. Lincoln was described by his contemporaries as agitated and nervous during these bursts of activity. He pushed himself hard. He was impulsive and slept little.

Family history. Having a close relative diagnosed with bipolar depression is *not* in itself a DSM-III-R criterion for this disorder. But as you know from Chapter 11, recent research shows that bipolar depression has a genetic predisposition. Accordingly, a positive family history may strengthen the diagnostician's confidence that a particular individual's symptoms exemplify this disorder. What about Abraham Lincoln's family? The evidence here is extremely weak. Fieve describes Lincoln's father as restless, moody, and impulsive, but he refrains from calling him bipolar.

THEODORE ROOSEVELT (1858–1919)

As the twenty-sixth President of the United States, Theodore Roosevelt at times seemed bigger than life. (Among other things, he inspired the teddy bear!) He was a bundle of energy, and his life story is a series of accomplishments, each greater than the preceding one. Here is a brief chronology:

- Although a sickly child, Roosevelt built up his body to become an excellent athlete and boxer.
- Attending college at Harvard, Roosevelt was regarded as too ambitious, too talkative, and in too much of a hurry; he had a good but not distinguished academic career.
- As a young politician in Albany, New York, he became a member of the State Assembly; again, he is remembered as doing too much and talking too much.
- He was appointed to the U.S. Civil Service Commission and set about to weed out corruption; he became famous for his quarrels with those who dared to contest him.
- In 1895, Roosevelt became the head of the police board in New York City; he worked during the days in the office, then patrolled the streets at night, on the lookout for policemen straying from their duties; he slept but one or two hours out of each twenty-four.
- When the Spanish-American War broke out, Roosevelt became a colonel and led the cavalry regiment that came to be known as the Rough Riders; he was an inspirational but reckless leader; losses in his regiment were incredibly high.
- In 1899, Roosevelt became governor of New York State.
- In 1900, he was elected Vice President, and following McKinley's assassination, Roosevelt became President.
- He worked eighteen hours a day, slept little, and pursued uncountable activities; for instance, it is estimated that he wrote some 150,000 letters while Governor and President.
- After stepping down from the presidency in 1908, he kept busy, touring Africa and Europe; he sent reports of his adventures back to newspapers in the states.
- In 1912, he ran again for president but did not succeed; he made strategic mistakes in his campaign and was at times inappropriate.

Are you exhausted just reading about this man's life?

Possible depressive episodes. Was Roosevelt ever depressed? According to Fieve, he had periods of depression at college and while in the New York Assembly. For the rest of his life, though, he showed no evidence of depression. Let us note that this does not rule out a diagnosis of bipolar depression. Although some individuals with this disorder show a regular and rapid cycle of depressive and manic episodes, there are many other individuals whose mood swings show no such pattern.

Possible manic episodes. Indeed, the historical record seems to show that Roosevelt's manic episodes lasted for decades at a time. There is little ambiguity in describing his activity, particularly when he came into national prominence, as manic. He had an expansive mood. He needed little sleep. He was reckless. He was argumentative. He was talkative. He was incredibly active. He charmed many of his contemporaries and alarmed others. Was Roosevelt indeed manic? We think there is no doubt that this fascinating and frenetic man can be so described.

WINSTON CHURCHILL (1874–1965)

Churchill is the third great man suggested by Fieve to suffer from bipolar depression. If you have forgotten your recent world history, Churchill was the Prime Minister of England during World War II, and his leadership is widely credited with helping the Allies prevail.

Churchill's early life shows some parallels to that of Roosevelt, as we have just described. He did not distinguish himself as a student. He enlisted in the army and fought in India. Then he served with the Nile expeditionary force. Once he got a taste of adventure, he took off on a career that made him the most important person in England throughout most of his life, a period when England was the most important nation in the world.

Churchill first made his mark as a brilliant writer, as he recounted his war experiences. Then he took on a series of political appointments, marking himself as energetic, confident, and tireless. His opponents found him aggressive and quarrelsome. Eventually, Churchill became Prime Minister and lead his country in its fight with Hitler. Needing almost no sleep and capable of working around the clock, he contributed more ideas than the rest of the Cabinet combined.

Possible depressive episodes. Despite his accomplishments, Churchill experienced frequent bouts with depression, which he termed "Black Dog" and made few efforts to disguise. He thought of suicide, became apathetic, and sat for hours in what Fieve characterizes as a stupor. During the episodes, Churchill was beset with self-doubt, complaining that he had accomplished nothing important in his life. His depressions were sometimes triggered by his political frustrations and defeats, but they at other times occurred spontaneously.

Possible manic episodes. As in the case of Roosevelt, there is little mistake in describing Churchill as manic. All viewed him as brilliant, but his critics added impetuous and hotheaded to their characterization. His decisions were sometimes questioned as reckless. Certainly, he was domineering and irritable. He talked nonstop and pursued numerous projects simultaneously.

Family history. Fieve firmly concludes that bipolar depression ran through the Churchill family, and hence Winston's disorder had a genetic predisposition. We see no reason to question this evidence.

EVALUATION

Fieve's thesis is provocative. How do we regard his examples? We agree that Churchill can be described as bipolar. We are less convinced in the case of Roosevelt, since depressive episodes are not well documented, and we are not at all convinced in the case of Lincoln, since manic episodes seem to be lacking altogether. What do you think?

Regardless, let us stress a distinction that DSM-III-R makes between mania and hypomania. In the former case, manic symptoms disrupt a person's social or occupational functioning, whereas in the latter case, symptoms are present but not overly disruptive. Indeed, as we have seen in these cases, they may facilitate a person's adaptation.

DISCUSSION QUESTIONS

1. Some writers "diagnose" contemporary celebrities just as Fieve diagnoses figures from history. Under what circumstances, if any, can this be done without being a sideshow? What are the ethical issues here?

2. In light of the cases we've presented, one might wonder whether political charisma has anything to do with hypomania. What do you conclude?

3. Some theorists speculate that unipolar depression is sometimes adaptive, because it ensures that an individual takes time out from frustrating pursuits to regroup. Is it possible that bipolar depression is sometimes adaptive? Put this disorder in an evolutionary context, and do your best to sketch a scenario in which natural selection would have chosen people with the capacity for mood swings.

4. Psychoanalytic accounts of bipolar depression propose that mania is a defense against depression. Is this persuasive to you? How might you test this hypothesis? Specify the sequencing of manic and depressive episodes that should be observed.

5. Some patients with bipolar depression do not comply with their lithium prescription. Part of their reason is that lithium may have uncomfortable physical side effects. But there are psychological effects as well that they dislike: obviously, the loss of symptoms

like boundless energy and enthusiasm. What can be done to encourage compliance with a medication that may make life less fun?

6. Suppose Lincoln, Roosevelt, and Churchill were given lithium. Would world history have been different?

7. In light of recent findings that support the biomedical conception of bipolar depression, some are tempted to dismiss the role of psychology in this disorder. Drawing on these three cases, why should we pay attention to psychological factors if we wish to understand this problem?

8. Should unipolar and bipolar depression be classed together? Specify your reasons.

9. At one time, but no longer, bipolar depression was considered a psychosis, and lumped together with schizophrenia as a psychotic disorder (cf. Chapter 12 of your text). What do you think was the basis for this classification? Why has it been abolished?

REFERENCE

Fieve, R. R. (1976). *Moodswing: The third revolution in psychiatry.* New York: Bantam.

Poor and Good Outcomes: Schizophrenia

When it was first described, schizophrenia was thought to be a progressive condition, meaning that if you had this disorder, your symptoms would inevitably worsen. This is no longer the case. Some schizophrenic individuals indeed show a poor prognosis, never fully recovering after their initial psychotic episode. But others make a good recovery.

As Chapter 12 of the text details, researchers have tried to discover factors that predict poor versus good outcome in schizophrenia. Bernheim and Lewine (1979) drew on this research to create two composite individuals with schizophrenia who show very different courses. In the present case, we will present their composites. These are fictitious individuals but nonetheless instructive.

JOHN: POOR PROGNOSIS

All of his life, John had struck his family as being a little off. He acted like an outsider even at home, never showing much enthusiasm or involvement with family activities. It should be noted that this was not an easy family for any child, much less John, because his mother was frequently gone on what the family called trips. In the fifth grade, John found out from the neighborhood children that these trips were really hospitalizations. They said his mother was crazy.

It was during these grade school years that John first experienced a strange sensation: his mind seemed to float out of his body. This was frightening to him at first but later comforting. John came to enjoy this sensation; it provided him with a refuge from the rest of his life.

John's life at school was for the most part uneventful; indeed, it was strikingly so. He never became part of the group. For the most part, he never tried. On the few occasions when he did reach out to others, his efforts were rebuffed: ignored or misinterpreted. John had no friends at all. The few people who would qualify as his acquaintances were social rejects like himself.

His life at home was undemanding. His mother did nothing around the house at all, and paid no attention to him. His father busied himself with all the tasks that needed to be done. John was not asked to help with any of these because his father became frustrated watching him fumble and move slowly. So, neither at school nor at home did John ever lay any foundation for responsibility or identity. He moved through his early life as a social nonentity:

> One cannot point to a dramatic event, a family problem, or personal tragedy as a reason for John's failure to mature socially. It was clear, however, that being a member of the group, belonging to anything or anyone, was simply not to be for him. John became the person who, in gym class, always turned right when everyone else turned left, who ate alone at a small corner of a large cafeteria table, and who made people laugh when being serious and was taken seriously when joking (Bernheim & Lewine, 1979, pp. 186–187).

Not surprisingly, perhaps, John lived more and more in an inner fantasy life.

John's inner world was populated with superhumans who spoke a special language known only to John. This world became more attractive to him than school or home, so he visited there frequently. Eventually, the time came when he simply did not return from his fantasies. He stopped taking care of himself, not bathing for weeks at a time. His family was unable to convince him to attend to his hygiene. Their threats and pleas, their rewards and punishments, all failed. He ignored them. What other people thought or did had little meaning to him. At age sixteen, John was hospitalized for the first time.

The next decade was marked by a series of hospitalizations for John. Those who treated him were at first optimistic about his outcome. Medication helped him concentrate. Various therapists taught him the skills for living that he had never acquired. Following his discharge, things would go well for a little while, and then John would start to neglect himself. He would feel worthless and lonely, and his fantasy life would beckon him again.

With each hospitalization, treatment, discharge, and rehospitalization, John felt more like he had failed. This feeling was paralleled by the reaction of his therapists, who lost their initial optimism, and that of his family, who made the difficult decision not to have John return home upon discharge.

When not hospitalized, John lives in a community halfway house. The patterns of his family are played out again in the halfway house. Most of the time, the other residents ignore John. When he needs attention, they send him back to the hospital. At some point, the halfway house may not take him back. John's choices at that point will be limited: stay in the hospital as a permanent resident or survive the best he can outside of the system.

SAM: GOOD PROGNOSIS

Sam was the second of three children born into a stable and supportive family. By reports, he was a healthy infant and an engaging child. He did his share of household chores, with some grumbling. He did well in school, receiving A's and B's for final grades in all of his courses. Sam had a circle of friends that stayed together throughout their school years.

Once in high school, Sam expanded his activities and horizons. He was a leader in school. He edited the school paper as a senior, and found that he loved this kind of work. He threw himself into each issue, writing, editing, and revising. He planned to attend a large college famous for journalism. He applied and was accepted.

Once at college, Sam felt a trifle homesick. He also felt somewhat overwhelmed by the demands of college life. The course work was a lot harder than he had expected. He did not meet too many new people. In a word, Sam found that college life was hectic.

Then came the first round of exams. Although he studied a great deal, he received an F on one of them. As you know, he had never failed an examination before, and somehow the grade didn't seem real to him. But he was extremely upset. He had difficulty concentrating on anything other than this failing grade. He began to entertain the belief that the purpose of college was to brainwash students like himself into thinking the same way. Grades were the instrument of this plot, and his F was a sign that he had been singled out for special attention.

Sam's beliefs about his college soon expanded to include the fear that the authorities were keeping a record of all of his activities. After all, he was capable of overthrowing the system, because he had figured out its purpose and method of operating. Sam stopped studying. He burned his notebooks and personal papers, in order not to leave any evidence. He started to keep irregular hours, in order to throw off anyone trying to follow him. He scrutinized the college newspaper for hidden messages about the suspected plot. He often found them. With increasing frequency, he also heard coded broadcasts on the local radio station.

Eventually, Sam started to tell others about the plot. His friends did not know what to make of it, so they did nothing. This might have continued indefinitely, except that he went to a television station and demanded free time to broadcast a warning to the general public. When he was refused, he became enraged and started to throw furniture. The police came, and Sam found himself in a psychiatric hospital.

Medication calmed him down. Once calm, he was unable to remember most of the events immediately preceding his hospitalization. He was soon discharged from the hospital, and he saw a therapist for several months on an outpatient basis. Then he returned to school.

He still has fleeting thoughts that others are out to get him, but these occur only during times of stress. For the most part, he is doing well. The major change in his life is that Sam tries to minimize potential disappointments. He knows that these are particularly stressful for him.

CONCLUSION

Bernheim and Lewine (1979, p. 212) offer the following conclusion about the outcome of schizophrenia:

> [It] can have many outcomes. At one extreme, the course of the disorder is slow and long, marked by an inability to survive on one's own. At the other extreme, some schizophrenics have a single psychotic episode and then recover. There is every possible outcome between these two extremes. Also, outcome may take may forms. Outcome may be measured by symptoms, hospitalization, need for outpatient treatment, level of interpersonal functioning, ability to work, and individual growth. Thus, when we ask, "What will be the outcome for schizophrenics?" the answer is, "Which outcome?" Recognition of these various aspects of pre- and post-psychotic functioning results in a complex collage.

DISCUSSION QUESTIONS

1. The cases of John and Sam were constructed to illustrate the factors that predispose poor outcome on the one hand and good outcome on the other. What specifically are these factors?

2. Most people who have a schizophrenic episode have a mixed prognosis. As a therapist working with a patient following an initial psychotic episode, what could you do to make the outcome as favorable as possible?

3. Using the terms in the book, describe the form of schizophrenia from which John suffers. Do the same for Sam.

4. Speculate on the possible etiology of John's disorder. Again, do the same for Sam's problem. What are the relative mixes of biological and environmental causes in each case?

5. Thomas Szasz (1961) argues that mental illness, including schizophrenia, is a myth, and that these disorders should be regarded as problems in living. Using the cases of John and Sam, examine this argument. What do you conclude?

REFERENCES

Bernheim, K. F., & Lewine, R. R. J. (1979). *Schizophrenia: Symptoms, causes, and treatments.* New York: Norton.

Szasz, T. (1961). *The myth of mental illness.* New York: Norton.

The Genain Quadruplets: Schizophrenia

As Chapter 12 of the text makes clear, psychologists have debated the causes of schizophrenia since the disorder was first delineated. Most of these debates have revolved around the issue of biological versus environmental causation, the familiar nature-versus-nurture issue played out so often in the biological and social sciences.

Family studies help us unravel the etiology of schizophrenia. Granted that individuals warrant the diagnosis, what is true about their parents or their offspring? Do they have the same problem? What about their brothers or sisters? And if they happen to have a twin, does their twin have schizophrenia? Do we see different patterns for identical versus fraternal twins?

One of the most interesting cases in the whole of abnormal psychology is that of the Genain children: identical quadruplets concordant for schizophrenia (Rosenthal, 1963). By the estimates we've read, the likelihood of such a coincidence is about one in fifteen billion, and we believe fewer than eight billion people have ever lived on the planet!

Estimates aside, the Genain quadruplets indeed exist, and have been studied by researchers at the National Institute of Mental Health. Perhaps the most important realization is that it is impossible to specify a simple and single cause of schizophrenia. Both biological and environmental factors apparently entwined to create the disorder shared by the Genains. Let us sketch their case for you, asking you to appreciate the complexity involved here.

THE CASE

The name "Genain" was made up by the researchers in order to protect the identity of the family. It is an acronym from Greek words meaning "dire birth." In all published reports, the four sisters are referred to as Nora, Iris, Myra, and Hester. These are made-up names as well, with the first letters coming from the initials NIMH. They were raised in a Midwestern town, and it is called Envira (for environment).

The Genain quadruplets were born in the 1930s, to great fanfare, as you might imagine. Their parents, Henry and Gertrude, were overwhelmed. Nothing in their background prepared them for the task of simultaneously raising four children.

Henry was the son of immigrants from Europe. His mother had a history of mental breakdowns and hospitalizations. She was manipulative and controlling. Henry was not a wanted child. When his mother became pregnant with him, she tried to induce an abortion by working herself to exhaustion and lifting heavy items. His father was meek and gentle, and he left the rearing of the children to his wife. Henry grew up a shy and fearful child. He stuttered, had a history of blacking out, and drank too much. He did not finish high school, and he worked at a series of unskilled jobs. At the time that the quadruplets were born, Henry was unemployed.

Gertrude was the daughter of farmers, the eldest child in a family of eight children. Her parents are described as kind and congenial, but neither spent much time with their older children. Gertrude did more than her share of household chores, and she helped care for her younger brothers and sisters. Her father greatly preferred his sons, and Gertrude resented the fact that he felt she needed little education. Indeed, she was kept at home until she was seven and a half years old, only then starting school. At about this time, both her parents became ill, so Gertrude went to live with her grandmother. When Gertrude expressed her preference to stay on with her grandmother, her father disowned her in an ugly scene. Supporting herself, Gertrude finished high school and started working as a practical nurse.

When Gertrude met Henry, she was not impressed. He annoyed her. But they eventually started to see each other. She was ambivalent about the courtship, but he threatened suicide if she would not marry him. Before they were married, they had a frank conversation. She asked him to stop drinking, which he did. He asked her to treat him as his mother had. Gertrude replied that she did not want to act in this way, but he apparently did not take her seriously. At any rate, they married.

Their married life did not start off on the right foot. Henry worked only occasionally. He was awkward around other people. He had little to say to Gertrude. Evenings were spent sitting alone at home, staring at each other but not talking. Neither of them particularly wanted to have children, but after three years of marriage, Gertrude became pregnant. According to her, Henry left for days at a time and neglected her. According to him, he helped with the cooking and housework.

In the fifth month of her pregnancy, her doctor predicted that she would have twins. He was wrong. She had quadruplets: four girls, weighing a total of 15 pounds, 1 ounce. The babies were small and sickly, and were difficult to feed. However, after six weeks in the hospital, all were in good condition and were sent home.

Gertrude and Henry could not afford to raise four babies, and so the local newspaper got involved with the family. There was a contest to name the children, and some modest contributions were raised. A new house was donated to them, and they moved in, along with Henry's mother. Gertrude shouldered the major burden in caring for the infants, and it was difficult work. Remember that this was before disposable diapers, paper towels, ready-made formula, automatic washers and driers, Sesame Street, and so on.

A steady stream of visitors came to see the babies, and the Genains started to charge each twenty-five cents per peek. Eventually visitors were turned away altogether, and Henry became worried about the safety and privacy of his family. He locked the doors and windows. Both Henry and Gertrude feared kidnappers, and an atmosphere of suspicion colored the household.

Although the four children were identical, they were treated by their family as two sets of twins. The two larger babies, Nora and Myra, were grouped together, as were the two smaller ones, Iris and Hester. Nora and Myra were favored by their parents. All four were weaned at five months apparently because Gertrude thought it would be funny to make this event coincide with a national holiday. (Yes, this is a strange thing to do.) She attempted to toilet train them at six months, but her efforts failed. Gertrude tried again when the quadruplets were nine months old, finally meeting with success after a year of trying. All four girls, however, continued to wet the bed at night until their middle teens.

Both parents accepted the belief that the four girls really represented one person split by unusual circumstance into four people. Accordingly, the girls were not expected to be particularly hardy. They were kept separate from other children. They never had playmates other than each other. Gertrude took a dislike to Hester, describing her as just like Henry, always trying to undermine her. At age three, Hester developed the habit of masturbating, causing her mother to see her as oversexed.

What was Henry up to during these first few years? He was in the basement of the new house, making illegal moonshine. He also started drinking again. Gertrude nagged at him to get a job, and he campaigned for public office in the town. With the fame that the quadruplets brought him, he was easily elected to a position he held for more than twenty years. He continued to drink heavily. This did not interfere with his job, but it created havoc at home. He frightened his children greatly when he was drunk.

Other problems plagued the household. Gertrude suffered a lengthy depression. She and Henry stopped having sex. Henry's mother had seizures and became senile. She criticized Gertrude and accused her of having affairs with other men. Henry had a series of rather open affairs. He contracted a venereal disease. Once, while drunk, he shot a revolver at his wife, thinking she was an intruder.

The girls started kindergarten at age five, and their first day of school was widely covered in the newspapers. Teachers considered them normal students, with the exception of Hester, who had some trouble with reading. The girls tried hard at school, doing average to somewhat less than average work. Henry and Gertrude, in contrast, believed that Nora and Myra—their favorites—were excellent students, whereas Iris and Hester were far behind. At the insistence of their teachers, all four girls repeated the fifth grade and part of the sixth. Everyone outside the family thought the girls were overprotected and highly restricted by their parents.

At school, the other children were never able to distinguish among the quadruplets. They made fun of them and called them dumb. At least some of this teasing came from resentment at the attention and privileges given to the girls. Also important is the fact that the girls did not know how to play any of the common childhood games. Hester continued to bear the brunt of criticism from Gertrude, who blamed her for the social problems of all four girls. In Gertrude's mind, Hester was too intent on masturbating to have any interest in developing friendships.

When the girls were about six, they started to take private dancing and singing lessons. And they performed around town. Then they appeared on radio shows and were featured in several Hollywood newsreels. They made a small amount of money, but most of it was used to buy costumes for them. The girls apparently enjoyed singing and dancing. They had some natural talent, and they were appealing to audiences when they performed in unison. They continued to perform until they were about twelve, when their schoolwork began to require more of their time.

Life at home became ever more stressful as the girls entered adolescence. Gertrude and Henry continued to fight. Each developed health problems. Henry's mother died, and Gertrude refused to go to the funeral. And the girls were faced for the first time with household chores.

The pairing of the girls into two sets continued, although often it was three against one, with Hester being the odd one out. The other three girls were always urged to "protect" her, which they did, but with more than a little resentment. Gertrude continued to worry about Hester's masturbation, and alerted all of her teachers to be on the outlook for it. She constantly punished the girl, once swabbing her clitoris with carbolic acid.

Gertrude brought Hester to a clinic, where she was assured that masturbation was normal and harmless. Nonetheless, Gertrude was not placated. She continued to punish Hester. Henry got into the act as well, telling the girls that masturbation led to insanity. The whole family became extremely upset about masturbation. Hester and Iris, still sleeping together at age twelve, were discovered by their mother engaged in mutual masturbation.

The parents found a doctor who would "circumcise" the two girls, i.e., remove part of the clitoris in the hope of deadening pleasurable sensations. But the girls continued to masturbate, breaking the stitches from the operation. For thirty days thereafter, their hands were tied to their beds when they were put to sleep. They continued to masturbate.

In junior high school, the girls did better work than in elementary school. Teachers regarded them as meek, and quiet, and shy. They were also too well behaved, in the eyes of some who were interviewed years later. Nora was the spokesperson for the quadruplets; Hester continued to be the most backward. The girls made few friends, and for the most part were ignored by the other students.

Gertrude and Henry were particularly adamant that the girls should have nothing to do with boys. Sex was a taboo topic except when its dangers were emphasized. The parents suspected that numerous boys and men were molesting their girls, especially Hester. It should be noted, though, that Henry insisted on watching his daughters dressing and undressing. He even watched when they changed their sanitary pads.

These patterns continued into high school, although the girls began to participate in some extracurricular activities and started to make some friends and take a few steps toward independent activity. Classmates warmed a bit toward them. Hester, however, began to have problems. She fell behind in her schoolwork. She became irritable and depressed. Her behavior became at times destructive and bizarre. Hester "confessed" to her mother about a series of sexual activities dating back to elementary school.

We can recognize Hester's actions as comprising a psychotic episode, but her parents thought that she had become mentally retarded from masturbation. Hester was removed from school, and kept at home. She complained of feeling lost and insecure. She was kept on sedatives. Nora and Iris started to experience physical symptoms: allergies, stomach spasms, menstrual irregularities, and fainting spells. They finished high school, though, and all the girls except Hester received their degrees.

Nora was the first to take a job, and she worked for two years as a stenographic clerk. Nora worked with a woman recently discharged from a tuberculosis sanatorium, and Henry insisted that she wash the office telephone with alcohol twice a day. He dropped in at her office several times a day, and he stood around watching her. Myra found a job as a legal secretary, at which she worked for four and a half years. Finally, Iris worked at a series of temporary jobs. She was overly slow and meticulous.

These three young women each had minor involvement in social groups. Henry fretted and fumed about this, warning his daughters of the dangers that other people represented. He forbade them to date. He started, however, to fondle both Nora and Myra, touching their breasts and buttocks, and he continued to watch all of his daughters dress and undress.

In the next few years, first Nora, then Iris, then Myra, and finally Hester had psychotic episodes requiring them to be hospitalized. They were all diagnosed with schizophrenia, and showed the gamut of symptoms described in your text: hallucinations, delusions, neglect of self-care, and so on. The family was unable to pay for the medical bills, and so the National Institute of Mental Health offered to provide free treatment in return for the opportunity to study them. Numerous studies have been carried out, resulting in the book from which we obtained their story (Rosenthal, 1963).

POSTSCRIPT

What happened to the Genain quadruplets? Twenty years after the initial NIMH investigations, a follow-up study was conducted (Buchsbaum, 1984). Although all four continued to have problems, they showed different outcomes. Hester and Iris spent most of the ensuing years in hospitals. Nora had successfully held several jobs, as had Myra. Myra was the only one of the four to marry and have children.

DISCUSSION QUESTIONS

1. In light of this case, discuss why the etiology of schizophrenia is so hard to articulate. What was responsible for the problems of the Genain quadruplets? What wasn't responsible?

2. The four sisters were all given an unambiguous diagnosis of schizophrenia, but the subtypes differed, from paranoid to disorganized to catatonic. Granted their identical genes, what is the significance of the differing diagnoses?

3. In light of our current knowledge, how might a therapist treat the Genain sisters following their initial psychotic episodes?

4. In light of our current knowledge, what might have been done to prevent the Genains from developing schizophrenia in the first place?

REFERENCES

Buchsbaum, M. S. (1984). The Genain quadruplets. *Psychology Today,* *18*(8), 46–51.

Rosenthal, D. (Ed.) (1963). *The Genain quadruplets.* New York: Basic Books.

Peter: Schizophrenia

R. D. Laing is a Scottish psychiatrist who takes a phenomenological approach to abnormality. He has directed his attention at schizophrenia in particular, and his well-known book *The Divided Self* tries to make madness comprehensible by depicting how one experiences it. What ensues is not so much a theory of schizophrenia as a description of it from the inside.

Laing feels that many of the concepts used to explain schizophrenia inadvertently serve as roadblocks to understanding because they make the schizophrenic individual seem to be a thing rather than a person. "Things" don't have experiences, and "things" don't assign meanings to events. If a schizophrenic is rendered a thing by a theory, and a broken thing at that, we are tempted not to listen to what he has to say. Consider such notions as word salad, loose associations, and cognitive slippage. These may be colorful metaphors, but Laing regards them as dangerous. After using them to describe a schizophrenic, are we likely to think of this individual as a human being?

Interestingly, according to Laing, one of the central problems of schizophrenia is that individuals regard themselves as things. When they act on this conception, the rest of society views them as abnormal. (Theories that regard them as things are considered scientifically sophisticated!) In *The Divided Self*, Laing (1965) describes how schizophrenics come to view themselves in these terms. Let us present one of the cases that Laing describes to make his point. It is the case of Peter.

THE CASE

Peter is a large and robust man in his middle twenties. When he first came to see Laing, he looked the picture of health. But Peter had an unusual complaint. An unpleasant smell constantly surrounded him. He was not sure that other people could detect the smell, but it was clear to him. (As a point of fact, olfactory hallucinations like this one are somewhat common in schizophrenia, although auditory hallucinations are by far the most typical. Olfactory hallucinations may also indicate the presence of a brain tumor.)

The smell seemed to emanate from the lower part of Peter's body, particularly his genitals. Sometimes it smelled like something was burning. Other times it smelled like something old and decayed. Although he bathed several times a day, Peter could not rid himself of the smell.

He later described frequent attacks of anxiety, centering around the conviction that he was a hypocrite. He knew himself to be a sham, someone whose "real" feelings consisted largely of sadistic sexual fantasies. It was just a matter of time before others found him out. In one incident that greatly frightened him, Peter masturbated in the bathroom at work, all the time thinking of assaulting one of his coworkers. When he left the bathroom, he immediately encountered the woman, who looked directly at him. He had a panic attack, fearing that she could read his mind and learn of his evil thoughts. He began to worry that people could smell his semen and thereby know that he had masturbated.

These beliefs and fears affected the way that Peter went about his daily life. He drifted, attempting to be as anonymous as possible. He was most comfortable in the role of the stranger. He would go to a place where he was unknown, always using a different name in his travels. Only as a stranger could he act spontaneously around other people. As long as he went incognito, Peter felt safe from his fear that others could see through him and detect his "real" nature.

A PHENOMENOLOGICAL DESCRIPTION

Based on what we have said so far about Peter, you can see that a diagnosis of schizophrenia might be warranted. He evidences hallucinations and delusions. His social functioning is less than optimal. He has been disturbed in these ways for years.

The typical psychiatric or psychological approach to schizophrenia would consider Peter's case closed. We have a diagnosis. Let's prescribe medication appropriate to the diagnosis and hope that his symptoms go away. Next?

But Laing tells the mental health professionals to slow down. The diagnosis of Peter is far from satisfactory. Whether or not his hallucinations and delusions have a biological underpinning, he is still a human being with experiences ignored by the diagnosis. What is it like to be Peter? And how did Peter develop his present way of being?

One starts to get a glimpse of Peter from the inside by knowing about his childhood. Here is Laing's (1965) account:

> His parents were not happy people but they stuck close to each other. They had been married ten years before he was born. They were inseparable. The baby, the only child,

made no difference to their life. He slept in the same room as his parents from birth until he left school. His parents were never openly unkind to him and he seemed to be with them and yet they simply *treated him as though he wasn't there.* . . . He was bottle-fed and put on weight well, but he was never cuddled or played with. . . . His mother . . . hardly noticed him at all. She was a pretty woman, and was always fond of dressing up and admiring herself . . . though the father was very fond of the boy in his way, something seemed to stop him from being able to show his affection to him. He tended to be gruff, to pick on faults, occasionally to thrash him for no good reason, and to belittle him with such remarks as, "Useless Eustace," "You're just a big lump of dough" (pp. 120–121, emphases in original).

We all have had episodes where other people have ignored us. Think about how we react when this happens. Then try to extrapolate these reactions to a lifetime of being ignored, and you'll have a sense of what Peter experienced.

Laing believes that Peter failed to learn what was real and what was not. His parents gave him no clues. Inner and outer reality were never particularly distinct for Peter. How could they be? When you are treated as if you are not there, you regard yourself as not really present. Some of his "symptoms" start to make sense. Most of us define reality as what is interpersonally validated. Smells that other people confirm are real ones; smells that only you detect are not. But if you were raised by parents who never confirmed any of your sensations as real, or disconfirmed others, then hallucinations are apt to occur.

Further, the hallucinated smell is not simply a byproduct of disordered biochemistry. It also has a meaning to Peter, to which Laing directs our attention. The smell symbolized Peter's shame. He later came to interpret the smell less literally: "'It was more or less the regard I had for myself. It was really a form of self-dislike.' That is to say, he stank so badly in his own nostrils that he could hardly endure it" (Laing, 1965, p. 130). Had Peter told others that he had an extremely low opinion of himself, he would not have been called schizophrenic. But this is what his "symptom" meant, which leads us to question whether schizophrenia can really be regarded as disordered biology.

A poignant episode from early in Peter's life further illustrates the usefulness of paying attention to a schizophrenic's experience, as opposed to his symptoms. Peter had but one friend when he was a child. So, we might say that he was socially estranged and leave it at that. But pause and discover that his friend was a little girl about his own age who had been blinded in an air raid (during World War II). For several years, Peter spent a great deal of time with the girl, showering her with patience and kindness, helping her adjust to life without sight. She later said that she owed her life to Peter's kindness, because no one else took any time to be with her.

Do you see the meaning of this relationship? If you were raised like Peter was raised, by parents who treated you like you were invisible, what would you look for in a friend? Like his mother, the little girl did not see him. But unlike his mother, she needed him.

On one level, Laing's account of Peter is consistent with some of the theories reviewed in Chapter 12 of your text, those that stress the causal role of disordered family communication in the origin of schizophrenia. But on another level, there is an important difference. Family theorists argue that particular styles of interaction can produce schizophrenia in a child. Laing's point is more subtle. We learn to think and act from the way our families treat us, however that may be. Some of these ways of behaving are regarded as normal; other ways of behaving are regarded as schizophrenic. But all of these ways make sense granted the way the individual sees himself and the world. Schizophrenia remains a closed book unless it is seen as part of a human experience.

DISCUSSION QUESTIONS

1. The text describes a number of therapies for schizophrenia. How would these treatments be different if they were informed by the sort of perspective that Laing urges?

2. Laing has developed his own approach to treating schizophrenia. What do you think it consists of?

3. Discuss Laing's description of Peter in light of the distinction in the text between positive and negative symptoms of schizophrenia. Is phenomenology incompatible with biology?

4. Laing can be described as an existentialist. Discuss the case of Peter in terms of the important existential concepts presented in Chapter 4 of your text.

5. Sketch a phenomenological approach to one or more of the other disorders discussed in the text.

6. In his more recent writings, Laing is a strong societal critic. Can you see the seeds of this criticism in the case of Peter?

REFERENCE

Laing, R. D. (1965). *The divided self: An existential study in sanity and madness.* New York: Penguin.

Please Tread on Me: Paraphilia

Throughout the text, the fuzziness of abnormality has been stressed. Nowhere is this easier to see than in the class of disorders called the paraphilias. DSM-III-R defines a paraphilia as a sexual response to an object or situation that is not part of "normative" patterns. But what does normative mean? Surveys of sexual activity, within our society as well as around the world, show that an incredible variety of objects and situations may become linked to arousal and gratification.

DSM-III-R further characterizes a paraphilia as interfering with reciprocated, affectionate sexual activity. In other words, a paraphilia is a disorder to the degree that it gets in the way of social relationships. This criterion strikes us as important, but it remains difficult to apply in the concrete.

The present case, described by Wilhelm Stekel (1930), is that of a man who is turned on when a woman walks on him while he is lying on his back. As she treads on his throat and chest, he becomes increasingly excited. When she eventually steps on his erect penis, he has an orgasm.

For most of us, this form of turn-on is unusual, if not unique. It seems to qualify as a paraphilia. Nonetheless, we believe that some might disagree. The individual in the case, Mr. P., is not at all distressed by what he likes. He is not psychotic. And he is not estranged from other people.

THE CASE

Mr. P. is a thirty-two-year-old man. Here is a description of his paraphilia in his own words:

> If I meet a woman who appears attractive to me . . . it is not my wish to have sexual contact with her in the usual sense of the word, but rather to lie down prone on the floor and have her walk over me and tread me underfoot. The curious wish occurs seldom and only when the woman in question is a

real lady and well built. She must be elegantly dressed, preferably in evening clothes with low shoes that have very high heels . . . Even though I may appreciate the spiritual or beautiful qualities of a woman, there is, after all, nothing about her that could arouse me like that part of her from the knee down, especially the foot. . . . Comparatively few women have a leg or ankle or foot beautiful enough to command my undivided or permanent attention. If such nevertheless turns out to be the case, I lose no time or energy in trying to get under her feet and then await being trod with most anxious anticipation.

The treading must last several minutes and must include the chest, abdomen . . . and finally the penis which is by then far too stiffly erect to suffer any damage thereby. I might say that I am also thrilled when a female foot compresses my throat. . . .

I imagine that the woman who treads upon me is my mistress and I her slave, and that she does it as a punishment for some transgression I have committed or perhaps out of pure pleasure for her self (pp. 277–278).

Mr. P. goes on to detail the ideal sexual experience of this sort, specifying particular types of shoes and stockings he likes the woman to wear, the range of weight that is optimal, and so on.

He occasionally has intercourse with women, and thereby experiences pleasure. But he derives greater satisfaction from being walked upon. He estimates that he has had about one hundred different partners in this activity. Few comply with his request more than once. Mr. P. believes that a small number of the women involved derive some pleasure from walking upon him, but that most initially comply without fully appreciating the sexual nature of what he has requested. He regards the process as a "conquest" of the woman in question and derives particular satisfaction when she is from the upper class. Most of his partners, however, have been prostitutes. He reports that three prostitutes he has hired were familiar with this form of sexual activity.

How did this practice begin? Mr. P. traces it to a sexual encounter when he was fourteen years old. Friends of his family had a pretty daughter, some years older than he. The two of them spent a great deal of time together. He found her ankles and feet extremely attractive, and she was aware of his attention. They would take walks together, and she seemed to go out of her way to step on things and crush them beneath her feet: flowers, fallen fruit, acorns, hay, and the like.

One evening Mr. P. was stretched out on a thick carpet in front of a fire. The young woman walked across the room. Instead of walking around him, she playfully stepped on him, and made a joke, saying that she was stepping on him just as she stepped on things during their walks. He laughed with her, and she remained standing on his body. He became aroused, grabbed her foot, and kissed it. The he pressed it against his erect penis, and he instantly had an orgasm.

They played out this scene many times in the next few years. She would buy lovely stockings and shoes, and demonstrate each new purchase to him by treading on his body and stimulating him to orgasm. She seemed to enjoy the activity as much as he did, although they never once talked about it. In her absence, Mr. P. would masturbate using one of her shoes. She eventually married someone else, and she and Mr. P. never again engaged in this sexual activity. Nor did they ever allude to it when they met. He wished to resume, but this was not to be. And so he turned his attention to other women. You know the rest.

DISCUSSION QUESTIONS

1. The text describes several theoretical accounts of how a paraphilia comes to be established. How does each apply to the present case? Do you find these compelling as explanations or just descriptions of his history? Remember that in the initial sexual episode with the young woman, Mr. P. was already turned on when it began. In other words, was this a critical event in the development of his paraphilia, or not?

2. Stekel hypothesizes that Mr. P.'s paraphilia and indeed all fetishes represent hostility toward women. He thinks that this is an unconscious process, and is alerted to it by Mr. P.'s preference for women of high social status. How would you test this hypothesis more definitively in the present case?

3. By his own reckoning, Mr. P. estimated that only a few of his partners derived any pleasure from treading on him. So, why would a woman freely choose to participate in this activity with him?

4. DSM-III-R specifies a number of specific paraphilias, including exhibitionism, fetishism, frotteurism, and masochism. Mr. P.'s paraphilia seems to have elements of all of these. What does this imply about attempts to classify the paraphilias?

5. Some theorists reserve the term fetish for a nonliving object. Other theorists say that a part of a body can be termed a fetish if a person is interested in the body part to the exclusion of the body to which it belongs. Does this make sense to you? What does this mean for someone with a preference that his partners, let us say, have green eyes or rippling muscles?

6. Why are some body parts more likely to be eroticized than others? (Feet, if you did not know this, are a common paraphilia.) Psychodynamic theorists stress the symbolic nature of these body parts. What might feet, shoes, and stockings symbolize for Mr. P. in the present case?

7. Suppose Mr. P. was distressed by his paraphilia and went to a behavior therapist for treatment. How would his therapy proceed?

8. Let's return to the issue of definition that we raised when introducing this case. Do you think that Mr. P.'s sexual preference

qualifies as a paraphilia? If so, let's imagine changing aspects of this activity. When does it stop being a paraphilia and start becoming just a variant of normal sexuality? For instance, suppose Mr. P. is naked. Does this make any difference? Suppose his partner is naked as well? Would your judgment of normality versus abnormality differ if she were not stepping on him but rather lying on top of him? Suppose she applied pressure to his body not with her feet but with her hands? Suppose Mr. P. had different fantasies about this activity? And so on.

9. Why are paraphilias apparently so rare among women?

REFERENCE

Stekel, W. (1930). *Sexual aberrations: The phenomena of fetishism in relation to sex.* New York: Liveright.

Homosexuality and American Psychiatry

An apt subtitle for this case would be "How and Why Homosexuality Stopped Being a Mental Illness." The history of how homosexuality has been regarded by the mental health professions is interesting and instructive. At one time, many psychiatrists considered the fact that someone was sexually attracted to members of his or her own sex as evidence in and of itself of a disorder. Indeed, this was the official stance of the American Psychiatric Association. This is no longer true. In DSM-III-R, homosexuality is no longer considered a disorder. There is of course a story about what took place in between. In the present case, we'll draw on Ronald Bayer's (1987) recent book *Homosexuality and American Psychiatry* to sketch this history. The subtitle that Bayer uses is "The Politics of Diagnosis," which conveys quite explicitly that the American Psychiatric Association's policy change did not take place simply because its members changed their minds.

SETTING THE STAGE

Western society has inherited many of its attitudes toward sexuality from the early Christians. Among the important tenets of early Christianity is the notion that sexuality without the intent of procreation is a sin. From this notion derive the positions that contraception is wrong, that abortion is wrong, and that homosexuality is wrong. Do you see the reasoning in the case of homosexuality? Sexual activity between two people of the same sex cannot possibly result in babies, and so it must be a sin. To further support this belief, one could point to the Biblical injunction: "If a man lies with a male as with a woman, both of them have committed an abomination; they shall be put to death, their blood is upon them" (Leviticus 20:13). One could also remember the lesson implicit in the story of Sodom and Gomorrah.

Biblical injunctions were supplemented in the Middle Ages with further warnings against the sinfulness of homosexuality. The negative attitude against homosexuality that would prevail in the Western world for centuries was crystallized by Thomas Acquinas, who branded it an unnatural practice.

(Here's an interesting tangent. Do you know the origin of the word "faggot," still used as a derogatory term for a homosexual? We'll explain it to you, and you will never hear this word in quite the same way again. As you know from Chapter 2, a suspected witch at one time was burned at the stake, to make her body inhospitable to the devil. The belief among those who burned the witches was that a particularly hot fire, one most appropriate to the task at hand, could be built by binding together with sticks of wood a homosexual plucked from a dungeon. The whole package—the sticks of wood and the homosexual—would then be set ablaze. The original meaning of "faggot" was the stick of wood used in such a fire, and the meaning came to apply as well to the hapless individual bound together with them.)

Following the Middle Ages, homosexuality gradually stopped being the sole province of the church and moved into secular law, and the negative attitude continued. In sixteenth-century England, homosexuality became a felony punishable by death. Not until 1861 was this particular punishment removed from the statutes of English law.

In the 1800s, scientists began to investigate homosexuality, "rescuing" the practice from the domains of sin and crime by branding it an illness and/or a constitutional weakness. Considerable debate ensued over whether homosexuality was inherited or not. We can recognize this as one more version of the familiar nature-nurture debate still of interest to psychologists (cf. Chapter 13 of your text). Regardless, homosexuality was always viewed as something deficient, whether inherited or acquired.

PSYCHIATRIC OPINIONS

Freud wrote on homosexuality, and was not particularly harsh in his opinions. Unflattering, yes; harsh, no. He regarded it as an arrest of development—a fixation, to use the technical term—but not in itself a pathology. In fact, Freud offered the opinion that homosexuality was a problem for someone only to the degree that it was accompanied by conflict and unhappiness. This was very much a modern view.

Other psychiatrists in the early twentieth century were not so far-sighted as Freud, and they called homosexuality an illness, a perversion, a phobia (toward the opposite sex), and so on. Research supported these opinions. In retrospect, these studies can be criticized for starting with the conclusion the researchers wished to support. That is, the strategy often followed was to compare homosexual individuals in therapy with heterosexual individuals not in therapy. Guess who fared worse on measures of mental health? So, the first two diagnostic manuals of the American Psychiatric Association, DSM and DSM-II, listed homosexuality as a bona fide mental disorder.

CHALLENGES

Eventually, the view of homosexuality as a mental disorder was challenged. First, Kinsey's surveys of sexual behavior revealed that fully 37 percent of American males reported at least some homosexual activity (to the point of orgasm) at some point in their lives. That's a lot of people having a mental disorder. Further, Kinsey's results showed that sexual preference did not fall into two discrete piles of homosexual versus heterosexual. Many people were in between. These findings further strained the position that homosexuality was a mental disorder.

Second, cross-cultural studies of human sexuality revealed incredible relativity with regard to what was considered normal. Although in no society is homosexuality the dominant sexual practice, there exist many cultures where homosexuality is considered perfectly normal. Children may be raised to be homosexuals. Homosexual acts may be part of adolescent rites of passage. And so on. Again, in the face of evidence like this, it became difficult to argue that homosexuality per se was a mental disorder.

Third, studies were undertaken that looked at the adjustment of homosexuals *not* in psychotherapy. In contrast to earlier studies, these investigations found no differences between homosexuals and heterosexuals. When Thomas Szasz, well known to us from his "myth of mental illness" arguments, began his attacks on conventional psychiatry, he used as examples the parallels between how the church had earlier persecuted homosexuals and the way the mental health professions were currently doing so. Szasz proposed that "mental illness" was simply the modern equivalent of "sin" and carried with it all the same connotations of evil and stigma.

Fourth, societal changes also occurred. Following the example of the black power movement in the 1960s, homosexual individuals became political activists and coined the slogan "gay is good" (just as "black is beautiful"). These activists took the stance that homosexuals were a persecuted minority. To the degree that they experienced psychological problems, the cause was their persecution, not their sexual preference.

CHANGES

These factors conspired to bring pressure on the American Psychiatric Association to change its stance concerning homosexuality as a disorder. Gay activists picketed meetings of the Association. They had allies within the group, as well as vocal opponents who continued to regard homosexuality as a disorder. In 1973, these issues came to a head, and the members of the American Psychiatric Association were asked to vote on the status of homosexuality.

The resolution here was a compromise, clearly political in nature. The organization tried to satisfy all parties to the debate. Homosexuality per se was no longer considered a disorder. But if someone with a homosexual preference felt unhappy or uncomfortable about his or her sexuality, then this "ego-dystonic homosexuality" was indeed a problem. As your text notes, this compromise was carried through into DSM-III. (Parenthetically, the architect of the compromise was a then-young psychiatrist named Robert Spitzer, who was later chosen—perhaps because of his political skills as well as his scientific ones—to preside over the creation of the DSM-III manual. We find this interesting.)

What is the current status of homosexuality? To very little fanfare, DSM-III-R (also under Spitzer's editorship) deleted the category of ego-dystonic homosexuality altogether. In its place is a new notion: ego-dystonic sexuality. Here, discomfort and displeasure with any sexual preference, for the same sex, for the opposite sex, or for no kind of sex at all, is considered a problem.

DISCUSSION QUESTIONS

1. The American Psychiatric Association was ridiculed by some for voting on whether homosexuality was or was not a disorder. Does voting strike you as strange? Defend your answer, and take into account the issues of definition presented in Chapter 1 of your text.

2. Is it fair to attribute current attitudes toward sexuality to the beliefs of individuals thousands of years ago? From what other sources might our sexual attitudes have come?

3. Why does homosexuality arouse in some people such strong feelings?

4. We believe that most theory and research (and controversy) pertaining to homosexuality focuses on male homosexuality rather than female homosexuality. Why is this so?

5. Should the origins of homosexuality (i.e., nature versus nurture) bear on our judgments of whether it is a psychological disorder? Apply your arguments to bipolar depression. To schizophrenia. To autism.

6. How has the AIDS epidemic affected our current societal attitudes toward homosexuality?

7. No theory of homosexuality is generally accepted. Some theorists believe that we first need a theory of sexuality. Only then can a

theory of homosexuality be specified. What questions should a theory of sexuality be able to answer?

REFERENCE

Bayer, R. (1987). *Homosexuality and American psychiatry: The politics of diagnosis.* Princeton, NJ: Princeton University Press.

Males, Females, and Others

One of the obvious things about the biological world is that a number of species come in two varieties, male and female. Indeed, we've read an esoteric argument that two sexes represent the optimal number needed to scramble genes without creating confusion in the process. But nonetheless, if we look for them in the biological world, we can also find patterns other than simply male and female. Some species come in three varieties: male, female, and neuter. Other species come in just one variety. And in still other species, the same organisms are first male and then female, or vice versa. Thus, we should be cautious in concluding that the arrangement of two and only two sexes is universal or natural.

What does this have to do with human beings? Everyone knows that there are males and females. That's the way it is, and that's the way it should be. Well, as usual, things are not quite this simple. We shouldn't expect them to be. With animals, we need merely concern ourselves with biological sex: the chromosomes or the sexual organs. But with people we additionally must consider sex as a psychological and sociological phenomenon. When choosing words carefully, theorists often use the term *gender* to refer to these aspects of sex. Further distinctions can be made between *gender identity*—the person's experience of the self as a male or female—and *gender role*—society's prescription of how people should behave granted that they are males or females. With people, we therefore can talk about the sexes in several ways: chromosomes; sex organs; gender identity; and gender role. You might still ask what this has to do with human beings. Everyone knows that these distinctions can be made, but that they all line up. Males have XY chromosomes, penises and testes, a masculine identity, and a man's role. Females have XX chromosomes, vaginas and ovaries, a feminine identity, and a woman's role. But consider the following phenomena:

Cytogenetic syndromes. Some people are born with sex chromosomes that depart from the typical XX or XY pattern. In Turner's syndrome, for instance, individuals have only one sex chromosome: X. In Klinefelter's syndrome, individuals have an extra sex chromosome: XXY. We tend to identify those with Turner's syndrome as females, and those with Klinefelter's syndrome as males, but note that when we do so, we are not basing our decision on their chromosomes.

Hermaphroditism. Some individuals are born with ambiguous genitals. Both ovarian tissue and testicular tissue are present. Or the tissue may not be sufficiently differentiated to say what it looks like. Regardless, these people are impossible to identify as males or females if we rely on their genitals for the judgment.

Transsexualism. In transsexualism, discussed in Chapter 13, a person's gender identity is at odds with his or her biological sexuality (i.e., chromosomes and/or genitals). A transsexual feels like a man in a woman's body, or a woman in a man's body. Here is yet one more example of how our various distinctions between males and females do not necessarily line up.

Androgyny. Some people combine within themselves stereotypically masculine and stereotypically feminine traits and interests. We speak of these people as androgynous, and in terms of the language we're using so far, we can say that they blend together male and female gender roles. Androgyny refers only to gender role, not to gender identity, genitals, and/or chromosomes.

With these complications as an introduction, the purpose of the present case is to speculate about what it would mean to live in a society that did not make the assumption that people come in only two varieties. Our speculation is aided by the fact that such societies apparently have existed. We will focus here on the berdache, a special group of people considered neither male nor female.

THE BERDACHE

The term "berdache" is reserved by anthropologists for aboriginal North Americans, but analogous groups have been described in Siberia, South Asia, Oceania, Australia, Africa, and South America. (If your geography isn't so great, that's every region of the world *except* Europe.)

How to characterize the berdache? In their book *Gender*, Kessler and McKenna (1978) stress the lack of consistency in anthropological definitions. Early European settlers of North America, and later anthropologists (who were European as well), used "berdache" to refer to transvestism, homosexuality, effeminacy, and/or prostitution. But Kessler and McKenna argue that these synonyms are all wrong. More profoundly, these synonyms miss the entire point of the berdache. This group provides an institutionalized role for those individuals who are—by virtue of filling that role—neither men nor women. The term "berdache" is used as a noun, not an adjective. It doesn't qualify one's maleness or femaleness.

What is known about the berdache that doesn't rest on preconceptions about gender? First, their genitals seem normal—they were not hermaphrodites. Second, they had a clearly defined role within their particular culture. Third, this role varied from society to society. In some, the berdache would totally embrace the role of men (or women). In others, they would partially embrace the role. In still others, they had their own role, playing a special function as healers or storytellers or go-betweens in love affairs. Fourth, within a given society, the berdache were regarded by others with widely different attitudes, from hatred to fear to embarrassment to pity to tolerance to respect to awe. Some societies believed that people became berdache through divine intervention. Other societies believed it to be a matter of personal choice.

WERE THE BERDACHE TRANSSEXUALS?

The term "berdache" is a perjorative one, derived from a French word meaning male prostitute. As we've already noted, the Europeans who first encountered this group of people could only make sense of what they saw using their own concepts, and so a label like berdache was chosen. The literal translations of the words used by the Native American societies to describe the berdache are more informative:

- man-woman
- pretend hermaphrodite
- soft man
- similar to woman
- half man–half woman
- neuter
- human it
- not man–not woman

These seem to support Kessler and McKenna's suggestion that the berdache indeed represented a third gender identity.

It's difficult to say whether or not the berdache were transsexuals. Perhaps this is an impossible question. Transsexuality is a phenomenon that makes sense only in our society, just as the phenomenon of the berdache makes sense only in their world. Let's remember that a transsexual has the gender identity of a man but the genitals of a woman, or vice versa. They can be described as intersexual—transcending male/female dichotomies—and so too can the berdache. But the transsexual additionally hates his (or her) genitals, wishing to be rid of them and to live like a member of the opposite sex. There are no reports that the berdache harbored similar feelings. Could this be simply because their society gave them an alternative—the gender identity of the berdache—that our society does not?

˙DISCUSSION QUESTIONS

1. We've suggested that our society makes distinctions between males and females on various levels, from biological to psychological to sociological. Are any of these distinctions more basic than the others?

2. Speculate as to why the berdache phenomenon appears throughout the entire world but not in Europe.

3. One implication of the present case is that transsexualism is culturally produced. What do you think?

4. Is the legitimization of a third (or fourth or fifth) gender identity a better answer to transsexualism than sex-change operations? How might this be done?

REFERENCE

Kessler, S. J., & McKenna, W. (1978). *Gender: An ethnomethodological approach.* New York: Wiley.

John Belushi: *Wired*

The present case describes the "short life and fast times" of a famous casualty of drug abuse, comedian John Belushi, in light of the DSM-III-R (American Psychiatric Association, 1987, pp. 167–168) definition of the syndrome of psychoactive *substance dependence*. For such a syndrome to be diagnosed, three or more of the following must be present for at least one month:

- substance often taken in larger amounts or over a longer period than the user intended
- unsuccessful efforts to cut down or control substance use
- great deal of time spent in activities necessary to obtain the substance and/or in recovering from the effects of using the substance
- frequent intoxication or withdrawal when expected to fulfill obligations at work or school or home
- important activities given up because of substance abuse
- continued substance use despite knowledge of the problems that it is causing
- tolerance—need for increased amounts to achieve the desired effects
- characteristic withdrawal symptoms
- substance taken to relieve or avoid withdrawal

John Belushi certainly fit many more than three of these criteria for substance abuse. Drawing on the details presented by Bob Woodward (1985) in his controversial book *Wired*, there can be no doubt that John Belushi died because he had a monstrous problem with drugs, particularly cocaine and eventually heroin. We have read that the book is currently being made into a movie, and perhaps you will have seen the movie by the time you read what we have written. How faithfully does the movie depict the degree to which Belushi exemplified the criteria for substance dependence?

THE CASE

John Belushi grew up in Wheaton, a small suburb of Chicago. He graduated from high school in 1967. As an adolescent, Belushi was a gifted athlete and actor. He was offered a football scholarship to college, but the opportunity of a summer job acting in a small company set him on his way to a show business career. His talent for comedy was soon apparent, and when he was just twenty-two years old, he became the youngest member of Chicago's famous Second City comedy troupe.

Belushi drew on the social and political events of the early 1970s for his material. Ten years younger than his fellow comedians, he was much more in contact with the anti-establishment attitudes of the nation's young people. He perfected a spectacular imitation of Chicago Mayor Daley. He added a number of bits to his comedic repertoire, which could be characterized as impatient, frenetic, and more than a little nasty. Belushi began to use drugs: marijuana and more potent hallucinogens. In the context of the time and place, this drug use was not unusual, except for two things that friends noticed retrospectively. He used drugs while working. And he used a prodigious amount before showing any outside effects.

His next notable career step was a major part in a satirical musical called *Lemmings*, which spoofed the Woodstock generation. The job took him to New York, and the musical was a great hit. Its highlight was John Belushi doing a Joe Cocker imitation. Here was where John was introduced to cocaine, and it quickly became his preferred substance. Again, he used the drug not only after the show—which was the "accepted" practice—but before as well. Sometimes it spoiled his performance. Friends suggested he not perform when he was high, but he resisted. "I can handle it," he assured them.

In 1975, NBC television executives decided that a live comedy show pitched at the counterculture might work. There was the danger that a live camera might let nasty words slip uncensored over the airwaves, and then there would be hell to pay. But this possibility made the show exciting as well. And so "Saturday Night Live" was born. A cast was assembled, including Jane Curtin, Dan Aykroyd, Chevy Chase, Gilda Radner, and John Belushi. None of these folks were at that time well known, and "Saturday Night Live" was their vehicle to fame. Chevy Chase became the first real star on the show, and Belushi was reportedly jealous.

But when Chevy Chase left the show to pursue movies, Belushi became the acknowledged star, and his various routines became the rage of the country: the Joe Cocker imitation, the buzzing bees, the samurai, the greasy diner that served only cheeseburgers and Pepsis, and the Blues Brothers. He helped make "Saturday Night Live" the hippest show on television. Some of the biggest names in comedy and show business appeared as guest hosts for the show: George Carlin, Richard Pryor, Candace Bergen, and so on. Even consumer advocate Ralph Nader hosted a show.

Belushi's drug use continued and increased. In 1976, John visited a doctor who specialized in drug addiction. The following summary appeared in the doctor's notes (Woodward, 1985, p. 111):

Smokes 3 packs a day.
Alcohol drinks socially.
Medications: Valium occasionally.
Marijuana 4 to 5 times a week.
Cocaine—snorts daily, main habit.
Mescaline—regularly.
Acid—10 to 20 trips.
No heroin.
Amphetamines—four kinds.
Barbiturates (Quaalude habit).

The doctor told him he had to stop because he was killing himself. Belushi refused. Drugs were his only relief in an otherwise hectic life.

Drug use pervaded the humor of "Saturday Night Live." Perhaps it was a more innocent time, or perhaps just a more hedonistic one. Regardless, the prevailing belief in the 1970s was that only drugs injected with a needle were harmful. Few thought cocaine addictive, and most thought that marijuana had no ill effects on one's physical health. As your text explains, and as public service announcements repeatedly stress, these are no longer the accepted beliefs.

We doubt that Belushi would have stopped using drugs even if at the time they had been widely recognized as harmful. But these prevailing notions perhaps explain why so many of his friends and associates stood to the side and watched him slowly poison himself. Perhaps they were awed by his growing success. As you probably know, Belushi moved from the television show to star in movies, including the highly successful *Animal House* and *The Blues Brothers*. He made a record album that sold well. He also did a sell-out concert tour. John Belushi was not only famous, he was wealthy.

As his drug use escalated, his reputation began to suffer. Some of his show business projects failed because his performances were hampered by intoxication. Belushi's drug use was clearly out of control, causing those closest to him to despair. It got so bad that his wife left him.

At this point, an around-the-clock bodyguard was hired by his manager to protect Belushi . . . not from other people but from himself. The guard labored mightily to keep drugs out of John's body. Mostly, he succeeded, but he eventually left the job. Babysitting is not easy work under any circumstances, much less when the baby is rich and powerful.

Then John discovered heroin. As a beginner, he had another person inject the drug for him. Like every other drug he had ever tried, he liked heroin very much. He once enthused that using heroin was "like kissing God" (Woodward, 1985, p. 321). In an ironic way, he was right, because heroin led him to his maker. On or about March 5, 1982, John Belushi died of an overdose. The coroner's report attributed his death to acute toxicity from heroin and cocaine. He was thirty-three years old.

DISCUSSION QUESTIONS

1. Woodward's book is highly engaging, but it is mostly a chronology of events. The reader gains little insight into Belushi's motives for drug use. What do you think might drive someone to the excesses detailed in this case?

2. Were Belushi's drug abuse and eventual death inevitable granted the situations in which he was placed? What could have been done to prevent his dependence from escalating as it did?

3. Evaluate current anti-drug campaigns in light of what you know about drug addiction. Which should be effective? Which should fall flat?

4. One of the few successful treatments for alcohol dependence is Alcoholics Anonymous. How might a similar approach be taken to help cocaine and heroin abusers?

5. As you may know, the individual who administered the lethal dose of heroin to John Belushi was charged with second-degree murder. Does this make sense to you?

6. One of the striking things about *Wired* is that there is almost no mention of the police. Although Belushi's drug abuse was hardly a secret, apparently there were never any attempts made to arrest him for possession, or to arrest those who sold or gave him drugs. How was this possible? Are drug laws completely ineffectual?

7. Much of the psychology of drug abuse focuses on a particular substance: alcohol, narcotics, tobacco, whatever. So, theories and treatment target one drug to the exclusion of others. But perhaps many individuals are like John Belushi, eclectic in the substances they abuse. Does psychology need special theories and treatments for these individuals?

REFERENCES

American Psychiatric Association (1987). *Diagnostic and statistical manual of mental disorders* (3rd ed.—revised). Washington, DC: author.

Woodward, B. (1985). *Wired: The short life and fast times of John Belushi*. New York: Pocket Books.

Adult Children of Alcoholics

The text describes recent research that documents the role of biological processes in alcoholism. One particularly intriguing finding is that the potential to become an alcoholic seems to be in part transmitted genetically. Results like these are important in furthering our understanding of substance abuse, but they should not blind us to the psychological processes involved. Whatever is passed through the genes from alcoholic parents to their offspring cannot be any more important than what is transmitted psychologically.

What is the impact on children of growing up in a family dominated by an alcoholic? All parents create a pervasive social environment for their children that profoundly shapes their development (Bandura, 1986). In the case of alcoholic parents, the environment stemming from their abuse affects the child in characteristic ways, some of them highly undesirable. The term "adult child of the alcoholic" has been coined to describe the resulting syndrome. The purpose of the present case is to expand on this syndrome.

Note that the complex of problems that may result from growing up with an alcoholic parent is not a DSM-III-R category. These problems—anxiety, depression, personality disorders, and sometimes substance abuse—can be described in terms of their own particular symptoms. But the route to these disorders might be the same, illustrating one more way in which alcohol abuse takes its toll on the well-being of society.

THE ALCOHOLIC HOME

Gravitz and Bowden (1985) described the typical home where one or more parents are chronic alcohol abusers. Family life is often:

- inconsistent
- unpredictable

- arbitrary
- chaotic

Granted the effect of alcohol on someone, these characteristics make sense. Remember that alcohol can be described as disinhibiting, not only in a neurological sense, but in a psychological one as well. Someone who is sober may act like a completely different person when drunk. Promises once made are no longer kept. Household rules change. Physical abuse occurs.

At the same time, the child of an alcoholic may be forced into great responsibility. An incapacitated parent means that the child must run the household: cleaning, cooking, shopping, and looking after younger children. In fact, the child is quite possibly the sole emotional support of the nonabusing parent.

Imagine being a child in these circumstances. Damage takes place at two levels. First is the obvious one: the myriad of slights and misfortunes that occur. Bad occurrences outnumber good ones. The child cannot invite friends to the house. Family outings are disastrous or nonexistent. Money is short.

Second in the more subtle yet more profound level: the inability of the child to conceptualize what is taking place. When an adult has a loved one who abuses alcohol or other drugs, at least the heartbreak can be explained. But the child lacks the understanding to attribute the experienced chaos to alcoholism. Indeed, there may be a taboo in such a family against acknowledging that anything is wrong when mother slurs her words, when father falls down in the living room, or when the police arrest one of the parents for driving under the influence. It is this resulting confusion that marks the personality of such a child.

Adult children of alcoholics are therefore perplexed about healthy family life. Never having seen it, they do not know how to recognize it, and they certainly do not know how to create it. As adults, when called upon to establish their own family, they are tentative. They make mistakes. Their children sometimes suffer. And so it goes.

REACTIONS TO THE ALCOHOLIC HOME

Besides possessing a general confusion about the way families should be, the adult child of the alcoholic tends to have a number of more specific characteristics. Here is a representative list presented by Woititz (1983). Adult children of alcoholics:

- guess at what normal behavior is
- have trouble following a project through from its beginning to its conclusion
- sometimes lie when it is just as easy to tell the truth
- judge themselves harshly
- have difficulty having fun

- take themselves very seriously
- feel awkward in intimate relationships
- respond poorly in situations where they lack control
- seek approval and affirmation
- feel stigmatized—different from other people
- show excesses of responsibility, taking on too much or too little
- are overly loyal to people who don't deserve loyalty
- act impulsively

These are generalizations, of course, and not all adult children of alcoholics should be expected to fit this profile. Nonetheless, we think you can see how these styles of acting represent a short-term solution to life in an alcoholic home. In the long run, these ways of behaving become problematic.

TREATMENT

Clinical psychologists are wrestling with the problem of how best to serve the adult child of the alcoholic. The stakes are high, because if uninterrupted, the syndrome can repeat itself across generations.

One possible solution lies in group therapy. Groups are therapeutic for several reasons, including the information they can provide to members. It sometimes comes as a revelation to adult children of alcoholics that others experienced exactly the same childhood as they did. This can be liberating. Here is a dramatization of an initial group therapy session for adult children of alcoholics:

> Leslie was mesmerized. The muscles around her eyes tightened as the shock of recognition crossed her face. The stories she was hearing sounded just like hers! The other people in this group, who looked so picture-perfect, had experienced the same abandonment, the same loss of childhood, the same sense of betrayal that she had felt in a home dominated by an alcoholic parent.
>
> Ann, who had recently celebrated her eighty-first birthday, relaxed as she heard others describe the embarrassment of their childhoods—the humiliations, the insults, the times they were afraid to come home, and those terrible holiday scenes. As the shrouds of silence slowly disappeared, she was no longer feeling isolated and alone. There were no secrets here. These were her stories too.
>
> Brian was trembling. He was thinking of his parents. Pangs of guilt pierced his stomach. For the first time he actually talked about what went on in his family. He dared say out loud to others that his parents were alcoholic. He fidgeted as he forced himself not to pretend anymore. But it was hard! Scary! Yet, somewhere at the edge of his awareness, there was a feeling, a real feeling, that he did not want to deny (Gravitz & Bowden, 1985, p. 1).

And of course group therapy involves more than people telling their stories. The group can devise and share solutions to problems, give feedback, and provide support.

DISCUSSION QUESTIONS

1. We've presented this case from the perspective of the environmentalist model, with a focus on how particular environments produce particular behaviors. What do the biological and psychodynamic approaches add to our understanding of adult children of alcoholics?

2. "Alcoholism runs through families." Explain this statement in light of the ideas we've presented in this case.

3. Attention to the impact of a disorder on children need not be limited to alcohol abuse. How might a fearful parent create a particular personality style in his or her child? How about a depressed parent? How about a schizophrenic parent?

4. Is there any problem for which group therapy would not help?

REFERENCES

Bandura, A. (1986). *Social foundations of thought and action.* Englewood Cliffs, NJ: Prentice-Hall.

Gravitz, H. L., & Bowden, J. D. (1985). *Recovery: A guide for adult children of alcoholics.* New York: Simon & Schuster.

Woititz, J. G. (1983). *Adult children of alcoholics.* Hollywood, FL. Heath.

Tom S.: Antisocial Behavior

Personality disorders are defined as persistent styles of thinking, feeling, and acting that impair an individual's functioning in the world and/or cause him significant distress. DSM-III-R describes various personality disorders, and probably the most coherent of these is the antisocial personality disorder. Technically, antisocial personality disorder is not used to describe someone younger than eighteen years of age, although there is considerable continuity between adolescence and adulthood in the sorts of activities that warrant this description. In the case we'll present here, described originally by Selling (1947), the central figure is only sixteen years old. So, we will not use the diagnosis of antisocial personality disorder. He nonetheless is an excellent example of what this disorder involves.

THE CASE

Tom S. came to the attention of the mental health authorities after his arrest for murder. He had broken into a woman's house, stolen sixty-five cents from her purse, and beaten her over the head with an iron fence stake. As part of his trial, the opinions of several psychologists were solicited. Here are some of the details they reported.

Tom's father had been arrested several times for theft and assault, and he was an alcoholic. The father and mother fought constantly and were divorced when Tom was only four years old. His mother went to work in a factory, and the boy's grandmother assumed his care. At about this time, Tom was involved in a serious accident. He mistakenly thought he saw his mother get into a car, and he ran after it. He jumped on the back of the then-moving car, but fell off and hit his head on the curb. He lost consciousness for at least three hours. Following this accident, he began to wet his bed at night, a habit that persisted into his teens. He also had spells that seemed like convulsions. He had permanent damage to one of his eyes, which became crossed, and both of his ears, which continually rang.

Tom slept in the same bed with his mother until she remarried, when he was about seven. The boy took a strong dislike to the second husband, who was a strong disciplinarian. He began to get in trouble around the neighborhood. Here are the "highlights" of his young criminal career:

- At age nine, Tom was arrested for stealing from a dime store.
- At age eleven, he was arrested for purse snatching.
- At age thirteen, he was arrested for assault and battery, with attempt to rob, when he went into a drug store and hit the female clerk over the head with a wrench.
- Following this incident, he was sent to a detention home, from which he ran away several times.
- At age fourteen, he was arrested for attempting to open a cash register in a gas station.
- Also at age fourteen, he assaulted a woman on the street, hitting her over the head with a wrench.
- In the next two years, he was arrested for seven burglaries, arson, and yet another assault on a woman he hit over the head with a weapon.

Although the assaults were all impulsive and irrational, it should be noted that all of the women Tom attacked were the same age as his mother. It doesn't seem too great a leap to suggest that this was not just a coincidence.

The murder he committed was senseless. Tom was looking for clothes. He had already stolen several pairs of pants off clotheslines where they hung to dry. At about midnight, he walked by the woman's house and saw an open window. He crawled through it, into what proved to be the woman's bedroom. Her purse was on the dresser, so he took it. As he started to leave, she woke up. He hit her over the head and escaped through the window.

Once outside, Tom discovered that the purse contained only sixty-five cents. He took the money and discarded the purse. But he also took her keys and decided to enter the house again, this time through the front door. When later questioned, he gave no explanation for this decision. He went back into her bedroom, where she was lying back on the bed—not moving. He took a hat. Then he left again. On his way home, he stole more clothes as well as a bicycle. He was arrested the next day.

Tom's acts in themselves are antisocial. They are reckless, irrational, and hurtful. Interviews with him further round out the characterization of him as antisocial. He reports no friends whatsoever. Indeed, his conceptions of other people are extremely shallow. He reports that he likes his mother and stepfather. He bears no ill will toward anyone. He didn't mean to kill the woman. He hit her because she was going to sit up.

Does Tom lack a conscience? In some ways, yes. He has little insight into his own actions. He says he steals things because he wants them. He attributes his more serious crimes to the "bad company" he has kept and the fact that he has been induced to stay out late. He also puts great stock on the automobile accident he suffered. Because it injured his eyes and ears, he is unable to pursue his goal of becoming an aviator. He can't think of doing anything other than flying as an occupation.

Tom was tried as an adult, and judged guilty of murder. He was sentenced to life imprisonment. One psychologist who testified described Tom as "a very dangerous, unpredictable, and impulsively vicious boy . . . literally the most dangerous type of criminal that can be conceived" because his manner seems so friendly and free of malice (Selling, 1947, pp. 470–471).

AN INTERPRETATION

Chapter 15 specifies a number of factors that make antisocial personality disorder more likely. Tom possessed literally all of these. His biological father was a criminal. His home life was characterized by strife and neglect. He had a head injury that may have affected his ability to plan ahead and foresee the consequences of his actions.

Note, though, that Tom's crimes were not completely random. There was a pattern that gives a clue to some of the motives behind them. Most of Tom's thefts, once he was an adolescent, were of clothes. He wanted to look right, and he didn't want to ask his mother or stepfather to pay for his clothing. All of Tom's assaults were directed against women the same age as his mother. Do these patterns suggest a rivalry with his stepfather and a resentment of his mother? Perhaps. The point we're trying to make doesn't hinge on this particular interpretation. Rather, we want you to appreciate that even if a disorder has underlying biological causes, it still manifests itself in a psychologically meaningful way.

DISCUSSION QUESTIONS

1. Drawing on the text, explain how Tom's risk factors led to his present style of life. Be sure to touch on his presumed deficits in avoidance learning.

2. One of the assumptions implicit in the notion of personality disorder is that people fall into rather discrete categories: those with disordered personalities and those without. Is this reasonable in the case of antisocial personality disorder, or should we speak of a continuum?

3. Tom's tested intelligence is reportedly normal. What does this say

about the ways in which psychologists conceive and measure intelligence?

4. What would a psychodynamic theorist make of the patterns to Tom's crimes? How about a cognitive theorist?

5. Is there anything that a therapist can do to rehabilitate Tom?

6. What could have been done to prevent Tom's antisocial behavior from occurring in the first place?

7. Does Tom fit the descriptions of any other personality disorders? Does he warrant any Axis One diagnosis?

8. Why aren't women nearly as apt as men to display antisocial behavior?

9. In a provocative and sometimes disturbing book titled *Crime and Human Nature*, James Wilson and Richard Herrnstein (1985) argue that social scientists interested in crime have largely ignored the possibility that biological factors make an important contribution. They argue that the typical criminal is a young mesomorphic male, who is extraverted and unable to hold his impulses in check. All of these characteristics are biological. What do you think of this argument? What implications does it have for the prevention of crime? For the punishment of crime?

REFERENCES

Selling, L. S. (1947). Psychopathic personality. II. In A. Burton & R. E. Harris (Eds.), *Case histories in clinical and abnormal psychology*. New York: Harper.

Wilson, J. Q., & Herrnstein, R. J. (1985). *Crime and human nature*. New York: Simon & Schuster.

Ms. W.'s Woes: Borderline Personality Disorder

The term "borderline" has appeared in the abnormal psychology literature for decades (Gunderson & Singer, 1975). Its original use stemmed from the days when psychiatrists and psychologists made an overarching distinction between psychotic disorders and neurotic disorders. The former disorders are marked by failure of reality testing, whereas the latter are not. Schizophrenia is a good example of a psychosis, and a simple phobia is a good example of a neurosis.

To assist in distinguishing psychotic from neurotic disorders, diagnosticians administered a variety of psychological tests, including structured tests like the WAIS and unstructured tests like the Rorschach (cf. Chapter 7). Their hope was that test results would converge on an individual's particular problem. Often they would. But sometimes a person would respond in an unremarkable way on structured tests but in an extremely disturbed way on unstructured ones. These results on the one hand showed intact reality testing (i.e., neurotic functioning), and on the other hand they showed impaired reality testing (i.e., psychotic functioning).

Because the psychosis-neurosis classification was thought to be mutually exclusive, people whose psychological test results placed them in both groups posed a problem in diagnosis. What to do? The decision was to place them metaphorically at the "border" or boundary between psychoses and neuroses.

And so the borderline category was created. It eventually came to have a more substantive meaning, and it was applied to people who functioned reasonably well when situations were simple and undemanding but who fell apart when matters became complex or ambiguous.

When psychoses and neuroses stopped being superordinate categories of disorders, the notion of borderline remained and accrued further meaning in its own right. In DSM-III-R, "borderline" is one of the Axis Two personality disorders, recognized generally by pervasive instability of moods, interpersonal relationships, and views of the self. More specifically, here are the relevant symptoms:

- intense relationships with others that alternate between putting them on a pedestal and knocking them off
- impulsivity in self-damaging areas like drug use, fast driving, and shoplifting
- marked shifts into depressed moods
- inappropriate anger and failure to control its expression
- recurrent suicidal threats or attempts
- identity disturbance characterized by uncertainty
- chronic feelings of boredom and emptiness
- efforts to avoid real or imagined boredom

The present case, Ms. W., is a good example of what is currently meant by a borderline personality disorder. We draw on Goldstein's (1985) detailed description of this case.

THE CASE

Ms. W. is twenty-three years old. She is a recent college graduate, unmarried, and working as a librarian at a local university. She sought out therapy, complaining of:

- fluctuating moods
- explosive rage, e.g., she would tear books and papers into shreds at the slightest provocation
- occasional boredom and numbness
- dangerous activities like shoplifting and reckless driving
- binges of drug and alcohol use, as well as periods of excessive eating
- dissatisfaction with her job
- dissatisfaction with her social life
- feelings that she was not a "whole" person

Right off the bat, we can see that Ms. W. satisfies well the DSM-III-R diagnostic criteria for borderline personality disorder.

According to Goldstein, Ms. W. is extremely attractive and intelligent. She graduated from an excellent college. She has what looks like a solid relationship with a twenty-four-year-old man; they spend a lot of time together, share many interests, talk well, and enjoy each other sexually.

But Ms. W. feels that something is missing. Her job is not "exciting" to her, and she can identify no "real" feelings for her boyfriend. When her therapist asked her if she liked him, she did not know how to answer. She finally said that he soothed her, keeping her from being bored.

> Ms. W. had met her boyfriend when he visited the library where she worked. He became very rapidly attracted to her, physically, sexually, and intellectually. Although she did not

experience any feelings for him, Ms. W. acted as if she liked him quite a bit and was very willing to date him frequently and to become sexually involved with him. . . . Ms. W.'s usual dating pattern was to become involved with one man at a time, usually for a number of months. She had had a large number of "close" relationships of this nature for a number of years now. Basically all the relationships were similar. Ms. W. acted as if she liked the men but could neither experience feelings toward them nor conceptualize them as people. She used the various men to help ward off boredom and other unpleasant affects, but this attempt was often unsuccessful. The typical relationship was considerably more stormy than the one just described (Goldstein, 1985, p. 155).

Ms. W. was always the one to end these relationships. Although saying she felt guilty about using men, guilt seemed not to be the operating motive behind the breakups. Instead, she felt bored and had found a new relationship that looked more exciting. Since high school, Ms. W. had repeated this pattern many times. She never had any female friends.

Ms. W. grew up in a family with seven children. Her father favored Ms. W., who was the most attractive of his daughters, but he was often out of town. He presented an inconsistent image to her, and she responded with inconsistency of her own. Sometimes she idolized him, and sometimes she wanted nothing to do with him. Her mother was explosive, constantly yelling at the children and threatening to divorce her husband. Again, inconsistency is an apt description, and again, Ms. W. reacted to her mother in an inconsistent fashion, alternating between attraction and repulsion.

The therapist noted that Ms. W. never spoke of her brothers and sisters as people in their own right. Instead, she viewed them solely in terms of how she related to them. She displayed a strong rivalry with several of her sisters, and kept close track of who received the nicest presents from their parents.

Ms. W.'s history corresponds to what self theorists hypothesize to be responsible for borderline personality disorder. Her parents treated her in ways that made it impossible for her to form a unified conception of them. Her own sense of self, based on her sense of her father and mother, was therefore just as fragmented. Her overt instability followed.

DISCUSSION QUESTIONS

1. What other diagnoses might be considered for Ms. W.? Some theorists speculate that borderline personality disorder is a version of unipolar depression. What do you think of this idea in light of Ms. W.'s case?

2. Psychodynamic theorists speak of the phenomenon of splitting: dividing people into their good and bad aspects, then relating to only one of these aspects at a time. How would this tendency produce the instability seen in individuals with borderline personality disorder?

3. Does the borderline personality disorder represent an either-or classification of people, or is it on a continuum?

4. Most explanations of borderline personality disorder come from psychodynamic theorists. What might a biomedical theory of this condition look like? How about a theory from the environmentalist model?

5. Inconsistency during childhood seems to explain why a person might show a borderline personality disorder as an adult, but let's examine this link more carefully. As you recall, inconsistency (unpredictability, uncontrollability, and so on) also seems to foreshadow a variety of other problems, like anxiety disorders, psychosomatic difficulties, depression, and schizophrenia. What's the lesson here?

6. How might therapy with Ms. W. proceed? (Note: therapists consider individuals with borderline personality disorders as extremely difficult to treat, because they tend to treat their therapists as they treat others in their life.)

7. Axis Two conditions are not disorders in their own right, but styles that exacerbate the clinical syndromes described on Axis One. Would a borderline style make *all* clinical syndromes worse?

REFERENCES

Goldstein, W. (1985). *An introduction to the borderline conditions.* Northvale, NJ: Aronson.

Gunderson, J., & Singer, M. (1975). Defining borderline patients: An overview. *American Journal of Psychiatry, 132,* 1–10.

Childhood Emotional Disorders

The text describes a variety of childhood emotional disorders. Many of them seem to resemble particular adult disorders, which is why both have usually been interpreted within the same frameworks—the popular models of abnormality featured in your text. More recently, though, clinical psychologists who work with children have cautioned against the assumption that children's problems are necessarily versions of adult's problems. In the field of developmental psychology, it has long been recognized that children are not miniature adults. The field of abnormal psychology is finally coming around to this same conclusion (cf. Achenbach, 1974).

Here we present two cases of children with problems. In the first case, the child seems anxious. In the second, the child seems depressed. Keep in mind while you read these cases the fact that these are young children. Can the models of adult psychopathology be applied to them? What needs to be taken into account about the age of these particular children in understanding their problems and how to treat them?

RACHEL: FEAR OF TAKING A BATH

Sarafino (1986) describes the case of Rachel, a three-year-old girl who developed a marked fear of taking a bath in the tub. As an infant, she was bathed in a bathinette, which she enjoyed. She at first made the transition to the larger tub with no difficulty. Indeed, she played enthusiastically with her toys while in the tub. Her mother and father watched her carefully, making sure she never fell or had an accident.

Nonetheless, Rachel suddenly began to protest over taking baths in the tub. At bathtime, she would begin to cry. If her parents put her in the tub, she stiffened and threw a tantrum. Why?

Sarafino (1986) reports that Rachel's father was able to remember when her fear first began. One evening, he had bathed her just before she was to go to bed. She opened the drain to the tub, which she had never done before. Because her bath was complete, her father left the drain open. While Rachel was still in the tub, the water ran down the drain. She watched intently as it vanished, making a swooshing noise at the last. Rachel started to cry and called to her father to pick her up. He though she merely wanted to go to bed, and didn't think anything about the incident until he realized some days later that it marked the beginning of her fear. It's perhaps important to mention the cartoons that Rachel repeatedly watched on television, one of which featured a genie who would withdraw into a small bottle, accompanied by the same swooshing noise as the water made when it went down the drain.

Although it was impossible to directly question Rachel, Sarafino (1986) speculated that particular thoughts on her part were at the root of her fear. Perhaps she was afraid because she thought that she would be sucked down the tub's drain along with the water, never to be seen again. An adult would not have such a fear, knowing that people are bigger than drains in tubs. But at her age, there was no way that Rachel could have grasped this fact. She didn't have the cognitive wherewithal to do so.

AETHELBERTA: ANACLITIC DEPRESSION

Spitz (1946) was studying infant behavior in a nursery when he discovered a striking syndrome among some of the children. Late in their first year of life, some of them would first become apprehensive, sad, and weepy. Then they would withdraw. These children would lose interest in their environment, showing in particular a reduced response to other people. They began to move slowly. They stopped sleeping well. Some refused to eat or ate poorly, and as a result lost weight. Indeed, these children began to fall behind others in their development.

A representative case presented by Spitz is that of a female infant named Aethelberta. We'll quote from his observations:

> From the beginning far advanced in her development, friendly, well-liked. At [seven months of age] . . . slightly depressive expression in the face noted, simultaneously with a decrease . . . [in developmental progress]. Inquiry elicits that she had been separated from her mother ten days before. In the following weeks, she becomes weepy; by the time she is nine months old the nursing staff observes that the child is getting thinner and suffering from insomnia. . . . She finally is isolated for the purpose of overcoming her insomnia. Approaching her becomes difficult; she is mostly sitting in her bed, her dress in her mouth, or sucking her hand. In the following weeks she refuses to touch toys and lies dejected on her bed, face averted. . . . The child, up to this point vigorously healthy, develops a stubbornly persisting cold. . . . At [eleven months of age] . . . the mother is returned. Si-

multaneously she has become friendly and positive (pp. 340–341).

As your text explains, Spitz termed this phenomenon anaclitic depression and regarded it as the earliest-appearing form of depressive disorder. As in the case of Aethelberta, anaclitic depression is brought about when the infant is separated from her primary caregiver. It is reversed by reuniting the two.

DISCUSSION QUESTIONS

1. In what ways is Rachel's fear of taking a bath similar to adult fear and anxiety disorders? In what ways is it different?

2. How would a psychologist working within the biomedical model account for Rachel's fear, and how would she treat it? How would a psychologist who ascribed to the psychodynamic approach explain and treat her fear? And how about a cognitive-behavioral psychologist?

3. What would a developmental psychologist say about these explanations?

4. In what ways is Aethelberta's depression similar to adult depression? In what ways is it different?

5. How would a psychologist working within the biomedical model account for Aethelberta's depression, and how would he treat it? How would a psychologist who ascribed to the psychodynamic approach explain and treat her depression? And how about a cognitive-behavioral psychologist?

6. What would a development psychologist say about these explanations?

7. Do any of the models of adult abnormality lend themselves more readily than the others to a developmental perspective?

8. Do some disorders require a developmental approach more than others?

9. Fears in childhood seem to have little link to fears in adulthood, whereas depression in childhood is correlated with depression in adults. Why do we see these patterns?

REFERENCES

Achenbach, T. M. (1974). *Developmental psychopathology.* New York: Ronald Press.

Sarafino, E. P. (1986). *The fears of childhood: A guide to recognizing and reducing fearful states in children*. New York: Human Sciences Press.

Spitz, R. A. (1946). Anaclitic depression: An inquiry into the genesis of psychiatric conditions in early childhood, II. *The Psychoanalytic Study of the Child, 2,* 313–357.

Mr. Duke's Daughter:
Anorexia Nervosa

The most obvious symptom of anorexia is extreme weight loss, at least 15 to 25 percent of the individual's "normal" weight. But anorexia is also characterized by various psychological symptoms, including an intense fear of becoming fat and a strong dislike of the way one looks. It occurs predominantly among females, and here there is yet one more symptom: cessation of menstrual cycles (when they otherwise would be expected to occur).

Epidemiological studies suggest that anorexia is rapidly increasing in our population, but it is not just a disorder of the twentieth century. Richard Morton, a seventeenth-century physician, gave a clear description of anorexia in his book on tuberculosis. In a chapter titled nervous consumption, he described several puzzling cases of people wasting away (as in tuberculosis) yet who did not have a fever or cough. He attributed these cases to the nervous system being put out of kilter by violent emotions and unwholesome air.

Today, we understand that Morton's cases were not bad examples of tuberculosis but rather good examples of anorexia. In the present case, we'll introduce you to one of Morton's patients, a young woman known to history only as Mr. Duke's daughter.

THE CASE

We begin our discussion with Morton's own description of Mr. Duke's daughter:

> Mr. Duke's daughter in St. Mary Axe, in the year 1684 and the eighteenth Year of her Age, in the month of July fell into a total suppression of her monthly courses from a multitude of Cares and Passions of her Mind, but without any Symptom of the Green-Sickness following it. From which time her appetite began to abate, and her Digestion to be bad; her flesh also began to be flaccid and loose, and her

looks pale, with other symptoms usual in an Universal Consumption of the Habit of the Body, and by the extream and memorable cold Weather which happened the Winter following, this consumption did seem to be not a little improved; for that she was wont by her studying at Night, and continual poring over books, to expose herself both Day and Night to the injuries of the Air, which was at that time extreamly cold, not without some manifest Prejudice to the System of her Nerves. The Spring followed by the Prescription of some Emperick, she took a Vomit, and after that I know not what Steel Medicines, but without any Advantage. So from the time loathing all sorts of Medicaments, she wholly neglected the care of her self for two full Years, till at last being brought to the last degree of a Marasmus, or Consumption, and thereupon subject to Frequent Fainting Fits, she apply'd her self to me for Advice.

I do not remember that I did ever in all my Practice see one, that was conversant with the living so much wasted with the greatest degree of a Consumption (like a Skeleton only clad with skin) yet there was no Fever, but on the contrary a coldness of the whole Body; no cough or difficulty of Breathing nor an appearance of any distemper of the Lungs, or of any other Entrail . . . Only her Appetite was diminished, and her Digestion uneasie, with Fainting Fits, which did frequently return upon her. Which Symptoms I did endeavor to relieve by the outward application of Aromatick Bags made to the Region of the Stomach . . . [and] by the internal use of Bitter Medicines, Chalybeates, and Juleps made of Cephalik and Antihysterick Waters, sufficiently impregnated with Spirit of Salt Aromoniack, and Tincture of Castor. . . . Upon the Use of which she seemed to be much better, but being quickly tired with Medicines, she beg'd that the whole Affair might be committed again to nature, whereupon . . . she was after three months taken with a Fainting Fit and died (Morton, 1694).

Did you make it through Morton's writing? If not, let us sketch the highlights of this case for you. Mr. Duke's daughter was eighteen years old when she lost her appetite. Over the next two years she steadily lost weight and developed fainting spells. She did not at all take care of her health and was wasting away. Dr. Morton prescribed various medicines for her, and these seemed to help a bit. But she didn't want to continue to take them. Shortly after she refused his further treatment, she died.

We think this young woman satisfies the DSM-III-R criteria for anorexia. Although Morton reported no exact weights, we can assume from his description of her as "a skeleton only clad with skin" that she was indeed greatly underweight. We don't know if she feared gaining weight, but it is striking that she sought Morton's help not because of her weight loss but because of her fainting spells. Further, she stopped his treatment because she didn't like medicines. Taken together, this information suggests that she was not aware that her weight loss threatened her life.

Elsewhere in his book, Morton wrote that this "disease" flatters and deceives patients; in other words, they like it. For this reason, he went on to say, physicians are rarely called until things have gone too far for them to help. Again, this information suggests that Mr. Duke's daughter had a disturbed view of her weight loss. At any rate, we do know that she ceased menstruating, because Morton says so.

It might be coincidental, but it is still interesting to speculate that this young woman fits the demographic and psychological profile of the modern anorexic. She was a female. She was from the upper class (which we know because she could read). The onset of her anorexia was during adolescence (remember that puberty occurred later in one's life in the seventeenth century). Morton speculated that "this Disease does almost always proceed from Sadness and anxious Cares," thereby implicating psychological risk factors. And Mr. Duke's daughter eventually refused treatment. We wish that Morton had commented on the Duke family, but alas, he did not.

At the same time, this woman and her problem are very much a part of her era—the seventeenth century. Note the frequent references to the air and how it can hurt someone's health. The germ theory of illness had not yet been proposed, and so other explanations of disease were in vogue. The air was particularly suspect. In fact, have you noticed how many of the older colleges in our country are built on top of hills? The goal in many cases was not to be picturesque but rather to keep the students and faculty safe from bad air! Dr. Morton probably viewed her disorder in terms of disturbed humours (remember Case 2). He probably prescribed medicine not to kill germs but to put her humours back in balance.

HOLY ANOREXIA

Let us conclude on a historical note. Fasting and weight loss have long been entwined with religious practice. In Christianity, for instance, the ability to subdue one's passions has traditionally been seen as a sign of piety. One battled not only the pleasures associated with sexuality but also those that came from eating. In a fascinating book, Rudolph Bell (1985) surveyed the lives of 261 Italian women who lived between the twelfth and twentieth centuries. All were honored by the Catholic Church for their exemplary lives. Some were made saints. In every case, they had demonstrated their venerability by starving themselves to death. Bell termed this phenomenon "holy anorexia."

He presented the lives of some of these women in great detail. Obviously, they did not consume very much food. But when they did eat, they used this as a further opportunity to triumph over the desires of the body. They chose extremely unappetizing substances to consume: seeds, bitter herbs, uncooked vegetables, even vomit and pus. (If you think this is disgusting, read Bell's book for the long version!)

On the face of it, holy anorexia differs from its counterpart in

DSM-III-R in that thinness per se is not the individual's goal but rather holiness. If we take a closer look, though, perhaps this distinction is fuzzy. In the twentieth century, being thin has achieved the status of an ideal, just as holiness was an ideal in centuries past. Perhaps all anorexics, holy and secular, are pursing an ideal state. So to speak, this idea provides much food for thought.

DISCUSSION QUESTIONS

1. Suppose Morton had been able to consult with you and your modern knowledge concerning the puzzling case of Mr. Duke's daughter. How would you advise him to proceed with her treatment?

2. Why did the medications that Morton prescribed to this young woman appear to help her?

3. Morton regarded anorexia as a type of tuberculosis, and it made little sense to him. This is an instructive mistake. Can you cite other examples from the field of abnormal psychology where our understanding of particular disorders has been hampered because they have been incorrectly classified with other disorders?

4. Suppose that anorexia does involve the pursuit of an ideal state. Does this theory explain the marked sex difference in prevalence? What other explanations of this sex difference do you find compelling?

REFERENCES

Bell, R. M. (1985). *Holy anorexia.* Chicago: University of Chicago Press.

Morton, R. (1694). *Phthisiologica—or a treatise of consumptions.* London.

Walter H.: Obesity

Obesity is not listed as a disorder in DSM-III-R, but it nonetheless is frequently associated with poor physical and mental health. Obesity is easy to define: excess weight, conventionally at least 20 to 40 percent over one's "normal" or expected weight. Its immediate cause is also easy to specify: consuming more calories than the body uses. But matters become more difficult when you begin to dig deeper into obesity.

What are the more distant causes that lead to obesity? The text cites a variety of biological, psychological, and sociological risk factors, but there is no consensus as to "the" ultimate cause of obesity. What can we do about it? Many interventions work in the short term, leading to weight loss, but few if any interventions seem to work in the long term to keep the excess weight off.

The present case illustrates some of the puzzles involved in the explanation and treatment of obesity. Its subject is Walter H., who has received much coverage in the popular media. Our information comes from a brief story in the *Chicago Tribune* (1988), a longer one in *People Weekly* (Plummer, 1987), and our recollection of information from a Phil Donahue show.

THE CASE

Walter H. is a forty-two-year-old man from Long Island who at one time weighed in excess of 1,200 pounds. He had a 103-inch waist. (That's almost nine feet around!) His weight was only able to be estimated, because Walter hadn't set foot outside his house in years. Actually, he had trouble taking a step anywhere because of his size. For the most part, he stayed in bed, where he spent his time reading the Bible.

Walter was the youngest of nine children. At age thirteen, he weighted 300 pounds. At about that time, he fell and hurt himself, then had to stay in bed for several months. He gained weight in even greater quantities and did not leave his house afterwards.

A sister and brother looked after him, providing him with the massive amounts of food he consumed. Any misgivings they had about hurting their brother's health were outweighed (so to speak) by their reluctance to disappoint him. He greatly enjoyed eating. Here is a typical day's food:

- two boxes of sausages
- one pound of bacon
- one dozen eggs
- a loaf of bread
- four Big Macs
- four double cheeseburgers
- three large ham steaks or two chickens
- four baked potatoes
- four sweet potatoes

Every meal was accompanied by six quarts of soda.

Walter rarely moved his bowels, because it was so difficult for him to walk to the bathroom. On one such journey, he slipped and fell. He couldn't get up, and his family couldn't get him up. An eight-person team of police, firefighters, and other emergency personnel was called in, and they spent three hours getting him back in bed.

Here is where Dick Gregory, the activist turned nutritionist, enters the story. Gregory helped Walter devise and follow and 1800-calorie-a-day diet. The procedure involved a powdered diet drink supplemented with vitamins and lots of water. The diet was successful, and Walter lost approximately 400 pounds in six months.

Gregory felt that the diet should be continued in the spa that he operates in the Bahamas, and so a date was set for Walter to leave his house. But when the day came, Walter refused to leave his house. He walked into the living room, with help, and said to the assembled photographers and reporters, "This is something I wanted to do, but the mental block in my head was so great I couldn't do it. I broke into tears. . . . I thought I would walk out. But when the moment comes, you just can't do it. . . . My legs wouldn't carry me."

Dick Gregory was saddened by this turn of events, and he removed himself from the treatment, citing Walter H.'s "psychological problem" as something he was not equipped to deal with.

DISCUSSION QUESTIONS

1. At one time, Walter weighed more than half a ton. Why do you think he didn't die?

2. What can be done to help this man lose weight? Is it possible that the special diet he followed contrasted too much with what he was used to?

3. Dick Gregory implied that there are two types of obesity: with and without psychological problems. Is this a reasonable distinction?

4. Speculate about the reasons Walter H. had for not leaving his home. Do analogous issues have to be addressed in the treatment of anyone's obesity?

5. How is obesity similar to other eating disorders? How is it different?

6. Should obesity be considered an addiction and treated accordingly?

7. What role was played by Walter's family in aiding and abetting his problem? Compare this to the role of family members in Case 24.

8. Why isn't obesity listed in DSM-III-R as a disorder?

REFERENCES

450 pounds lighter, he won't take next step. *Chicago Tribune,* February 5, 1988, p. 4.

Plummer, W. (1987). After 27 years in his bedroom, 1,200 lb. Walter Hudson decides to take a load off. *People Weekly,* October 26, pp. 60–61.

Nate G.: Down's Syndrome

There are two types of mental retardation. The first stems from a demonstrable injury or illness to an individual, and the second is attributed to a somewhat murky combination of social and cultural factors. One example of the former type of retardation is Down's syndrome, caused by a chromosomal abnormality. Although Down's syndrome cannot be cured in the sense of making it go away, recent years have seen a drastic rethinking of the capabilities of an individual with this syndrome. The subject of this case is Nate G., a teenager with Down's syndrome, who was featured in a newspaper story we recently read (Ogintz, 1988). But first, here's some background information to help you better understand this case.

BACKGROUND

Down's syndrome was first described in 1866 by the English physician Langdon Down. The condition was originally called "Mongolism" because Down thought the children resembled Asians due to their slanting eyes. In retrospect, this is regarded as a misguided and possibly racist analogy. Asian children with Down's syndrome are as easy to recognize as their counterparts among Caucasian children. At any rate, the physical characteristics associated with Down's syndrome are described in your text.

On the whole, children with this disorder have lower IQs than other children and show less ability to fend for themselves when they become adults. But the exact "limits" of what these children can do are not as fixed as was once thought. At one time, their parents were routinely advised to institutionalize them, and so many did. Research then began to show, however, that institutionalized children fared much worse than those kept at home (Edgerton, 1979). Presumably, a stimulating home environment boosts the intellectual and interpersonal attainments of children with Down's syndrome, just as it can for other children.

Another boost for this group of individuals came from the 1975 federal law mandating public education for handicapped people. Children with Down's syndrome began to receive instruction heretofore withheld from them, with new plateaus being reached all the time. For instance, those with Down's syndrome may show difficulties with language. One obvious interpretation is that these difficulties reflect intellectual deficiencies, but a recent and less obvious explanation points to peculiarities of the tongue and related muscles that characterize those with Down's syndrome. So, the problems that these children have with language may be as much mechanical as intellectual. Speech therapy indeed helps them to acquire language skills.

THE CASE

Nate G. is a fifteen-year-old male with Down's syndrome. He is an eighth-grade student at a suburban school in the Chicago area. In many ways, his activities are the same as those of his classmates. He uses a computer to do his schoolwork, and he uses its graphics capacity to create his own comic strips. He likes girls, and basketball, and acting. (Sounds a bit like a young Jack Nicholson.)

Nate's condition was obvious at birth, but his parents never considered treating him as anything but normal. He was the first child with Down's syndrome to attend his elementary school, but he has since been joined by four other Down's children. He learned to read and write, and he takes some regular classes as well as some special education classes. His parents report that he has a good image of himself. He is aware that he is different from other children. He doesn't like having Down's syndrome, but he does accept that some things will be hard for him to master. He simply persists at them.

For the most part, Nate's classmates accept him. He has been teased occasionally, and one must realistically expect that at least some of the gaps between Nate and his peers will widen in the years to come. It is difficult enough to be an adolescent, much less one with Down's syndrome. Whether Nate will someday find work and how he will then live are matters that understandably concern his parents.

THE FUTURE FOR THOSE WITH DOWN'S SYNDROME

As we've noted, there is currently much more reason to be optimistic about the prognosis of Down's syndrome than ever before. One expert quoted in the story we read predicted that "The majority will be able to go to school and read and write and do a job" (Ogintz, 1988, p. 1). Life expectancy has greatly increased as well. Not too long ago, most of those with Down's syndrome died in their early twenties, which explains why previous discussions of this disorder almost always focused on Down's children. There were no adults to talk about.

But now most of these individuals are expected to live into their fifties. In large part, the increased life expectancy reflects earlier and more aggressive medical intervention. We can read between the lines, perhaps, and deduce that earlier generations saw no good reason to try to increase the life expectancy of those with the syndrome. Moreover, today, people with Down's syndrome are no longer locked away in institutions, which means that the rest of us are more familiar with them. With familiarity comes greater acceptance on our part. Perhaps this contributes as well to their greater mental and physical well-being.

Some experts raise a flag of caution amid all this optimism, pointing out that the extra chromosome that marks Down's syndrome has a host of effects not so easily undone by psychological and educational interventions. Is it a service to children and their parents to raise hopes that may not be realized? This of course is a philosophical issue far broader than Down's syndrome itself and how to conceive it. We are of the opinion that people are usually better off erring on the side of optimism. What do you think?

DISCUSSION QUESTIONS

1. Further insight into Down's syndrome can be found in two published diaries kept by young men with this condition (Seagoe, 1964; Hunt, 1967). If you can, read one or both of these diaries and discuss the implications for how we ought to think about Down's syndrome and those with it.

2. Mental retardation is usually defined by two criteria: (1) low IQ as revealed by intelligence tests; and (2) inability to achieve personal independence and social responsibility. What does the first criterion (IQ) tell us that the second criterion (adaptation) does not? Do you agree with this definition of mental retardation?

3. Is "mental retardation" a meaningful category, or is it a jumble of disparate phenomena?

4. Does the topic of mental retardation belong in an abnormal psychology book or course? (Remember matters of definition as discussed in Chapter 1.)

5. What can be done to make the world in general more hospitable for people like Nate, whose physical and intellectual characteristics set them apart from most others?

6. Discuss the ethical issues raised by the availability of prenatal testing for Down's syndrome.

7. Men with Down's syndrome are apparently all infertile, but some women with Down's syndrome can bear children. About half of these children have the syndrome. Should these women be allowed to have a family?

REFERENCES

Edgerton, R. B. (1979). *Mental retardation.* Cambridge, MA: Harvard University Press.

Hunt, N. (1967). *The world of Nigel Hunt: The diary of a mongoloid youth.* New York: Garrett.

Ogintz, E. (1988). In the mainstream. *Chicago Tribune*, May 3, Section 5, pp. 1–2.

Seagoe, M. V. (1964). *Yesterday was Tuesday, all night and all day.* Boston: Little, Brown.

Mrs. Johnson: Alzheimer's Disease

The most common cause of dementia is Alzheimer's disease, a progressive loss of higher mental functions that usually occurs in old age. As your text points out, Alzheimer's disease has a gradual onset, which means that it may not be recognized at first. Confusion and error may be dismissed as inevitable aspects of aging, which they are not. In the present case, we'll draw on Gruetzner's (1988) description of the course of Alzheimer's disease in a woman named Jewell Johnson. Note how her friends and family members do not consider the possibility that her problems result from a neurological disease until a physician makes the diagnosis.

THE CASE

Jewell Johnson is a seventy-four-year-old woman. Her husband died several years ago, but after grieving, she has carried on well with her life. She involves herself in community and church activities. She strikes her friends and family as a strong and healthy individual—a model senior citizen. But Mrs. Johnson has started to act in slightly uncharacteristic ways. She stopped going to church after a mishap involving money. Mrs. Johnson served as the church treasurer, and somehow Mrs. Johnson neglected to deposit several hundred dollars in cash. The money could not be found. She insisted that someone had stolen the money, but there was no evidence for this.

She also started to stay at home more than usual, and she began discouraging visitors. To those who insisted on calling, she was rude. She stopped taking care of her home. Unraked leaves accumulated in the yard. Newspapers thrown on the porch stayed there for several days. When her neighbors checked in on her, she never let them into the house. She dismissed them abruptly.

A neighbor finally called Mrs. Johnson's daughter to ask if she knew what was going on. The daughter, who lived hundreds of miles away, was surprised at the question. Her recent phone conversations with her mother, although on the brief side, had seemed to her to be completely normal. But the daughter then called Mrs. Johnson to discuss the neighbor's concerns. Mrs. Johnson was unpleasant to her, denying any problems and accusing both the daughter and the neighbor of being meddlers. She went off on what could only be called a paranoid tirade. Then Mrs. Johnson hung up. Her daughter was now quite upset, and she made plans to visit her mother as soon as possible.

Meanwhile, the utility companies turned off Mrs. Johnson's gas and electricity because the bills had not been paid for several months. When neighbors rang her bell, she would peer through the window but not answer the door. Then one night Mrs. Johnson awakened her neighbors with loud screams. She was out in her yard, clad only in a nightgown. She said her husband was roaming about in the attic, and she was afraid to go into the house. The police were called, and in light of Mrs. Johnson's agitation, she was taken to a hospital. The neighbors entered her house and found it a shambles. There was no food to be found. Papers were piled everywhere. Clothes were scattered on the floor. The toilet had not been flushed in days.

The doctors in the hospital soon arrived at a diagnosis: Mrs. Johnson was suffering from Alzheimer's disease.

INTERPRETATION

Mrs. Johnson shows the characteristic signs of dementia: impaired memory, thinking, and judgment. Her personality has changed. In terms of the DSM-III-R criteria for describing the severity of dementia, she qualifies for the "severe" category, because she is unable to live without continual supervision.

Her age of onset is typical for Alzheimer's disease. Very few cases occur among those less than fifty years of age. There are slightly more cases of Alzheimer's disease among women than men, but this may reflect the fact that women tend to live longer. The course of this disease is progressive and deteriorating, as Mrs. Johnson exemplifies. Death eventually occurs, and the average amount of time between initial onset of symptoms and death is about five years.

Why did Mrs. Johnson develop Alzheimer's disease? There is no firm answer at the present time. Your text suggests that excess aluminum in the body might play some role. Also possible, and not incompatible, is a chromosomal abnormality. Yesterday on the television news, we heard speculation that a virus may be involved.

TREATMENT

Treatment for Alzheimer's disease is mostly in an experimental phase. Researchers are particularly interested in two lines of possible intervention. The first looks at drugs and dietary supplements that presumably increase levels of acetylcholine in the brain. Some studies report that such treatment slows the deterioration associated with Alzheimer's disease; other studies report a slight reversal of dementia. Other studies, however, show no real benefit from these treatments.

The second type of intervention is the possibility of grafting one's own healthy neuronal tissue onto impaired areas of the brain. These operations have already been performed in a small number of cases of people suffering from Parkinson's disease, with positive results reported (e.g., Moore, 1987). If these transplant operations stand up as an effective treatment for neurological disease, then they raise some difficult ethical questions. After all, the healthy tissue might someday come from another person. Some fear that fetuses will become the "donors" of choice, making abortion an even more controversial procedure than it already is.

DISCUSSION QUESTIONS

1. As our population ages, the number of people with Alzheimer's disease will only increase. Because there are no cures at the present time, this means that our societal resources will be severely taxed. What will happen to those with Alzheimer's disease?

2. Depression frequently co-occurs with Alzheimer's disease. Speculate on the possible biological and psychological links between the two.

3. What is gained by early identification of Alzheimer's disease?

4. Suppose research finds that Alzheimer's is genetically based, and that it is possible to test for the predisposition long before onset of the disease. (This is already possible for Huntington's chorea, a genetically transmitted disease.) Discuss the social implications of the availability of such a test. Would you want to know the results of your own test? How about for your spouse? Your unborn child? Your employee?

5. What do you think about the idea of neuronal transplants? What are the ethical issues to be addressed if these become feasible?

REFERENCES

Gruetzner, H. (1988). *Alzheimer's: A caregiver's guide and sourcebook.* New York: Wiley.

Moore, R. Y. (1987). Parkinson's disease—A new therapy? *New England Journal of Medicine, 316,* 872–873.

Witty Ray: Tourette's Syndrome

Your text covers the majority of disorders that people may experience, but there are some inevitable gaps. Not featured is a discussion of tic disorders. A *tic* is an involuntary, sudden, recurrent, nonrhythmic motor movement or vocalization. Tics can be suppressed by an individual, but only for a brief period of time. They are exacerbated by stress and decreased by sleep or participation in a fully engaging activity.

Tics take various forms, and when chronic or severe, they are considered a bona fide disorder. DSM-III-R classifies tic disorders with problems first evident in childhood and adolescence. This is usually when they show up. Some tic disorders prove to have an organic basis, which means we can look to the nervous system for an explanation.

THE SYNDROME

One tic disorder is Tourette's syndrome, first described in 1885 by the French neurologist Gilles de la Tourette, one of Charcot's students (cf. Chapter 2). Tourette's syndrome is quite an unusual example of a tic disorder. The person who suffers from it experiences multiple tics, usually both motor and vocal. The motor tics involve the head and upper body. A person so afflicted snaps and jerks himself about. The vocal tics are sounds like yelps, barks, sniffs, or coughs. Words may also occur, blurted out with great force, and in about one-third of the cases, these are obscenities. The tics occur many times throughout the day—every day. Typically, Tourette's syndrome begins at age seven and lasts a lifetime.

It is hard to picture someone with Tourette's syndrome from this brief listing of symptoms. But try. Imagine a person who has an excess of uncontrollable nervous activity, and whose tics may be grotesque to the observer, particularly when they include a stream of profanity.

When it was first described, Tourette's syndrome seemed to demand a biological explanation, because a purely psychological account just on the face of it was implausible. This line of thinking still seems reasonable. Current speculation about the biological basis of the syndrome centers on an excess of the neurotransmitter dopamine. At the same time, theorists stress that excess dopamine is hardly the entire picture. There may well be subtle changes in one's brain structure, possibly in the thalamus and hypothalamus, additionally involved in Tourette's syndrome.

The purpose of this case is to describe Witty Ray, a young man with an extreme case of Tourette's disorder. We encountered Ray in an essay by the well-known medical writer Oliver Sacks (1985), who always reminds his readers that people with problems are first and foremost human beings, no matter how bizarre or severe their difficulties. The case of Witty Ray is striking because Ray eventually was able to integrate his "normal" and "abnormal" aspects.

THE CASE

At twenty-four years of age, Ray was an intelligent young man with a profound problem. Since the age of four, he had experienced multiple tics of great severity every few seconds of his waking life. The diagnosis of Tourette's syndrome was unambiguous. In the face of a disorder that might have proven completely debilitating, he had achieved some remarkable accomplishments. Ray had finished high school and college. He had several close friends and a wife who greatly valued him, tics and all. But the Tourette's syndrome created incredible difficulties for him. Most people shunned him. He had lost a series of jobs, always because of the tics. His marriage had problems. When Ray would become sexually excited, his involuntary profanities would increase. Needless to say, cries of "Fuck!" and "Shit!" get in the way of making love.

Witty Ray was an impatient and pugnacious individual, known for his sudden wit and clowning manner. These personality traits are not part of Tourette's syndrome, but in Ray's case at least, they seem related, either as a compensation for his disorder or simply as an extension of it. Regardless, Ray and his tic disorder had in many ways accommodated each other. One example of this accommodation was Ray's weekend activity as a jazz drummer. He was quite accomplished and had a reputation for his wild improvisations, which would start as an uncontrollable tic but then be turned into an appropriate and exciting aspect of the music.

TREATMENT

Because so many problems followed in the wake of his tics, Ray came to Dr. Sacks asking for help. Haldol—a major tranquilizer used to treat schizophrenia—was administered in the hope that Ray's dopamine level would be decreased and his tics thereby controlled. He proved to be highly sensitive to the Haldol, and indeed his tics became less severe.

This is not the end of the story. Ray was not entirely pleased with the outcome of his treatment. He found his entire approach to life thrown off. Not only did the Haldol affect his tics, the medicine also affected everything else, including those aspects of Ray that he liked and considered central to his identity. As a trifling example of this, Ray found himself unable to navigate revolving doors. Before he had been able to dart in and out of them, and he enjoyed doing so. Now he had a black eye and a broken nose! As a serious example, Ray lost his ability to improvise as a drummer. Most generally, he lost the spark and playfulness that defined who he was. Ray expressed the fear that he was nothing but tics. If these were taken away, nothing would be left but a shell.

Dr. Sacks took Ray off the medication, and the two of them embarked on several months of talking therapy. They explored a number of concerns revolving around Ray's "true" personality and his dependency on the symptoms with which he had lived for twenty years. Only when Ray knew that he would be able to replace his Tourette's syndrome symptoms with something positive was he able to go back on Haldol and be successfully treated.

POSTSCRIPT

At the time that Sacks (1985) described Witty Ray, he had been on Haldol for nine years. Ray held a steady job. His marriage had stabilized, and he was now a father. But Ray had made a decision several years ago that he missed the excitement that accompanied Tourette's syndrome, and so he didn't take Haldol on the weekends, becoming frenetic and frivolous. During the week, he resumed his medication, leading a calm and sober life. Sacks describes the situation as strange, and we agree, but it also seems that today Ray is a healthy person, with and without Tourette's syndrome.

DISCUSSION QUESTIONS

1. How might the other models of abnormality featured in your text explain tic disorders?

2. Note that both schizophrenia and Tourette's syndrome are linked to excess dopamine (cf. Chapter 12). Obviously, these are different disorders, which means that dopamine level per se cannot fully explain either. Several questions suggest themselves. First, what do

schizophrenia and Tourette's syndrome share in common? Might this be the effect of excess dopamine? Second, what else is going on to produce schizophrenia in the one case and Tourette's syndrome in the other?

3. The case of Witty Ray reminds us of the "great men" discussed in Case 16 because the symptoms of Ray's disorder intermingle with his personality and seem at least partly responsible for some of his achievements in life. Is this sort of accommodation generally true for people with disorders? Relate your answer to the difficulties inherent in defining abnormality as discussed in Chapter 1 of your text.

4. The text observes that the field of neurology is much further along in diagnosis than in treatment. But perhaps this is true only when therapists try to treat the nervous system rather than the person with the nervous system. Wouldn't all patients with neurological disorders benefit from the sort of talking therapy that Ray and Dr. Sacks pursued? Consider this question with respect to the specific neurological problems described in Chapter 17: aphasia, amnesia, and so on.

REFERENCE

Sacks, O. (1985). Witty Ticcy Ray. In *The man who mistook his wife for a hat and other clinical tales*. New York: Summit.

Johnson versus Johnson: Determining Child Custody

Chapter 18 of your text presents several examples of how psychology and the legal system may come into contact: the insanity plea, involuntary commitment, right to treatment, and so on. One topic not considered that is becoming increasingly important is the role of the psychologist in helping adjudicate child custody following a divorce.

As you know, divorce is a frequent occurrence in contemporary America. Perhaps as many as 40 percent of recent marriages will end in divorce. And perhaps as many as 20 percent of these divorces will entail disputed custody of the children. The purpose of this case is to raise some of the issues involved in determining child custody. We'll include a sample case that Richard Gardner (1982) originally described in his book *Family Evaluation in Child Custody Litigation.*

THE BEST INTERESTS OF THE CHILD

According to the law, the overriding concern in awarding custody following a divorce is "the best interests" of the child. In other words, what will benefit the son or daughter takes precedence over what will benefit the father or mother. This is consistent with the general tenor of our legal system. We afford special protection to minors because they are not able to fully fend for themselves.

Although the details differ from jurisdiction to jurisdiction in the United States, the current (1988) Michigan Child Custody Act is representative in how it characterizes the child's best interest. Here are some extracts from this act:

> "Best interests of the child" means the sum total of the following factors . . .
>
> (a) The love, affection, and other emotional ties existing between the parties involved and the child.

(b) The capacity and disposition of the parties involved to give the child love, affection, and guidance and continuation of the educating and raising of the child in its religion or creed, if any.

(c) The capacity and disposition of the parties involved to provide the child with food, clothing, medical care or other remedial care recognized and permitted under the laws of the state in place of medical care, and other material needs.

(d) The length of time the child has lived in a stable, satisfactory environment, and the desirability of maintaining continuity.

(e) The permanence, as a family unit, of the existing or proposed custodial home or homes.

(f) The moral fitness of the parties involved.

(g) The mental and physical health of the parties involved.

(h) The home, school, and community record of the child.

(i) The reasonable preference of the child, if the court deems the child to be of sufficient age to express preference.

(j) The willingness and ability of each of the parents to facilitate and encourage a close and continuing parent-child relationship between the child and the other parent.

(k) Any other factor considered by the court to be relevant to a particular child custody dispute.

... When the dispute is between the parents, between agencies, or between third parties the best interests of the child shall control. When the dispute is between the parent or parents and an agency or a third person, it is presumed that the best interests of the child are served by awarding custody to the parent or parents, unless the contrary is established by clear and convincing evidence.

It is far easier, however, to define a child's best interests than to recognize them. The decision is rarely clear-cut. Each contesting parent, or third party, presents a mixture of strengths and weaknesses, and the wisdom of Solomon is needed to make the appropriate judgment.

WHO SHALL DECIDE?

The law makes it clear that the final decision in child custody is a legal one, not a psychological one. That is, courts decide custody, not psychologists. But the language with which a child's best interests are defined is psychological language, as you can see from the act we just showed you. Psychologists increasingly are asked to testify concerning a child's best interests.

How is this testimony regarded? Let's take a broad view in answering this question. Appreciate that our legal system is adversarial in nature. Two parties argue over a matter, and the person who argues better wins. This approach may be useful for determining the outcome of criminal cases, but it may not be useful in determining child custody. Gardner (1982) therefore recommends that the psychologist is much better off when entering into these disputes as an impartial expert and not an advocate of one party over another.

THE ROLE OF THE PSYCHOLOGIST

As an impartial expert, the psychologist should meet with both parties involved in the custody dispute, in order to arrive at a recommendation that one is the *better* parent. First, she gathers information, much like a diagnostician. She uses interviews, observations, tests, reports from others, and so on. Then, she tries to combine all of it into an overall judgment. It's important that she be on the alert for factors that bias the information available and thus her conclusions.

SAMPLE CASE

Gardner (1982) presents several sample reports summarizing custody evaluations. These reports are forwarded to the judge presiding over the case in question. Here, we paraphrase and abbreviate one such report, to give you an idea of the form these can take:

November 17, 19—

Honorable Roberta Barnes
Superior Court

Re: Johnson vs. Johnson

Dear Judge Barnes:

This report is submitted in compliance with your court order requesting that I evaluate the Johnson family in order to provide the court with information to be used in deciding which of the parents should have custody of their three children, Tara, Elaine, and Charles.

My findings and recommendations are based on interviews conducted as described below: . . . [names, dates, times, etc.] . . .

Mr. Frank Johnson is forty-three years old and works as an airplane pilot. His first wife died soon after giving birth to Tara, who is now sixteen years old. He married Mrs. Carol Barnes when Tara was two years old. Mrs. Johnson is now a housewife, forty years old, and formerly worked as a teacher. There are two children from the Johnson marriage: Elaine, age eleven, and Charles, age seven . . .

In October, 19— Mr. Johnson initiated divorce proceedings because he felt Mrs. Johnson was a poor mother, particularly to Tara. Both parents are requesting custody of all three children. My recommendation is that Mr. Johnson be awarded custody of Tara, and that Mrs. Johnson be awarded custody of Elaine and Charles. Let me present the observations from which these recommendations are derived by dividing them into four categories.

1. *Mr. Johnson's assets as a parent.* Mr. Johnson is Tara's biological father. The special psychological tie that this engenders is not present with Mrs. Johnson. It is not the biological relationship per se that is critical but the psychological attachment that follows from this bond. . . . At the present, Tara has a closer relationship with her father than her mother. . . . In every interview, Tara openly expresses the wish to live with her father . . .

2. *Mr. Johnson's liabilities as a parent.* Mr. Johnson states that he would not have participated in this evaluation if he had to pay for it. It is financed solely by Mrs. Johnson, and I conclude that his position is less strong than hers. . . . Mr. Johnson tends to make sweeping judgments without being able to specify examples of them. He says that Mrs. Johnson is "a very poor mother," but backs this up with no incidents. I consider this a manifestation of his difficulty in communicating. . . . Mr. Johnson's profession as an airline pilot has not allowed him predictable hours. . . . Both Charles and Elaine stated that they want to live with their mother and not their father. . . . Mr. Johnson plans to move to California, and I believe this would lead to further absences. . . .

3. *Mrs. Johnson's assets as a parent.* She is more committed to the custody evaluation than her husband. . . . She is more available to the children, and is a more accurate and clearer communicator than Mr. Johnson. Mrs. Johnson is recognized by her husband as having a closer relationship with Elaine than he does.

4. *Mrs. Johnson's liabilities as a parent.* Mrs. Johnson and Tara have a poor relationship at this point. I found that Tara views her mother with scorn and resents her authority. "She has a lot of nerve telling me how to act." . . . Mrs. Johnson cannot provide a male role model to Charles. . . . I believe that Mrs. Johnson is a little too punitive with the children. . . .

Conclusions. I believe the evidence strongly favors Mr. Johnson being given custody of Tara and Mrs. Johnson custody of Elaine. There are arguments both ways in the case of Charles, although I think the balance is tipped toward awarding his custody to Mrs. Johnson as well. . . .

DISCUSSION QUESTIONS

1. "The best interests of a child" should probably be regarded as a family resemblance, as your text in Chapter 1 recommends for

conceiving the notion of abnormality. Compare and contrast these two family resemblances.

2. Do you agree with all the criteria listed in the Michigan Child Custody Act? Comment specifically on the criterion of "mental health" in light of what you know about abnormality. Which criteria does Mr. Johnson meet? Which are met by Mrs. Johnson? Does the recommendation reflect the preponderance of criteria met?

3. How is the assessment of "the best interests" different than the diagnosis of abnormality?

4. How might bias creep into the process of determining child custody?

5. In what other domains concerning the welfare of children does the legal system enlist the advice of mental health professionals?

6. Should potential parents be licensed by the state before they are allowed to raise children?

7. Do you think that psychologists can predict with any accuracy who will be a better parent?

8. Take a critical attitude toward the sample case we presented here. What information seems to be missing? What conclusions strike you as wrong?

REFERENCE

Gardner, R. A. (1982). *Family evaluation in child custody litigation.* Cresskill, NJ: Creative Therapeutics.

Classifying Schizophrenia
in the Soviet Union

Chapter 18 of your text describes how the field of abnormal psychology can be abused by the state. One way is by "diagnosing" someone who dissents, thereby undercutting what may be legitimate disagreement and criticism and justifying the removal of the individual from society. Rather blatant examples of this practice sometimes occur in the Soviet Union. Our purpose in this case is not to document these examples (but see, for example, Fireside, 1979). Instead, we'll briefly describe the current system of classifying schizophrenia used in the Soviet Union; this system lends itself to abuse, as you will see.

The more general purpose of this case is to raise your awareness about the political nature of diagnostic schemes in general. As stressed throughout your text, judgments of abnormality inherently involve social considerations. When mental health professionals specify the categories with which to conceive abnormality, their schemes cannot help but reflect larger societal values.

CLASSIFICATION SYSTEM

The World Health Organization in 1973 reported a worldwide study of how schizophrenia was variously defined and recognized. As you might imagine, considerable differences occurred across different nations. Although in each country that was studied, something like schizophrenia was recognized, there was quite a range in how narrowly or broadly the boundaries of this phenomenon were drawn. Among those nations where narrow definitions prevailed, there was substantial agreement. As definitions became more broad, and applied to a greater variety of people and problems, agreement fell off, so that "schizophrenia" was increasingly culture-bound.

The Soviet Union uses a broad definition of schizophrenia. (And let us in the United States not feel too righteous on this score, because the

American definition—though differing in detail from the Soviet definition—resembles it in breadth and hence idiosyncrasy.) The Soviets recognize three forms of schizophrenia (Bloch & Reddaway, 1985):

- periodic—occasional psychotic episodes occurring to a person who is "normal" between episodes
- shiftlike—occasional psychotic episodes with a progressive course; in other words, the person shows incomplete remission following each episode and steadily worsens
- continuous—progressive deterioration with no remissions

Note that this basic classification relies on the history of one's problems rather than the symptoms per se, as does the DSM-III-R classification.

The continuous schizophrenia category is further subdivided into several forms according to the speed of deterioration:

- rapid (or malignant)
- moderate
- sluggish (or mild)

These different forms can be further recognized by the particular symptoms that characterize each. So, in the case of rapid deterioration, we find flagrant hallucinations. In moderate cases, paranoia predominates. And in sluggish schizophrenia, individuals retain their ability to function socially but tend to overvalue their self-importance. Frequently, they wish to reform the world.

In the Soviet Union, the diagnosis of schizophrenia stays with someone forever, even if he returns to a normal state, as in periodic schizophrenia. Continuous schizophrenia is regarded as irreversible, and prospects for any improvement are thought to be nil. Also, the Soviets believe that if someone is diagnosed as schizophrenic, then he is not responsible for any of his actions.

ABUSE

What's the relevance of this classification scheme and its underlying rationale to abuse by the state? First, consider the fact that anyone bearing the diagnosis is considered to be not responsible. "Symptoms" in the DSM-III-R sense are not pertinent. A person can seem normal but still be nonresponsible. And someone who is not responsible can be ordered to undergo compulsory medical treatment.

Second, dissent per se can be seen as a sign of the sluggish variety of continuous schizophrenia. "Reformism" by definition becomes delusional. Bloch and Reddaway (1985, p. 147) argue that Soviet forensic psychiatrists frequently use expressions like the following in their reports:

- "paranoid reformist delusional ideas"
- "opinions . . . [with] moralizing character"

- "overestimation of his own personality"
- "poor adaptation to the social environment"

These sound pathological in the abstract. But in the concrete, they may refer to an individual's beliefs that Soviet minorities should have greater rights, that the Soviet constitution should be changed, or that Soviet excursions into Czechoslovakia, Afghanistan, and so on, should be regretted.

Third, in the cases taken up by international human rights organizations, diagnoses are invariably of continuous schizophrenia—sluggish variety. If these diagnoses are made in a nonbiased way, one would expect to see at least some of the other diagnoses occasionally represented. Because the pattern is so pronounced, there is good reason to suspect that abuse is taking place.

On occasion, Soviet dissenters carrying a diagnosis of schizophrenia have been released to Western nations. Of note is the fact that these individuals almost always make a good social, occupational, and political adjustment to their new way of life. Remember that in the Soviet Union, they were thought to have suffered from a chronic and progressive mental disorder. The fact that they "recover" in spectacular fashion upon leaving their country is also good reason to suspect that their original diagnosis reflected political abuse by the state.

THE MOTIVES OF SOVIET PSYCHIATRISTS

As we see it, black-and-white thinking on the issue of state abuse of psychology is not too useful. We are arguing here that such abuse does take place in the Soviet Union, and we think this is bad. But let's refrain from categorically condemning the mental health professionals involved in the process. There is a temptation to see "them" as having bad motives of which they are completely aware. But it's not a good idea to judge their motives or their consciousness from afar.

On the other hand, Bloch and Reddaway (1985) argue that regardless of a Soviet psychiatrist's motives in diagnosing a dissenter as schizophrenic, the frequent recommendation that they be sent to so-called "special psychiatric hospitals" can be criticized from afar. These hospitals differ from regular psychiatric hospitals, because they are run by the same agency that presides over the police and prison system. Treatment differs accordingly, and so it is impossible for a psychiatrist to be blind to the political nature of these institutions.

DISCUSSION QUESTIONS

1. Does the Soviet system of classifying schizophrenia map in any simple way into the system proposed by DSM-III-R?

2. Compare and contrast Soviet versus American delusions of grandeur.

3. Remember that mental health professionals in the United States define schizophrenia broadly. Where do you think the "excess" in our categorization of schizophrenia occurs?

4. In general, how do the conditions that we consider disorders reflect American values and ideals?

5. Psychology may be abused by the state in ways other than by stifling dissent. What are some other ways?

6. Do you think that psychology is abused in the United States like it is in the Soviet Union? Or are the possible abuses different? Or are there no abuses at all?

7. Diagnoses and treatments differ depending on one's social class, gender, religion, and/or race. Does this reflect bias? Does this reflect abuse?

8. How can a mental health professional *not* serve political purposes, or is this inevitable?

9. Can there be a value-free field of abnormal psychology? How about a value-free diagnostic system?

REFERENCES

Bloch, S., & Reddaway, P. (1985). Psychiatrists and dissenters in the Soviet Union. In E. Stover & E. O. Nightingale (Eds.), *The breaking of bodies and minds: Torture, psychiatric abuse, and the health professions.* New York: Freeman.

Fireside, H. (1979). *Soviet psychoprisons.* New York: Norton.

World Health Organization (1973). *The international pilot study of schizophrenia.* Geneva: author.

Psychotherapies with Mr. Jones

A large number of different psychotherapies exist, and the number is growing all the time (Garfield & Bergin, 1986). In the 1960s, we could identify approximately 60 versions of therapy. In the early 1970s, this number had increased to 130. By the late 1970s, there were 250 different approaches to therapy. And who knows how many therapies exist today?

Still, most therapies can be placed within just a few broad categories corresponding to the major models of abnormality discussed in your text. Herein lies an important point: therapy is theoretically motivated. One does not arbitrarily choose a therapy, but rather bases one's choices on a particular conception of human nature (i.e., psychology) and a specific sense of how problems can develop (i.e., psychopathology).

Many clinical psychologists believe that given problems are better treated with some therapies than with others, but this position—sometimes called the matching hypothesis—is merely plausible. It has not yet been fully verified. So, in actuality, a person with a specific problem may well seek therapy with a variety of therapists who represent a range of orientations.

The purpose of the present case is to describe how Mr. Jones, a man with difficulties surrounding gambling, might be treated by therapists of differing orientations. We encountered this case originally as an example of behavior modification (Fitchett & Sanford, 1976). We paraphrase how that approach to therapy was used with Mr. Jones, and then go on to speculate how therapy might have proceeded if he had received instead other forms of psychotherapy.

THE CASE

Mr. Jones was a thirty-one-year-old man with a strong interest in betting on horse races. This interest led him into trouble, because he had embezzled almost $30,000 from his employer in order to pay his gambling debts. He was caught, charged, and convicted. He was sent to prison, where he continued to gamble. Even incarcerated, he found ways to follow the results of horse races and to place illegal bets. He became concerned with his own behavior, fearing that upon his release from prison, he would repeat the pattern that landed him there in the first place. In the language of DSM-III-R, Mr. Jones seems to suffer from an impulse control disorder centering on gambling.

BEHAVIOR MODIFICATION

Mr. Jones sought out treatment with a behavior therapist. The first step in therapy was to cast Mr. Jones's problems in terms of constituent behaviors. "Listening to a race broadcast" was a critical response. Mr. Jones did not attend actual races, even when he was out of prison, but instead listened to races on the radio. The behavior therapist decided to decrease this particular response by pairing it with aversive stimuli.

By talking to Mr. Jones, the therapist discovered that he cared greatly for his wife. So, she was asked to help out. She recorded several messages to Mr. Jones, including "please don't bet on the races" and "I love you." The former message was spliced several times into a tape describing a horse race, along with the sound of a woman periodically screaming. The latter message was incorporated at random intervals into a tape of light music.

Mr. Jones then participated in several sessions in which he sat before a simulated radio and listened to the horse race tape, along with his wife's pleas that he not bet, as well as the periodic screams. He was not allowed to turn the radio off or to leave the room. The point of these sessions was for him to associate broadcasts of horse races with aversive stimuli.

Next there were several sessions in which Mr. Jones was allowed to turn the nob on the radio and switch from the horse race tape to the light music tape. These sessions allowed him to escape the aversive stimuli, and be further rewarded by hearing his wife say that she loved him.

Finally, there were sessions where not all his escape responses were reinforced. As you know, "partial reinforcement" makes a response highly resistant to extinction, which was the goal for these final sessions. Once released from prison, Mr. Jones could not realistically be expected to win rewards each and every time he turned away from a horse race broadcast, and so it was imperative that resistance to extinction be established.

BIOMEDICAL THERAPY

Suppose Mr. Jones sought out treatment with a biologically oriented therapist. Of course there is no "anti-gambling" drug available, but that doesn't mean that biomedical therapy has nothing to offer. Here are some possibilities. First, Mr. Jones's gambling may stem directly from a biologically based problem. Undiagnosed bipolar depression is a possibility, for instance, with gambling as one of the reckless activities characterizing a manic episode. Assuming that other signs of bipolar disorder are present as well, perhaps lithium could be prescribed.

Second, Mr. Jones's gambling may stem indirectly from a biological problem. Gambling shares at least a superficial similarity with addictions, and we know that excessive indulgence in food, drugs, sex, or alcohol may be someone's attempt to "self-medicate" an underlying anxiety or depressive disorder. Maybe gambling makes Mr. Jones feel less anxious or less depressed. Unfortunately, because he runs up large debts in the course of gambling, he has even more reasons to feel anxious or depressed, which means that his gambling is a vicious circle. In fact, one common pattern among compulsive gamblers is to keep increasing the stakes, because a given wager soon loses its ability to deliver a thrill. This is consistent with the idea that gambling is a short-term distraction from underlying emotional problems. A therapist might be able to help Mr. Jones by giving him medications that reduce his anxiety or depression.

Third, some biological theorists suggest that gambling is linked to the level of endorphins in one's brain (Rosenfeld, 1985). As you know from the text, endorphins are chemicals akin to narcotics that are produced naturally in our brains, where they help to alleviate stress and pain. The argument here is that compulsive gamblers have an abnormally low baseline level of endorphins, which makes them particularly susceptible to distress. Gambling gives a jolt to their systems, so to speak, elevating endorphins and thereby producing good feelings. This theory is speculative, but it suggests that a gambler like Mr. Jones could be helped if it were possible to alter his endorphin level. Maybe he could be encouraged to jog, for instance, or become a weight lifter. These activities would boost his endorphins just like gambling, without such dire consequences. He could even be given drugs like naloxone that block the euphoric effects of the endorphins presumably stimulated by gambling.

PSYCHODYNAMIC THERAPY

If Mr. Jones sought out treatment with a psychodynamic therapist, his problem would be viewed as the manifestation of an unconscious conflict, perhaps one originating early in childhood. The gambling per se would be considered a symptom of this conflict, and it would probably bear some symbolic relationship to it. The psychodynamic therapist would explore Mr. Jones's associations to gambling, to horses, to listening to races on the radio. (My goodness, maybe Mr. Jones is Little Hans all grown up!) The therapist would be alert to any dreams concerning gambling that Mr. Jones might report.

There may be a temptation to offer a single psychodynamic interpretation for all forms of compulsive gambling. Certainly, some theorists have done so (Greenberg, 1980), variously regarding it as:

- symbolic intercourse
- symbolic masturbation
- a manifestation of the death instinct
- the triumph of the id over the superego
- anal sadism
- infantile omnipotence

But the more reasonable conclusion from a psychodynamic perspective is that gambling is overdetermined. The motives of any particular individual, like Mr. Jones, reflect an idiosyncratic blend of several contributing factors.

What would his treatment entail? First, he would be made aware of what lies behind his behavioral patterns. The therapist would expect Mr. Jones to resist. Indeed, one likely area where problems might occur is in the payment of fees for therapy. If he didn't settle up promptly with his therapist, this transference issue could become a good topic for discussion.

COGNITIVE THERAPY

Suppose Mr. Jones sought out treatment with a cognitive therapist. As we have seen with the other approaches to therapy, the first step here is to describe his problem in terms compatible with the cognitive model. For the sake of our example, let's assume that Mr. Jones shows the pattern of emotions that many compulsive gamblers show: tension or anxiety prior to gambling and release or gratification while gambling. A cognitive therapist might target these emotions for change, and do so by getting at the underlying thoughts that (presumably) produce them.

According to cognitive theorists, anxiety can be caused by a belief in one's particular vulnerabilities (Beck & Emery, 1985). If anxiety precedes gambling, then the therapist would take a look at Mr. Jones's thoughts of pending threat. The cognitive therapist seen by Mr. Jones would explain this link between thoughts and impulses, and encourage Mr. Jones to "capture" the automatic thoughts that flash through his mind when he feels like placing a bet. Some possibilities include "I don't make enough money on my job to support my family" or "I have so many gambling debts I'll never pay them off unless I win big" and so on. Are these beliefs warranted by the facts? The cognitive therapist would instruct Mr. Jones to consider this question. Perhaps yes, perhaps no.

In either case, the therapist would then know what to do: change the situation or change Mr. Jones.

The other emotional aspect of Mr. Jones's gambling is the pleasure he experiences while gambling. Again, a cognitive therapist would tie these feelings to particular thoughts. Maybe Mr. Jones believes he is going to win. Maybe he believes he is an important person. The therapist can help him detect and challenge these thoughts as warranted.

DISCUSSION QUESTIONS

1. Do you find any of these treatments more compelling than the others? Does your answer reflect *your* conception of human nature and how it can go awry?

2. How would "cure" be ascertained in each of these forms of therapy with Mr. Jones?

3. What common ingredients do you see in these different strategies of treating compulsive gambling?

4. Use the terms introduced in Chapter 19 of your text to describe these different psychotherapies.

5. Suppose you wanted to combine the different therapies described in this case, and treat Mr. Jones with a "multi-therapy" approach. What form would this take? Would it be coherent or confused?

6. How would a client-centered therapist approach the treatment of Mr. Jones?

7. How would a therapist using rational-emotive therapy approach this case?

8. How would a family therapist help Mr. Jones with his gambling problem?

9. Research on therapy outcome implies that in the short run, all these treatments of Mr. Jones will work, but none will be dramatically superior to the others. But what about relapse? Which therapy do you believe will help Mr. Jones to refrain from gambling in the long run?

10. Besides compulsive gambling, DSM-III-R describes several other impulse control problems:
    - intermittent explosive disorder (uncontrollable loss of one's temper)
    - kleptomania (uncontrollable stealing)
    - pyromania (deliberate setting of fires)
    - trichotillomania (uncontrollable impulse to pull out one's own hair)

What do these disorders share in common with compulsive gambling?

How are they different? Would therapy proceed in the same way with each of these disorders?

REFERENCES

Beck, A. T., & Emery, G. (1985). *Anxiety disorders and phobias: A cognitive perspective.* New York: Basic Books.

Fitchett, S. M., & Sanford, D. A. (1976). Treatment for habitual gambling. In J. D. Krumboltz & C. E. Thoreson (Eds.), *Counseling methods.* New York: Holt, Rinehart, & Winston.

Garfield, S. L., & Bergin, A. E. (Eds.) (1986). *Handbook of psychotherapy and behavior change.* 3rd ed. New York: Wiley.

Greenberg, H. R. (1980). Psychology of gambling. In H. I. Kaplan, A. M. Freedman, & B. J. Sadock (Eds.), *Comprehensive textbook of psychiatry.* 3rd ed. Baltimore: Williams & Wilkins.

Rosenfeld, A. H. (1985). Brain chemicals and gambler's high. *Psychology Today, 19*(5), 8.

CHAPTER 1

The Meanings of Abnormality

CHAPTER OVERVIEW

The textbook begins with a discussion of abnormality. How is it best to define it? Abnormality, like many concepts in ordinary language, has fuzzy boundaries. Although it is easy to recognize extreme examples of abnormality, it is not as easy to classify less extreme instances—the gray areas. The notion of "family resemblance" is introduced to help explain the fuzzy nature of abnormality. When instances of a concept like abnormality are said to have a family resemblance, they have elements in common. However, no given element is necessary or sufficient to define that concept.

For abnormality, these elements include (a) suffering; (b) maladaptiveness; (c) irrationality and incomprehensibility; (d) unpredictability and loss of control; (e) vividness and unconventionality; (f) observer discomfort; and (g) violation of moral and ideal standards. The more of these elements present, the more confident we are that abnormality is present.

Abnormality is a social judgment, and, like all such judgments, it is fallible. Disagreement sometimes occurs about who or what is abnormal. However, this does not mean that abnormality does not exist or that it is not a useful concept.

Normality is defined here simply as the absence of abnormality—i.e., possessing few of the elements that count toward a judgment of abnormality. There is more to life than the mere absence of abnormality, though, and the positive side of life is termed *optimal living*. Optimal living includes (a) positive attitudes toward oneself; (b) ability to grow and develop; (c) autonomy; (d) accurate perception of reality; (e) competence at life's tasks; and (f) satisfying relationships with other people.

ESSENTIAL TERMS

family resemblance	notion that instances of a concept possess elements in common, but no given element is necessary or sufficient
flexible control	ability to retain control or to give it up as self and situation require
intern's disease	illness created by suggestion, as by reading of symptoms and "discovering" their presence
necessary condition	property that all instances of a given concept possess
normality	absence of abnormality
optimal living	pleasures, maturities, insights, achievements, and wisdoms of life
residual rules	unwritten rules of behavior
sufficient condition	property that only instances of a given concept possess

SAMPLE EXAM

1. Which of these statements was made about abnormality?
   a. It is easy to define abnormality.
   b. Abnormality exists in all cultures.
   c. There is no such thing as abnormality.
   d. Although it is difficult to define abnormality, it is easy to recognize it.

2. Which of these is a necessary condition for "dog"?
   a. four legs
   b. bark
   c. fur
   d. domesticated

3. Which of these is a sufficient condition for "triangle"?
   a. equal angles
   b. three sides
   c. each angle less than 90 degrees
   d. equal sides

4. Which of these is a necessary condition for "abnormality"?
   a. suffering
   b. irrationality
   c. unpredictability
   d. observer discomfort
   e. none of the above

5. Which of these is a sufficient condition for "abnormality"?
   a. suffering
   b. irrationality
   c. unpredictability
   d. observer discomfort
   e. none of the above

6. The idea of a family resemblance is that
   a. first cousins look more alike than second cousins.
   b. there are necessary and sufficient conditions for belonging to a family.
   c. members of a family tend to share characteristics in common.
   d. identical twins look alike.

7. The more elements of abnormality present,
   a. the more abnormal a person is.
   b. the more complex abnormality is.
   c. the more certain it is that abnormality is present.
   d. the more difficult it is to cure abnormality.

8. Which of these statements is true?
   a. Abnormality always implies suffering.
   b. Suffering always implies abnormality.
   c. Abnormality never implies suffering.
   d. Suffering never implies abnormality.
   e. Abnormality sometimes implies suffering.
   f. Suffering sometimes implies abnormality.

9. In biology, adaptiveness involves all except
   a. survival of species.
   b. population growth.
   c. well-being of individual.
   d. well-being of society.

10. Which of these is most incomprehensible?
    a. grief
    b. thought disorder
    c. arson
    d. ingratiation

11. Flexible control is the ability to
    a. bend but not break.
    b. change one's mind about the causes of behavior.
    c. retain or relinquish control as required.
    d. control actions in several ways.

12. Unconventionality characterizes all but
    a. genius.
    b. abnormality.
    c. trend-setters.
    d. high moral standards.

13. When broken, residual rules of behavior result in
    a. judgments of abnormality.
    b. misdemeanors.
    c. observer discomfort.
    d. felonies.

14. Violation of moral standards
    a. may be conventional.
    b. always results in observer discomfort.
    c. always is abnormal.
    d. always is normal.

15. The *Diagnostic and Statistical Manual* (Third Edition—Revised) is a
    a. list of fees charged by psychiatrists.
    b. set of criteria for different mental disorders.
    c. discussion of global abnormality.
    d. specification of necessary and sufficient conditions for different mental disorders.

16. Which one of the following statements is *not* a hazard of the family-resemblance approach?
    a. Society may be wrong about abnormality.
    b. There may be no family resemblance for abnormality.
    c. Observers may disagree about abnormality.
    d. Actors and observers may disagree about abnormality.

17. Normality is
    a. absence of abnormality.
    b. adaptation.
    c. conventionality.
    d. lack of suffering.

18. Optimal living is
    a. self-actualization.
    b. normality.
    c. the positive side of life.
    d. different in kind from normality.

19. Optimal living involves all of the following but
    a. positive attitudes toward self.

    b. autonomy.
    c. conventionality.
    d. environmental competence.

20. Interns' syndrome is caused by
    a. stress.
    b. germs.
    c. congenital defect.
    d. suggestion.

Answer Key for Sample Exam

1.	b	(p. 5)	11.	c	(p. 10)
2.	a	(p. 6)	12.	d	(p. 11)
3.	b	(p. 6)	13.	c	(p. 11)
4.	e	(p. 7)	14.	a	(p. 12)
5.	e	(p. 7)	15.	b	(p. 15)
6.	c	(p. 7)	16.	b	(p. 16)
7.	c	(p. 7)	17.	a	(p. 17)
8.	e, f	(p. 8)	18.	c	(p. 19)
9.	b	(p. 9)	19.	c	(p. 19)
10.	b	(p. 9)	20.	d	(p. 21)

SELF-TEST

1. Abnormality is recognized in _____ cultures.

2. If all cases of abnormality shared some single property, the property would be a _____ for abnormality.

3. If only cases of abnormality shared some single property, the property would be a _____ for abnormality.

4. Just because abnormality is difficult to define does not mean _____ or _____.

5. The idea that cases of abnormality share elements in common, although none of these elements is necessary or sufficient, is called _____.

6. The more elements of abnormality present, the more _____.

7. The elements of abnormality include _____, _____, _____, _____, _____, _____, and _____.

8. An instance of loss of control that is not abnormal is _____.

9. Unwritten rules of behavior are called _____.

10. Unlike many judgments in science, the judgment of abnormality is a _____.

11. The catalog currently in use of ways in which people are abnormal is _____.

12. The three hazards of the family resemblance approach to abnormality are _____,

    _____, and _____.

13. Normality is _____.

14. The positive side of life is _____ _____.

15. The elements of optimal living are _____ _____, _____, _____,

    _____, and _____.

16. Illness brought about by suggestion is _____ _____.

Answer Key for Self-Test

1. all
2. necessary condition
3. sufficient condition
4. it does not exist; it cannot be recognized
5. family resemblance
6. certain we are that abnormality is present
7. suffering; maladaptiveness; irrationality and incomprehensibility; unpredictability and loss of control; vividness; observer discomfort; violation of moral and ideal standards
8. flexible control
9. residual rules of behavior
10. social judgment
11. *Diagnostic and Statistical Manual of Mental Disorders* (Third Edition-Revised) (or DSM-III-R)
12. society may be wrong; observers may disagree; observers and actors may disagree
13. absence of abnormality
14. optimal living
15. positive attitudes toward self; growth and development; autonomy; accurate perception of reality; environmental competence; positive interpersonal relations
16. interns' syndrome

TYING IT TOGETHER

This chapter introduces two important ideas that will aid in understanding the material presented in the rest of the textbook. First, abnormality is described as a category with fuzzy boundaries. There are neither necessary nor sufficient conditions for abnormality. Instead, instances of abnormality bear a family resemblance to each other; they tend to share elements in common, although no given element is critical in defining abnormality. The idea of family resemblances should be kept in mind throughout your reading of the textbook. It helps explain why clinical research (Chapter 6) and clinical diagnosis (Chapter 7) are less than exact. It helps explain why treatment (Chapter 19) is less than 100 percent successful.

The disorders described in Chapters 8 through 17 are also characterized by family resemblances. Any given disorder has a number of elements that count toward its diagnosis, but in most cases these elements are neither necessary nor sufficient. Further, elements may count toward more than one diagnosis. Anxiety, for instance, is pertinent not just to the anxiety disorders (Chapters 8 and 9), but also to such difficulties as psychosomatic disorders (Chapter 10), sexual dysfunctions (Chapter 13), and the schizophrenias (Chapter 12).

Chapters 3 through 5 describe popular approaches to understanding and treating abnormality. Most of these approaches propose that some factor is a necessary and sufficient cause of abnormality. The family resemblances idea suggests that none of these approaches will always be reasonable. Indeed, it is frequently concluded throughout the textbook that a combination of models is needed to explain a given disorder.

The examples given of each disorder tend to be good examples—i.e., they possess many of the elements that count toward a diagnosis. However it should be realized that such good examples are rarely encountered. In reality, most instances of a disorder lack some of the important elements.

The second important idea introduced in this first chapter is that identification of abnormality is a social judgment. Theory (Chapters 3 through 5), research (Chapter 6), and assessment (Chapter 7) aid this judgment, but inherently it involves one person making a decision about another person, even in the case of neurological disorders (Chapter 17). Mistakes may occur (Chapter 18). The social context of abnormality and its identification (Chapter 2) should not be forgotten even though attention is usually drawn to the so-called abnormal individual.

FURTHER READINGS

Barnes, M., & Berke, J. (1973). *Mary Barnes: Two accounts of a journey through madness.* New York: Ballantine.

Campbell, A. (1976). Subjective measures of well-being. *American Psychologist, 31,* 117–124.

Chesler, P. (1972). *Women and madness.* New York: Doubleday.

Foulks, E. F., Wintrob, R. M., Westermeyer, J., & Favazza, A. R. (1977). *Current perspectives in cultural psychiatry.* New York: Spectrum.

Greenblatt, M. (1978). *Psychopolitics.* New York: Grune & Stratton.

Kozol, R. (1988). *Rachel and her children: Homeless families in America.* New York: Crown.

Scott, W. A. (1958). Research definition of mental health and mental illness. *Psychological Bulletin, 55,* 29–45.

Scott, W. A. (1968). Conceptions of normality. In E. G. Borgotta & W. W. Lambert (Eds.), *Handbook of personality theory and research* (pp. 974–1006). Chicago: Rand McNally.

TERM-PAPER TOPICS

1. Critics of the mental health professions, like Thomas Szasz, argue that diagnoses of abnormality constitute moral judgments in the guise of scientific statements. Evaluate this claim. Discuss the idea of family resemblances and its pertinence to your thesis.

2. It can be argued that the family resemblances idea is too easy a way out for psychologists who have been unable to discover the essence of abnormality. The natural sciences—physics, chemistry, and biology—have proceeded without resorting to family resemblances. What about the field of abnormal psychology? Take a strong stand, and defend it.

3. The textbook does not discuss positive mental health (optimal living) in much detail. However, other writers have devoted considerable thought to the topic. Review some of these formulations. Can positive mental health be actively brought about, or can it at best merely not be inhibited?

EXERCISES

Exercise One—The Elements of Abnormality

The purpose of this exercise is to illustrate the idea that the elements of abnormality are neither necessary nor sufficient.

Consider the following descriptions. Most people would consider at least some of the actions described to be abnormal. In each case, which elements of abnormality are present? Which are absent? Compare your judgments with those of your classmates.

a. Your neighbors encourage their children to watch twelve hours of television per day.

b. Your uncle consumes a quart of whiskey per day; he has trouble remembering the names of those around him.

c. Your ten-year-old neighbor calls the police to tell them that her parents keep marijuana in the house.
d. Your neighbor divorces her husband in order to devote more time to her career.
e. All visitors to your parents' home must wash their hands immediately upon arriving, or else they are not allowed to stay.
f. Your neighbors allow their children to watch while they make love.
g. Your cousin is pregnant, and she smokes three packs of cigarettes per day.
h. Your roommate is a highly successful college football player who uses steroids to increase his strength, despite their negative effects on his long-term health.

Exercise Two—Actor-Observer Differences in Explanation

The purpose of this exercise is to show that people often explain their own behaviors differently than do people who observe these behaviors. Specifically, "actors" often point to situational demands or requirements, while "observers" often point to dispositions of the actor.

Ask several different individuals you know to explain (a) why they received a poor grade on an exam; (b) why they went to a party; (c) why they have a part-time job. Then ask other people who know these individuals to explain the same events. Do actor-observer differences occur?

Jones, E. E., & Nisbett, R. E. (1971). *The actor and observer: Divergent perceptions of the causes of behavior.* Morristown, NJ: General Learning Press.

Exercise Three—Examples of Concepts: Family Resemblances

The textbook introduced the idea of family resemblances to explain why instances of abnormality do not always have elements in common. The purpose of this exercise is to show that the idea of family resemblances has wide application.

Think of a large number of examples of common concepts like these:
a. fruit (e.g., apple, orange)
b. dog (e.g., collie, shepherd)
c. game (e.g., baseball, billiards)
d. joke (e.g., cartoon, pun)

For each concept, what appear to be critical elements? Does every example possess these elements?

Wittgenstein, L. (1953). *Philosophical investigations.* New York: Macmillan.
Rosch, E., & Mervis, C. B. (1975). Family resemblances: Studies in the internal structure of categories. *Cognitive Psychology, 7,* 573–605.

CHAPTER 2

Abnormally across Time and Place

CHAPTER OVERVIEW

This chapter provides a brief history of abnormality. How has it been explained across time and place? How has it been treated? Changing conceptions of madness underscore the point of the first chapter: abnormality is not some invariant thing. Rather, it is explained and treated within a cultural and historical context.

Over the years, the causes of abnormality have variously been viewed as (a) animistic; (b) physical; and (c) psychological. Animistic explanations included the belief that madness resulted from possession by evil spirits as well as the notion that madness could be caused by witches. Such explanations largely gave way to physical-illness explanations and psychological explanations, which remain the prevalent conceptions today.

Each explanation of madness has an associated strategy for treatment. When thought to be animistic in origin, madness was treated by religious means such as exorcism. When thought to be an illness, it is treated medically—with drugs, operations, and diet. And when thought to be psychological, it is treated psychologically.

Important in the history of abnormality is the rise of the psychiatric hospital. Hospitals originated as asylums for the underprivileged, which included the mad. These individuals were given worse treatment than other inmates, especially severer physical abuse, since it was believed that they were like animals and experienced little pain. Eventually, this belief was replaced by the idea that humane treatment was more ethical and more effective.

ESSENTIAL TERMS

animalism	belief that animals and mad people are similar
animism	belief in spirits
animal magnetism	according to Mesmer, "universal magnetic fluid" which causes physical disease when distributed unequally in the body
baquet	large wooden tub filled with water and magnetized iron filings, used by Mesmer to restore the health of patients in whom animal magnetism was unequally distributed
catharsis	release of psychic energy resulting from uncovering and reliving early traumatic conflicts

exorcism	ceremonial ritual during which demons are thought to be dispelled from the victim's body
hospital	charitable institution for the needy, infirm, or young
hypnotism	techniques originally associated with Mesmer's theory of animal magnetism
hysteria	disorder with symptoms such as fits, pains, paralysis, blindness, lameness, listlessness, and melancholia; at one time thought to be caused by a wandering uterus
lycanthropy	form of psychopathology in the Middle Ages in which groups of people believed themselves to be wolves and acted accordingly
mesmerism	another term for animal magnetism
moral treatment	approach to treating mental disorders emphasizing kindness and the virtues of work
ostracism	casting out of a person believed to be possessed by demons
tarantism	form of dancing mania in the Middle Ages thought to be caused by the tarantula
Witches' Hammer (Malleus Maleficarum)	1486 manual describing how to identify and dispose of witches

SAMPLE EXAM

1. All of these have changed across time except
   a. elements of abnormality.
   b. theories of abnormality.
   c. concern with abnormality.
   d. treatment of abnormality.

2. Which of these disorders is uncommon today?
   a. depression
   b. schizophrenia
   c. hysteria
   d. phobia

3. Over time, explanations of abnormality fall into which categories?
   a. animistic, physical, and psychological
   b. historical, political, and economic
   c. religious, racial, and ethnic
   d. pessimistic, optimistic, and neutral

4. What is a trephine?
   a. stick with which to find water
   b. hole bored in skull to let out demons
   c. sacred vessel to hold talismans
   d. irrigation ditch into which the mad were thrown

5. How were evil spirits thought to cause abnormality?
   a. by upsetting brain chemistry
   b. by leading to faulty learning
   c. by inhabiting the brain and controlling actions
   d. by stealing one's possessions

6. Which of these disorders was not common in the Middle Ages?
   a. tarantism
   b. anorexia
   c. animal possession
   d. lycanthropy

7. All of these historical events provided the context of the witch hunts in the Middle Ages except
   a. decay of cities.
   b. rise of capitalism.
   c. schism in the Roman Catholic church.
   d. breakdown of the family.

8. The Witches' Hammer was a
   a. machine used in exorcism rituals.
   b. tool used by a witch's familiar.

c. manual for hunting witches.
d. cookbook for magical brews.

9. At the heart of *The Witches' Hammer* is
a. fear of women's sexuality.
b. distrust of ethnic minorities.
c. intolerance of socialism.
d. disgust with conventional morality.

10. All of these were considered evidence of witchcraft in the Middle Ages except
a. confessions.
b. body marks.
c. accidents to neighbors.
d. due process.

11. The Salem witch trials seemed to begin in
a. disagreement over tobacco tariffs.
b. children's games.
c. suggestions in a sermon.
d. letters from England.

12. Historically, hysteria was most common among
a. children.
b. elderly men.
c. women who were virgins or widows.
d. adolescent boys.

13. According to the Greeks, hysteria was caused by
a. an inadequate diet.
b. a ruptured spleen.
c. fallen arches.
d. a wandering uterus.

14. Galen believed that hysteria was caused by
a. lack of exercise.
b. sexual abstinence.
c. red meat.
d. interpersonal conflict.

15. Proponents of animalism pointed to all of these characteristics of the mad except that
a. the mad could live without protest in miserable surroundings.
b. the mad could not control themselves.
c. the mad could be unusually loyal.
d. the mad could be suddenly violent.

16. When abnormality began to be regarded as a physical illness, it was treated with all of the following except
a. purges.
b. rebirthing.
c. bleeding.
d. forced vomiting.

17. The view that abnormality has psychological causes is

a. a twentieth-century idea.
b. a nineteenth-century idea.
c. present in Roman writings.
d. present in Stone Age cave paintings.

18. Which of these terms does not belong?
a. anthropomorphism
b. animal magnetism
c. hypnotism
d. mesmerism

19. How did Mesmer define animal magnetism?
a. musk-based perfume
b. universal magnetic fluid
c. communication among animals
d. sexual pheromones

20. What was the purpose of a baquet?
a. to concentrate magnetic fluid
b. to distract hysterics from their symptoms
c. to provide nourishment to anemics
d. to exorcise evil spirits

21. Mesmer was criticized for his
a. therapy success.
b. theory of animal magnetism.
c. taste in clothes.
d. fees.

22. Charcot was all of the following except a
a. physician
b. neurological researcher.
c. clinical psychologist.
d. teacher.

23. Charcot used the technique of hypnosis to
a. redistribute universal magnetic fluid.
b. distinguish hysteria from epilepsy.
c. bring unconscious conflicts to the surface.
d. see whether or not an accused criminal was guilty.

24. Charcot's research into hypnotism was sabotaged by
a. overzealous students.
b. cuts in government funding.
c. overprotective ethics committees.
d. jealous fellow scientists.

25. Over time, treatment of abnormality has often
a. not been considered possible.
b. reflected theories of underlying causes.
c. followed the suggestions of the patient.
d. treated body and mind simultaneously.

26. Which of the following does not belong?
    a. exorcism
    b. ostracism
    c. anomie
    d. prayer

27. All of the following were treatments for hysteria except
    a. garlic and burning dung.
    b. lithium.
    c. massage.
    d. perfume.

28. Mesmer's theory of hysteria is an example of
    a. a supernatural explanation.
    b. an illness explanation.
    c. a cognitive explanation.
    d. a psychological explanation.

29. Who first introduced catharsis?
    a. Galen
    b. Cotton Mather
    c. Josef Breuer
    d. Sigmund Freud

30. Catharsis belongs with
    a. "A stitch in time saves nine."
    b. "Thanks, I needed that."
    c. "Walk softly but carry a big stick."
    d. "I am not a crook."

31. Freud showed that catharsis results from
    a. hypnosis.
    b. early sexual experience.
    c. neurological disorder.
    d. talking about problems.

32. Historically, hospital meant
    a. an asylum for the underprivileged.
    b. a workplace for physicians.
    c. an inn for travelers.
    d. a spa for workers.

33. The Hôpital Général of Paris was founded in
    a. 1532.
    b. 1606.
    c. 1656.
    d. 1789.

34. Inmates of early hospitals had what in common?
    a. illness
    b. insurance
    c. unemployment
    d. abnormality

35. The first hospital in the United States was founded in
    a. New York.
    b. Virginia.
    c. Pennsylvania.
    d. Maryland.

36. Treatment of the mad in the early hospitals embodied what belief about abnormality?
    a. lycanthropy
    b. animalism
    c. medical model
    d. psychogenic explanation

37. Gheel is best known
    a. for its humane treatment of abnormality.
    b. for using exorcism as a cure of abnormality.
    c. for first using psychosurgery.
    d. as the source of Freud's patients.

38. Philippe Pinel advocated
    a. liberty and equality.
    b. a supernatural explanation of abnormality.
    c. catharsis.
    d. the psychological control of abnormality.

39. The Retreat at York was founded by
    a. secular authorities.
    b. physicians.
    c. Quakers.
    d. mesmerists.

40. Moral treatment embodied
    a. a supernatural view of abnormality.
    b. an illness view of abnormality.
    c. a psychological view of abnormality.
    d. Mesmer's view of abnormality.

Answer Key for Sample Exam

1.	c	(p. 23)	21.	b	(p. 32)
2.	c	(p. 23)	22.	c	(p. 33)
3.	a	(p. 24)	23.	b	(p. 33)
4.	b	(p. 25)	24.	a	(p. 33)
5.	c	(p. 25)	25.	b	(p. 34)
6.	b	(p. 25)	26.	c	(p. 34)
7.	a	(p. 26)	27.	b	(p. 35)
8.	c	(p. 26)	28.	b	(p. 35)
9.	a	(p. 26)	29.	c	(p. 36)
10.	d	(p. 27)	30.	b	(p. 36)
11.	b	(p. 28)	31.	d	(p. 36)
12.	c	(p. 29)	32.	a	(p. 36)
13.	d	(p. 29)	33.	c	(p. 37)
14.	b	(p. 29)	34.	c	(p. 37)
15.	c	(p. 29)	35.	c	(p. 38)
16.	b	(p. 30)	36.	b	(p. 38)
17.	c	(p. 30)	37.	a	(p. 39)
18.	a	(p. 32)	38.	d	(p. 40)
19.	b	(p. 32)	39.	c	(p. 41)
20.	a	(p. 32)	40.	c	(p. 42)

SELF-TEST

1. Over the years, concepts of abnormality have _____ .

2. Treatment of abnormality reflects _____ .

3. Over the years, the three major explanations of abnormality have been _____ , _____ , and _____ .

4. Holes drilled in skulls of Paleolithic cave dwellers are called _____ and are thought to have been drilled in order to _____ .

5. Abnormality thought to be caused by supernatural forces was treated by _____ .

6. Witch hunts in Europe resulted from _____ _____ occurring _____ .

7. The 1486 manual for recognizing witches was _____ .

8. Most "witches" persecuted in Europe were _____ .

9. *The Witches' Hammer* seems to reflect a strong fear of _____ .

10. Evidence regarding a suspected witch was obtained by _____ and _____ .

11. One of the first psychological disorders thought to have a physical cause was _____ ; the cause was believed to be _____ .

12. The belief stressing the similarity between animals and mad people was _____ ; it was in part responsible for the seemingly cruel _____ .

13. Abnormality thought to be caused by physical factors was treated by _____ .

14. The theory of animal magnetism was proposed by _____ .

15. Mesmer used a device called a _____ to treat hysteria; the device was thought to cure hysteria by _____ .

16. Mesmer came under criticism not for _____ but for _____ .

17. Mesmerism came to be known as _____ .

18. Charcot used hypnosis to distinguish between _____ and _____ .

19. Abnormality thought to be caused by psychological factors was treated by _____ .

20. The first psychological therapy was used to treat _____ .

21. Emotional relief that accompanies the reliving of painful experiences is _____ .

22. Freud discovered that catharsis could occur without the use of _____ .

23. Hospitals date as far back as _____ .

24. Inmates of the first hospitals shared one common characteristic: _____ .

25. Compared to the treatment of other inmates, the treatment of the insane in the first hospitals was _____ .

26. The idea that the insane should not be treated like animals was called _____ .

27. The Belgium town that pioneered humane treatment was _____ .

28. The director of the Paris Hospital who removed the chains from the insane was _____ .

29. The approach emphasizing the therapeutic value of work and the need for self-esteem was called _____ .

30. Moral treatment in the United States resulted in _____ percent of patients being discharged within one year as recovered or improved.

Answer Key for Self-Test

1. changed
2. the perceived cause of abnormality
3. animistic explanations; physical explanations; psychological explanations
4. trephines; let demons escape from the skull
5. supernatural means
6. social upheaval; at the end of the fifteenth century
7. *The Witches' Hammer (Malleus Maleficarum)*
8. women
9. women's sexuality
10. body marks; confessions
11. hysteria; wandering uterus
12. animalism; ways mad people were treated
13. physical means
14. Franz Anton Mesmer
15. baquet; redistributing magnetic fluid
16. his cures; his theories
17. hypnosis
18. hysteria; epilepsy
19. psychological means
20. hysteria
21. catharsis
22. hypnosis
23. the seventeenth century
24. unemployment
25. brutal
26. humane treatment
27. Gheel
28. Philippe Pinel
29. moral treatment
30. 70

TYING IT TOGETHER

This chapter illustrates the idea introduced in Chapter 1 that judgments of abnormality are social. The history of how abnormality has been explained and treated underscores the idea that abnormality is not an invariant property of an individual. Rather, explanation and treatment reflect the particulars of a given social and historical context. As the disorders in Chapters 8 through 17 are described, you should entertain the possibility that some are mainly problems of contemporary Americans. For instance, drug abuse (Chapter 14), anorexia nervosa (Chapter 16), and infantile autism (Chapter 16) are relatively "new" disorders that may reflect reactions to aspects of contemporary society. Schizophrenia (Chapter 12) may be similarly interpreted. And perhaps depression (Chapter 11) is the psychological manifestation of twentieth-century alienation.

Treatment of abnormality usually reflects theories about underlying causes. This strategy seems to have been followed by primitive people who drilled holes in the skulls of their fellows to let demons escape. Similarly, today's treatments (Chapter 19) for the various disorders (Chapter 8 through 17) usually attempt to undo their presumed causes. Thus, if schizophrenia is viewed as a biologically determined disorder, it is treated with drugs (see Chapter 12). Although this strategy is often reasonable, it is not guaranteed to be. There are biological disorders that can be treated psychologically (see Chapter 17) and psychological disorders that can be treated biologically. As emphasized in Chapter 3, one of the dangers in adhering to a given model of abnormality is blindness to better ways of conceiving and treating disorders.

Chapter 2 describes the rise of humane treatment in psychiatric hospitals. Compare humane treatment with the factors that characterize successful psychotherapy (Chapter 19). They are strikingly similar. One of the important elements that characterize abnormality is observer discomfort (Chapter 1). To the degree that individuals with psychological difficulties can be approached without discomfort, the better off they may be.

FURTHER READINGS

Hare, E. H. (1974). The changing content of psychiatric illness. *Journal of Psychosomatic Research, 18,* 283–289.

Jackson, S. W. (1986). *Melancholia and depression from Hippocratic times to modern times.* New Haven, CT: Yale University Press.

Kuhn, T. S. (1970). *The structure of scientific revolutions* (2nd ed.). Chicago: University of Chicago.

Maher, W. B., & Maher, B. (1982). The Ship of Fools: Stultifera Navis or Ignis Fatuus.

American Psychologist, 37, 756–761.

Roosens, E. (1979). *Mental patients in town life: Gheel, Europe's first therapeutic community.* Beverly Hills, CA: Sage.

Spanos, N. P., & Gottlieb, J. (1979). Demonic possession, mesmerism, and hysteria: A social psychological perspective on their historical interrelations. *Journal of Abnormal Psychology, 88,* 527–546.

Zilboorg, G. (1941). *A history of medical psychology.* New York: Norton.

TERM-PAPER TOPICS

1. What were the causes of the witch hunts in the Middle Ages? In Salem? Were psychological factors of overriding importance?

2. Why did Mesmer run afoul of French authorities? Was his theory that much at odds with dominant thought, or did political factors enter into his difficulties?

3. Transposing present trends to the future, speculate about psychiatric hospitals in the year 2050.

EXERCISES

Exercise One—Animistic Accounts of Abnormality

This exercise has the purpose of illustrating how abnormality can be explained and treated from an animistic point of view.

Go to a popular horror movie. What are the abnormal things that the characters in the movie are driven to do? How are animistic forces depicted as responsible for these instances of abnormality? How are these forces combated?

Exercise Two—Mental Health Treatment

The purpose of this exercise is to illustrate the close relationship between theories of abnormality and treatments of abnormality. As Chapter 2 of the textbook stresses, through history these have usually been congruent. They still are today.

Contact local mental health facilities and arrange tours for the class. Inquire about the philosophy of each facility. Do treatment philosophies reflect assumptions about the causes of abnormality?

Exercise Three—Beliefs about Mental Illness

The purpose of this exercise is to show how diverse beliefs about mental illness—its causes and its treatments—can be.

Ask acquaintances questions like "What is mental illness?" "Who is at risk for mental illness?" "How is mental illness treated?" "What are people like after treatment for mental illness?" Try to talk to a variety of people. What range of opinions is represented? As you read the rest of the textbook, keep in mind these opinions. Which are consistent with current knowledge in psychology? Which are inconsistent?

Nunnally, J. C. (1961). *Popular conceptions of mental health.* New York: Holt, Rinehart & Winston.

CHAPTER 3

The Biomedical Model

CHAPTER OVERVIEW

This chapter is the first of three that deal respectively with the most prevalent contemporary approaches to abnormality: (a) the biomedical model; (b) the psychodynamic and existential approaches; and (c) the environmentalist model, including behavioral and cognitive approaches. A model helps in approaching abnormality. It suggests how to describe, explain, and treat. However, the risk in using models is that important aspects of abnormality may be overlooked.

The chapter describes the biomedical model, which views abnormality as something wrong with the body—an illness, an injury, a defect. Described in detail is the account of how general paresis—a psychological disorder—was discovered to result from untreated syphilis—a physical disorder. Also described is the contemporary search for the cause of schizophrenia in biological factors. Research linking manic-depression to genes is one more example of the biomedical approach.

ESSENTIAL TERMS

concordant twins	both members of a set of twins have the same disorder
discordant twins	one member of a set of twins has a disorder, and the other does not
dopamine hypothesis	explanation of schizophrenia proposing that the disorder results from too much dopamine (a neural transmitter) in the brain
electroconvulsive shock (ECT)	therapy for depression in which an electric current is passed through the brain of a patient
environmentalist model of abnormality	model of abnormality that stresses situational determinants; outgrowth and combination of behavioral and cognitive models
etiology	causal explanation of a disorder
general paresis	disorder characterized by delusions of grandeur, mental deterioration, and eventual paralysis and death; caused by untreated syphilis
lithium	drug used to treat bipolar depression and mania
model	approach to defining and explaining some phenomenon by emphasizing presumably critical aspects of the phe-

nomenon while de-emphasizing other, presumably non-critical aspects

behavioral model of abnormality — model of abnormality conceiving it as learned behavior

biomedical model of abnormality — model of abnormality holding that it is an illness or malfunction of the body

cognitive model of abnormality — model of abnormality holding that it is the product of certain thoughts and beliefs

psychodynamic model of abnormality — model of abnormality regarding it as the result of unconscious conflicts within the person

PET (positron emission tomography) scan — assessment of brain metabolism

syndrome — a group of diverse symptoms that tend to co-occur

SAMPLE EXAM

1. A model of abnormality is
   a. psychopathology in children caused by parents.
   b. a pictorial representation of unconscious conflicts.
   c. a means of defining and approaching abnormality.
   d. unnecessary if the causes of abnormality are of primary interest.

2. The risk in using models of abnormality is that
   a. society may be wrong about abnormality.
   b. actors and observers may disagree about abnormality.
   c. investigators may be blinded to other possibilities.
   d. biological determinants may be de-emphasized.

3. The idea that abnormality results from unconscious conflicts within the self is the
   a. biomedical model.
   b. psychodynamic model.
   c. behavioral model.
   d. cognitive model.
   e. existential model.

4. The idea that abnormality results from illness or injury to the body is the
   a. biomedical model.
   b. psychodynamic model.
   c. behavioral model.
   d. cognitive model.
   e. existential model.

5. The idea that abnormality results from the failure to confront successfully fundamental questions about living is the
   a. biomedical model.
   b. psychodynamic model.
   c. behavioral model.
   d. cognitive model.
   e. existential model.

6. The idea that abnormality results from certain thoughts and beliefs is the
   a. biomedical model.
   b. psychodynamic model.
   c. behavioral model.
   d. cognitive model.
   e. existential model.

7. The idea that abnormality results from the acquisition of certain ways of acting is the
   a. biomedical model.
   b. psychodynamic model.
   c. behavioral model.
   d. cognitive model.
   e. existential model.

8. If an individual acting abnormally were found to have a brain tumor, this would support the
   a. biomedical model.
   b. psychodynamic model.
   c. behavioral model.
   d. cognitive model.
   e. existential model.

9. If an individual acting abnormally were found to have deep doubts about the

meaning of life, this would support the
a. biomedical model.
b. psychodynamic model.
c. behavioral model.
d. cognitive model.
e. existential model.

10. If an individual acting abnormally were found to have idiosyncratic beliefs about the ways things should be if happiness is to be achieved, this would support the
a. biomedical model.
b. psychodynamic model.
c. behavioral model.
d. cognitive model.
e. existential model.

11. A syndrome is
a. a set of symptoms that cohere.
b. an illness with an unknown cause.
c. a pathological way of behaving.
d. an instance of thought disorder.

12. An advocate of the biomedical model looks for the cause of abnormality among all these except
a. germs.
b. genetics.
c. biochemistry.
d. church attendance.

13. Abnormality with a physical etiology might be treated in any of these ways except
a. catharsis.
b. drugs.
c. fumigations.
d. massage.

14. Which discovery provided important support for the biomedical model of abnormality?
a. Patients exposed to the moral treatment often improved dramatically.
b. Hysteria was not caused by a wandering uterus.
c. General paresis resulted from untreated syphilis.
d. Penicillin was isolated.

15. General paresis is characterized by all these symptoms except
a. delusions of grandeur.
b. paralysis.
c. forgetfulness.
d. low self-esteem.

16. One reason why the link between general paresis and syphilis was not discovered earlier is that
a. many individuals with general paresis denied ever having syphilis.

b. abnormality was thought to be caused by psychological factors.
c. most cases of syphilis had been successfully cured.
d. general paresis had a social stigma.

17. The experiment showing that untreated syphilis caused general paresis was based on the
a. careful use of a control group.
b. fact that general paresis was more common among cigar smokers than nonsmokers.
c. fact that one could contract syphilis only once.
d. fact that general paresis was more common among men than women.

18. The experiment showing that untreated syphilis caused general paresis was conducted by
a. Sigmund Freud.
b. Richard von Krafft-Ebing.
c. Josef Breuer.
d. August von Wassermann.
e. Sir Randolph Churchill.

19. Nowadays, the prevalence of general paresis is
a. as common as always.
b. more common than it used to be.
c. less common than it used to be.
d. difficult to estimate.

20. Fraternal twins have
a. the same genes.
b. more genes in common than non-twin siblings, but fewer in common than identical twins.
c. two-thirds of their genes in common.
d. as many genes in common as non-twin siblings.

21. Twins have been studied extensively by researchers interested in the role of
a. communication in schizophrenia.
b. genetics in schizophrenia.
c. birth order in schizophrenia.
d. facial appearance in schizophrenia.

22. Which pattern of results provides support for the biomedical model?
a. Fraternal twins and identical twins are equally concordant for schizophrenia.
b. Identical twins are concordant for schizophrenia.
c. Identical twins are more concordant for schizophrenia than are fraternal twins.
d. Fraternal twins are discordant for schizophrenia.

23. Which pattern of results would disprove the biomedical model?
   a. if fraternal twins and identical twins were equally concordant for schizophrenia
   b. if identical twins were concordant for schizophrenia
   c. if fraternal twins were discordant for schizophrenia while identical twins were concordant for schizophrenia
   d. if fraternal twins were discordant for schizophrenia

24. Schizophrenia research using twins makes a number of simplifying assumptions, including all of the following except that
   a. identical and fraternal twins have the same environment.
   b. identical twins have the same genes.
   c. diagnosis of schizophrenia is reliable.
   d. all instances of schizophrenia have the same causes.

25. The current view about genetics and schizophrenia is that
   a. schizophrenia is caused by genes.
   b. schizophrenia is caused by the environment.
   c. schizophrenia is caused by both genes and the environment.
   d. there is not enough known to make any conclusions.

26. The dopamine hypothesis proposes that schizophrenia
   a. involves diminished intellectual ability.
   b. results from untreated general paresis.
   c. is caused by too few neurons in the brain.
   d. results from too much neural transmitter.

27. Support for the dopamine hypothesis comes largely from
   a. drug research.
   b. twin studies.
   c. epidemiological research.
   d. psychosurgery investigations.

28. The dopamine hypothesis is an example of the
   a. biomedical model.
   b. psychodynamic model.
   c. behavioral model.
   d. cognitive model.
   e. existential model.

29. Recent research that compares cerebral blood flow in the brains of schizophrenics with that in the brains of normal individuals finds
   a. less blood to the left hemisphere of schizophrenics.
   b. less blood to the right hemisphere of schizophrenics.
   c. more blood to the left hemisphere of schizophrenics.
   d. more blood to the right hemisphere of schizophrenics.

30. A recent study among the Old Order Amish in Pennsylvania linked genes to
   a. bipolar depression.
   b. language difficulty.
   c. schizophrenia.
   d. unipolar depression.

31. The treatment of choice for bipolar depression is
   a. antidepressive medication.
   b. electroconvulsive shock.
   c. lithium.
   d. major tranquilizers.
   e. minor tranquilizers.

32. Electroconvulsive shock is an effective treatment for
   a. bipolar depression.
   b. language difficulty.
   c. schizophrenia.
   d. unipolar depression.

33. Strengths of the medical model include all but one of the following
   a. concepts are objective.
   b. methods are well defined.
   c. its history is one of successes.
   d. the side effects of drugs are minimal.

Answer Key for Sample Exam

1.	c	(p. 48)	18.	b	(p. 52)
2.	c	(p. 49)	19.	c	(p. 53)
3.	b	(p. 48)	20.	d	(p. 53)
4.	a	(p. 48)	21.	b	(p. 54)
5.	e	(p. 48)	22.	c	(p. 54)
6.	d	(p. 48)	23.	a	(p. 54)
7.	c	(p. 48)	24.	b	(p. 54)
8.	a	(p. 48)	25.	c	(p. 54)
9.	e	(p. 48)	26.	d	(p. 54)
10.	d	(p. 48)	27.	a	(p. 55)
11.	a	(p. 49)	28.	a	(p. 55)
12.	d	(p. 49)	29.	c	(p. 55)
13.	a	(p. 49)	30.	a	(p. 57)
14.	c	(p. 50)	31.	c	(p. 58)
15.	d	(p. 50)	32.	d	(p. 59)
16.	a	(p. 51)	33.	d	(p. 60)
17.	c	(p. 52)			

SELF-TEST

1. An approach to identifying, explaining, and treating abnormality is a _____.

2. The danger of adhering to a given model is that one may _____.

3. The model that views abnormality as an illness or injury of the body is the _____.

4. The model that views abnormality as the product of unconscious conflicts is the _____.

5. The model that views abnormality as the result of learning is the _____.

6. The model that views abnormality as caused by thoughts and beliefs is the _____.

7. The model that views abnormality in terms of the failure to confront fundamental questions about life is the _____.

8. Diverse symptoms that tend to occur together are a _____.

9. Proponents of the biomedical model look for the cause of abnormality to involve _____, _____, and/or _____.

10. The sixteenth-century disorder characterized by delusions of grandeur and caused by untreated syphilis was _____.

11. The cause of a disorder is referred to as its _____.

12. Syphilis is like measles in that once someone has contracted it, he or she _____.

13. The crucial experiment linking syphilis to general paresis was conducted by _____. In this experiment, individuals with _____ were exposed to _____. The result was that they _____.

14. The current treatment of general paresis is to treat syphilis with _____.

15. Schizophrenia afflicts about _____ percent of the world's population.

16. Twins who have all the same genes are _____ twins, while twins who do not have all the same genes are _____ twins.

17. If schizophrenia is genetically transmitted, the _____ for schizophrenia would be greater among _____ twins than among _____ twins.

18. The concordance rate of schizophrenia among identical twins is approximately _____ percent.

19. The concordance rate of schizophrenia among fraternal twins is approximately _____ percent.

20. The neurotransmitter thought to be involved in schizophrenia is _____. Schizophrenia may involve too _____ of this neurotransmitter in the brain.

21. Drugs used to treat schizophrenia seem to work by _____ dopamine receptors in the brain.

22. The blood flow to the _____ hemisphere in schizophrenics may be _____ , suggesting damage there that the body is trying to repair.

23. Recent research links manic-depression to a particular _____ .

24. People with the genetic predisposition for manic-depression develop this disorder in _____ of cases.

25. Manic-depression can often be treated with _____ .

26. Problems with the biomedical model include _____ and _____ .

Answer Key for Self-Test

1. model of abnormality
2. overlook other possibilities
3. biomedical model
4. psychodynamic model
5. behavioral model
6. cognitive model
7. existential model
8. syndrome
9. germs; genetics; biochemistry
10. general paresis
11. etiology
12. cannot contract it again
13. Richard von Krafft-Ebing; general paresis; syphilis; did not contract syphilis
14. penicillin
15. 1
16. identical; fraternal
17. concordance; identical; fraternal
18. 50
19. 10
20. dopamine; much
21. blocking
22. left; excessive
23. chromosome
24. 63%
25. lithium
26. neglect of psychological factors; side effects of medication

TYING IT TOGETHER

The biomedical model was the first cohesive approach to abnormality. The successful identification of untreated syphilis as the cause of general paresis provides an example still followed by researchers who hope to find biological bases—illness, injury, genetics, biochemistry—for other disorders. In some cases, their search has uncovered biological factors: psychosomatic disorders (Chapter 10), depression (Chapter 11), personality disorders (Chapter 15), schizophrenia (Chapter 12), childhood disorders (Chapter 16), and neurological disorders (Chapter 17). In other cases, an understanding of biology is essential to an understanding of what otherwise are psychological problems: neuroses (Chapter 8 and 9), sexual dysfunctions (Chapter 13), and drug abuse (Chapter 14). However, in almost no case are biological factors alone responsible for a disorder. The contemporary view of many disorders is a diathesis-stress model, which attributes the disorder to a constitutional weakness (diathesis) coupled with an environmental trauma (stress).

The biomedical model is at the base of several well-known treatments—in particular, drugs and electroconvulsive shock therapy (Chapter 19). Again, though, these treatments are rarely 100 percent effective in themselves. The case of drug treatment and rehabilitation (Chapter 14) illustrates this well. Biological treatments of drug abuse are often of limited effectiveness, since they ignore the reasons that an individual has for using drugs. Drug abuse is like an illness, but it is not quite the same thing. No one has pneumonia for a reason, but everyone who drinks too much alcohol does have a reason. Successful treatment must address not just the biological aspect of drug abuse but also the psychological aspect (Chapter 14). The same seems to be true for schizophrenia; the neuroleptics alleviate certain schizophrenic symptoms, but they do not solve the psychological problems faced by the schizophrenic patient (Chapter 12).

As you read about disorders that have been conceptualized in terms of the biomedical model, keep in mind its limitations. Because the biomedical model is the oldest of the contemporary approaches to abnormality, its problems are the easiest to recognize.

FURTHER READINGS

Andreasen, N. C. (1984). *The broken brain: The biological revolution in psychiatry.* New York: Harper & Row.

Dubos, R. J. (1950). *Louis Pasteur: Free lance of science.* Boston: Little, Brown.

Engel, G. L. (1980). The clinical application of the biopsychosocial model. *American Journal of Psychiatry, 137,* 535–544.

Mazur, A., & Robertson, L. S. (1972). *Biology and social behavior.* New York: Free Press.

Painter, T. I. (1981). Tuskegee experiment. *Encore, 10*(11), 32–33.

Sochurek, H. (1987). Medicine's new vision. *National Geographic, 171*(1), 2–41.

Wrightsman, L. S. (1974). *Assumptions about human nature: A social-psychological approach.* Monterey, CA: Brooks/Cole.

TERM-PAPER TOPICS

1. Is the biomedical model outmoded in medicine? Compare and contrast the biomedical model as described in your textbook with current ideas about holistic medicine.

2. Was the Krafft-Ebing experiment in which he exposed individuals suffering from general paresis to syphilis really necessary? Why did he not include a comparison group?

3. Consider this statement: All models of abnormality embrace the medical model in the sense that they look for a metaphorical "germ" or "deficiency" within the person. Do you agree or disagree with this statement? Defend your answer with examples.

4. As particular diseases are linked to genetic predispositions, the possibility of testing people for these genes must be considered. Discuss the ethical issues involved here.

5. Twin studies are used to isolate genetic versus environmental causes of disorders like schizophrenia. What are the simplifying assumptions necessary for such studies to serve their stated purpose? Are these overlimiting assumptions?

EXERCISES

Exercise One—Working with a Model

The purpose of this exercise is to illustrate one of the consequences of working within a given model of abnormality—in this case the biomedical model. If one believes abnormality to be an illness or injury of the body, then one tends to treat it with medical means.

Look at recent issues of a psychiatry journal that accepts advertising, like *Archives of General Psychiatry.* Notice the treatments of abnormality that are advertised (drugs) and the benefits that are touted (rapid relief). How might ads be different if the journal did not adhere to the biomedical model of abnormality?

Exercise Two—Twins and the Environment

Twin studies are frequently used to disentangle the effects of nature (heredity) and nurture (environment). In order for these studies to serve their stated purpose, several assumptions must be made. The purpose of this exercise is to examine critically one of these assumptions: that the "environment" of identical twins is the same as the "environment" of fraternal twins.

One person of every eighty-six people is a twin. Find some of these individuals, and talk to them about being a twin. Ask these individuals if they are identical or not. Ask about their social environment—which includes their twin—as they were growing up. Do identical twins describe a different environment than fraternal twins?

Scheinfeld, A. (1967). *Twins and supertwins.* Philadelphia: Lippincott.

CHAPTER 4

Psychodynamic and Existential Approaches

CHAPTER OVERVIEW

This chapter describes one of the important psychological approaches to abnormality, the psychodynamic model, which originated in the work of the Viennese physician Sigmund Freud. The psychodynamic model views abnormality as resulting from unconscious conflicts within the individual. These conflicts typically occur between instinctive sexual impulses and societal prohibitions internalized by the individual. Conflicts produce anxiety, which is thought to be at the root of abnormality.

Psychodynamic explanation is complex because of Freud's assumption that behavior is overdetermined, the product of numerous factor. Important to all of these factors is psychic energy, which seeks an outlet in pleasurable activities. The developing individual is thought to use this energy differently as maturation occurs. Development involves the passage through psychosexual stages defined by that part of the body with which pleasure is obtained: the mouth, the anus, the genitals.

Present at birth is the *id*, the seat of the instincts. As a result of socialization, there emerges the *superego*, or the conscience, and the *ego*, the arbitrator between id and superego. Because id impulses are threatening to the superego, the ego has at its disposal a variety of techniques called defense mechanisms that disguise one's true motives from one's conscious self.

Abnormality occurs when the individual's ego is weak relative to the id or the superego. Psychic energy is tied up in symptoms and is not available for more constructive purposes. Psychodynamic therapy attempts to bring underlying conflicts into consciousness.

Freud inspired a number of other theorists to propose energy-based conflict theories of abnormality, notably Carl Jung and Alfred Adler. These theorists did not emphasize sexuality to the degree that Freud did. Other theorists—the Neo-Freudians Karen Horney, Harry Stack Sullivan, and Erik Erikson— were also inspired by Freud and proposed theories that viewed people as inherently social.

Psychoanalytic theory suffers from two problems. First, it is difficult to verify. Second, it was based on observations of a small number of individuals: clients in psychoanalytic therapy. Modern approaches have tried to correct these flaws and in particular concern themselves with the self, which gives personality its unity.

This concern overlaps with the existential approach, which sees abnormality resulting from one's failure to deal successfully with fundamental questions about life and existence. People are viewed as responsible for their actions and their destinies; and they are seen as intrinsically motivated to fulfill their inner potentials.

ESSENTIAL TERMS

anal character	personality traits of orderliness, stinginess, and stubbornness thought to result from fixation at the anal stage of psychosexual development
anxiety	in psychoanalytic theory, psychic pain
realistic anxiety	expectation that real-world events may be harmful
neurotic anxiety	expectation that one will be overwhelmed by one's own unconscious impulses
moral anxiety	expectation that one's behavior will violate one's moral standards
archetype	in Jung's psychodynamic theory, a universal idea obtained in the collective unconscious
authenticity	in existential theories, acting to achieve attainable goals
castration anxiety	fear among young boys that their father will castrate them because of their incestuous desire
catharsis	in psychoanalytic theory, the release of psychic energy resulting from uncovering and reliving early traumatic conflicts (*see* Chapter 2, "Essential Terms")
client-centered therapy	therapy founded by Carl Rogers that attempts to change the self-regard of an individual through unconditional positive regard and empathy on the part of the therapist
collective unconscious	in Jung's psychodynamic theory, memory traces of experience of past generations
core self	sense of physical separateness and unity
counterphobia	a reaction formation in which individuals pursue deeply feared activities
death anxiety	in existential theories, the central human fear: fear of dying
defense mechanism	in psychoanalytic theory, the technique used by the mind to cope with painful psychological events
denial	in psychoanalytical theory, active ignoring of distressing external events
dereflection	logotherapy technique in which the client's attention is turned from symptoms to what may be done for oneself and others in the absence of preoccupation with problems
displacement	in psychoanalytic theory, replacement of a true objective with a less threatening objective
ego	in psychoanalytic theory, mental representation of reality requirements
exhortative will	in existential theories, the ability to force oneself to do things at odds with immediate desires

fixation	in psychoanalytic theory, not progressing from one stage of psychosexual development to the next
fusion	in existential theories, a way to deal with death anxiety by attaching oneself to others and making oneself indistinguishable from them
Gestalt therapy	therapy founded by Fritz Perls that attempts to help the client confront, accept, and take responsibility for feelings, thereby allowing the client to live in the present, not the past
goal-directed will	in existential theories, the ability to work toward future goals, to make specific wishes come true
hypochondriasis	conviction in the absence of medical evidence that one is ill or about to become ill
id	in psychoanalytic theory, mental representation of biological processes
identification	process by which characteristics of others are internalized
intellectualization	in psychoanalytic theory, repression of emotional components of experience and their restating in abstract and analytic terms
introcosm	subjective psychological space that is the storehouse of personal experience within each person
isolation	in psychoanalytic theory, repression of affective components of a threatening experience and retention of informational components
libido	psychic energy associated with a variety of pleasurable activities
logotherapy	therapy founded by Viktor Frankl that attempts to help clients control their life and endow it with meaning
Neo-Freudians	theorists like Horney, Sullivan, and Erikson who followed Freud, emphasizing unconscious motives but downplaying sexuality and stressing the social nature of people
Oedipus complex	desire among young children to do away with the same-sex parent and to take the opposite-sex parent for themselves
oral character	personality traits of dependence and distrust thought to result from fixation at the oral stage of psychosexual development
overdetermined behavior	in psychoanalytic theory, the notion that every behavior has numerous determinants
paradoxical intention	logotherapy technique in which clients are encouraged to indulge and exaggerate symptoms, thereby learning that control over them is possible
penis envy	desire among young girls to have a penis
pleasure principle	immediate impulse gratification that characterizes the id

projection	in psychoanalytic theory attribution of private understandings and meanings to others
assimilative projection	projection of a quality of which one is aware
disowning projection	projection of a quality that one denies having
psychic energy	in psychoanalytic theory, energy that fuels psychological life
psychoanalysis	Freud's psychodynamic theory; also, his methods of studying and changing personality
psychodynamic theory	theory of behavior concerned with unconscious psychological forces
psychosexual development	in psychoanalytic theory, description of development emphasizing passage through stages defined by the means by which pleasure is achieved: oral, anal, phallic, latency, and genital
psychosocial development	in psychodynamic theory, description of development emphasizing passage through stages defined by dominant means of interaction with others.
rationalization	in psychoanalytic theory, assignment to behavior of socially desirable motives
reaction formation	in psychoanalytic theory, repression of one impulse and substitution of its opposite
reality principle	delayed and realistic impulse gratification that characterizes the ego
repression	in psychoanalytic theory, active deflection of material from consciousness
responsibility	in existential theories, awareness that one has created one's own self, life, and destiny
self-coherence	sense that one is physically unified
self-history	perception of one's continuity through time
self-objects	people and things providing support to personality cohesiveness
self theory	contemporary psychodynamic theory that emphasizes the self: how it develops, is experienced, and is defended
specialness	in existential theories, a way to deal with death anxiety by regarding oneself as special and not subject to the laws of nature
sublimation	in psychoanalytic theory, transfer of libido to socially valued activities
subjective self	sense of understanding each others' intentions and feelings, as well as the sharing of experiences about things and events
superego	in psychoanalytic theory, conscience and ideals
transference	in psychoanalytic theory, transfer by clients of emotions, conflicts, and expectations from diverse sources on to their therapist

unconditional positive regard

in client-centered therapy, the therapist's acceptance of and respect for the client regardless of what is said or done

unconscious

material not available to awareness

verbal self

self as a storehouse of knowledge and experience

SAMPLE EXAM

1. Psychodynamic theories are so named because of their concern with
   a. strong personalities.
   b. biological processes.
   c. psychological forces.
   d. personality disorders.

2. Sigmund Freud was
   a. a Viennese physician.
   b. a Berlin psychologist.
   c. a Parisian neurologist.
   d. a Leipzig scientist.

3. Among the most important concern of Freud was
   a. physical forces.
   b. psychic energy.
   c. will power.
   d. mental telepathy.

4. Which of the following terms does not belong?
   a. psychic energy
   b. libido
   c. lust
   d. IQ

5. A child gains pleasure from sucking. In what stage of psychosexual development is this child?
   a. oral
   b. anal
   c. phallic
   d. genital

6. A child gains pleasure from eliminating. In what stage of psychosexual development is this child?
   a. oral
   b. anal
   c. phallic
   d. genital

7. A child gains pleasure from masturbating. In what stage of psychosexual development is this child?
   a. oral
   b. anal
   c. phallic
   d. genital

8. In *The Odd Couple*, Felix is fixated at what stage of psychosexual development?
   a. oral
   b. anal
   c. phallic
   d. genital

9. In *The Odd Couple*, Oscar is fixated at what stage of psychosexual development?
   a. oral
   b. anal
   c. phallic
   d. genital

10. All of the following are part of the Oedipal complex except
    a. desire to do away with same-sex parent.
    b. desire to possess opposite-sex parent.
    c. stiff-legged gait resulting from guilt.
    d. fear of retaliation.

11. Who was Oedipus?
    a. a character of Greek legends
    b. one of Freud's first patients
    c. the mayor of Vienna
    d. an elderly uncle of Garfield

12. Castration anxiety is to little boys as what is to little girls?
    a. hysteria
    b. penis envy
    c. genital fixation
    d. womb worry

13. According to Freud, the result of the Oedipal complex is
    a. schizophrenia.
    b. hysteria.
    c. identification.
    d. deviance.

14. The Oedipal complex occurs during which stage of psychosexual development?
    a. oral
    b. anal

c. phallic
d. latency
e. genital

15. In which stage of psychosexual development is sexuality repressed?
a. oral
b. anal
c. phallic
d. latency
e. genital

16. Which of these processes is present first?
a. id
b. ego
c. superego
d. none of the above

17. Id is to pleasure principle as what is to reality principle?
a. libido
b. ego
c. superego
d. sublimation

18. Freud characterized the relationship among id, ego, and superego as
a. harmonious.
b. hierarchical.
c. independent.
d. conflicting.

19. Most of the time, one's telephone number is
a. conscious.
b. pre-conscious.
c. unconscious.
d. subconscious.

20. According to Freud, material is unconscious because it
a. has been poorly learned.
b. has been forgotten.
c. is not interesting.
d. has been repressed.

21. The fear of real-world events is termed
a. realistic anxiety.
b. high anxiety.
c. neurotic anxiety.
d. moral anxiety.

22. The fear of one's impulses is termed
a. realistic anxiety.
b. high anxiety.
c. neurotic anxiety.
d. moral anxiety.

23. The fear that one's behavior will violate one's standards is termed
a. realistic anxiety.
b. high anxiety.
c. neurotic anxiety.
d. moral anxiety.

24. The text criticizes early psychoanalytic theory on grounds of
a. generalizability.
b. verifiability.
c. both.
d. neither.

25. The collective unconscious is associated with
a. Sigmund Freud.
b. Fritz Perls.
c. Carl Jung.
d. Alfred Adler.

26. According to Jung, an archetype is
a. a universal idea.
b. *The Witches' Hammer.*
c. a trephine.
d. a baquet.

27. Who among the following does not belong?
a. Alfred Adler
b. Karen Horney
c. Fritz Perls
d. Harry Stack Sullivan

28. The Neo-Freudians differed from Freud by
a. de-emphasizing sexuality.
b. de-emphasizing social aspects of people.
c. ignoring defense mechanisms.
d. downplaying consciousness.

29. Modern psychodynamic theories focus mainly on
a. development.
b. instincts.
c. needs.
d. the self.

30. The first "self" to emerge is the
a. core self.
b. intersubjective self.
c. *Self* magazine.
d. subjective self.
e. verbal self.

31. Physical unity is the province of the
a. core self.
b. intersubjective self.
c. subjective self.
d. verbal self.

32. The "self" that allows us to understand others is the
a. core self.
b. *Self* magazine.
c. subjective self.
d. verbal self.

33. Self theory terms the important others in one's life
    a. meaningful relationships.
    b. other objects.
    c. self objects.
    d. them.

34. A defense mechanism is a
    a. technique pioneered by Tom Landry.
    b. coping strategy of the ego.
    c. biochemical process that combats infection.
    d. means of winning arguments with others.

35. An individual forgets the details of a painful experience. This is an example of what defense mechanism?
    a. repression
    b. sublimation
    c. regression
    d. projection
    e. reaction formation
    f. displacement
    g. denial
    h. isolation
    i. rationalization
    j. intellectualization

36. An individual keeps the bedroom of a dead relative intact. This is an example of what defense mechanism?
    a. repression
    b. sublimation
    c. regression
    d. projection
    e. reaction formation
    f. displacement
    g. denial
    h. isolation
    i. rationalization
    j. intellectualization

37. An individual pursues medicine as a career. This is an example of what defense mechanism?
    a. repression
    b. sublimation
    c. regression
    d. projection
    e. reaction formation
    f. displacement
    g. denial
    h. isolation
    i. rationalization
    j. intellectualization

38. An individual says that she hates someone who is dear. This is an example of what defense mechanism?
    a. repression
    b. sublimation
    c. regression
    d. projection
    e. reaction formation
    f. displacement
    g. denial
    h. isolation
    i. rationalization
    j. intellectualization

39. Counterphobia is an example of what defense mechanism?
    a. repression
    b. sublimation
    c. regression
    d. projection
    e. reaction formation
    f. displacement
    g. denial
    h. isolation
    i. rationalization
    j. intellectualization

40. An individual who cannot play professional sports becomes a Little League coach. This is an example of what defense mechanism?
    a. repression
    b. sublimation
    c. regression
    d. projection
    e. reaction formation
    f. displacement
    g. denial
    h. isolation
    i. rationalization
    j. intellectualization

41. Identification is the opposite of what defense mechanism?
    a. repression
    b. sublimation
    c. regression
    d. projection
    e. reaction formation
    f. displacement
    g. denial
    h. isolation
    i. rationalization
    j. intellectualization

42. Identification with the aggressor is thought to
    a. be a way to ridicule powerful others.
    b. occur frequently among happy individuals.
    c. help overcome fear and inadequacy.
    d. result from jealousy.

43. An individual matter-of-factly discusses the recent death of her child. This is an

example of what defense mechanism?
a. repression
b. sublimation
c. regression
d. projection
e. reaction formation
f. displacement
g. denial
h. isolation
i. rationalization
j. intellectualization

44. An individual argues against clear evidence that his child is seriously ill. This is an example of what defense mechanism?
a. repression
b. sublimation
c. regression
d. projection
e. reaction formation
f. displacement
g. denial
h. isolation
i. rationalization
j. intellectualization

45. A student studies hard but fails a test. He then claims that the material was not worth knowing. This is an example of what defense mechanism?
a. repression
b. sublimation
c. regression
d. projection
e. reaction formation
f. displacement
g. denial
h. isolation
i. rationalization
j. intellectualization

46. A recently divorced individual provides an elaborate explanation of why her marriage failed. This is an example of what defense mechanism?
a. repression
b. sublimation
c. regression
d. projection
e. reaction formation
f. displacement
g. denial
h. isolation
i. rationalization
j. intellectualization

47. Which of these defense mechanisms is the most mature?
a. denial
b. sublimation

c. projection
d. displacement

48. Which of these defense mechanisms is the least mature?
a. denial
b. sublimation
c. projection
d. displacement

49. The study of Harvard graduates between 1939 and 1942 revealed that mature defense mechanisms were associated with
a. psychological adjustment in later life.
b. social adjustment in later life.
c. medical adjustment in later life.
d. all of the above.

50. According to existential psychologists, the central human fear is
a. castration fear.
b. fear of death.
c. fear of self-actualization.
d. fear of childhood.

51. How are specialness and fusion similar?
a. Both are means of self-actualization.
b. Both are ways to cope with fear of death.
c. Both are innate defense mechanisms.
d. Both are instances of Pavlovian conditioning.

52. The workaholic may be exemplifying
a. specialness.
b. catharsis.
c. dereflection.
d. fusion.

53. The individual who identifies himself as a Jaycee may be exemplifying
a. specialness.
b. catharsis.
c. dereflection.
d. fusion.

54. Existential psychology is particularly opposed to psychoanalysis and behaviorism with regard to
a. the role of responsibility.
b. the role of the environment.
c. the role of thought processes.
d. the role of conflict.

55. All of the following ways of talking avoid responsibility except
a. the use of the passive voice.
b. the avoidance of first-person pronouns.
c. reference to freedom.
d. mention of the past.

56. Goal-directed will is concerned with
a. the past.

b. the present.
c. the future.
d. death.

57. According to existential psychologists, all of the following are true about wishes except that
   a. wishes are general.
   b. wishes make willing possible.
   c. wishes may be confused.
   d. wishes create vulnerability.

58. Psychoanalytic therapy attempts to free psychic energy because
   a. psychic energy can be used in other, more constructive ways.
   b. neurotic individuals have no libido.
   c. there is an energy crisis.
   d. conscious conflicts are harmful.

59. A client confesses that he loves his therapist. This is an example of
   a. sublimation.
   b. transference.
   c. repression.
   d. moral anxiety.

60. Client-centered therapy is characterized by all of the following except concern with
   a. early experiences.
   b. responsibility.
   c. experience.
   d. freedom.

61. The client-centered therapist usually is
   a. active.
   b. passive.
   c. inscrutable.
   d. remote.

62. Who does not belong?
   a. Fritz Perls
   b. Carl Rogers
   c. Albert Bandura
   d. Viktor Frankl

63. Which one of the following is *not* important for client-centered therapy?
   a. diagnosis
   b. unconditional positive regard
   c. empathy
   d. reflection

64. Gestalt therapy is most concerned with
   a. the past.
   b. the present.
   c. the future.
   d. death.

65. Gestalt therapy is most concerned with
   a. thought.
   b. feeling.
   c. behavior.
   d. memory.

66. According to Frankl, the meaning of life resides in
   a. gratification of sexual drive.
   b. self-actualization.
   c. assistance to other people.
   d. survival.

67. If a client is afraid of cats, how could you treat him with paradoxical intention?
   a. Help him relax in the presence of cats.
   b. Encourage him to talk freely about his fear.
   c. Ask him to scream and run when he sees a cat.
   d. Tell him to buy a dog.

68. If a client is afraid of cats, how could you treat him with dereflection?
   a. Tell him to avoid cats.
   b. Suggest that he stare at cats.
   c. Encourage him to forget about cats.
   d. Ask him to do volunteer work for the local humane society.

69. Among the shortcomings of psychoanalytic theory are all these except
   a. reliance on individual cases.
   b. demystification of abnormality.
   c. neglect of situation.
   d. relative inefficacy of psychoanalytic therapy.

70. Overdetermined behavior means that
   a. lower mental abilities are caused by higher mental abilities.
   b. each behavior has numerous determinants.
   c. all behavior is determined by an overriding sexual drive.
   d. important behaviors have causes, but unimportant behaviors do not.

Answer Key for Sample Exam

1. c (p. 62)	17. b (p. 67)	
2. a (p. 62)	18. d (p. 69)	
3. b (p. 62)	19. b (p. 69)	
4. d (p. 63)	20. d (p. 69)	
5. a (p. 63)	21. a (p. 70)	
6. b (p. 64)	22. c (p. 70)	
7. c (p. 64)	23. d (p. 70)	
8. b (p. 64)	24. c (p. 71)	
9. b (p. 64)	25. c (p. 72)	
10. c (p. 65)	26. a (p. 72)	
11. a (p. 65)	27. c (p. 73)	
12. b (p. 65)	28. a (p. 72)	
13. c (p. 66)	29. d (p. 73)	
14. c (p. 65)	30. a (p. 74)	
15. d (p. 66)	31. a (p. 74)	
16. a (p. 67)	32. c (p. 75)	

33.	c	(p. 76)	43.	h	(p. 82)	53.	d	(p. 89)	62.	c	(p. 100)
34.	b	(p. 77)	44.	g	(p. 82)	54.	a	(p. 90)	63.	a	(p. 98)
35.	a	(p. 77)	45.	i	(p. 83)	55.	c	(p. 91)	64.	b	(p. 99)
36.	g	(p. 78)	46.	j	(p. 83)	56.	c	(p. 91)	65.	b	(p. 99)
37.	b	(p. 84)	47.	b	(p. 84)	57.	a	(p. 93)	66.	c	(p. 100)
38.	e	(p. 80)	48.	a	(p. 84)	58.	a	(p. 93)	67.	c	(p. 100)
39.	e	(p. 81)	49.	d	(p. 86)	59.	b	(p. 96)	68.	d	(p. 100)
40.	f	(p. 84)	50.	b	(p. 88)	60.	a	(p. 98)	69.	b	(p. 102)
41.	d	(p. 81)	51.	b	(p. 89)	61.	a	(p. 98)	70.	b	(p. 101)
42.	c	(p. 82)	52.	a	(p. 89)						

SELF-TEST

1. Psychodynamic theories are concerned with inner _____ that are _____ to the individual.

2. Freud's psychodynamic theory is called _____.

3. The most important psychoanalytic concept is that of _____.

4. The five psychosexual stages are _____, _____, _____, _____, and _____; they are defined by the way in which _____ is obtained.

5. If an individual does not pass through a stage of psychosexual development, he is _____ at that stage.

6. People fixated at the oral stage show _____ as adults.

7. People fixated at the anal stage show _____, _____, and _____ as adults.

8. The important conflict during the phallic stage of psychosexual development is the _____, in which the child wishes to _____ the same-sex parent and _____ the opposite-sex parent.

9. Accompanying the Oedipus complex is _____ among boys and _____ among girls.

10. The outcome of the Oedipus complex is thought to be _____ with the _____ parent.

11. The transfer of libidinal energy to socially valued activities is called _____ and occurs during the _____ stage of psychosexual development.

12. Freud described three interacting processes that comprise personality. The _____ is the source of instincts; the _____ is the internalization of societal demands; and the _____ arbitrates between the two.

13. The id operates according to the _____ principle, while the ego operates according to the _____ principle.

14. The three levels of consciousness described by Freud are _____, _____, and _____.

15. Material is unconscious because it has been _____.

16. According to Freud, conflicts are accompanied by the signal of _____.

17. Fear of real-world events is _____ anxiety.

18. Fear of one's impulses is _____ anxiety.

19. Fear that one will violate one's personal standards is _____ anxiety.

20. Theorists who build upon the ideas of Freud are called _____.

21. Jung proposed that we not only have a personal unconscious but also a _____ made up of memories from our ancestors; among these memories are universal ideas called _____.

22. In contrast to Freud's psychosexual stages, the Neo-Freudians describe development in terms of _____ stages.

23. Modern psychodynamic theories emphasize the _____.

24. According to self theory, the three aspects of the self are the _____, _____, and _____ selves.

25. The coping strategies deployed against anxiety are _____.

26. The defense mechanism that forces undesired thoughts into the unconscious is _____.

27. The defense mechanism in which undesired characteristics and impulses are attributed to others is _____.

28. The defense mechanism in which an impulse is substituted for its opposite is _____.

29. The defense mechanism in which the target of an impulse is replaced with a less threatening target is _____.

30. The defense mechanism that is the opposite of projection is _____.

31. The striking phenomenon observed in concentration camps in which some Jewish inmates imitated the Nazi guards is _____.

32. The defense mechanism in which objective facts are ignored is _____.

33. The defense mechanism in which only the affective components of experience are deleted from consciousness is _____.

34. The defense mechanism in which a painful experience is given an elaborate interpretation is _____.

35. The defense mechanism in which implausible excuses are offered is _____.

36. Research suggests that _____ defense mechanisms such as _____ result in social, psychological, and medical well-being.

37. The issues of primary concern to the existential psychologists are _____, _____, and _____.

38. According to existential psychologists, people cope with fear of death through _____ and _____.

39. A false mode of acting, one that attempts to achieve unattainable goals, is _____.

40. Existential psychologists are strongly opposed to traditional psychoanalysts and behaviorists on the issue of whether people have _____ for their lives.

41. One of the ways in which people seem to avoid taking responsibility is through their _____.

42. The two forms of will are _____ will and _____ will.

43. Goal-directed willing arises from the capacity to _____.

44. Psychoanalytic therapy attempts to make conflicts _____.

45. When clients transfer their own emotions, conflicts, and expectations to their therapists, this is called _____.

46. In _____ therapy, the therapist attempts to provide unconditional positive regard.

47. _____ developed Gestalt therapy, which is concerned with the immediate _____.

48. Viktor Frankl's therapy is _____; it is based on the idea that life is made meaningful when one _____.

49. The logotherapy technique in which clients are asked to turn their attention from their own symptoms is _____.

50. The logotherapy technique in which clients are asked to exaggerate their symptoms is _____.

51. Shortcomings of the psychodynamic model of abnormality include _____, _____, _____, _____, and _____.

52. According to psychoanalytic theory, behavior is _____.

Answer Key for Self-Test

1. conflicts; unconscious
2. psychoanalysis
3. psychic energy
4. oral; anal; phallic; latency; genital; pleasure
5. fixated
6. dependency
7. orderliness; stinginess; stubbornness
8. Oedipus complex; do away with; possess
9. castration anxiety; penis envy

10. identification; same-sex
11. sublimation; genital
12. id; superego; ego
13. pleasure; reality
14. perceptual consciousness; preconscious; unconscious
15. repressed
16. anxiety
17. realistic
18. neurotic
19. moral
20. Neo-Freudians
21. collective unconscious; archetypes
22. psychosocial
23. self
24. core; subjective; verbal
25. defense mechanisms
26. repression
27. projection
28. reaction formation
29. displacement
30. identification
31. identification with the aggressor
32. denial
33. isolation
34. intellectualization
35. rationalization
36. mature; sublimation
37. fear of dying; responsibility; will
38. specialness; fusion.
39. inauthenticity
40. responsibility
41. language
42. exhortative; goal-directed
43. wish
44. conscious
45. transference
46. client-centered
47. Frederick Perls; present
48. logotherapy; helps others
49. dereflection
50. paradoxical intention
51. reliance on individual cases; difficulty of proof; lack of scientific support; neglect of situation; ineffectiveness of therapy
52. overdetermined

TYING IT TOGETHER

Although Freud discovered that disorders could have psychological causes instead of physical causes, the psychodynamic approach shares some characteristics with the biomedical approach (Chapter 3). Both look beyond the behavior of a troubled individual to pre-sumed underlying causes. Psychic energy is analogous to physical energy, and Freud wrote about mental processes as if they were literal "things" within a person, like viruses or bacteria. Clinical case histories (Chapter 6) were patterned after medical histories. Freud's training as a neurologist is shown in the psychodynamic approach, which embodies many neurological principles (Chapter 17).

Psychological assessment and testing have been greatly influenced by the psychodynamic model (Chapter 7). In particular, projective tests like the Rorschach and past diagnostic schemes like DSM-II look beyond what the individual is doing on the surface to find an underlying basis to his or her "symptoms." To a large degree, the diagnostic scheme currently in use, DSM-III-R, embodies less of a biomedical/psychodynamic flavor. However, it still retains terminology originating with Freud, particularly in his theorizing about anxiety disorders (Chapters 8 and 9).

The psychodynamic model proposes explanations of most of the disorders covered in Chapters 8 and 17. Some of these explanations seem more reasonable than others. In particular, psychodynamic explanations fare well when applied to disorders with some "depth" to them: hysteria (Chapter 9), amnesia (Chapter 9), and depression (Chapter 11). Like biomedical explanations, psychoanalytic explanations can be faulted for neglecting the role of environmental factors and conscious thought (Chapter 5). To the degree that disorders reflect the influence of these, psychoanalytic explanations fall short.

The existential approach is more interested in psychological health than in psychological disorder, in experience than in research. Accordingly, it is not surprising that this approach has little to say about how to explain disorders (Chapters 8 through 17) or how to remediate them (Chapter 19). Indeed, since the existential approach usually disavows any strict determinism, it has not given rise to much traditional research, which is concerned with the isolation of causes (Chapter 6).

Nevertheless, the existential approach offers an important criticism of what is neglected by the other models. Other approaches sometimes fail because they neglect the questions of choice and meaning deemed important by the existential approach. Thus, drug abuse is not fully understood until an individual's reasons for choosing to use drugs are addressed (Chapter 14). Schizophrenia may be as much a statement about the meaning of life in an insane world as it is an insufficiency of neurotransmitter (Chapter 12). Successful psychotherapies are those in which the client and the therapist treat each other as human beings (Chapter 19).

Of all the models surveyed in the textbook, the existential approach is most compatible with common-sense notions. Not surprisingly, it is the only model that seems to fit with legal aspects of abnormality (Chapter 18) since the legal system is importantly based on the idea of free will and individual responsibility. As you read about how the other models explain and treat disorders, you should consider whether these disorders involve deficiencies in will and responsibility, perhaps occasioned by an oppressive environment. The existential approach shares with the psychodynamic approach a view of the environment as coercive. Both models assume a human nature that is easily thwarted by others.

FURTHER READINGS

Allport, G. W. (1955). *Becoming: Basic considerations for a psychology of personality.* New Haven, CN: Yale University.

Bettelheim, B. (1976). *The uses of enchantment: The meaning and importance of fairy tales.* New York: Knopf.

Blum, G. S. (1953). *Psychoanalytic theories of personality.* New York: McGraw-Hill.

Brown, J. A. C. (1966). *Freud and the Post-Freudians.* Baltimore: Penguin.

Camus, A. (1946). *The stranger.* New York: Vintage.

Erikson, E. H. (1963). *Childhood and society* (2nd ed.). New York: Norton.

Erikson, E. H. (1968). *Identity: Youth and crisis.* New York: Norton.

Fancher, R. (1973). *Psychoanalytic psychology: The development of Freud's thought.* New York: Norton.

Frankl, V. (1971). *Man's search for meaning: An introduction to logotherapy.* New York: Pocket Books.

Freud, S. (1952). *On dreams.* New York: Norton.

Freud, S. (1963). *Jokes and their relation to the unconscious.* New York: Norton.

Freud, S. (1963). *Three case histories.* New York: Collier.

Freud, S. (1966). *Introductory lectures on psychoanalysis.* New York: Norton.

Freud, S. (1976). *The interpretation of dreams.* New York: Norton.

Fromm, E. (1941). *Escape from freedom.* New York: Rinehart.

Fromm, E. (1974). *The art of loving.* New York: Perennial Library.

Greenberg, J. R., & Mitchell, S. A. (1983). *Object relations in psychoanalytic theory.* Cambridge, MA: Harvard University Press.

Hall, C. S. (1954). *A primer of Freudian psychology.* New York: New American Library.

Jones, E. (1953–57). *The life and work of Sigmund Freud* (3 vols.). New York: Basic Books.

May, R. (1969). *Existential psychology* (2nd ed.). New York: Random House.

Perls, F. S., Hefferling, R. F., & Goodman, P. (1951). *Gestalt therapy: Excitement and growth in the human personality.* New York: Julian Press.

Perls, F. S. (1969). *Gestalt therapy verbatim.* Moab, UT: Real People Press.

Vaillant, G. E. (1977). *Adaptation to life.* Boston: Little, Brown.

Wertheimer, M. (1978). Humanistic psychology and the humane but tough-minded psychologist. *American Psychologist, 33,* 739–745.

TERM-PAPER TOPICS

1. Compare and contrast Freud and the Neo-Freudians. Does the work of the Neo-Freudians represent an extension of Freud's work or a drastic break from Freud's work?

2. Existential psychology is antagonistic to research. Evaluate this claim. Take a strong stand, and defend it with examples.

3. Why is the effectiveness of psychoanalytic therapy so difficult to ascertain?
4. Compare and contrast DSM-II and DSM-III-R. The former clearly embodies psychodynamic theory. What about the latter?

EXERCISES

Exercise One—Dream Analysis

This exercise allows you to evaluate an important Freudian hypothesis: dreams represent unconscious wishes.

Keep a notebook and pencil next to your bed. For a week, write down the dreams that you remember. Do this immediately upon awakening, and provide as much detail as you can. After the week, analyze what you have written. Are there recurrent themes? Do these themes pertain to important aspects of your life—parents, romance, achievement? Do they seem to represent wishes that you may have? Do any of your dreams illustrate Freudian defense mechanisms such as displacement or reaction formation?

Freud, S. (1952). *On dreams*. New York: Norton.

Exercise Two—Freudian Slips

In this exercise you will evaluate another important Freudian hypothesis: "errors" such as slips of the tongue or slips of the pen reveal one's true motives.

Talk to individuals about "errors" they have made while speaking or writing. Are these slips sexual or aggressive in nature? Do they correspond with motives that these individuals would prefer not to acknowledge?

A favorite example of mine comes from a student's paper of several years ago. The student was writing an essay on the absurdity of Freudian symbolism. His sentence "A pen is not a phallic symbol" was typed without a space between "pen" and "is"—perhaps the result of the very process against which he was arguing!

Freud, S. (1965). *The psychopathology of everyday life*. New York: Norton.

Exercise Three—Prejudice and Projection

The defense mechanism of projection involves the attribution to others of characteristics one does not like in oneself. In this exercise, you will look for examples of projection.

Talk to some individuals you know well about people or groups that they dislike. Ask them what it is that they dislike. Do these characteristics have anything to do with their own make-up?

Freud, S. (1936). *The problem of anxiety*. New York: Norton.

Exercise Four—Language and Responsibility

In this exercise, you will investigate an important existential hypothesis—that individuals may avoid taking responsibility for events in their life by the use of certain expressions.

Talk to graduate students about their thesis or dissertation research, and unobtrusively note if they refer to their research as *the* thesis or *the* dissertation—e.g., "When *the* dissertation is done, I can get a good job." Also ask them about their progress. Do students who objectify their research, who speak of it as if they have little to do with its start or finish, also have difficulties doing the research, as the existentialists predict?

I saw a similar phenomenon well illustrated when I worked as a psychologist on a rehabilitation ward in a hospital. Patients had all suffered some loss of bodily function, through a stroke, an accident, and so on. Patients with paralyzed limbs sometimes referred to their arm or leg as *the* arm or *the* leg, as if it were no longer part of them. In one way this was a psychologically healthy way of speaking, because it helped the patients make a short-term adjustment to a serious loss. But in another way this was not a helpful way of speaking, because it encouraged the patients not to take responsibility for solving their problems.

Exercise Five—Choice and Responsibility

The purpose of this exercise is to illustrate the existential idea that some individuals do not make choices because they are afraid of being wrong.

Talk to friends who are graduating seniors about what they will be doing in the next few years. Pay attention to students who speak of "keeping options open." Are these the same individuals who do not have a good idea about what they will be doing? Are these the same individuals who are traumatized at the thought of leaving college?

Fromm, E. (1941). *Escape from freedom*. New York: Rinehart.

Exercise Six—Being a Good Listener

In this exercise, students will practice an empathic technique suggested by Carl Rogers.

When you talk to a friend, "reflect" back to him things that he says. That is, if he mentions that he is worried about a pending event, ask him to elaborate on his feelings about the event. If he says that he is happy, ask him to tell you about his happiness. And so on.

According to Rogers, by accepting what your friend says, you will help your friend accept himself. Above and beyond this possibility, I suspect that your friend will find you a good "conversationalist" since good conversationalists are usually those who help other people talk.

Rogers, C. R. (1951). *Client-centered therapy: Its current practice, implications, and theory.* Boston: Houghton Mifflin.

CHAPTER 5

The Environmentalist Model:
Behavioral and Cognitive
Approaches

CHAPTER OVERVIEW

This chapter is concerned with behavioral and cognitive approaches to abnormality. According to the behavioral view, abnormal behavior is determined by the environment: it is the result of learning. The behavioral model thus regards therapy as a process of relearning, and it is optimistic that all disorders can thereby be treated.

The roots of the behavioral model lie in animal learning research, which distinguishes between two types of learning. The first is Pavlovian conditioning, in which individuals come to learn what goes with what as a result of pairings among stimuli in the environment. For instance, in Pavlov's original experiments, dogs learned to salivate at the sight of the experimenter since his presence had previously been paired with food, which reflexively elicits salivation. The second type of learning is operant conditioning, in which individuals come to learn what to do in order to obtain rewards and avoid punishments as a result of environmental response to behaviors. Thus, a child may learn to help with housework because he is given a special dessert after doing so.

Each type of learning gives rise to several therapy techniques. Pavlovian techniques such as flooding and desensitization are usually deployed against undesired emotional reactions. Operant techniques such as selective positive reinforcement and behavioral contracting are used to increase desired behaviors and decrease undesired ones.

The cognitive model regards abnormality as due to maladaptive thoughts. Cognitive therapy attempts to change the thoughts that give rise to abnormality. Among the targets of cognitive therapy are unrealistic and irrational expectations, appraisals, attributions, and beliefs. Depressed individuals may believe, for instance, that they are responsible for all the bad events in the world. Cognitive therapy would attempt to dissuade these people from their depressing beliefs.

ESSENTIAL TERMS

acquisition	process by which learning occurs; in Pavlovian conditioning, pairing of conditioned stimulus with unconditioned stimulus; in operant conditioning, pairing of an operant with reinforcement or punishment
associationism	movement that believes ideas congeal in the mind because they have been experienced together

attribution	individual's conception of why an event occurred
avoidance learning	form of learning that involves both Pavlovian conditioning (learning what stimulus predicts an aversive event) and operant conditioning (learning to escape the stimulus, thereby avoiding the aversive event)
BASIC ID	notion of Arnold Lazarus that disorder occurs at seven different levels (B = behavior; A = affect; S = sensation; I = imagery; C = cognition; I = interpersonal relations; D = drugs) and that there are therapies appropriate to each level
behaviorism	movement within psychology that stresses overt actions and their shaping by the environment
cognitive-behavioral therapy	approach to therapy employing techniques based on the learning model and the cognitive model
cognitive therapy	therapy techniques based on the cognitive model of abnormality, which views mental events as causing disorder
conditional reflex (conditioned response; CR)	behavior acquired by Pavlovian conditioning
continuous reinforcement	reinforcement that occurs after every operant
discriminative stimulus	stimulus that signals that reinforcement is available if an operant is made
efficacy expectancy	person's estimate that he or she can successfully execute behavior necessary to produce a desired outcome
empiricism	movement that regards all ideas as resulting from experience
environmentalism	movement that regards all organisms, including humans, as being shaped by the environment
epiphenomenon	process that is not causal but that reflects an underlying process that is causal
extinction	process by which learning is "lost"; in Pavlovian conditioning, cessation of pairing of a conditioned stimulus with an unconditioned stimulus; in operant conditioning, cessation of pairing of an operant with reinforcement or punishment
flooding	therapy technique based on Pavlovian conditioning in which stimuli that elicit fear are repeatedly encountered
law of effect	Thorndike's principle of learning: when a response is followed by positive consequences, it tends to be repeated; when it is followed by negative consequences, it tends not to be repeated
nature-nurture issue	debate whether behavior is determined by heredity (nature) or environment (nurture)
negative reinforcer	stimulus that by its removal increases probability that a response preceding it will occur again
operant	response whose probability can be either increased by positive reinforcement or decreased by negative reinforcement

operant conditioning	form of learning described by Edward Thorndike and B. F. Skinner in which behaviors come to be associated with environmental consequences (rewards and punishments); trial-and-error learning
outcome expectancy	person's estimate that a given behavior will lead to a desired outcome
partial reinforcement	reinforcement that occurs after only some operants
Pavlovian conditioning	form of learning described by Ivan Pavlov in which environmental events (stimuli) come to elicit behaviors (responses) because they have been paired with other environmental events that do so reflexively
positive reinforcer	stimulus that by its presentation increases probability that a response preceding it will occur again
rational-emotive therapy	therapy founded by Albert Ellis that attempts to change the irrational beliefs of an individual
rationalism	movement that regards certain basic ideas as inborn or innate
selective positive reinforcement	therapy technique based on operant conditioning in which probability of a desired target behavior is increased by delivering positive reinforcement contingent on this behavior
selective punishment	therapy technique based on operant conditioning in which the probability of an undesired target behavior is decreased by delivering punishment contingent on this behavior
stimulus generalization	tendency of a response conditioned to one stimulus to occur to similar stimuli
systematic desensitization	therapy technique based on Pavlovian conditioning in which stimuli that elicit fear are paired with relaxation or other pleasant experiences

SAMPLE EXAM

1. What is the stance of the behavioral model with respect to the nature-nurture issue?
   a. agrees with the nature position
   b. agrees with the nurture position
   c. agrees with both positions
   d. agrees with neither position

2. Descartes is to Locke as
   a. mind is to body.
   b. dopamine is to schizophrenia.
   c. rationalism is to empiricism.
   d. Freud is to Erikson.

3. Which of the following terms does not belong?
   a. empiricism
   b. associationism

   c. materialism
   d. behaviorism

4. Which of the following terms does not belong?
   a. environmentalism
   b. rationalism
   c. experimentalism
   d. optimism

5. The bahavioral model of abnormality regards abnormal behavior and normal behavior as
   a. different in kind.
   b. learned in the same way.
   c. similar only on the surface.
   d. related by association learning.

6. Ivan Pavlov's initial interest was in
   a. mental phenomena.
   b. learning.
   c. digestion.
   d. obedience.

7. When Pavlov's dog learned to salivate to the sight of Pavlov, what was the conditional reflex?
   a. the sight of Pavlov
   b. food
   c. the taste of food
   d. salivation to the sight of Pavlov

8. Suppose you ate too many cookies and became ill. If you became nauseated the next day when you saw the cookie jar, what was the conditional reflex?
   a. sight of the cookie jar
   b. cookies
   c. the taste of cookies
   d. nausea

9. For the situation in question 8, how could you extinguish this learning?
   a. ignore the cookie jar
   b. wait until time passed
   c. continue to see the cookie jar
   d. eat more cookies

10. Pavlovian conditioning best explains
    a. thought.
    b. memory.
    c. emotion.
    d. libido.

11. According to the Pavlovian conditioning model of phobias, an individual afraid of cats
    a. does not know why he or she has the fear.
    b. has had past experiences with cats.
    c. really likes cats.
    d. has always avoided cats.

12. According to the behavioral model, abnormality resides in
    a. the symptoms of the disorder.
    b. underlying drives.
    c. one's conflict with the environment.
    d. personality traits.

13. Which of the following types of therapy does not belong?
    a. flooding
    b. behavioral contracting
    c. systematic desensitization
    d. Pavlovian extinction

14. Systematic desensitization is effective with
    a. schizophrenia.
    b. general paresis.
    c. phobias.
    d. anorexia.

15. In systematic desensitization, what is the conditional reflex?
    a. fear in the presence of the feared object
    b. the feared object
    c. relaxation in the presence of the feared object
    d. early learning

16. If you wished to treat someone who was afraid of mice with the technique of flooding, you would
    a. expose the individual to mice.
    b. have the individual read about Disneyland.
    c. ask the individual to speak freely about mice.
    d. discover if the person has had experience with mice.

17. Which of the following corresponds to the "law of effect"?
    a. "A stitch in time saves nine."
    b. "Pretty is as pretty does."
    c. "You can catch more flies with honey than with vinegar."
    d. "It don't rain in Indianapolis."

18. Your cat learns to ring the doorbell to be let in when she sees your car in the driveway. In this example, what is the operant?
    a. ringing the doorbell
    b. your car in the driveway
    c. being let in
    d. seeing your car

19. In question 18, what is the reinforcer?
    a. ringing the doorbell
    b. your car in the driveway
    c. being let in
    d. seeing your car

20. In question 18, what is the discriminative stimulus?
    a. ringing the doorbell
    b. your car in the driveway
    c. being let in
    d. seeing your car

21. In question 18, you could decrease the frequency with which your cat rang the doorbell by all of these except
    a. selling your car.
    b. stopping answering the door.
    c. kicking the cat when she comes in.
    d. feeding the cat when she comes in.

22. Intermittent reinforcement results in all of the following except
    a. behavior that is learned slowly.
    b. behavior that is extinguished quickly.
    c. behavior that is persistent.
    d. behavior that is maintained with little payoff.

23. Selective positive reinforcement as a treatment of anorexia involves
    a. ignoring bizarre behaviors.
    b. convincing the client to eat.
    c. finding a desired reinforcer.
    d. prescribing minor tranquilizers.

24. Avoidance learning involves
    a. only Pavlovian conditioning.
    b. only operant conditioning.
    c. both Pavlovian and operant conditioning.
    d. neither Pavlovian nor operant conditioning.

25. In avoidance learning, what is the reinforcer?
    a. avoidance
    b. fear
    c. decrease of fear
    d. signal

26. The cognitive model of abnormality views abnormality as residing in
    a. faulty learning.
    b. demonic possession.
    c. irrational thoughts.
    d. bodily injury.

27. Behaviorists may concede that mental life exists, but they further argue that it is
    a. epiphenomenal.
    b. literal.
    c. norepinephral.
    d. dual.

28. A cognitive therapist is mainly interested in the
    a. early childhood experiences of clients.
    b. physical well-being of clients.
    c. thought and beliefs of clients.
    d. unconscious impulses of clients.

29. All of the following are cognitive processes except
    a. expectation.
    b. reuptake.
    c. attribution.
    d. appraisal.

30. What is the difference between an outcome expectancy and an efficacy expectation?
    a. An outcome expectancy is a belief about what will happen, and an efficacy expectation is a belief about how hard one will try.
    b. An outcome expectancy is an optimistic belief, and an efficacy expectation is a pessimistic belief.
    c. An outcome expectancy is a belief about whether a given response leads to an outcome, and an efficacy expectation is a belief about whether one can perform a given response.
    d. An outcome expectancy is a belief about end states, and an efficacy expectation is a belief about processes.

31. You are taking an examination, and another student turns in her test after a few minutes and leaves. You think: "I must be stupid. I'm going to flunk." This is an example of
    a. appraisal.
    b. attribution.
    c. epiphenomenon.
    d. castration fear.

32. You go out on a date, and you have a bad time. You explain your bad time by saying: "I was too tired this evening to enjoy a movie." This causal attribution is
    a. internal, stable, and global.
    b. external, unstable, and global.
    c. internal, unstable, and specific.
    d. external, stable, and specific.

33. You cannot finish all the work given to you. You explain this failure by saying: "The boss is overly thorough when it comes to this kind of project." This causal attribution is
    a. internal, stable, and global.
    b. external, unstable, and global.
    c. internal, unstable, and specific.
    d. external, stable, and specific.

34. You give a speech, and the audience reacts negatively. You explain this reaction by saying: "I am an inept person." This causal attribution is
    a. internal, stable, and global.
    b. external, unstable, and global.
    c. internal, unstable, and specific.
    d. external, stable, and specific.

35. Cognitive therapy for depression attempts to change the way people explain bad events. This involves changing
    a. external attributions to internal attributions.
    b. internal attributions to external attributions.
    c. specific attributions to global attributions.
    d. unstable attributions to stable attributions.

36. Which of the following is *not* an irrational belief identified by Albert Ellis?
    a. One should take the bad with the good.
    b. One should be thoroughly competent in all respects.
    c. One must be loved by all people.
    d. There is a right way to do everything.

37. Cognitive therapy and behavior therapy
    a. are similar.
    b. are not incompatible.
    c. are both concerned with underlying causes.
    d. are unsuccessful.

38. Arnold Lazarus suggests the mnemonic BASIC ID to describe the seven different levels of disorder. The A refers to
    a. autonomy.
    b. assertion.
    c. affect.
    d. adrenaline.

39. Arnold Lazarus suggests the mnemonic BASIC ID to describe the seven different levels of disorder. The I stands for
    a. id.
    b. independence.
    c. indolamine.
    d. interpersonal relations.

40. Arnold Lazarus suggests the mnemonic BASIC ID to describe the seven different levels of disorder. The D stands for
    a. drugs.
    b. dependence.
    c. displacement.
    d. discomfort.

41. Which one of the following is *not* a strength of the cognitive approach?
    a. Cognitive therapy is usually brief.
    b. Cognitive therapy is often successful.
    c. Cognitive therapy addresses the whole person.
    d. Cognitive therapy is based on research.

Answer Key for Sample Exam

1.	b	(p. 106)	22.	b	(p. 114)
2.	c	(p. 106)	23.	c	(p. 116)
3.	c	(p. 106)	24.	c	(p. 117)
4.	b	(p. 107)	25.	c	(p. 118)
5.	b	(p. 107)	26.	c	(p. 118)
6.	c	(p. 108)	27.	a	(p. 119)
7.	d	(p. 108)	28.	c	(p. 119)
8.	d	(p. 108)	29.	b	(p. 120)
9.	c	(p. 109)	30.	c	(p. 121)
10.	c	(p. 110)	31.	a	(p. 121)
11.	b	(p. 110)	32.	c	(p. 123)
12.	a	(p. 110)	33.	d	(p. 123)
13.	b	(p. 112)	34.	a	(p. 123)
14.	c	(p. 112)	35.	b	(p. 123)
15.	c	(p. 112)	36.	a	(p. 124)
16.	a	(p. 111)	37.	b	(p. 125)
17.	c	(p. 112)	38.	c	(p. 126)
18.	a	(p. 113)	39.	d	(p. 126)
19.	c	(p. 112)	40.	a	(p. 126)
20.	b	(p. 113)	41.	c	(p. 128)
21.	d	(p. 114)			

SELF-TEST

1. The sixteenth-century French philosopher _____ proposed that basic ideas were innate. This position is termed _____ .

2. The position that all ideas are acquired through experience is _____ and is associated with the philosophers _____ and _____ .

3. According to the empiricists, the "mental glue" that holds together ideas is called an

_____ .

4. Behaviorism is a world view based on assumptions of _____ , _____ , and _____ .

5. The two major forms of learning are _____ conditioning and _____ conditioning.

6. The major difference between Pavlovian conditioning and operant conditioning is that in Pavlovian conditioning one learns _____ , while in operant conditioning one learns _____ .

7. Pavlov was originally interested in the _____ reflex.

8. When Pavlov's dogs began to salivate at the sight of him, it was because he had become a _____ .

9. A treatment for alcoholism based on Pavlovian conditioning consists of pairing the taste of alcohol with a drug that makes the individual _____ .

10. _____ is the process by which one learns that a CS is associated with a US. The opposite process is _____ .

11. According to the behavioral model, emotional states and emotional disorders are acquired through _____ .

12. The behaviorists feel that symptoms of a disorder _____ .

13. Behavior therapies attempt to rid the client of _____ .

14. Joseph Wolpe developed the therapy technique known as _____ .

15. In systematic desensitization, the phobic object is paired with _____ .

16. Flooding is based on Pavlovian _____ .

17. Thorndike discovered that learning among cats was not sudden but rather _____ .

18. According to the "law of effect," behaviors with positive consequences are _____ , while behaviors with negative consequences are _____ .

19. An event that increases the probability that a response preceding it will occur again is a _____ .

20. An event that decreases the probability that a response preceding it will occur again is a _____ .

21. A signal that reinforcement is available if the operant is made is a _____ .

22. Reinforcement delivered after every operant is _____ reinforcement, while reinforcement delivered only after some operants is _____ reinforcement.

23. Partial reinforcement makes responses more difficult to learn, but it also makes them more resistant to _____ .

24. Selective positive reinforcement is a therapy technique in which a target behavior is chosen to be _____ .

25. A type of learning that involves both Pavlovian conditioning and operant conditioning is _____ .

26. Behaviorists may concede the existence of mental events, but they dismiss them as _____ .

27. According to the cognitive model of abnormality, thoughts and beliefs _____ disorders.

28. The approach to therapy that attempts to change what a client believes is _____ .

29. Short-term cognitive processes include _____ (anticipations about future events), _____ (evaluations), and _____ (causal explanations).

30. _____ expectancy is a person's estimate that a given behavior will lead to the desired outcome, while _____ expectancy is the belief that he or she can successfully execute the behavior that produces the desired outcome.

31. An attribution for an event that points to an individual's lack of intelligence is _____ , _____ , and _____ .

32. _____ developed rational-emotive therapy, which is based on the argument that psychological disorder stems largely from beliefs that are _____ .

33. When therapy combines techniques from the behavioral approach and the cognitive approach, it is called _____ therapy.

34. Arnold Lazarus has argued that disorder exists on seven levels; _____ , _____ , _____ , _____ , _____ , _____ , and _____ .

35. Cognitive therapy has been criticized for being too _____ .

Answer Key for Self-Test

1. René Descartes; rationalism
2. empiricism; John Locke; David Hume
3. association
4. environmentalism; experimentalism; optimism
5. Pavlovian (classical); operant (instrumental)
6. what goes with what; what to do to get what one wants
7. salivary
8. conditional stimulus
9. sick (nauseous)
10. Acquisition; extinction
11. Pavlovian conditioning
12. are the disorder
13. symptoms
14. systematic desensitization
15. relaxation
16. extinction
17. gradual
18. repeated; not repeated
19. reinforcer
20. punishment
21. discriminative stimulus
22. continuous; partial (intermittent)
23. extinction
24. increased in frequency
25. avoidance learning
26. epiphenomena
27. cause

28. cognitive therapy
29. expectations; appraisals; attributions
30. Outcome; efficacy
31. internal; stable; global
32. Albert Ellis; irrational
33. cognitive-behavioral
34. behavior; affect; sensation; imagery; cognition; interpersonal relations; drugs
35. narrow

TYING IT TOGETHER

The behavioral model was the first approach to abnormality to be identified mainly with psychologists and not with physicians or biologists. It is based largely on experimental research (Chapter 6). Historically, advocates of the behavioral model have been less interested in diagnosis than in careful description of the behaviors involved in abnormality (Chapter 7). Thus, the behavioral model does not regard behaviors as symptoms of an underlying biological or psychodynamic cause; instead, behaviors are regarded as the problem itself. The behavioral model is associated with careful studies of therapy outcome in which the frequencies of target behaviors are assessed following treatments.

The behavioral approach seems to do its best job in explaining and changing problems that involve circumscribed behaviors with emotional components: fears and phobias (Chapter 8), obsessive-compulsive disorders (Chapter 9), paraphilias (Chapter 13), sexual dysfunctions (Chapter 13), and drug abuse (Chapter 14). It is less successful when difficulties are "deeper" or more diffuse.

In part a reaction against psychoanalysis, the behavioral model also has served as a foil for the cognitive approach and the existential approach. According to cognitive psychologists, behaviorists inappropriately ignore mental life. According to existential psychologists (Chapter 4), behaviorists are guilty of a narrow determinism that overlooks essential aspects of human experience. The emergence of a cognitive-behavioral approach suggests that these criticisms have been valid, and that they can be answered within the behavioral framework.

One of the achievements of the behavioral approach has been the development, implementation, and evaluation of a number of simple and successful therapy techniques to treat problems that have defied previous therapeutic attempts (Chapter 19).

The cognitive approach to abnormality developed both from the behavioral model and in reaction to it. Like the behavioral model, it is largely associated with psychologists. It has generated its own assessment devices, like the Rep Test (Chapter 7), and it is closely tied to empirical research (Chapter 6).

The cognitive model is at its best when explaining disorders in which conscious thought plays a causal role. Thus, fear and anxiety disorders (Chapter 9) and depression (Chapter 11) are clarified by the cognitive approach since these disorders are partly brought about by characteristic ways of thinking. Cognitively based therapies have been successfully used to treat such disorders (Chapter 19), and in some cases they may be as effective as drug therapy without the side effects of medication.

The psychodynamic model is concerned with mental processes, but it differs from the cognitive model in emphasizing the unconscious (Chapter 4). In contrast, the cognitive approach is concerned largely with conscious thought. Accordingly, it co-exists more easily with existential approaches (Chapter 4) than do the other models of abnormality. However, there is a tendency for cognitive explanations to focus on "small" aspects of thought, such as expectations and appraisals, rather than on "larger" belief systems. Perhaps this is the reason why the cognitive model is largely silent about schizophrenia, a so-called thought disorder (Chapter 12).

The cognitive model is the most recently articulated psychological approach to abnormality. Its applicability to the range of disorders has not been fully explored. As you read Chapter 8 through 17, you may speculate about which disorders could be profitably approached in terms of an individual's thoughts and beliefs. Sexual behavior is inherently symbolic behavior, not just an activity of the physical body; accordingly, the sexual dysfunctions (Chapter 13) may merit reexamination from a cognitive perspective. Similarly, drug use and abuse (Chapter 14) are embedded in a life style that includes a belief system. Couldn't this belief system help maintain drug-related behavior? Perhaps cognitive therapy could be effective in dissuading individuals from a destructive life-style.

FURTHER READINGS

Bandura, A. (1969). *Principles of behavior modification*. New York: Holt, Rinehart & Winston.

Beck. A. T. (1976). *Cognitive therapy and the emotional disorders*. New York: International Universities Press.

Begelman, D. A. (1975). Ethical and legal issues of behavior modification. In M. Hersen, R. Eisler, & P. Miller (Eds.), *Progress in behavior modification* (vol. 1, pp. 159–189). New York; Academic Press.

Burns, D. D. (1980). *Feeling good: The new mood therapy*. New York: Morrow.

Carrera, F., & Adams, P. L. (1970). An ethical perspective on operant conditioning. *Journal of the American Academy of Child Psychiatrists, 9,* 607–634.

Ellis, A. (1962). *Reason and emotion in psychotherapy*. New York: Stuart.

Huxley, A. (1946). *Brave new world.* New York: Harper & Row.

Kelly, G. A. (1963). *A theory of personality: The psychology of personal constructs.* New York: Norton.

Mahoney, M. J. (1974). *Cognition and behavior modification.* Cambridge, MA: Ballinger.

Meichenbaum, D. (1977). *Cognitive-behavior modification.* New York: Plenum.

Skinner, B. F. (1971). *Beyond freedom and dignity.* New York: Knopf.

Skinner, B. F. (1976). *Walden two.* New York: Macmillan.

Wachtel, P. (1977). *Psychoanalysis and behavior therapy: Toward an integration.* New York: Basic Books.

Watson, J. B. (1970). *Behaviorism.* New York: Norton.

TERM-PAPER TOPICS

1. How does social learning theory build upon the behavioral model? How does it break with this model? Does social learning theory have more to do with the cognitive model than with the behavioral model?

2. Consider this statement: Behavior therapy techniques are effective only for mild problems. Do you agree or disagree? Support your answer with examples from research.

3. What are the ethical issues raised by behavior modification? Are they any different than the ethical issues raised by other approaches to therapy?

4. Read the first chapter in Gilbert Ryle's *Concept of Mind* (1949). In light of his arguments, evaluate the cognitive model's claims that thoughts and beliefs are at the basis of psychological disorders.

5. It has been claimed that cognitive therapy for depression is as effective as antidepressant medication. Read some of the original studies that made this comparison. What qualifications need to be made? What factors may be considered in pursuing cognitive therapy versus drug therapy?

6. *Irrational* is a complex term with several meanings. In what sense does Albert Ellis use the term? In what sense does Aaron Beck use the term? Does cognitive therapy as practiced by Ellis and Beck make clients more rational, or is there a better way to describe its effects?

EXERCISES

Exercise One—Taste Aversion and Pavlovian Conditioning

In this exercise you will evaluate the Pavlovian-conditioning explanation of taste aversions.

According to Pavlovian conditioning, if a taste is paired with an unpleasant experience, that taste will become unpleasant. Talk to people about tastes of foods or drinks that make them nauseous. Were these tastes originally associated with illness or some other aversive experience?

Logue, A. W., Logue, K. R., & Strauss, K. E. (1983). The acquisition of taste aversions in humans with eating and drinking disorders. *Behaviour Research and Therapy, 21,* 275–289.

Seligman, M. E. P., & Hager, J. L. (1972). Biological boundaries of learning: The sauce-Béarnaise phenomenon. *Psychology Today, 6*(3), 59–61; 84–87.

Exercise Two—Increasing the Frequency of Your Studying

In this exercise you will use principles of operant conditioning to increase the frequency of an important operant—your studying.

A reinforcer is any stimulus that increases the probability of an operant that precedes it. This is a circular definition, and a number of attempts have been made to characterize a reinforcer in noncircular terms. One of these attempts is the Premack principle, which proposes that the opportunity to engage in a high-frequency behavior will reinforce any low-frequency behavior. If this is the case, then you can increase your studying in a simple way. Identify some behavior that you perform a great deal (e.g., watching television, playing sports). Impose on yourself the rule that you will only perform this behavior if you have first studied, say, one hour more per day than you have been studying in the past. According to the Premack principle, your studying should increase.

Premack, D. (1959). Toward empirical behavior laws: I. Positive reinforcement. *Psychological Review, 66,* 219–233.

Exercise Three—Thoughts and Mood

In this exercise, you will test the premise of the cognitive model that thoughts cause emotions.

Have some of your friends read the following statement out loud:

> I have just failed an examination. It is entirely my fault that I failed this test. The teacher made her help available, but I did not take it. The course material was interesting, and my classmates said that it was

simple, but I could not understand the ideas no matter how hard I tried. My failure on this examination is just one of many disappointments that I have had throughout my life. I have no close friends, and even my family takes no interest in what I do. There is nothing that I'm good at, and there is nothing that I'll ever be good at. Failure seems to result from everything I do.

Have other friends read this statement out loud:

> I have just failed an examination. It was a hard test, and the teacher didn't help in making the ideas easier to understand. I guess I could have studied a bit harder, but I had some other things to do that were more important. They turned out fine, so I can't look at the failed exam as a big deal. What's really important to me are my friends and my family, and doing things with them that are rewarding. So I can't complain. Anyway, I usually do well on exams and in my courses in general, so I'm pretty sure that I'll pull my grade up before the course is over. Things usually turn out pretty successfully for me.

Ask your friends about how they feel after they have read the statements. Do the two statements have different effects on mood?

Velten, E. (1968). A laboratory task for the induction of mood states. *Behaviour Research and Therapy, 6,* 473–482.

Exercise Four—Test Anxiety and Automatic Thoughts

According to the cognitive model, emotions like guilt and sadness are brought about by negative statements that people make to themselves, almost without being aware of what they are doing. The purpose of this exercise is to demonstrate this idea.

Arrange this exercise with the instructor of a large class. During an examination, have a student hand in her test in the front of the classroom shortly after receiving it. She should do so confidently, as if she breezed through all the questions. Thirty seconds later, the instructor should ask the other students in the class to write down what they thought when the test was handed in so early. How many students wrote down self-deprecating statements? Are these the same individuals who experience a great deal of anxiety while taking tests?

Sarason, I. G. (1980). *Test anxiety: Theory, research, and applications.* Hillsdale, NJ: Erlbaum.

Exercise Five—Depression and Attributions

The purpose of this exercise is to test the prediction of learned helplessness theory that depression is associated with a characteristic style of explaining bad events.

Talk to individuals who are sad and individuals who are not. (You may gauge their mood by administering the questionnaire below.) Ask them to explain the causes of several recent bad events they have experienced. Are the sad individuals more apt to offer internal, stable, and global attributions as explanation for bad events?

Ask people to respond to these questions in terms of how they have been feeling for the last two weeks:

1. My mood has been sad.
   a. not at all
   b. sometimes
   c. all the time
2. My appetite has been poor.
   a. not at all
   b. sometimes
   c. all the time
3. My sleep has been irregular.
   a. not at all
   b. sometimes
   c. all the time
4. My interest in activities has decreased.
   a. not at all
   b. sometimes
   c. all the time
5. My concentration has been poor.
   a. not at all
   b. sometimes
   c. all the time
6. My self-esteem has been low.
   a. not at all
   b. sometimes
   c. all the time

Score each question a = 1, b = 2, and c = 3. The higher the score, the more depressed the person is.

Peterson, C., & Seligman, M. E. P. (1984). Causal explanations at a risk factor for depression: Theory and evidence. *Psychological Review, 91,* 347–374.

CHAPTER 6

Investigating Abnormality

CHAPTER OVERVIEW

There are a number of ways in which abnormality and its causes may be investigated, and these are described in Chapter 6. The hope of all abnormality researchers is that effective means for preventing and/or curing disorders will result from discovery of their causes.

The two principal methods of investigation, which possess complementary strengths and weaknesses, are clinical case histories and experimental studies. A clinical case history is a record of part of the life of an individual seen during therapy. Case histories are useful as a source of hypotheses and as a nonartificial means of studying rare phenomena. However, case histories cannot definitively isolate causes. In contrast, an experimental study is able to evaluate possible causes of a disorder by manipulating them and assessing the consequences. Among the drawbacks of experiments are artificiality as well as practical and ethical limitations in applying them to certain disorders.

To overcome some of these limitations, researchers use three other techniques of investigation. All attempt to isolate causes, but they cannot do so definitively. Correlational studies observe the relationships among variables without manipulating them. Experiments of nature capitalize on striking accidents to provide a "manipulation" of some factor of interest, the consequences of which are assessed. Finally, laboratory models of psychopathology attempt to create in the laboratory under controlled circumstances phenomena analogous to disorders that can be studied with fewer limitations than the disorders themselves.

What is the best method of investigation? There is none. Different questions and different circumstances require different research approaches. Method is a means to an end. In the case of methods for studying abnormality, the desired end is an understanding of disorders that allows assistance to those suffering from them. If research using different methods converges in the understanding provided, then a good research strategy has been followed.

ESSENTIAL TERMS

clinical case history	record of part of the life of an individual seen during therapy
confound	factor other than the independent variable that could produce an experimental effect
correlation	linear covariation of two variables
negative correlation	correlation in which increases in one variable are associated with decreases in the other variable

positive correlation	correlation in which increases in one variable are associated with increases in the other variable
uncorrelated correlation	correlation in which changes in one variable are not associated with changes in the other variable
correlational study	alternative to experimental studies in which the co-occurrence of two factors is assessed without manipulation
correlation coefficient	strength of correlation between two variables, ranging from +1.00 (perfect positive correlation) through 0.00 (no correlation) to –1.00 (perfect negative correlation)
demand characteristics	clues in an experimental setting which may induce subjects to invent hypotheses about how they should behave
dependent variable	in an experimental study, the effect, appearance of which depends on whether the cause precedes it
double-blind experiment	experiment in which both subject and experimenter are "blind" as to which drug or treatment has been provided
experimental effect	change in a dependent variable determined by manipulation of an independent variable
experimental study	method of isolating causes by manipulating possible causes and assessing the consequences
experimenter bias	subtle influence of the experimenter on subjects, producing an expected result
experimenter-blind experiment	experiment in which the experimenter is "blind" as to which drug or treatment has been provided
experiment of nature	alternative to experimental studies in which the occurrence of a striking event is regarded as a "manipulated" factor and its consequences are assessed
false alarms	conclusions that effects are true when they are actually false
independent variable	in an experimental study, the hypothesized cause, which is manipulated by the experimenter
laboratory model of psycho-pathology	production under controlled conditions of phenomena analogous to naturally occurring mental disorders
longitudinal study	investigation that follows the same subjects over time
meta-analysis	statistical technique for combining the results of different investigations
misses	conclusions that effects are false when they are actually true
operational definition	set of observable and measurable conditions under which a phenomenon is said to occur
placebo	useless drug or treatment that produces an effect because of subject bias
prospective study	longitudinal investigation in which subjects are chosen at one point in time and followed into the future
random assignment	in an experimental study, an equal chance of each subject to be assigned to each condition

single-blind experiment

experiment in which the subject is "blind" as to which drug or treatment has been provided

single-subject experiment

experimental study with only one subject

statistical significance

probability that a given result occurred by chance; when sufficiently low, it is concluded that the effect is real

subject bias

in an experimental study, the subtle tendency of a subject to produce an expected result

SAMPLE EXAM

1. The benefit of an experimental study as opposed to a clinical case history is that
   a. experiments are richer in detail.
   b. experiments are more scientific.
   c. experiments isolate causes.
   d. experiments have greater applicability.

2. All of the following are alternatives to experimental studies except
   a. correlational studies.
   b. introspective studies.
   c. experiments of nature.
   d. laboratory models of psychopathology.

3. The best method of investigating abnormality is
   a. correlational studies.
   b. experiments of nature.
   c. laboratory models of psychopathology.
   d. none of the above.

4. Sigmund Freud used which method of investigation?
   a. clinical case histories
   b. correlational studies
   c. experiments of nature
   d. laboratory models of psychopathology

5. Which one of the following is a disadvantage of the clinical case history?
   a. It is not artificial.
   b. It studies mundane phenomena.
   c. It is a rich source of hypotheses.
   d. It can provide evidence that disconfirms a generally accepted theory.

6. Which one of the following is *not* a disadvantage of the clinical case history?
   a. It uses retrospective evidence.
   b. It lacks repeatability.
   c. It lacks generality.
   d. It overemphasizes causality.

7. In an experimental study, the scientist manipulates
   a. the hypothesized cause.
   b. the hypothesized effect.
   c. the number of subjects.
   d. the dependent variable.

8. Which of these is an operational definition of temperature?
   a. the movement of atoms
   b. the lack of cold
   c. the reading of a thermometer
   d. the amount of heat

9. Which of these is an operational definition of happiness?
   a. the number of smiles per hour
   b. the amount of joy
   c. the degree of pleasure
   d. the operation of brain processes

10. Which of these does not belong?
    a. independent variable
    b. dependent variable
    c. effect
    d. experimental effect

11. How would you conduct an experiment to see if ice cream causes happiness?
    a. Feed individuals ice cream and see if they are happy.
    b. Do not feed individuals ice cream and see if they are unhappy.
    c. Feed some individuals ice cream, and do not feed other individuals; see which group of individuals is more happy.
    d. Conduct a survey in which individuals are asked if ice cream causes them to be happy.

12. A factor that occurs along with the independent variable is
    a. a cause.
    b. a confound.
    c. an overdetermined behavior.
    d. an operational definition.

13. Why do experimenters employ control groups?
    a. to achieve symmetry
    b. to check for random error
    c. to rule out confounds
    d. to replicate findings

14. The ideal control group in an experiment
    a. is exactly the same as the experimental group.
    b. is one that introduces the suspected confound.
    c. is studied before the experimental group is studied.
    d. is exactly the same as the experimental group except that the hypothesized cause is not present.

15. Meta-analysis is a(n) _____ technique.
    a. assessment
    b. deductive
    c. epidemiological
    d. statistical
    e. therapy

16. According to meta-analysis, the average client in psychotherapy does better than _____ of untreated clients.
    a. 1%
    b. 25%
    c. 50%
    d. 75%
    e. 99%

17. All of the following are potential confounds except
    a. nonrandom assignment.
    b. experimenter bias.
    c. yoking.
    d. demand characteristic.

18. In the "executive" monkey study, what was the confound?
    a. nonrandom assignment
    b. experimenter bias
    c. yoking
    d. demand characteristic

19. Placebo treatments work because of
    a. experimenter bias.
    b. nonrandom assignment.
    c. subject bias.
    d. sublimation.

20. What confound does a double-blind experiment attempt to avoid?
    a. experimenter bias
    b. subject bias
    c. nonrandom assignment
    d. a and b
    e. a and c
    f. b and c

21. What confound does an experimenter-blind experiment attempt to avoid?
    a. experimenter bias
    b. subject bias
    c. nonrandom assignment
    d. a and b
    e. a and c
    f. b and c

22. What confound does a single-blind experiment attempt to avoid?
    a. experimenter bias
    b. subject bias
    c. nonrandom assignment
    d. a and b
    e. a and c
    f. b and c

23. Demand characteristics assume that an experimental subject usually tries to be
    a. objective.
    b. helpful.
    c. belligerent.
    d. humorous.

24. Sensory-deprivation experiments have sometimes been subject to what confound?
    a. experimenter bias
    b. nonrandom assignment
    c. demand characteristics
    d. yoking

25. Statistics are used to make inferences about
    a. whether a population represents a sample.
    b. whether a sample represents a population.
    c. both a and b.
    d. neither a nor b.

26. At statistically significant effect is one that
    a. occurs more than 95 percent of the time.
    b. has a less than 95 percent chance of occurring by chance.
    c. has greater than a 5 percent chance of occurring by chance.
    d. has a less than 5 percent chance of occurring by chance.

27. If a scientist concludes that a therapy technique is successful when it is not successful, she has made what kind of mistake?
    a. a statistically significant error
    b. a false alarm
    c. a miss
    d. an experimenter bias

28. If a scientist concludes that a therapy technique is unsuccessful when it really is successful, she has made what kind of mistake?
    a. a statistically significant error
    b. a false alarm
    c. a miss
    d. an experimenter bias

29. What is the biggest drawback of a single-subject experiment?
    a. It does not isolate causes.
    b. It lacks repeatability.
    c. It lacks generality.
    d. It is liable to subject bias.

30. A scientist may not conduct an experiment for all these reasons except
    a. ethical considerations.
    b. financial considerations.
    c. time considerations.
    d. scientific considerations.

31. Correlational studies involve
    a. manipulation without observation.
    b. observation without manipulation.
    c. both manipulation and observation.
    d. neither manipulation nor observation.

32. The correlation between height and weight is
    a. positive.
    b. negative.
    c. zero.
    d. none of the above.

33. Individuals who study a lot also receive good grades. This means that
    a. studying results in good grades.
    b. good grades result in studying.
    c. conscientiousness results in studying and good grades.
    d. none of the above.

34. Which correlation coefficient is most likely to describe the correlation between height and weight?
    a. $r = +1.00$
    b. $r = +0.50$
    c. $r = 0.00$
    d. $r = -0.50$
    e. $r = -1.00$

35. Which one of the following is *not* an advantage to the correlational method?
    a. It is quantitative and rigorous.
    b. It is not artificial.
    c. It can avoid ethical problems.
    d. It can isolate causes.

36. Are confounds more likely in experiments or in experiments of nature?
    a. experiments
    b. experiments of nature
    c. equally likely
    d. none of the above

37. In an experiment of nature, what corresponds to the independent variable?
    a. the effect
    b. the operational definition
    c. the accident
    d. the confound

38. A longitudinal study explicitly incorporates
    a. childhood factors.
    b. manipulations.
    c. projective tests.
    d. survey questions.
    e. the element of time.

39. Which one of the following is *not* a strength of experiments of nature?
    a. They are not artificial.
    b. They are repeatable.
    c. They avoid ethical problems.
    d. They isolate gross causes.

40. Laboratory models are based on
    a. simplicity.
    b. analogy.
    c. animals.
    d. physiology.

41. Which one of the following is *not* a strength of laboratory models?
    a. They isolate causes.
    b. They are repeatable.
    c. They avoid ethical problems.
    d. They are not artificial.

42. If one were most interested in conveying the reality of a disorder, one would use which method of investigation?
    a. clinical case history
    b. experimental study
    c. correlational study
    d. laboratory model

43. Research using different methods is most useful when it
    a. supports experimental findings.
    b. converges.
    c. diverges.
    d. supports insights from clinical case histories.

Answer Key for Sample Exam

1.	c	(p. 133)	12.	b	(p. 139)	23.	b	(p. 141)
2.	b	(p. 133)	13.	c	(p. 139)	24.	c	(p. 142)
3.	d	(p. 134)	14.	d	(p. 139)	25.	b	(p. 142)
4.	a	(p. 134)	15.	d	(p. 139)	26.	d	(p. 143)
5.	b	(p. 136)	16.	d	(p. 140)	27.	b	(p. 143)
6.	d	(p. 136)	17.	c	(p. 141)	28.	c	(p. 143)
7.	a	(p. 137)	18.	a	(p. 140)	29.	c	(p. 145)
8.	c	(p. 137)	19.	c	(p. 141)	30.	d	(p. 146)
9.	a	(p. 137)	20.	d	(p. 141)	31.	b	(p. 147)
10.	a	(p. 137)	21.	a	(p. 141)	32.	a	(p. 147)
11.	c	(p. 138)	22.	b	(p. 141)	33.	d	(p. 149)

34.	b	(p. 149)
35.	d	(p. 150)
36.	b	(p. 150)
37.	c	(p. 150)
38.	e	(p. 151)
39.	b	(p. 151)
40.	b	(p. 152)
41.	d	(p. 153)
42.	a	(p. 153)
43.	b	(p. 153)

SELF-TEST

1. The two principle methods of investigating abnormality are _____ and _____ .

2. Case histories cannot isolate _____ .

3. Alternatives to experimental studies include _____ , _____ , and _____ .

4. Sound method is a _____ , not an _____ .

5. Clinical case histories have several strengths. First, they are not _____ ; second, they can be used to study _____ phenomena; and third, they are a rich source of _____ .

6. Clinical case histories have several disadvantages. First, their evidence may be _____ ; second, they lack _____ ; third, they lack _____ ; and fourth, they cannot identify _____ .

7. In an experiment, the hypothesized cause is the _____ and the effect of interest is the _____ .

8. An _____ is the set of observable conditions under which a phenomenon occurs.

9. Factors other than the independent variable that may produce an experimental effect are _____ .

10. To eliminate confounds in an experiment, one uses _____ groups.

11. Meta-analysis has been used to investigate _____ .

12. Among the common experimental confounds are _____ , _____ , _____ , and _____ .

13. Statistical inference is used to decide whether the _____ truly represents the _____ .

14. Conclusions that say x is false when it is true are _____ , while conclusions that say x is true when it is false are _____ .

15. Single-subject experiments can demonstrate _____ but not _____.

16. The experimental method has several strengths. First, it is the foremost method for _____ ; second, it is _____ ; and third, it is _____ .

17. Among the weaknesses of the experimental method are that it is _____ ; inferences are _____ ; and it is sometimes _____ or _____ .

18. Studies in which variables are observed without being manipulated are _____ .

19. If variable A increases while variable B decreases, and vice versa, then the correlation between variables A and B is _____ .

20. If variable C increases while variable D also increases, and vice versa, then the correlation between variables C and D is _____ .

21. The strength of the relationship between two variables can be expressed by a _____ .

22. On the positive side, correlational studies are not _____ ; they are _____ ; they are _____ ; and they avoid _____ problems; on the negative side, they are not able to _____ .

23. Studies that capitalize on the occurrence of a striking event are _____ .

24. Experiments of nature have several strong points. First, they are not _____ ; second, they avoid _____ problems; and third, they isolate gross _____ .

25. There are several weaknesses in experiments of nature. First, they cannot specify _____ in the gross cause; second, they are not _____ ; and third, they may be subject to _____ bias.

26. The production under controlled conditions of a phenomenon analogous to an actual psychopathology is a _____ .

27. The strengths of laboratory models are: first, they specify _____ ; second, they are _____ ; and third, they minimize problems with _____ .

28. On the negative side, laboratory models are _____ , and _____ is limited.

29. The best method is _____ .

Answer Key for Self-Test

1. clinical case histories; experimental studies
2. causes
3. correlational studies; experiments of nature; laboratory models of psychopathology
4. means; end
5. artificial; rare; hypotheses
6. selective; repeatability; generality; causes

7. independent variable; dependent variable
8. operational definition
9. confounds
10. control (comparison)
11. psychotherapy effectiveness
12. nonrandom assignment; experimenter bias; subject bias; demand characteristics
13. sample; population

14. misses; false alarms
15. repeatability; generality
16. isolating causes; repeatable; general
17. artificial; probabilistic; impractical; unethical
18. correlational studies
19. negative
20. positive
21. correlation coefficient
22. artificial; quantitative; repeatable; ethical; isolate causes
23. experiments of nature
24. artificial; ethical; causes
25. active elements; repeatable; retrospective
26. laboratory model
27. causes; repeatable; ethics
28. artificial; generality
29. none

TYING IT TOGETHER

This chapter surveys the ways in which abnormality is investigated. The first major strategy of investigation is the clinical case history, which is associated with the psychodynamic approach as well as with the existential approach (Chapter 4). You will encounter clinical case histories throughout the text as they are used to illustrate the various disorders (Chapter 8 through 17). For rare disorders such as multiple personality (Chapter 9), transsexuality (Chapter 13), and certain forms of aphasia (Chapter 17), they provide the only information available.

The second major strategy of investigation is the experiment, which is associated mainly with the behavioral model (Chapter 5) but also with the biomedical (Chapter 3) and cognitive (Chapter 5) approaches. The more circumscribed a disorder, the more amenable it is to investigation with experimentation.

Correlational investigations are frequently cited throughout the text. You have already seen how such a strategy led researchers to suspect that general paresis may be linked to syphilis and to conduct the critical experiment described in Chapter 3. Correlations are at the basis of epidemiological research, which has shed light on the origins of psychosomatic disorders (Chapter 10), depression (Chapter 11), sexual difficulties (Chapter 13), drug abuse (Chapter 14), and schizophrenia (Chapter 12). The elegant twin studies and adoption studies, undertaken to unravel nature and nurture, are essentially correlational investigations.

Experiments of nature also occur throughout the textbook. They have provided important information about post-traumatic stress disorders (Chapter 8), dissociative disorders (Chapter 9), depression (Chapter 11), childhood disorders (Chapter 16), and neurological disorders (Chapter 17). Biological accidents such as hermaphroditism (Chapter 13) and the XYY chromosome disorder (Chapter 15) should be recognized as experiments of nature.

Finally, laboratory models of psychopathology have been used to investigate phobias (Chapter 8), peptic ulcers (Chapter 10), hypertension (Chapter 10), sudden death (Chapter 10), schizophrenia (Chapter 12), obesity (Chapter 16), and so on. In many cases, these models have suggested therapy techniques that have proven successful in the clinic (Chapter 19).

This chapter makes the point that the best research metaphorically resembles a woven fabric; it occurs when results from different strategies converge in the understanding provided. As you read about the disorders and their treatments, decide which disorders seem most understandable. Are these the ones that have converging research?

FURTHER READINGS

American Psychological Association (1973). *Ethical principles in the conduct of research with human subjects.* Washington, DC: Author.

Barber, T. X. (1976). *Pitfalls in human research: Ten pivotal points.* New York: Pergamon.

Becker, H. (1986). *Writing for social scientists.* Chicago: University of Chicago Press.

Huff, D. (1954). *How to lie with statistics.* New York: Norton.

Jung, J. (1971). *The experimenter's dilemma.* New York: Harper & Row.

Kazdin, A. E. (1980). *Research design in clini-

cal psychology. New York: Harper & Row.

Kazdin, A. E. (1981). Drawing valid inferences from case studies. *Journal of Consulting and Clinical Psychology, 49,* 183–192.

Maser, J. D., & Seligman, M. E. P. (1977). *Psychopathology: Experimental models.* San Francisco: Freeman.

Runyan, W. M. (1984). *Life histories and psychobiography: Explorations in theory and method.* New York: Oxford.

Smith, M. L., & Glass, G. V. (1977). Meta-analysis of psychotherapy outcome studies. *American Psychologist, 32,* 752–760.

TERM-PAPER TOPICS

1. Describe the pros and cons of experimentation as a means to understanding complex human behavior. What are the implications of these arguments for the use of experiments in understanding abnormality?

2. Describe the pros and cons of laboratory models of psychopathology. When are models most useful? When are they least useful?

3. Is the relationship between laboratory research and therapy techniques based on this research really as straightforward as the textbook suggests? Evaluate the evidence with respect to a particular therapy technique. Take a stand, and defend it.

EXERCISES

Exercise One—Find the Confound

In this exercise, you will criticize the research designs of hypothetical investigations.

In a few sentences describe what is wrong with the conclusion of the researcher in each of the following:

1. A psychology teacher hypothesized that students who know little in the first place will learn more effectively than students who known a great deal to begin with. Thus, he administered to his students the identical multiple-choice test at the beginning and end of a course. He subtracted the number correct at the beginning from the number correct at the end to obtain a measure of improvement. This measure was negatively correlated with the number of correct answers on the first test. The instructor concluded that his hypothesis was therefore correct.

2. A hospital director approached her hospital board with a request to continue a program of deep muscle massage for depressed patients. She provided statistics showing that among patients who had been massaged within the preceding five years, 20 percent were able to leave the hospital within one month after the massage and another 50 percent were able to leave within two months.

3. A group of elementary school children first learned a list of ten five-letter words and then a list of ten two-digit numbers. Two days later, they were asked to recall as many words and numbers as they could. The mean number of words recalled was 5.3, while the mean number of numbers was 1.2. It was concluded that numbers are more difficult to recall than words.

4. A study used a large number of clinical tests and interviews to show that 37 of 112 patients given a new drug for hypertension exhibited inappropriate aggressiveness. It was, therefore, concluded that the drug should be discontinued because of its dangerous effect on behavior.

5. In a follow-up of patients treated with a new form of psychotherapy, it was found that 68 percent of the individuals treated with the new approach reported that they were satisfied with its effects. In contrast, 43 percent of the patients in a comparison group given traditional psychotherapy by the same therapists reported satisfaction. The researchers concluded that the new psychotherapy approach was an improvement over the traditional approach.

Exercise Two—Designing Psychological Research

Many questions of interest to psychologists can be approached with a variety of research strategies. In this exercise, you will demonstrate this idea to yourself.

For each of the following questions, design a brief experiment, correlational study, experiment of nature, and laboratory model to answer it.

1. Is depression the result of insufficient positive reinforcement?
2. Can phobias result from classical conditioning?
3. What are the characteristics of a good psychotherapist?
4. Does drug use cause psychopathology, or does psychopathology cause drug use?
5. Does loneliness lead to overeating?

Exercise Three—The Human Side of Research

The purpose of this exercise is to take you behind the scenes of psychological research by asking you to read some autobiographies by famous psychologists.

These volumes contain autobiographies by important researchers:

Boring, E. G., & Lindzey, G. (Eds.). (1967). *A history of psychology in autobiography* (Vol. 5). New York: Appleton-Century-Crofts.

Boring, E. G., Werner, H., Yerkes, R. M., & Langfeld, H. S. (Eds.). (1952). *A history of psychology in autobiography* (Vol. 4). Worcester, MA: Clark University Press.

Lindzey, G. (Ed.). (1974). *A history of psychology in autobiography* (Vol. 6). Englewood Cliffs, NJ: Prentice-Hall.

Murchinson, C. (Ed.). (1930–1936). *A history of psychology in autobiography* (3 vols.). Worcester, MA: Clark University Press.

As you read a given autobiography, contrast the life depicted with the common stereotype of the detached and eccentric scientist.

Exercise Four—Research by Psychologists and Others

In this exercise, you will compare and contrast the goals and methods of research by psychologists with the goals and methods of research by other scientists.

Arrange for your class a panel discussion by a research psychologist, biologist, chemist, physicist, and anthropologist. Have these scientists discuss research in their respective fields. What is common? What is different?

CHAPTER 7

Psychological Assessment and Classification

CHAPTER OVERVIEW

This chapter explains how psychologists diagnose abnormality. Diagnosis—or classification—is unavoidable in treating disorders, and when done well, it serves several purposes: (a) communication shorthand; (b) treatment recommendation; (c) etiology suggestion; and (d) scientific investigation. Psychologists use a variety of assessment devices in diagnosis, and these devices should be reliable (giving the same information on different occasions) and valid (serving the purpose intended).

A number of assessment techniques are described in this chapter, among them clinical interviews, psychological tests (inventories, projective tests, and intelligence tests), behavioral assessments, and psychophysiological assessments.

The diagnostic system in widest current use is the *Diagnostic and Statistical Manual of Mental Disorders,* Third Edition, Revised, of the American Psychiatric Association, DSM-III-R. This system is described along with its strengths and weaknesses. The chapter ends with a discussion of factors that may bias diagnosis.

ESSENTIAL TERMS

behavioral assessment	record of the behaviors and thoughts targeted for change in therapy
clinical interview	assessment technique in which a clinical psychologist or psychiatrist obtains information by face-to-face talking with a patient
structured interview	clinical interview in which questions are predetermined
unstructured interview	flexible clinical interview in which questions are not predetermined
diagnosis	classification into categories of disorder based on information about a pattern of symptoms for purposes of efficient communication, selection of treatment, suggestion of etiology, and/or facilitation of scientific investigation
clinical diagnosis	diagnosis given to patient in therapy
research diagnosis	diagnosis given to subject in scientific research

Diagnostic and Statistical Manual of Mental Disorders (DSM)	diagnostic system adopted by the American Psychiatric Association in 1952
Diagnostic and Statistical Manual of Mental Disorders, Second Edition (DSM-II)	revision of DSM adopted by the American Psychiatric Association in 1968
Diagnostic and Statistical Manual of Mental Disorders, Third Edition (DSM-III)	revision of DSM-II adopted by the American Psychiatric Association in 1980
Diagnostic and Statistical Manual of Mental Disorders, Third Edition, Revised (DSM-III-R)	revision of DSM-III adopted by the American Psychiatric Association in 1987, currently in use
Diagnostic Interview Schedule (DIS)	structured diagnostic interview that can be used by lay interviewers as well as professionals
electromyograph (EMG)	psychophysiological assessment instrument for measuring muscle contractions
functional analysis	behavioral assessment that includes a record of stimuli presumed to increase or decrease behaviors of interest
genital plethysmograph	psychophysiological assessment instrument for measuring sexual excitement
illusory correlation	in psychological tests, the false belief that certain responses indicate certain disorders
intelligence quotient (IQ)	score from Wechsler intelligence tests
performance IQ	score reflecting nonverbal skills, such as design comprehension, ability to associate symbols with numbers
verbal IQ	score reflecting verbal skills, such as vocabulary, verbal comprehension, general information
intelligence test	psychological test that samples behaviors that predict success in school; used by clinicians to assess mental retardation and brain damage
interview schedule	protocol for a structured clinical interview
Kappa	statistic for estimating agreement between two interviews that corrects for chance
mental disorder	behavioral or psychological pattern that causes an individual distress or disables the individual in one or more significant areas of functioning, distinct from social deviance
Minnesota Multiphasic Personality Inventory (MMPI)	widely used personality inventory
personality inventory	psychological test in written form that inquires about conscious experiences and feelings; e.g., MMPI
projective test	psychological test that presents individuals with ambiguous stimuli to which they respond; so named because respondents are thought to project their unconscious conflicts on to the ambiguous stimuli; e.g., Rorschach
psychological test	standardized assessment technique, usually highly reliable

psychophysiological assessment	psychological testing that measures physiological characteristics
Q-sort	psychological test used to assess clients' perceptions of their real and ideal selves; cards containing adjectives are sorted into piles ranging from "unlike me" to "like me" in accord with their perceived real self and in accord with their perceived ideal self
reliability	characteristic of an assessment device: capacity to generate the same findings on repeated use
Renard Diagnostic Interview (RDI)	structured diagnostic interview that can be used by lay interviewers as well as professionals
Role Construct Repertory Test (Rep Test)	psychological test used to elicit the ways in which people interpret or construct experience; patients are presented with names of three objects, usually people, and asked to describe the ways in which two are alike and different from the third
Rorschach test	projective test consisting of ten bilaterally symmetric inkblots; patients are asked to describe everything each inkblot resembles
Schedule for Affective Disorders and Schizophrenia (SADS)	structured interview used for diagnosing affective and schizophrenic disorders
Thematic Apperception Test (TAT)	projective test consisting of a series of ambiguous pictures; patients are asked to look at each picture and make up a story about it
validity	characteristic of an assessment device: utility for intended purposes
descriptive validity	ability of an assessment device to differentiate patients in one category from those in another
predictive validity	ability of an assessment device to predict the course and outcome of treatment
Wechsler Adult Intelligence Scale—Revised (WAIS-R)	intelligence test for adults
Wechsler Intelligence Scale for Children—Revised (WISC-R)	intelligence test for children
Wechsler Preschool and Primary Scale of Intelligence (WPPSI)	intelligence test for young children

SAMPLE EXAM

1. An assessment device generates the same findings with repeated use. It is, therefore,
   a. reliable.
   b. valid.
   c. both reliable and valid.
   d. neither reliable nor valid.

2. An assessment device proves useful for the purpose intended. It is, therefore,
   a. reliable.
   b. valid.
   c. both reliable and valid.
   d. neither reliable nor valid.

3. In general, the reliability of an assessment device used in clinical diagnosis
   a. should be as high as the reliability of an assessment device used in research.
   b. should be higher than the reliability of an assessment device used in research.
   c. should be lower than the reliability of an assessment device used in research.
   d. is not as important as its validity.

4. In a clinical interview, information is obtained from
   a. what people say.
   b. how people say what they say.
   c. body posture.
   d. all of the above.

5. An interview schedule is
   a. a list of daily appointments for a clinical psychologist.
   b. a list of possible diagnoses to be ascertained during an interview.
   c. a list of questions to be asked during an interview.
   d. a list of techniques for increasing the flexibility of an interview.

6. All of the following are strengths of an unstructured interview except
   a. reliability.
   b. spontaneity.
   c. flexibility.
   d. sensitivity.

7. Kappa is used to estimate
   a. inter-judge reliability.
   b. inter-judge validity.
   c. intra-judge reliability.
   d. intra-judge validity.

8. Which does not belong?
   a. DIS
   b. MMPI
   c. RDI
   d. SADS

9. Which does not have computer scoring?
   a. DIS
   b. MMPI
   c. RDI
   d. SADS

10. In general, compared to interviews, psychological tests are
    a. more valid.
    b. less valid.
    c. more reliable.
    d. less reliable.

11. Which is an example of a personality inventory?
    a. MMPI
    b. SNAFU
    c. SADS
    d. WAIS-R

12. If you were asked by a psychologist to put cards into piles, you would be taking a
    a. WAIS-R.
    b. Q-sort.
    c. Rep Test.
    d. SADS.

13. The MMPI was developed by
    a. writing questions that operationalized DSM-III-R categories.
    b. seeing how people with known characteristics responded to questions.
    c. choosing statements reported verbatim in Freud's case histories.
    d. borrowing questions from WAIS-R.

14. The validity scales of the MMPI
    a. ascertain the reliability of the test.
    b. distract the respondent from the true purpose.
    c. contain items that are not scored.
    d. check for distortions.

15. If you were asked by a psychologist to compare and contrast people you know, you would be taking a
    a. WAIS-R.
    b. Q-sort.
    c. Rep Test.
    d. SADS.

16. The Q-sort tends to be used by psychologists who favor the
    a. biomedical model.
    b. psychodynamic model.
    c. behavioral model.
    d. cognitive model.
    e. existential model.

17. The Rep Test measures
    a. social roles.
    b. intelligence.
    c. personal constructs.
    d. conflicts.

18. Projective tests are used by psychologists who favor the
    a. biomedical model.
    b. psychodynamic model.
    c. behavioral model.
    d. cognitive model.
    e. existential model.

19. If a psychologist asked you to look at inkblots, you would be taking a
    a. TAT.
    b. BDI.
    c. Rorschach.
    d. Rep Test.

20. Why are projective tests called projective tests?
    a. They are administered on 35-mm slides.
    b. The psychologist uses her imagination to score them.
    c. The respondent is thought to reveal his unconscious conflicts.
    d. They ask about future events.

21. The Rorschach inkblots are all
    a. black.
    b. multicolored.
    c. round.
    d. symmetric.

22. Which one of the following is *not* scored from the Rorschach?
    a. what is seen
    b. where it is seen
    c. how common the response is
    d. the order of the cards

23. Interpretation of the Rorschach is plagued by difficulties with
    a. reliability.
    b. validity.
    c. distortion.
    d. literacy.

24. Rorschach interpretations may be distorted by
    a. negative correlations.
    b. zero correlations.
    c. nonsignificant correlations.
    d. illusory correlations.

25. If a psychologist asked you to tell a story about a fuzzy picture, you would be taking a
    a. TAT.
    b. WPPSI.
    c. SADS.
    d. GRE.

26. The TAT has been frequently used to measure
    a. intelligence.
    b. motives.
    c. attributions.
    d. hallucinations.

27. The TAT is used by psychologists who favor the
    a. biomedical model.
    b. psychodynamic model.
    c. behavioral model.
    d. cognitive model.
    e. existential model.

28. Intelligence tests tend to be
    a. reliable.
    b. valid.
    c. reliable and valid.
    d. reliable but not valid.

29. Intelligence tests are most useful for predicting success at
    a. a profession.
    b. school.
    c. interpersonal relations.
    d. telling jokes.

30. Clinical psychologists sometimes use intelligence tests to assess
    a. sexual conflicts.
    b. brain damage.
    c. norepinephrine depletion.
    d. creativity.

31. If you wished to give an intelligence test to a twenty-five-year-old man, you would administer a
    a. WAIS-R.
    b. WISC-R.
    c. WPPSI.
    d. WHAT.

32. If you wished to give an intelligence test to a ten-year-old boy, you would administer a
    a. WAIS-R.
    b. WISC-R.
    c. WPPSI.
    d. WHAT.

33. If you wished to give an intelligence test to a three-year-old girl, you would administer a
    a. WAIS-R.
    b. WISC-R.
    c. WPPSI.
    d. WHAT.

34. Behavioral assessment tends to be used by psychologists who favor the
    a. biomedical model.
    b. psychodynamic model.
    c. behavioral model.
    d. cognitive model.
    e. existential model.

35. Functional analysis is to behavioral assessment as what is to operant?
    a. instincts
    b. personal constructs
    c. rewards and punishments
    d. discriminative stimuli

36. Psychophysiological assessment has been used to assess all of the following problems except
    a. anxiety.
    b. sexual disorder.
    c. schizophrenia.
    d. headaches.

37. If a psychologist wished to measure contractions of your muscles, she might employ a
    a. EKG.
    b. EMG.
    c. EEG.
    d. EFG.

38. An assessment device that is different for men and women is
    a. Rorschach.
    b. Q-sort.
    c. plethysmograph.
    d. WAIS-R.

39. Which one of the following is *not* a reason to make a diagnosis?
    a. Diagnosis aids communication.
    b. Diagnosis guides treatments.
    c. Diagnosis suggests etiology.
    d. Diagnosis increases vigilance.

40. All of the following are diagnostic schemes except
    a. *The Witches' Hammer.*
    b. DSM.
    c. DSM-II.
    d. Aesop's fables.

41. Who does not belong?
    a. Pinel
    b. Peterson
    c. Kraepelin
    d. Kretchmer

42. DSM-III-R improves on previous diagnostic schemes because it
    a. is contemporary.
    b. provides precise criteria.
    c. specifies necessary and sufficient conditions for mental disorders.
    d. recommends preferred treatments.

43. Mental disorder is not the same as
    a. mental illness.
    b. emotional disturbance.
    c. social deviance.
    d. behavioral disability.

44. DSM-III-R describes mental disorders along how many dimensions?
    a. two
    b. three
    c. five
    d. seven

45. Which one of the following is *not* a strength of DSM-III-R?
    a. More diagnoses are possible.
    b. Reliability has been ascertained.
    c. Reliability is acceptably high.
    d. It aids in planning treatment.

46. Reliability studies of DSM-III are criticized for all these reasons except
    a. Axis II disorders are more reliable than Axis I diagnoses.
    b. judges are not always independent.
    c. reliabilities are reported for clusters of diagnoses only.
    d. all of these are criticisms.

47. DSM-III-R has good
    a. descriptive validity.
    b. outcome validity.
    c. both *a* and *b*.
    d. neither *a* nor *b*.

48. All of these conditions bias diagnosis except
    a. context.
    b. reliability.
    c. expectation.
    d. source credibility.

49. Patients in mental hospitals tend to
    a. engage in writing behavior.
    b. hear voices.
    c. be regarded as abnormal.
    d. be seen as malingering.

50. Psychological diagnosis is plagued by all of these except
    a. suspect reliability.
    b. suspect validity.
    c. bias.
    d. lack of treatments.

51. On the whole, psychological diagnosis is
    a. useless.
    b. unavoidable.
    c. accurate.
    d. simple.

Answer Key for Sample Exam

1.	a	(p. 157)	11.	a	(p. 162)
2.	b	(p. 157)	12.	b	(p. 165)
3.	b	(p. 158)	13.	b	(p. 162)
4.	d	(p. 159)	14.	d	(p. 163)
5.	c	(p. 160)	15.	c	(p. 165)
6.	a	(p. 160)	16.	e	(p. 165)
7.	a	(p. 159)	17.	c	(p. 165)
8.	b	(p. 161)	18.	b	(p. 166)
9.	d	(p. 161)	19.	c	(p. 166)
10.	c	(p. 162)	20.	c	(p. 166)

21. d (p. 166)	29. b (p. 170)	37. b (p. 173)	45. c (p. 178)
22. d (p. 167)	30. b (p. 170)	38. c (p. 173)	46. a (p. 178)
23. b (p. 168)	31. a (p. 169)	39. d (p. 174)	47. d (p. 180)
24. d (p. 168)	32. b (p. 169)	40. d (p. 175)	48. b (p. 183)
25. a (p. 168)	33. c (p. 169)	41. b (p. 175)	49. c (p. 181)
26. b (p. 169)	34. c (p. 171)	42. b (p. 176)	50. d (p. 184)
27. b (p. 169)	35. c (p. 171)	43. c (p. 176)	51. b (p. 184)
28. c (p. 169)	36. c (p. 171)	44. c (p. 177)	

SELF-TEST

1. Without _____ , science is impossible.

2. Classification of psychological disorders is also called _____ .

3. If an assessment device gives the same results on repeated occasions, it is _____ .

4. If an assessment device serves its stated purpose, it is _____ .

5. How reliable an assessment device should be depends partly on the consequences of _____ .

6. The favorite assessment technique of clinicians is the _____ .

7. The Schedule for Affective Disorders and Schizophrenia (SADS) is a _____ interview.

8. Advantages of personality inventories include _____ and the _____ with which they can be administered.

9. The most commonly used personality inventory is the _____ ; its results are presented in terms of a _____ .

10. If a psychologist wished to assess a client's perceptions of his real self and his ideal self, she could use the _____ .

11. To assess how a client interprets significant events, a psychologist can use the _____ .

12. Psychodynamic clinicians tend to favor _____ tests to measure _____ conflicts; two of the most common of these tests are the _____ and the _____ .

13. Interpretations of the Rorschach may be distorted by _____ correlations.

14. When a client takes the TAT, she is asked to _____ .

15. The most reliable and valid psychological tests are _____ .

16. The Wechsler test for adults is the _____ ; for children it is the _____ ; and for preschoolers it is the _____ .

17. Wechsler tests provide two scores, the _____ IQ and the _____ IQ.

18. Intelligence tests were originally developed to distinguish _____ from _____ ; psychologists may also use these tests to diagnose _____ and _____ .

19. Psychologists who favor the behavioral model tend to use _____ assessment, which usually is done in conjunction with _____ .

20. The electromyograph and the plethysmograph are used in _____ assessment.

21. Reasons for diagnosis include _____, _____, _____, and _____ .

22. Diagnosis of psychological disorders is modeled on the example of _____ classification.

23. The first comprehensive system of classifying psychological disorders was created by _____; he based diagnosis on _____ .

24. The current system of diagnosis endorsed by the American Psychiatric Association is _____ .

25. DSM-III-R attempts to improve DSM-II by making the criteria for diagnosis more _____ .

26. DSM-III-R diagnoses employ _____ axes.

27. According to DSM-III-R, mental disorders should be distinguished from _____ .

28. The reliabilities of DSM-III-R diagnoses are _____ than the reliabilities of DSM-II.

29. The reliability and validity of DSM-III-R diagnoses are an _____ .

30. Conditions that may bias diagnosis include _____, _____, and _____ .

31. The reliability of research diagnoses may be _____ than the reliability of clinical diagnoses. The validity of research diagnoses may be _____ than the validity of clinical diagnoses.

Answer Key for Self-Test

1. classification
2. diagnosis
3. reliable
4. valid
5. errors
6. clinical interview
7. structured
8. reliability; efficiency
9. MMPI; profile
10. Q-sort
11. Rep Test
12. projective; unconscious; Rorschach; TAT
13. illusory
14. tell a story
15. intelligence test
16. WAISR; WISCR; WPPSI
17. verbal; performance

18. bright students; dull students; mental retardation; brain damage
19. behavioral; treatment
20. psychophysiological
21. communication shorthand; treatment recommendation; etiology suggestion; scientific investigation
22. biological
23. Emil Kraepelin; symptoms
24. DSM-III-R
25. precise
26. five
27. social deviance
28. higher
29. open question
30. context; expectation; source credibility
31. less; less

TYING IT TOGETHER

Diagnostic approaches reflect models of abnormality. Each approach surveyed in Chapters 3 through 5 is associated with characteristic assessment techniques. Thus, the biomedical approach (Chapter 3) gives rise to psychophysiological assessment (see also Chapter 17), the psychodynamic approach to projective tests (Chapter 4), the behavioral approach (Chapter 5) to functional analysis, and the cognitive approach (Chapter 5) to the Rep Test. Even the supernatural approach (Chapter 2) had an associated diagnostic strategy presented in *The Witches' Hammer*.

Regardless of the type of assessment, the fuzzy nature of abnormality must be remembered. The family resemblance idea puts upper limits on the reliability and validity of an assessment device that measures a single sign of abnormality (Chapter 1). To the degree that this idea is neglected, problems in research (Chapter 6) and legal decisions (Chapter 18) may seem more puzzling than they may otherwise.

As you read the remaining chapters, keep in mind how the various assessment devices described in Chapter 7 can be used to make a diagnosis (Chapter 8 through 17), to justify involuntary commitment (Chapter 18), and to assess the effectiveness of psychotherapy (Chapter 19). Remember the less-than-perfect reliability and validity of any assessment device.

DSM-III-R attempts to make assessment easier. It proposes behavioral criteria (see Chapter 5) for most disorders, and it rarely proposes necessary and sufficient conditions (see Chapter 1) for diagnosis. Again, as you read the remaining chapters, keep in mind the clarity of DSM-III-R criteria for a given diagnosis. In some cases, such as phobias (Chapter 8), diagnosis is simple. In other cases, such as personality disorders (Chapter 15), diagnosis is more complicated and may ultimately prove nonviable. As illustrated in Chapter 2, conceptions of abnormality have changed over the years. Perhaps the future will see further change in diagnostic categories in response to difficulties in reliable and valid diagnoses.

FURTHER READINGS

Chapman, L. J., & Chapman, J. P. (1969). Illusory correlation as an obstacle to the use of valid psychodiagnostic signs. *Journal of Abnormal Psychology, 74*, 271–287.

McLemore, C. W., & Benjamin, L. S. (1979). Whatever happened to interpersonal diagnosis? A psychosocial alternative to DSM-III. *American Psychologist, 34*, 17–34.

Persons, J. B. (1986). The advantages of studying psychological phenomena rather than psychiatric diagnoses. *American Psychologist, 41,* 1252–1260.

Schact, T., & Nathan, P. E. (1977). But is it good for psychologists? Appraisal and status of DSM-III. *American Psychologist, 32,* 1017–1025.

Singerman, B. (1981). DSM-III: Historical antecedents and present significance. *Journal of Clinical Psychiatry, 42,* 409–410.

Zigler, E., & Phillips, L. (1961). Psychiatric diagnosis: A critique. *Journal of Abnormal and Social Psychology, 63,* 607–618.

TERM-PAPER TOPICS

1. The use of intelligence tests in the school system is controversial, yet this is where they seem to be most valid. How are intelligence tests used in diagnosis of abnormality? What is controversial about this use?

2. Describe the evidence for the reliability and validity of a particular projective test.

3. How has illusory correlation been investigated? Do these investigations convince you that psychological testing should be viewed with skepticism?

4. Review the popular approaches to interviewing. Identify which model of abnormality is most compatible with which interviewing approach.

EXERCISES

Exercise One—Invalidity of Trait Description

In this exercise, you will see how "personality" sketches that describe people in terms of their traits may not capture their unique selves as well as you may think.

Ask a group of five or six people who know each other well to describe each other in terms of his or her striking traits. Remove the names from these descriptions, and show them to all the group members. Ask them to identify who has been described. You may find that correct identification is no better than chance.

Forer, B. R. (1949). The fallacy of personal validation: A classroom demonstration of gullibility. *Journal of Abnormal and Social Psychology, 44,* 118–123.

Mischel, W. (1968). *Personality and assessment.* New York: Wiley.

Rodin, M. J. (1972). The informativeness of trait descriptions. *Journal of Personality and Social Psychology, 21,* 341–344.

Exercise Two—Validity of Behavior Description

The purpose of this exercise is to assess the validity of behavioral assessment compared to "personality" assessment.

Repeat Exercise One, but this time ask the individuals to describe each other in terms of characteristic actions and behaviors. It may be that correct identification is greatly increased by the use of descriptions based on discrete and observable characteristics.

What do you conclude about behavioral assessment versus more traditional "personality" assessment?

Exercise Three—Psychological Assessment

The purpose of this exercise is to gain some first-hand knowledge about the use of psychological tests.

Arrange a class presentation by a clinical psychologist about his or her use of psychological assessment. What tests are used by this psychologist? What tests are not used? Does the psychologist adhere to a given model of abnormality?

Exercise Four—Expectations and Assessment

The textbook describes how expectations can bias assessment. In this exercise, you will demonstrate this.

Introduce someone to several of your friends. To some of your friends, mention that this individual has just returned from a year abroad in which he traveled widely. To your other friends, mention that the individual has just returned from a year abroad in which he stayed in a mental hospital. Pay attention to how the individual is treated during the ensuing conversation. What is said about him after he leaves?

Before I took my previous job teaching, I worked as a psychologist on an inpatient psychiatric ward. When I arrived in Blacksburg and began to meet people, I at first would say matter-of-factly, "Oh, I just spent two years on a psychiatric ward, and now it's interesting to be in such a different place." Strange reactions always ensued, and it finally occurred to me that my new acquaintances had not heard me say what I intended to say.

Farina, A., Holland, C. H., & Ring, K. (1966). The role of stigma and set in interpersonal attraction. *Journal of Abnormal Psychology, 71,* 421–428.

Langer, E. J., & Abelson, R. P. (1974). A patient by any other name . . . : Clinician group difference in labelling bias. *Journal of Consulting and Clinical Psychology, 42,* 4–9.

CHAPTER 8

Fear and Phobia:
Anxiety Felt

CHAPTER OVERVIEW

This is the first of ten chapters that describe the major types of abnormality. The subject of this chapter is disorders in which fear or anxiety is consciously experienced. Subsequent chapters describe disorders in which anxiety is not consciously experienced but is inferred.

Disorders in which anxiety is consciously experienced are of two major types: fear disorders (phobias and post-traumatic stress disorders) and anxiety disorders (panic disorders and generalized anxiety disorders). A phobia involves fear of an object out of all proportion to the actual danger posed. Post-traumatic stress disorders are reactions to a catastrophic experience in which the individual suffers anxiety, depression, numbness, and reliving of the catastrophe. In a panic disorder, an individual is suddenly overwhelmed by apprehension and terror that are unattached to any specific object in the environment. Generalized anxiety disorders are the chronic experience of anxiety.

The chapter describes the four components of fear: (a) cognitive, (b) somatic, (c) emotional, and (d) behavioral. The components of anxiety are the same except for cognitive component. In fear expectation of harm is associated with a specific danger, but in anxiety expectation of harm is general.

Phobias are the best understood of these disorders and are described in some detail in this chapter. The psychodynamic account and the behavioral account of phobias are explained. When the idea of prepared classical conditioning is introduced, the behavioral model better handles the evidence regarding phobias than does the psychodynamic model. Successful therapies for phobias are based on the behavioral model: systematic desensitization, flooding, and modeling.

The other fear and anxiety disorders are briefly described.

ESSENTIAL TERMS

adrenal glands	glands that secrete hormones involved in emergency reaction
adrenergic system	physiological system using adrenaline and noradrenaline as chemical messengers to produce an emergency reaction; e.g., SNS
agoraphobia	phobia characterized by fear of places of assembly and open spaces

anxiety

emotion involving expectation of diffuse danger, physiological emergency reaction, and fight-or-flight behavior (cf. fear)

state anxiety

transient anxiety

trait anxiety

anxiety displayed across time and situation

anxiety disorder

disorder in which no specific object is feared (cf. fear disorder)

autonomic nervous system (ANS)

part of the nervous system that controls internal organs composed of sympathetic and parasympathetic nervous systems

avoidance responding

flight response in which a harmful event is fled from before it is encountered

central nervous system (CNS)

brain and spinal cord

cholinergic system

physiological system using acetycholine as a chemical messenger to produce the relaxation reaction; e.g., PNS

counterconditioning

therapy technique for fear disorders in which responses that are incompatible with fear are caused to occur at the same time as the fear object; e.g., systematic desensitization

emergency reaction

physiological response to danger; increased heart beat, breathing, sweating; contraction of spleen; blood-content change

escape responding

flight response in which a harmful event actually occurs and then is fled from

fear

emotion involving expectation of specific harm, physiological emergency reaction, and fight-or-flight behavior (cf. anxiety)

fear disorder

disorder characterized by dread of specific objects (cf. anxiety disorder)

flooding

therapy technique for fear disorders in which stimuli that elicit fear are repeatedly encountered (*see* Chapter 5, "Essential Terms")

generalized anxiety disorder

disorder characterized by chronic anxiety

hypothalamus

brain structure influencing eating, drinking, and sexual behavior, and regulating fundamental bodily processes

incidence

rate of new cases of a disorder in a given time period (cf. prevalence)

modeling

therapy technique for fear disorders in which client watches someone who is not fearful perform a behavior of which the client is not capable

nosophobia

phobia of a specific illness or injury; not the same as hypochondria (*see* Chapter 4, "Essential Terms"), which is anxiety about a variety of illnesses

panic disorder

disorder characterized by recurrent attacks of sudden and intense anxiety

parasympathetic nervous system (PNS)	part of the autonomic nervous system responsible for producing the relaxation response, which counteracts the emergency reaction
phobia	disorder characterized by fear of an object out of all proportion to the reality of danger
post-traumatic stress disorder	following a catastrophic event, a disorder characterized by numbness, reliving of event, and symptoms of anxiety
prepared classical conditioning	rapidly acquired Pavlovian conditioning thought to be predisposed by natural selection
prevalence	percentage of population having a disorder at any given time (cf. incidence)
rape trauma syndrome	post-traumatic stress disorder following rape, including acute (disorganization) and long-term (reorganization) reactions
social phobia	phobia characterized by fear of social situations
survival guilt	aspect of post-traumatic stress disorder in which the individual feels guilty for having survived a traumatic event while others did not
sympathetic nervous system (SNS)	part of the autonomic nervous system responsible for producing emergency reaction
systematic desensitization	therapy technique for fear disorder in which stimuli that elicit fear are paired with relaxation or other pleasant experiences (*see* Chapter 5, "Essential Terms)

SAMPLE EXAM

1. All of these are neuroses in which anxiety is experienced except
   a. phobia.
   b. hysteria.
   c. post-traumatic stress disorder.
   d. panic disorder.

2. Anxiety disorders are broken into what two categories?
   a. phobia and schizophrenia
   b. mild and severe
   c. panic disorder and generalized anxiety disorder
   d. obsessive-compulsive disorder and phobia

3. The fear disorders include
   a. phobias and post-traumatic stress disorders.
   b. hysteria and obsessive-compulsive disorders.
   c. factitious disorders and paranoia.
   d. panic disorders and generalized anxiety disorders.

4. All of these are disorders in which anxiety is *not* experienced except
   a. amnesia.
   b. fugue.
   c. phobia.
   d. multiple personality.

5. The most important element of fear is
   a. cognitive.
   b. somatic.
   c. emotional.
   d. behavioral.
   e. none of the above.

6. What is the cognitive component of fear?
   a. appraisal
   b. expectation
   c. attribution
   d. belief

7. All of the following are reactions to fear except
   a. flushed skin.
   b. goosebumps.
   c. sweat.
   d. tense muscles.

8. What is the emergency reaction?
   a. flight or fight response
   b. body's reaction after danger has passed
   c. response to sudden infection
   d. resolution of the approach-avoidance conflict

9. The emergency reaction follows which order?
   a. danger to SNS to hypothalamus to cortex
   b. danger to cortex to hypothalamus to SNS
   c. danger to cortex to SNS to hypothalamus
   d. danger to hypothalamus to cortex to SNS

10. The parasympathetic nervous system is to the sympathetic nervous system as what is to the emergency reaction?
    a. vigilance
    b. excitation
    c. exhaustion
    d. relaxation

11. The SNS is to the PNS as
    a. cholinergic is to adrenergic.
    b. behavioral is to cognitive.
    c. adrenergic is to cholinergic.
    d. cognitive is to behavioral.

12. What is the difference between escape responding and avoidance responding?
    a. Escape responding occurs frequently, while avoidance responding does not.
    b. Escape responding is easily learned, while avoidance responding is not.
    c. Escape responding is easily extinguished, while avoidance responding is not.
    d. Escape responding occurs when an event is encountered, while avoidance responding does not.

13. Which element of abnormality do phobias have?
    a. suffering
    b. maladaptiveness
    c. observer discomfort
    d. all of the above

14. All of the following are common phobias except
    a. agoraphobia.
    b. anthophobia.
    c. social phobia.
    d. animal phobia.

15. At any given time, 20 percent of the population has a certain disorder. Every year, 1 percent of the population acquires this disorder. What is its prevalence?
    a. 20 percent
    b. 1 percent per year
    c. 19 percent
    d. 21 percent

16. In the above question, what is the incidence of the disorder?
    a. 20 percent
    b. 1 percent per year
    c. 19 percent
    d. 21 percent

17. What is the most common phobia?
    a. animal phobia
    b. claustrophobia
    c. agoraphobia
    d. nosophobia

18. Agoraphobics are afraid of all of the following except
    a. open spaces.
    b. traveling.
    c. the dark.
    d. streets.

19. Most agoraphobics are
    a. children.
    b. adolescents.
    c. men.
    d. women.

20. Social phobics are afraid of all of the following except
    a. crowds.
    b. the dark.
    c. being seen.
    d. speaking.

21. Animal phobias begin during
    a. early childhood.
    b. puberty.
    c. early adulthood.
    d. middle age.

22. Which is *not* true about animal phobics?
    a. Most are women.
    b. Most outgrow their phobia.
    c. Most have other problems.
    d. Most can point to a precipitating trauma.

23. Which one of the following is *not* true about nosophobics?
    a. Most are healthy.
    b. Most are not hypochondriacs.
    c. Most are women.
    d. Most have other problems.

24. According to Freud, the development of a phobia involves all but

a. castration fear.
b. displacement.
c. sublimation.
d. anxiety.

25. According to Freud, the phobic object is a
    a. real danger.
    b. symbol.
    c. non sequitur.
    d. fantasy.

26. According to Freud, phobias are cured through
    a. desensitization.
    b. flooding.
    c. insight.
    d. tricyclics.

27. Little Hans was afraid of
    a. dogs.
    b. homosexuals.
    c. horses.
    d. lightning.

28. Which one of the following is *not* true about the psychoanalytic account of phobias?
    a. Psychoanalytic therapy does not cure phobias.
    b. There exist better explanations.
    c. It explains only phobias among men.
    d. It is based on loose reasoning.

29. According to the behavioral account, phobias arise by
    a. classical conditioning.
    b. operant conditioning.
    c. modeling.
    d. desensitization.

30. Little Albert was afraid of
    a. horses.
    b. Lucky Strikes.
    c. white rats.
    d. the dark.

31. Little Hans is to Little Albert as
    a. Stevie Wonder is to Little Stephen.
    b. psychoanalysis is to behaviorism.
    c. Little Mo is to Moses Malone.
    d. cognitive theory is to psychoanalysis.

32. The Little Albert investigation was an early example of
    a. clinical case history.
    b. experimental study.
    c. correlational study.
    d. experiment of nature.
    e. laboratory model of psychopathology.

33. How does the behavioral model account for the persistence of phobias?

a. escape learning
b. avoidance learning
c. modeling
d. it cannot

34. All of these are effective therapies of phobias except
    a. flooding.
    b. insight.
    c. desensitization.
    d. modeling.

35. In desensitization, the phobic object is paired with
    a. drugs.
    b. terror.
    c. relaxation.
    d. social support.

36. The cure rate of specific phobias by systematic desensitization is approximately
    a. 10 percent.
    b. 33 percent.
    c. 50 percent.
    d. 85 percent.

37. Symptom substitution following treatment of phobias by systematic desensitization is predicted by the
    a. biomedical model.
    b. psychodynamic model.
    c. behavioral model.
    d. cognitive model.
    e. existential model.

38. Flooding involves
    a. modeling.
    b. escape responding.
    c. avoidance responding.
    d. extinction.

39. Modeling involves
    a. behavioral change.
    b. cognitive change.
    c. both behavioral and cognitive change.
    d. neither behavioral nor cognitive change.

40. Antidepressant drugs may be used to treat phobics who
    a. have specific fears.
    b. have spontaneous panic attacks.
    c. have illness phobias.
    d. have little insight.

41. Which one of the following is *not* a problem with the behavioral account of phobias?
    a. It fails to explain which therapies prove effective.
    b. It fails to explain the selectivity of phobias.

c. It fails to explain the irrationality of phobias.
d. It fails to explain the lack of a traumatic event for some phobias.

42. Prepared classical conditioning is thought to be "prepared" by
a. learning.
b. evolution.
c. briefing.
d. drugs.

43. Which one of the following is *not* true about prepared classical conditioning?
a. It is involved in taste aversions.
b. It has been demonstrated with people.
c. It is rational.
d. It may be a model of phobias.

44. The prepared-classical-conditioning account does not explain
a. why phobias persist.
b. why phobias occur in some people but not in others.
c. why phobias are irrational.
d. why phobias entail suffering.

45. Post-traumatic stress disorders are characterized by all of the following except
a. numbness.
b. reliving the trauma.
c. loss of contact with reality.
d. anxiety.

46. Survival guilt occurs among those with
a. agoraphobia.
b. nosophobia.
c. post-traumatic stress disorder.
d. panic disorder.

47. The rape trauma syndrome is an example of
a. agoraphobia.
b. nosophobia.
c. post-traumatic stress disorder.
d. panic disorder.

48. The difference between fear disorders and anxiety disorders is that
a. fear disorders are serious, but anxiety disorders are not.
b. fear disorders involve emotions, but anxiety disorders do not.
c. fear disorders involve bodily changes, but anxiety disorders do not.
d. specific objects are feared in fear disorders, but not in anxiety disorders.

49. Fear and anxiety are the same with respect to all of the following components except

a. cognitive.
b. somatic.
c. emotional.
d. behavioral.
e. all of the above.

50. A panic disorder consists of anxiety that is
a. chronic.
b. infrequent.
c. spontaneous.
d. rational.

51. Recent explanations of panic disorders emphasize _____ factors.
a. biological
b. cognitive
c. both
d. neither

52. Cognitive explanations of panic disorders point to _____ bodily sensations.
a. absence of
b. exaggerated
c. fluctuating
d. misinterpreted

53. A generalized anxiety disorder consists of anxiety that is
a. chronic.
b. infrequent.
c. spontaneous.
d. rational.

54. Panic disorder is to generalized anxiety disorder as
a. Freud is to Beck.
b. mind is to body.
c. state is to trait.
d. Freud is to Jung.

Answer Key for Sample Exam

1.	b	(p. 189)	17.	c	(p. 198)
2.	c	(p. 190)	18.	c	(p. 198)
3.	a	(p. 189)	19.	d	(p. 199)
4.	c	(p. 189)	20.	b	(p. 200)
5.	e	(p. 191)	21.	a	(p. 201)
6.	b	(p. 191)	22.	c	(p. 201)
7.	a	(p. 191)	23.	c	(p. 203)
8.	a	(p. 192)	24.	c	(p. 204)
9.	b	(p. 193)	25.	b	(p. 204)
10.	d	(p. 193)	26.	c	(p. 204)
11.	c	(p. 193)	27.	c	(p. 204)
12.	d	(p. 195)	28.	c	(p. 206)
13.	d	(p. 196)	29.	a	(p. 207)
14.	b	(p. 199)	30.	c	(p. 208)
15.	a	(p. 198)	31.	b	(p. 208)
16.	b	(p. 198)	32.	e	(p. 208)

33. b (p. 208)	39. c (p. 212)	45. c (p. 218)	50. c (p. 228)
34. b (p. 209)	40. b (p. 213)	46. c (p. 220)	51. c (p. 230)
35. c (p. 210)	41. a (p. 215)	47. c (p. 222)	52. d (p. 230)
36. d (p. 211)	42. b (p. 215)	48. d (p. 228)	53. a (p. 231)
37. b (p. 211)	43. c (p. 215)	49. e (p. 228)	54. c (p. 231)
38. d (p. 211)	44. b (p. 217)		

SELF-TEST

1. There are two types of "neuroses"—those in which anxiety is _____ and those in which anxiety is _____ .

2. Fear disorders include _____ and _____ .

3. Anxiety disorders include _____ and _____ .

4. A phobia involves fear of an object; this fear is _____ of the danger represented by the object.

5. The four elements of fear are _____ , _____ , _____ , and _____ .

6. The cognitive component of fear is an expectation of _____ .

7. The internal state that accompanies fear is the _____ ; it prepares the body for _____ or _____ .

8. The chain of command in fear proceeds from the cortex to the _____ to the _____ to the _____ .

9. The autonomic nervous system is composed of the _____ nervous system and the _____ nervous system.

10. The SNS is an _____ system, and the PNS is a _____ system.

11. In _____ responding, a bad event is actually encountered, and in _____ responding, it is not.

12. The percentage of people with a disorder at a given time is _____ , and the rate of new cases in a given time period is _____ .

13. The most common phobias are _____ , social phobias, and specific phobias.

14. The specific phobias include fear of _____ and fear of _____ .

15. The most crippling phobia is _____ , and it tends to occur among _____ .

16. Most animal phobias occur among _____ and _____ .

17. Fear of illness is _____ .

18. Comprehensive theories of phobias have been proposed by the _____ model and by the _____ model.

19. The famous psychoanalytic case in which Freud proposed his theory of phobias was the _____ case.

20. According to Freud, Little Hans was not really afraid of horses. Instead, he was afraid of his _____ .

21. The psychoanalytic account of phobias is _____ .

22. In Pavlovian conditioning terms, the phobic object is a _____ .

23. In their study of _____, Watson and Rayner showed that fear could be learned.

24. The behavioral account of phobias explains their persistence in terms of _____ responding.

25. The three behavioral treatments of phobias are _____ , _____ , and _____ .

26. _____ drugs may be helpful in treating phobias that involve _____ .

27. Problems with the Pavlovian conditioning account of phobias are several. First, phobias are usually _____; second, they are _____; and third, they are not always preceded by _____ .

28. The problems with the Pavlovian conditioning account of phobias are solved by _____ .

29. Prepared classical conditioning is thought to be "prepared" by _____ .

30. The behavioral account of phobias does not explain _____ .

31. In contrast to phobias, the event feared in post-traumatic stress disorders is not _____ .

32. The symptoms of post-traumatic stress disorder are _____ to the world, _____ the trauma, and symptoms of _____ .

33. When an individual feels guilty for surviving a trauma in which others died, he is experiencing _____ .

34. Reactions to rape follow a sequence known as the _____ .

35. Prognosis for post-traumatic stress disorders appears _____ .

36. Unlike fear disorders, anxiety disorders do not involve fear of a _____ object.

37. Panic disorders are more common among _____ .

38. Panic disorders have recently been explained by _____ theorists.

39. In generalized anxiety disorders, anxiety is _____ .

40. Transient anxiety is called _____ anxiety, and chronic anxiety is called _____ anxiety.

Answer Key for Self-Test

1. experienced; inferred
2. phobias; post-traumatic stress disorders
3. panic disorders; generalized anxiety disorders
4. out of proportion to the reality of the danger
5. cognitive; somatic; emotional; behavioral
6. specific impending harm
7. emergency reaction; flight; fight
8. hypothalamus; sympathetic nervous system; adrenal medulla
9. sympathetic; parasympathetic
10. adrenergic; cholinergic
11. escape; avoidance
12. prevalence; incidence
13. agoraphobias
14. animals; illness
15. agoraphobia; women
16. children; women
17. nosophobia
18. psychodynamic; behavioral
19. Little Hans
20. father
21. unsatisfactory
22. CS (conditioned stimulus)
23. Little Albert
24. avoidance
25. systematic desensitization; flooding; modeling
26. Antidepressant; spontaneous panic attacks
27. selective; irrational; trauma
28. prepared classical conditioning
29. evolution
30. who becomes a phobic
31. commonplace
32. numbness; reliving; anxiety
33. survival guilt
34. rape trauma syndrome
35. bleak
36. specific
37. women
38. biological and cognitive
39. chronic
40. state; trait

TYING IT TOGETHER

Freud wrote extensively about neurosis (Chapter 4), and used the term to refer not just to symptoms of a disorder, but also to the presumed underlying process; defense against anxiety. However, research (Chapter 6) and therapy (Chapter 19) suggest that the behavioral account (Chapter 5) of neurosis is more reasonable. Symptoms are regarded as the problem, and they are assumed to arise because they have been learned. Therapy consists of new learning. Laboratory models of psychopathology (Chapter 6), often employing animals, have been fruitful in the study of neurosis.

Fear and anxiety are present in a number of other disorders as well: obsessions (Chapter 9), psychosomatic disorders such as peptic ulcers and hypertension (Chapter 10), sexual dysfunction (Chapter 13), drug abuse (Chapter 14), and childhood disorders (Chapter 16). Not surprisingly, the behaviorally based therapy techniques often prove useful in treating these disorders as well as the fear disorders (Chapter 19). Antisocial personality disorder may involve too little fear and anxiety (Chapter 15). Although neuroses have historically been contrasted with the psychoses, schizophrenia (Chapter 12) often is associated with fear and anxiety. The neuroleptic drugs used to treat schizophrenic symptoms are tranquilizers. Deficits caused by neurological damage (Chapter 17) are exacerbated by anxiety.

Fear and anxiety are often experienced by "normal" people. These emotions are part of the observer discomfort that counts toward a judgment of abnormality (Chapter 1). To the degree that an individual's behavior is unconventional and inexplicable, it will be reacted to with trepidation. Erroneous diagnoses may be made (Chapter 7), and involuntary commitment (Chapter 19) and other extreme measures may be undertaken (see Chapter 2). Some have observed that even research may be distorted if experimental subjects are overly fearful and anxious; subject bias is increased, and demand characteristics are potentiated (Chapter 6).

FURTHER READINGS

Burgess, A. W., & Holmstrom, L. L. (1974). *Rape: Victims of crisis.* Bowie, MD: Brady.

Figley, C. R. (1977). *The American Legion study of psychological adjustment among Vietnam veterans.* Lafayette, IN: Purdue University.

Figley, C. R., & Leventman, S. (1980). *Strangers at home: Vietnam veterans since the war.* New York: Praeger.

Holmstrom, L. L., & Burgess, A. W. (1978). *The victim of rape: Institution reactions.* New York: Wiley.

Laughlin, H. P. (1967). The soterial reactions: Security from an external object choice. In *The neuroses* (pp. 607–638). Washington, DC: Butterworth.

Marks, I. M. (1969). *Fears and phobias.* New York: Academic Press.

Marks, I. M. (1970). Agoraphobic syndrome (phobic anxiety state). *Archives of General Psychiatry, 23,* 538–553.

Tuma, A. H., & Maser, J. D. (1985). *Anxiety and the anxiety disorders.* Hillsdale, NJ: Erlbaum.

TERM-PAPER TOPICS

1. What is the evidence against the behavioral account of phobias? (Include evidence against the preparedness idea.)

2. Agoraphobia is mainly a problem experienced by women, and it has been argued that the "disorder" reflects sexism in our society. Review these arguments, and then agree or disagree with them.

3. How was combat fatigue treated in World War II? With which model of abnormality was this treatment compatible?

4. Of recent interest is the plight of Vietnam veterans. In particular, these individuals may suffer from post-traumatic stress disorders to a greater degree than have veterans from other eras. Is this true? If so, what about the Vietnam War may be responsible for this? If not, why has the claim been made?

EXERCISES

Exercise One—Phobias and Classical Conditioning

In this exercise, you will evaluate the classical conditioning explanation of phobias.

Talk to individuals who have phobias. What were the circumstances under which their fears first appeared? Do these correspond to the Pavlovian account?

For years, I was afraid of dogs. According to my parents, when I was three years old, the family pet, a collie who looked like Lassie, developed the un-Lassie-like habit of knocking me down as I explored the backyard. This may have been the origin of my fear of dogs. Almost twenty years later, I was "cured" through flooding occasioned by my summer job: a letter carrier in the suburbs of Chicago. Almost every house to which I delivered mail was guarded by a large dog, and I quickly became used to them. The only time I was bitten was by a three-year-old girl. However, I did not develop a fear of children.

Seligman, M. E. P. (1971). Phobias and preparedness. *Behavior Therapy, 2,* 307–320.

Exercise Two—Sex Differences in Fears

The purpose of this exercise is to ascertain whether men and women fear different things.

Ask men and women of your acquaintance to list the objects and situations of which they are afraid. What are the sex differences? How do you explain them?

Cornelius, R. R., & Averill, J. R. (1983). Sex differences in fear of spiders. *Journal of Personality and Social Psychology, 45,* 377–383.

Marks, I. M. (1969). *Fears and phobias.* New York: Academic Press.

Wilson, G. D. (1967). Social desirability and sex differences in expressed fear. *Behaviour Research and Therapy, 5,* 136–137.

CHAPTER 9

Obsession, Hysteria, and Dissociation: Anxiety Inferred

CHAPTER OVERVIEW

Disorders in which underlying anxiety has often been inferred as the cause—i.e., obsessive-compulsive disorders, somatoform disorders, and dissociative disorders—are the subject matter of this chapter.

Obsessive-compulsive disorders involve uncontrollable, repulsive thoughts (obsessions) and senseless rituals (compulsions). Obsessions and compulsions are thought to be defenses against anxiety. The psychodynamic model attempts to explain vulnerability to obsessive-compulsive disorders, while the behavioral model attempts to explain their persistence. Recent studies find a biological predisposition to obsessive-compulsive disorders. Behavioral therapies for these disorders are described.

Somatoform disorders (hysterical conversion, somatization disorder, and somatoform pain disorder) are characterized by the loss of physical functioning in the absence of any physical problem. Instead, somatoform disorders are thought to result from psychological factors. Cautions in diagnosing somatoform disorders are discussed since they often resemble other problems. Two theories of somatoform disorders—the psychodynamic model, which proposes that these disorders symbolize underlying conflicts, and the communicative model, which suggests that they communicate global distress—are described along with treatments.

Dissociative disorders entail problems with memory. In amnesia, an individual forgets who he or she is. In the fugue state, the individual suffers amnesia and assumes a new identity. In multiple personality, more than one self exists within the same individual, and "they" may not always be aware of each other. Like obsessive-compulsive disorders and somatoform disorders, dissociative disorders are thought to be ways of dealing with anxiety.

ESSENTIAL TERMS

alexithymic	being unable to express feelings in words
amnesia	sudden loss of memory caused by severe psychological trauma
anterograde amnesia	amnesia in which events after a trauma are forgotten
global amnesia	amnesia in which all details of one's personal memory are lost
retrograde amnesia	amnesia in which events prior to a trauma are forgotten

selective amnesia (categorical amnesia)	amnesia in which only events related to a particular theme vanish
belle indifference, la	symptom of somatoform disorders, wherein there is a lack of concern with physical symptoms
clavus	somatoform disorder common at the time of World War I characterized by the painful sensation of a nail being driven into the head and severe low back pain producing a forwardly bent back
communicative model	theory of somatoform disorder proposing that symptoms are used to deal with distressing emotions and to negotiate difficult interpersonal transactions
dissociative disorder	mental disorder in which some area of the memory is split off or dissociated from conscious awareness; e.g., amnesia, fugue, multiple personality
factitious disorder (Münchhausen syndrome	disorder resembling a somatoform disorder; in this disorder symptoms are voluntarily produced
fugue	amnesic state, wherein a new identity is assumed
glove anesthesia	somatoform disorder in which nothing can be felt in the hand and fingers although sensation is intact from the wrist up
malingering	faking; symptoms are under the person's voluntary control
multiple personality	more than one personality existing in the same individual, each with a life of its own
obsessive-compulsive disorder	mental disorder in which the individual is plagued by the uncontrollable, repulsive thoughts (obsessions) and engages in seemingly senseless rituals (compulsions)
obsessive-compulsive personality	personality style characterized by methodical, meticulous, and ordered behavior
psychosomatic disorder	disorder resembling a somatoform disorder but with a physical basis that can explain the symptom, e.g., peptic ulcer
response prevention	therapy technique for obsessive-compulsive disorders in which the compulsive act is not allowed to occur
secondary gain	benefits from the environment as a consequence of abnormal symptoms
somatization disorder	mental disorder involving a dramatic and complicated medical history for a variety of bodily complaints not physically caused (cf. somatoform disorder)
somatoform disorder	mental disorder characterized by loss of physical functioning in the absence of physical cause (cf. somatization disorder)
somatoform pain disorder	pain not caused physically

SAMPLE EXAM

1. All of the following are disorders in which anxiety is *not* experienced except
   a. panic disorder.
   b. obsessive-compulsive disorder.
   c. somatoform disorder.
   d. dissociative disorder.

2. Obsession is to compulsion as
   a. Lennon is to McCartney.
   b. behaviorism is to psychoanalysis.
   c. thought is to deed.
   d. cholinergic is to adrenergic.

3. Obsessions are different from recurring thoughts in all of the following ways except that they
   a. are unwelcome.
   b. are difficult to control.
   c. are cognitive.
   d. arise from within.

4. Common contents of obsessions today include all of the following except
   a. religion.
   b. illness.
   c. violence.
   d. orderliness.

5. Howard Hughes suffered from
   a. schizophrenia.
   b. depression.
   c. amnesia.
   d. obsessive-compulsive disorder.

6. How do obsessives deal with anxiety?
   a. by crossing the street
   b. by acting out their compulsions
   c. by panic attacks
   d. by flooding

7. Obsessive-compulsive disorders are made worse by
   a. depression.
   b. illness.
   c. alcoholism.
   d. schizophrenia.

8. Obsessive-compulsive disorders
   a. are more common among men than women.
   b. are more common among women than men.
   c. are equally common among men and women.
   d. none of the above.

9. If you were told that you would soon meet an individual with an obsessive-compulsive personality, you would expect to encounter someone who is
   a. meticulous.
   b. sloppy.
   c. tall.
   d. flexible.

10. Which statement is true?
    a. Obsessive-compulsive personality leads to obsessive-compulsive disorder.
    b. Obsessive-compulsive disorder leads to obsessive-compulsive personality.
    c. Obsessive-compulsive personality and obsessive-compulsive disorder are the same thing.
    d. Obsessive-compulsive personality and obsessive-compulsive disorder are not related.

11. People with obsessive-compulsive disorders may have abnormal
    a. brain metabolism.
    b. brain structure.
    c. cognitive styles.
    d. learning strategies.
    e. perceptual habits.

12. The cognitive-behavioral account of obsessive-compulsive disorders does a good job explaining
    a. the genesis of the disorders.
    b. the maintenance of the disorders.
    c. both the genesis and maintenance of the disorders.
    d. neither the genesis nor maintenance of the disorders.

13. The psychoanalytic account of obsessive-compulsive disorders does a good job explaining
    a. the genesis of the disorders.
    b. the maintenance of the disorders.
    c. both the genesis and maintenance of the disorders.
    d. neither the genesis nor maintenance of the disorders.

14. According to the cognitive-behavioral model of obsessive-compulsive disorders, which one of the following is *not* true about obsessions?
    a. They are made worse by depression.
    b. They involve a vicious circle.
    c. They are temporarily relieved by compulsive rituals.
    d. They are eventually extinguished.

15. Psychoanalysts see obsessions as all of the following except as
    a. a defense against more threatening thoughts.

b.   an instance of sublimation.
c.   a symbol of an underlying conflict.
d.   a neurosis.

16. The most effective treatment for obsessive-compulsive disorders seems to be
a.   electroconvulsive shock.
b.   drugs.
c.   insight therapy.
d.   behavioral therapy.

17. Which one of the following is *not* evidence that obsessive-compulsive disorders involve anxiety?
a.   Anxiety-reducing therapies are effective.
b.   Anxiety is common among those with obsessive-compulsive personalities.
c.   Anxiety is experienced if compulsive acts are not performed.
d.   Anxiety is reduced if compulsive acts are performed.

18. Somatoform disorders include
a.   hysterical conversions.
b.   psychosomatic disorders.
c.   factitious disorders.
d.   malingering.

19. Somatoform disorders are characterized by all of the following except
a.   loss of physical functioning.
b.   lack of neurological damage.
c.   fear.
d.   lack of voluntary control.

20. All of the following are somatoform disorders except
a.   somatization disorder.
b.   somatoform pain disorder.
c.   hysterical conversion.
d.   thought disorder.

21. Hysterical conversion is to somatization disorder as
a.   phobia is to schizophrenia.
b.   one is to many.
c.   behaviorism is to psychoanalysis.
d.   East is to West.

22. The most frequent somatoform disorder seems to be
a.   somatization disorder.
b.   somatoform pain disorder.
d.   hysterical conversion.
d.   thought disorder.

23. All of the following may be confused with somatoform disorders except
a.   phobias.
b.   malingering.
c.   factitious disorders.

d.   psychosomatic disorders.
e.   undiagnosed physical illnesses.

24. Conversion disorders are particularly uncommon among
a.   children.
b.   adolescents.
c.   middle-aged individuals.
d.   old people.

25. According to the psychodynamic model, hysterical conversion involves all except
a.   defense against anxiety.
b.   transformation of psychic energy.
c.   symbolic symptoms.
d.   fear.

26. What is "la belle indifference"?
a.   indifference of individuals to their conversion symptoms
b.   inability of diagnosticians to distinguish somatoform disorders from psychosomatic disorders
c.   ideas that hysterics are likely to be young women
d.   confusion accompanying somatoform pain disorder

27. Which model best explains "la belle indifference"?
a.   biomedical model
b.   psychodynamic model
c.   behavioral model
d.   cognitive model
e.   existential model

28. According to the communicative model of hysterical conversion, hysterics
a.   can tell you what is wrong.
b.   can be cured through social support.
c.   use their symptoms to communicate.
d.   are nonstop talkers.

29. The communicative model does a good job of explaining
a.   "la belle indifference."
b.   sex differences in hysterical conversions.
c.   changing hysterical symptoms over time.
d.   double-binds.

30. Someone who is alexythimic has difficulty expressing
a.   abstractions.
b.   emotions.
c.   motives.
d.   thoughts.

31. The mechanism of hysterical conversion may involve
a.   blocking of a percept from awareness.

b.   excess dopamine in the brain.
c.   too little serotonin in the brain.
d.   sensory overload.

32. All of the following seem to be successful treatments for hysterical conversion except
a.   suggestion.
b.   electroconvulsive shock.
c.   insight.
d.   antidepressant drugs.

33. All of these are dissociative disorders except
a.   amnesia.
b.   fugue.
c.   multiple personality.
d.   somatoform pain disorder.

34. Dissociative disorders all involve
a.   forgetting.
b.   willing.
c.   learning.
d.   concentrating.

35. Psychogenic amnesia is thought to result from
a.   genetic factors.
b.   learning.
c.   anxiety.
d.   errors in logic.

36. An individual cannot remember events immediately before a bad automobile accident that he caused. He is experiencing
a.   global amnesia.
b.   retrograde amnesia.
c.   anterograde amnesia.
d.   categorical amnesia.

37. An individual cannot remember events immediately after a bad automobile accident that he caused. He is experiencing
a.   global amnesia.
b.   retrograde amnesia.
c.   anterograde amnesia.
d.   categorical amnesia.

38. An individual cannot remember events related to a prior unhappy romance. She is experiencing
a.   global amnesia.
b.   retrograde amnesia.
c.   anterograde amnesia.
d.   categorical amnesia.

39. An individual can remember nothing since joining the navy. She is experiencing
a.   global amnesia.
b.   retrograde amnesia.

c.   anterograde amnesia.
d.   categorical amnesia

40. Which one of the following is false?
a.   Organic amnesia is caused by physical trauma, while psychogenic amnesia is not.
b.   Organic amnesia is not associated with prior life stresses, while psychogenic amnesia is.
c.   Organic amnesia involves forgetting the distant past, while psychogenic amnesia does not.
d.   Organic amnesia involves loss of both personal and general knowledge, while psychogenic amnesia does not.

41. Which of these statements is true?
a.   Amnesia involves multiple personality.
b.   Multiple personality involves amnesia.
c.   Amnesia and multiple personality are the same thing.
d.   Amnesia and multiple personality have no relation.

42. Which is an example of multiple personality?
a.   Lenin and Marx
b.   Howard Hughes
c.   Dr. Jekyll and Mr. Hyde
d.   Little Hans and Little Albert

43. Which one of the following is *not* true about multiple personality?
a.   One of the personalities is aware of the other(s).
b.   One of the personalities is unaware of the other(s).
c.   The different personalities are essentially the same along important dimensions.
d.   The dominant personality is not always the most psychologically healthy.

44. All of the following seem involved in the etiology of multiple personality except
a.   tendency toward schizophrenia.
b.   severe trauma.
c.   susceptibility to self-hypnosis.
d.   relief of emotional burden through the creation of a different personality.

45. Therapy for multiple personality is
a.   usually successful.
b.   usually unsuccessful.
c.   of unknown success.
d.   none of the above.

Answer Key for Sample Exam

1.	a	(p. 235)	13.	a	(p. 243)	25.	d	(p. 253)
2.	c	(p. 236)	14.	d	(p. 243)	26.	a	(p. 254)
3.	c	(p. 236)	15.	b	(p. 244)	27.	b	(p. 254)
4.	a	(p. 237)	16.	d	(p. 245)	28.	c	(p. 254)
5.	d	(p. 237)	17.	b	(p. 247)	29.	c	(p. 255)
6.	b	(p. 238)	18.	a	(p. 248)	30.	b	(p. 255)
7.	a	(p. 239)	19.	c	(p. 248)	31.	a	(p. 256)
8.	c	(p. 239)	20.	d	(p. 249)	32.	b, d	(p. 257)
9.	a	(p. 240)	21.	b	(p. 249)	33.	d	(p. 259)
10.	d	(p. 240)	22.	b	(p. 250)	34.	a	(p. 259)
11.	a	(p. 241)	23.	a	(p. 250)	35.	c	(p. 261)
12.	b	(p. 243)	24.	a, d	(p. 252)			

36.	b	(p. 260)
37.	c	(p. 260)
38.	d	(p. 260)
39.	a	(p. 260)
40.	c	(p. 260)
41.	b	(p. 261)
42.	c	(p. 261)
43.	c	(p. 263)
44.	a	(p. 265)
45.	a	(p. 266)

SELF-TEST

1. Disorders in which anxiety is inferred include _____ , _____ , and _____ .

2. Dissociative disorders include _____ , _____ , and _____ .

3. _____ are uncontrollable, repulsive thoughts, and _____ are senseless rituals.

4. Obsessions are distinguished from harmless recurring thoughts in three ways. First, they are not _____ ; second, they arise from _____ ; and third, they are _____ .

5. The _____ of obsessions has changed over time.

6. If an obsessive does not act out her compulsion, she experiences _____ .

7. Obsessions are _____ among men and women.

8. A methodical and meticulous person is said to have an _____ personality; such as a person is _____ to develop an obsessive-compulsive disorder than other people.

9. Obsessive-compulsive disorders tend to co-occur with _____ disorders, perhaps because of _____ .

10. According to recent biological studies, obsessive-compulsive disorders may be predisposed by problems with _____ .

11. According to the cognitive-behavioral view of obsessive-compulsive disorders, compulsions serve to _____ .

12. The cognitive-behavioral explanation of obsessive-compulsive disorders does a good job accounting for their _____ , but a poor job accounting for _____ .

13. According to the psychodynamic model, obsessions are _____ against more threatening impulses.

14. Psychodynamic theory explains _____ to obsessive-compulsive disorders as well as their _____ .

15. The prognosis for obsessive-compulsive disorders is _____ .

16. Among the behavioral therapy techniques for obsessive-compulsive disorders are
    _____, _____, and _____ .

17. There are four reasons why anxiety is thought to underlie obsessive-compulsive disorders.
    First, therapy techniques that _____ are effective. Second, when an individual with
    an obsessive-compulsive disorder is not allowed to _____, anxiety is experienced.
    Third, obsessives experience some _____ during the obsession. And fourth, the
    content of the obsession can often be seen as a _____ of an underlying conflict.

18. Somatoform disorders are marked by loss of _____ in the absence of _____ .

19. Three types of somatoform disorder are _____, _____, and _____ .

20. Somatoform disorders are difficult to diagnose. They must be distinguished from
    _____, _____, and _____, as well as from _____ .

21. Conversion disorders are _____ likely to occur among men than women.

22. About _____ percent of conversion disorders disappear within two years.

23. According to the psychodynamic model, conversions are _____ .

24. _____ is the puzzling lack of concern among hysterics for their symptoms.

25. The _____ model of conversion disorders proposes that symptoms are a means of
    negotiating difficult interpersonal transactions.

26. One theory of conversion disorders suggests that they involve the blocking of perceptions
    from _____ .

27. Among the treatments for somatoform disorders are _____ and _____ .

28. All the dissociative disorders involve loss of _____, presumably to reduce
    _____ .

29. Amnesia in which all memories are lost is _____ amnesia; when events immediately
    prior to a trauma are forgotten, it is _____ amnesia; when events immediately after
    a trauma are forgotten, it is _____ amnesia; and when events pertaining to a certain
    theme are forgotten, it is _____ amnesia.

30. In cases of multiple personality, one personality is usually _____ of the other per-
    sonalities.

31. Multiple personality is often confused with _____, but these are different disorders.

32. Individuals susceptible to multiple personality are high _____; as children, they of-
    ten had _____ and experienced _____ .

Answer Key for Self-Test

1. obsessive-compulsive disorders; somatoform disorders; dissociative disorders
2. amnesia; fugue; multiple personality
3. obsessions; compulsions
4. welcome; within; difficult to control
5. content
6. anxiety
7. equally common
8. obsessive-compulsive; no more likely
9. depressive; helplessness
10. brain metabolism
11. reduce anxiety
12. persistence; individual susceptibility
13. defenses
14. individual susceptibility; content
15. not particularly good
16. response prevention; flooding; modeling
17. reduce anxiety; perform the ritual; anxiety; symbol
18. physical functioning; neurological damage
19. conversion disorders; somatization disorder; somatoform pain disorder
20. malingering; psychosomatic disorders; factitious disorders; undiagnosed physical illnesses
21. less
22. 50
23. defenses against anxiety
24. "La belle indifference"
25. communicative
26. awareness
27. suggestion; insight
28. memory; anxiety
29. global; retrograde; anterograde; categorical
30. unaware
31. schizophrenia
32. suggestible; imaginary playmates; sexual abuse

TYING IT TOGETHER

This chapter covers disorders in which anxiety is inferred to be the cause. These disorders—hysteria in particular—are historically important, since early workers debated whether they were biologically or psychologically caused (Chapter 2; see Chapter 17). Pioneers in the field of abnormal psychology such as Mesmer, Charcot, Janet, Breuer, and Freud were all concerned with hysteria (Chapter 2 and 4). These disorders are still explained with the psychodynamic model, although the behavioral model (Chapter 5) has made important contributions to our understanding of them.

Hysteria seems to be less common now than it was at the turn of the century. This may be due to increased sophistication on the part of individuals who "know" that physical functions do not suddenly cease without cause. It may also result from an increasingly liberal society in which conflicts around sexuality and aggression are not as prevalent as they once were (Chapter 2). Yet another factor contributing to the decline in hysteria is the increase in use of tranquilizing drugs and alcohol (Chapter 14). To the degree that "self-medication" decreases fear and anxiety, it also decreases disorders in which these are underlying causes. Of course, drug abuse may create more problems than it solves.

Obsessions and compulsions are sometimes components of other disorders, where they may serve a role in decreasing anxiety. Depressives (Chapter 11) often suffer repetitive thoughts involving themes of self-recrimination. Schizophrenic delusions (Chapter 12) are repetitive and may give rise to ritualistic behavior. Neurological disorders are sometimes associated with perseveration (Chapter 17).

The behavioral treatments are among the most successful for disorders brought about by fear an anxiety (Chapter 19).

FURTHER READINGS

Bliss, E. L. (1980). Multiple personalities: A report of 14 cases with implications for schizophrenia and hysteria. *Archives of General Psychiatry, 37,* 1388–1397.

Freud, S. (1963). Notes upon a case of obsessional neurosis. In *Three case histories.* New York: Collier.

Hirst, W. (1982). The amnesic syndrome: Descriptions and explanations. *Psychological Bulletin, 91,* 435–460.*

Schreiber, F. R. (1973). *Sybil.* New York: Warner Books.

Stevenson, R. L. (1906). *The merry men, and other tales and fables; Strange case of Dr. Jekyll and Mr. Hyde.* New York: Scribner's.

Thigpen, C. H., & Cleckley, H. M. (1957). *The three faces of Eve.* New York: Popular Library.

TERM-PAPER TOPICS

1. One of Freud's patients, known as the Wolf Man, has been the subject of two contemporary books—Gardiner, M. (1971). *The Wolf-Man.* New York: Basic Books; Obholzer, K. (1982). *The Wolf-Man—Sixty years later: Conversations with Freud's controversial patient.* New York: Continuum. Read these books and Freud's original case study. Evaluate Freud's account of neuroses and their treatment with psychoanalysis.

2. Evaluate the psychoanalytic explanation of psychogenic amnesia on the basis of case histories.

3. Cases of multiple personality are rare and exciting. Therapists can make a great deal of money by writing about such cases. Could these therapists ever be guilty of encouraging a patient to evidence multiple personalities? In short, decide if multiple personality is real.

EXERCISES

Exercise One—Superstitious Rituals and Sports

The purpose of this exercise is to investigate the rituals followed by athletes to reduce their anxiety while performing.

Talk to men and women of your acquaintance about superstitions they have while playing sports. Do these involve behaviors? Cognitions? How did these superstitions develop? Do these athletes experience anxiety if their rituals are interrupted?

Skinner, B. F. (1948). "Superstition" in the pigeon. *Journal of Experimental Psychology, 38,* 168–172.

Exercise Two—Superstitious Rituals and Tests

The purpose of this exercise is to investigate the rituals followed by students taking examinations to reduce their anxiety.

Repeating the procedure of the above exercise, talk to your classmates about their test-taking superstitions.

Exercise Three—Imaginary Playmates

According to the textbook, multiple personalities may develop from imaginary playmates that a child invents in stressful situations. The purpose of this exercise is to ascertain the frequency of imaginary playmates and the circumstances under which they "come out to play."

Talk to your friends about imaginary playmates they had when they were young. If possible, talk to young school children who may still have them. What are the characteristics of these playmates? Are they similar or different from the people who create them? What kinds of things do people do with imaginary playmates? Are these done in stressful situations?

I did not have a typical imaginary playmate when I was young. Rather, my twin brother was always available as a playmate. When I was mad at him, I used to wish that he were imaginary. Now that I'm older, my imaginary playmates are more conventional. Like anyone who has ever lived in Chicago, my imaginary playmates now bear an uncanny resemblance to Michael Jordan.

Pines, M. (1978). Invisible playmates. *Psychology Today, 12*(9), 38–42, 106.

Exercise Four—Reactions to Stress

The purpose of this exercise is to ascertain if one's own aches and pains reflect stress reactions.

Among the possible responses to stress are headaches, stomach aches, insomnia, lower back pains, diarrhea, sore throats, and so on. Keep a daily log of such minor physical disturbances for at least a month. At the same time, keep track of how stressful each day was. You may want to rate each day on a scale like the following

1 = an incredibly laid-back day
2 = a relaxing day
3 = a somewhat relaxing day
4 = a somewhat stressful day
5 = a moderately stressful day
6 = a pretty stressful day
7 = an incredibly stressful day

Is there a relationship between the stressfulness of the day and the number of minor aches and pains you experienced? Try representing the information in graph form. Consider the possibility that you respond to stress several days following it. (Beware of illusory correlations in interpreting the information you have recorded!)

Kanner, A. D., Coyne, J. C., Schaefer, C., & Lazarus, R. S. (1981). Comparison of two modes of stress measurement: Daily hassles and uplifts versus major life events. *Journal of Behavioral Medicine, 4,* 1–39.

CHAPTER 10

Health Psychology and Psychosomatic Disorders

CHAPTER OVERVIEW

In contrast to somatoform disorders, psychosomatic disorders involve actual physical problems influenced by psychological factors. Peptic ulcers and coronary heart disease are two important examples of psychosomatic disorders. Each is interpreted in terms of a diathesis-stress model, in which a physical weakness (diathesis) is coupled with an environmental event (stress) to bring about the disorder.

A peptic ulcer is an erosion of the mucous lining of the stomach or esophagus. There are constitutional risk factors for peptic ulcers—oversecretion of gastric juice and weak mucous membrane—as well as environmental risk factors—conflict, unpredictability, and uncontrollability.

One risk factor for coronary heart disease is the Type A personality pattern, characterized by hostility, time urgency, and competitiveness. Research suggests that hostility is the active ingredient leading to heart disease, perhaps because it leads to chronic engagement of the body's emergency reaction.

A new area within psychosomatics is currently taking form: psychoneuroimmunology, which studies how psychological factors influence the body's ability to recognize and fight off disease. Described in detail is a line of research linking stressful events, helplessness, depression, and pessimism to poor immune function and hence to increased illness and death.

ESSENTIAL TERMS

anti-hypertensive drug	drug that reduces blood pressure
approach-avoidance conflict	situation with aspects encouraging both approach and avoidance; thought to produce peptic ulcers
asthma	condition in which the air passages of the bronchia narrow, swell, and secrete excess fluid in response to a variety of stimuli, resulting in difficulty breathing
blood pressure	pressure exerted by the blood on the walls of blood vessels
cimetidine	drug that reduces stomach acid; treatment of choice for peptic ulcers
continual emergency reaction	constant state of anxiety and readiness for danger

diathesis-stress model	idea that disorder results from a combination of constitutional weakness (diathesis) and traumatic event (stress)
executive monkey study	well-known but confounded study ostensibly showing that monkeys given control (executives) develop more ulcers than monkeys not given control; subsequent research suggests lack of control produces ulcers
general adaptation syndrome	theory of stress proposed by Hans Selye that describes a sequence of three stages in response to stress: alarm reaction (i.e., emergency reaction), resistance, and exhaustion)
hardiness	personality characteristic associated with robust physical health
health psychology	field that investigates the psychological causes and consequences of health and disease
hypertension	technical term for high blood pressure
immune system	bodily system that recognizes and removes foreign material
antibody	material that inactivates antigens
antigen	material foreign to one's body
lymphocytes	cells that recognize antigens
macrophages	cells that eat antigens
neutrophils	cells that eat antigen-antibody complexes
life stressors	theory of psychosomatic disorders proposing that illness follows stressful life events
entrances	life events involving gains
exits	life events involving losses, thought to result in more problems than entrances
uncontrollable events	events for which no response an individual can make changes their chances of occurring
unpredictable events	unsignaled life events
peptic ulcer	circumscribed erosion of the mucous membrane of the stomach (gastric ulcer) or duodenum (duodenal ulcer)
psychoneuroimmunology	field that investigates how psychological states influence the immune system
psychosomatic disorder	disorder of the body (soma) influenced by the mind (psyche); e.g., peptic ulcer
specific organ vulnerability	theory of psychosomatic disorders holding that an individual inherits a tendency to react to stress with a characteristic part of the body
stigmata	marks on skin, usually bleeding or bruising, often of religious or personal significance, brought on by an emotional state
sudden death	death in the face of threat, thought to result from hopelessness and giving up

Type A behavior pattern   personality style that predisposes an individual to cardio-vascular difficulties; the pattern consists of exaggerated time urgency, competitiveness and ambition, aggression and hostility in response to frustration

Type B behavior pattern   personality style in contrast to Type A pattern; such a pattern consists of no time urgency, as well as relaxation and serenity

ulcer-prone personality   personality style characterized by disguised need for nurturance, including exaggerated self-sufficiency, driving ambition, and inappropriate shows of strength; it is thought to predispose individuals to peptic ulcers, although evidence support this only for men

SAMPLE EXAM

1. Psychosomatic disorders involve
   a. the mind.
   b. the body.
   c. both the mind and the body.
   d. neither the mind nor the body.

2. All of the following are psychosomatic disorders except
   a. stigmata.
   b. somatoform disorder.
   c. peptic ulcer.
   d. high blood pressure.

3. Stigmata usually possess
   a. religious significance.
   b. political significance.
   c. economic significance.
   d. historical significance

4. DSM-III-R describes psychosomatic disorders as
   a. physical factors affecting a psychological condition.
   b. psychological factors affecting a physical condition.
   c. conscious factors affecting an unconscious condition.
   d. unconscious factors affecting a conscious condition.

5. Diathesis is to stress as
   a. mild is to severe.
   b. phobia is to schizophrenia.
   c. nature is to nurture.
   d. conscious is to unconscious.

6. All of the following may destroy the stomach lining except
   a. antacids.
   b. aspirin and alcohol.
   c. hydrochloric acid.
   d. pepsin.
   e. bile.

7. The most obvious symptom of peptic ulcers is
   a. abdominal pain.
   b. fever.
   c. flushed skin.
   d. painful bowel movements.

8. In general,
   a. peptic ulcers are more frequent among men than women.
   b. peptic ulcers are more frequent among women than men.
   c. peptic ulcers are equally frequent among men and women.
   d. sex differences in peptic-ulcer frequency have changed over the years.

9. Which of the following statements are true?
   a. Social class does not influence the incidence of peptic ulcers.
   b. Peptic ulcers are less frequent after age thirty-five.
   c. Peptic ulcers run in families.
   d. Boys have more peptic ulcers than girls.

10. According to research, gastric secretions increase during all of the following emotions except
    a. anxiety.
    b. anger.
    c. resentment.
    d. sadness.

11. Animal research has shown that all of
the following situations increase the
likelihood of ulcers except
    a. conflict.
    b. extinction.
    c. unpredictability.
    d. uncontrollability.

12. What was the confound in the "executive
monkey" study?
    a. nonrandom assignment
    b. experimenter bias
    c. subject bias
    d. demand characteristics

13. Suppose you were told that you were to
meet someone with an ulcer-prone personality. You would expect this person to
be all of the following except
    a. ambitious.
    b. dependent.
    c. unassertive.
    d. fixated at the oral stage.
    e. fixated at the anal stage.

14. The idea that an ulcer-prone personality
indeed predisposes peptic ulcers has
    a. no evidence in favor of it.
    b. evidence in favor of it.
    c. evidence in favor of it, but only for
       men.
    d. evidence in favor of it, but only for
       women.

15. The best treatment for a peptic ulcer is
    a. antacids.
    b. a bland diet.
    c. cimetidine.
    d. thorazine.
    e. steroids.

16. Psychological treatment for a peptic ulcer has
    a. been conclusively proven effective.
    b. been conclusively proven ineffective.
    c. not been attempted.
    d. not been appropriately tested.

17. Blood pressure increases under conditions of
    a. threat.
    b. anxiety.
    c. depression.
    d. hostility.

18. Hypertension is most likely to occur
when an individual is
    a. constantly threatened and can
       retaliate.
    b. constantly threatened and cannot
       retaliate.

    c. periodically threatened and can
       retaliate.
    d. periodically threatened and cannot
       retaliate.

19. The Type A behavior pattern is a
    a. personality prone to cardiovascular
       troubles.
    b. way to resolve approach-avoidance
       conflicts.
    c. tracking strategy for elementary
       education.
    d. defense against sexual inadequacy.

20. All of the following are characteristics of
the Type A behavior pattern except
    a. time urgency.
    b. forgetfulness.
    c. competitiveness.
    d. hostility.

21. Suppose you were told that you would
meet someone for lunch who had a Type
A personality. You would be surprised if
this individual
    a. arrived late.
    b. ate quickly.
    c. sent food back to the kitchen.
    d. had a heart attack while eating
       French fries.

22. _____ kills more people in the Western
world than any other disease.
    a. AIDS
    b. cancer
    c. coronary heart disease
    d. pneumonia

23. Which of these is a risk factor for coronary heart disease?
    a. female
    b. smoking cigarettes
    c. physical activity
    d. Type B personality
    e. low serum cholesterol

24. Type A personality predicts heart disease among
    a. males only.
    b. females only.
    c. the general population.
    d. people selected to be at risk for heart
       disease only.

25. The active ingredient making Type A
personality a risk factor for coronary
heart disease is
    a. anger.
    b. competitiveness.
    c. time urgency.
    d. all of the above.
    e. none of the above.

26. Compared to Type B individuals, Type A's seem to be more involved in a
   a. struggle for control.
   b. conflict with unconscious impulses.
   c. need to self-actualize.
   d. desire to help others.

27. Compared to Type B individuals, Type A's respond to helplessness by
   a. desperately trying to gain control and then by giving up.
   b. half-heartedly trying to gain control and then by giving up.
   c. giving up for a while and then by trying to gain control.
   d. giving up immediately and then by leaving the situation.

28. When a person shows a chronic emergency reaction, his or her heart becomes
   a. efficient.
   b. overloaded.
   c. sluggish.
   d. unresponsive.

29. Can Type A behavior be changed?
   a. yes
   b. no

30. Foreign materials that invade the body are
   a. antibodies.
   b. antigens.
   c. lymphocytes.
   d. T-cells.

31. The psychological state of helplessness makes tumors
   a. grow faster.
   b. be rejected less.
   c. both.
   d. neither.

32. All of these psychological states except _____ have been linked to poor immune function among people.
   a. anxiety
   b. depression
   c. helplessness
   d. pessimism

33. Sudden death seems to result from
   a. hopelessness and helplessness.
   b. fear and loathing.
   c. approach and avoidance.
   d. illness and exhaustion.

34. When one's spouse dies, one's risk of death is
   a. increased.
   b. increased but only for six months.
   c. decreased.
   d. decreased but only for six months.

35. Which one of the following factors may be involved in the development of cancer?
   a. significant loss
   b. job instability
   c. lack of meaning in life
   d. all of the above

36. Research in nursing homes suggests that
   a. choice and control result in longer life.
   b. support and assistance result in longer life.
   c. rest and relaxation result in longer life.
   d. respect and deference result in longer life.

37. Asthma always results from
   a. infection.
   b. allergy.
   c. psychological factors.
   d. none of the above.

38. All of the following have proposed accounts of psychosomatic disorders except the
   a. biomedical model.
   b. psychodynamic model.
   c. behavioral model.
   d. cognitive model.
   e. existential model.

39. Specific organ vulnerability is an instance of the
   a. biomedical model.
   b. psychodynamic model.
   c. behavioral model.
   d. cognitive model.
   e. existential model.

40. The idea of specific organ vulnerability is that
   a. after repeated psychosomatic disorders, individuals develop weakness in a specific part of the body.
   b. with repeated use, individuals develop weakness in a specific part of the body.
   c. without repeated use, individuals develop weakness in a specific part of the body.
   d. individuals inherit weakness in a specific part of the body.

41. According to Selye's general adaptation syndrome, stress results in which one of the following sequence of responses?
   a. alarm reaction to exhaustion to resistance
   b. alarm reaction to resistance to exhaustion

c. resistance to alarm reaction to exhaustion

d. resistance to exhaustion to alarm reaction

42. The psychodynamic account of psychosomatic disorders emphasizes all of the following except
a. vulnerable organ.
b. underlying conflict.
c. precipitating event.
d. adaptation.

43. The conditioning account of asthma has
a. received good research support.
b. received minimal research support.
c. not been investigated.
d. not been investigated properly.

44. The life-events account of illness has
a. received good research support.
b. received minimal research support.
c. not bee investigated.
d. not been investigated properly.

45. Life events that are most likely to result in illness are those that are
a. controllable entrances.
b. controllable exits.
c. uncontrollable entrances.
d. uncontrollable exits.

Answer Key for Sample Exam

1.	c	(p. 271)	24.	c	(p. 284)
2.	b	(p. 273)	25.	a	(p. 284)
3.	a	(p. 271)	26.	a	(p. 285)
4.	b	(p. 273)	27.	a	(p. 286)
5.	c	(p. 273)	28.	b	(p. 287)
6.	a	(p. 275)	29.	a	(p. 288)
7.	a	(p. 274)	30.	b	(p. 292)
8.	d	(p. 275)	31.	c	(p. 293)
9.	c	(p. 276)	32.	a	(p. 293)
10.	d	(p. 277)	33.	a	(p. 290)
11.	b	(p. 278)	34.	b	(p. 290)
12.	a	(p. 279)	35.	d	(p. 290)
13.	c, e	(p. 281)	36.	a	(p. 291)
14.	c	(p. 281)	37.	d	(p. 296)
15.	c	(p. 281)	38.	e	(p. 295)
16.	d	(p. 282)	39.	a, b	(p. 295)
17.	a, d	(p. 284)	40.	d	(p. 295)
18.	b	(p. 284)	41.	b	(p. 297)
19.	a	(p. 283)	42.	d	(p. 298)
20.	b	(p. 283)	43.	b	(p. 299)
21.	a	(p. 283)	44.	a	(p. 300)
22.	c	(p. 282)	45.	d	(p. 300)
23.	b	(p. 282)			

SELF-TEST

1. Unlike somatoform disorders, psychosomatic disorders involve actual _____.

2. Among the psychosomatic disorders are _____ and _____.

3. Marks on the skin produced by an emotional state and having religious significance are _____.

4. The model used to explain psychosomatic disorders is the _____ model.

5. The process causing psychosomatic effects seems to be _____ for different organs.

6. A peptic ulcer is an erosion of the _____ of the _____ or the _____.

7. The most salient symptom of a peptic ulcer is _____.

8. Among the constitutional weaknesses that predispose peptic ulcers are an excess of _____, a weak _____, and a slow _____ stomach lining.

9. Twin studies suggest that peptic ulcers are _____.

10. Emotional states like _____ and _____ cause excess stomach acid. These states may be brought about by conditions of _____, _____, and _____.

11. The "executive monkey" study suggested that _____ causes peptic ulcers. However this study was confounded by _____, and its conclusion should really have been _____.

12. According to Franz Alexander, an ulcer-prone personality involves an unconscious conflict between _____ and _____. Research suggests that this personality style predisposes ulcers, but only for _____.

13. _____ is the treatment of choice for peptic ulcers.

14. The Type A behavior pattern characterizes individuals at risk for _____ difficulties. It involves exaggerated _____, _____ and _____, and _____ and _____.

15. Type A behavior pattern predicts coronary disease among _____.

16. _____ is probably the component of Type A personality that puts one at increased risk for heart disease, through _____.

17. The field that looks at how psychological states affect the body's immune system is _____.

18. The two tasks of the immune system are _____ and _____.

19. Animals that are _____ fail to reject tumors.

20. _____, _____, _____, and _____ affect immune functioning among people.

21. Sudden death seems to be caused by the psychological state of _____.

22. Following the loss of a spouse, one's chances of death are increased for about _____ months.

23. Cancer may involve the psychological state of _____.

24. Hopelessness may be promoted in nursing homes that deprive individuals of _____.

25. Pessimistic _____ may be a risk factor for illness.

26. Emotional factors play a role in about _____ percent of asthma cases.

27. The notion of specific organ vulnerability proposes that people inherit _____ in a _____.

28. Research support for the notion of specific organ vulnerability is _____.

29. Hans Selye's general adaptation syndrome theory hypothesizes that psychosomatic disorders are _____.

30. Life events may influence illness if they are _____.

Answer Key for Self-Test

1. physical damage
2. peptic ulcers; coronary heart disease
3. stigmata
4. diathesis-stress
5. similar
6. mucous lining; stomach; duodenum
7. abdominal pain
8. hydrochloric acid; mucous membrane; regenerating
9. genetic
10. anger; anxiety; conflict; unpredictability; uncontrollability
11. control; nonrandom assignment; the opposite
12. dependence; independence; men
13. Cimetidine
14. cardiovascular; time urgency; competitiveness; ambition; aggressiveness; hostility
15. the population at large
16. Hostility; chronic arousal of the emergency reaction
17. psychoneuroimmunology
18. recognizing foreign materials; removing them from the body
19. helpless
20. Depression, helplessness, hopelessness, and stressful events
21. hopelessness
22. six
23. hopelessness
24. control
25. explanatory style
26. 33
27. weakness; specific organ
28. mixed
29. general stress reactions
30. uncontrollable exits

TYING IT TOGETHER

The psychosomatic disorders are explained with a diathesis-stress model, which combines the biomedical approach (Chapter 3) with the behavioral approach (Chapter 5). This may become an increasingly popular way to explain other psychological disorders—e.g., depression (Chapter 11) and schizophrenia (Chapter 12)—and it may become a popular way to view physical disorders as well (Chapter 17). Chapter 10 describes how feelings of hopelessness may underlie illness. Similar feelings have been implicated in post-traumatic stress disorders (Chapter 8), depression, and suicide (Chapter 11).

The day may come when "psychological" disorders and "physical" disorders are seen as overlapping, as possessing fuzzy boundaries (Chapter 1). The idea behind holistic medicine is that all disorders—physical and psychological—are psychosomatic disorders. Treatments may become more eclectic, and therapists may become more broadly trained (Chapter 19). Contemporary models of abnormality (Chapter 3 through 5) may become outmoded and replaced with more integrative explanations.

The personality disorders described in Chapter 15 lead to social and occupational maladjustment. Perhaps these disorders should be expanded to include any pervasive life-style that results in problems. Thus, the Type A behavior pattern, shown by research to be associated with hypertension and other cardiovascular difficulties, is as much a disorder of personality as is sociopathy. Similarly, life-styles that entail drug abuse (Chapter 14) could be viewed as being akin to life-styles that result in psychosomatic difficulties.

Many of the psychosomatic disorders described in this chapter involve fear and anxiety (Chapter 8 and 9), and animal models of psychopathology have been used to understand them better (Chapter 6) and to develop effective treatments (Chapter 19).

FURTHER READINGS

Alexander, F. (1950). *Psychosomatic medicine: Its principles and applications.* New York: Norton.

Cannon, W. B. (1942). "Voodoo" death. *American Anthropologist, 44,* 169–181.

Cousins, N. (1979). *Anatomy of an illness.* New York: Norton.

Friedman, N., & Rosenman, R. H. (1974).

Type A behavior and your heart. New York: Knopf.

Jaret, P. (1986). Our immune system: The wars within. *National Geographic, 169*(6), 702–735.

Locke, S., & Colligan, D. (1986). *The healer within.* New York: Dutton.

Ornstein, R., & Sobel, R. (1987). *The healing*

brain. New York: Simon & Schuster.

Richter, C. P. (1957). On the phenomenon of sudden death in animals and man. *Psycho-*

somatic Medicine, 19, 191–198.

Selye, H. (1956). *The stress of life.* New York: McGraw-Hill.

TERM-PAPER TOPICS

1. Does asthma fit a diathesis-stress model? Review the evidence, and come to a conclusion.

2. The textbook describes how feelings of hopelessness can be involved in cancer. What other psychological factors have been shown to foreshadow cancer? Is cancer a psychosomatic disorder?

3. How does the prevalence of ulcers vary across different occupational and economic groups? What theory of ulcer formation does the pattern support?

4. It has been suggested that so-called "crib death" may be an instance of sudden death. What is the evidence for and against this claim?

5. Suppose research continues to support the role of psychological factors in predisposing immunological disease. What role might psychologists play in the prevention and treatment of such illnesses?

EXERCISES

Exercise One—Type A Behavior Pattern and Achievement

The textbook described the Type A behavior pattern in terms of its negative effects on cardiovascular health. However, this way of living also has positive effects on achievement. The purpose of this exercise is to demonstrate the often superior academic performance of Type A individuals.

Categorize a number of your friends as Type A or Type B. Remember that Type A individuals are characterized by (a) an exaggerated sense of time urgency; (b) competitiveness and ambition; and (c) aggressiveness and hostility when things get in their way. Type B individuals are the opposite—relaxed and serene. Talk to these individuals about their approach to schoolwork. How much time do they spend studying? Do they study as much for courses they like as for courses they dislike? How well do they do? What are their future academic goals? You will probably find striking differences between Type A individuals and Type B individuals.

Glass, D. C. (1976). Pattern A and achievement striving. In *Behavior patterns, stress, and coronary disease* (pp. 36–50). Hillsdale, NJ: Erlbaum.

Exercise Two—Blood Pressure

In this exercise you will have your blood pressure checked. This will give you a better understanding of hypertension and how it is diagnosed. This may also start a habit that is life-long and life-protecting.

Contact your physician at home or at school and make an appointment to have your blood pressure checked. Is your blood pressure normal?

You may also be able to arrange a classroom demonstration by the American Red Cross in which the blood pressure of everyone in your class can be measured. What is the range of scores? What sorts of people have the highest blood pressure? What sorts of people have the lowest?

Exercise Three—Stomach aches and Ulcers

The purpose of this exercise is to learn about the causes and consequences of ulcers.

Talk to several individuals of your acquaintance who suffer or have suffered from stomach aches and ulcers. Does their experience correspond to what your textbook describes as the case about people with peptic ulcers? For instance, do their family members have similar problems? Does stress exacerbate their ulcer?

Kapp, F. T., Rosenbaum, M., & Romano, J. (1947). Psychological factors in men with peptic ulcers. *American Journal of Psychiatry, 103,* 700–704.

CHAPTER 11

Depression and Suicide

CHAPTER OVERVIEW

The depressive disorders, the most common form of abnormality, are covered in this chapter. These are disorders of mood and include unipolar depression (characterized by sadness), mania (characterized by euphoria), and bipolar depression (characterized by swings between sadness and euphoria). Depression is also associated with specific cognitive, motivational, somatic, and behavioral symptoms. Women are more apt to become depressed than men, and recent studies show that depression is much on the rise among both men and women.

The biological model of depression points to an insufficiency of the neurotransmitter norepinephrine as the cause of depression. Antidepressant medication, which is successful in combating depression, increases the availability of this brain chemical. The psychodynamic model proposes that depression results when excessively dependent and help-less individuals turn anger inward against the self. Psychodynamic therapy encourages depressed individuals to recognize and change their anger, dependency, and helplessness. Cognitive models emphasize negative thoughts, erroneous logic, and learned helplessness, and cognitive therapies try to undo these ways of thinking. Each model seems to capture something about depression.

Bipolar depression and mania are not as well understood as unipolar depression, but they involve a genetic component. Lithium is successful in controlling manic episodes, but in light of its serious side effects it is to be used with caution.

The chapter ends with a discussion of suicide, which is frequently preceded by depression. Descriptive information about suicide and suicide attempts is presented, and the presumed motives of suicidal individuals are discussed.

ESSENTIAL TERMS

affective disorder	mental disorder involving disturbance in mood; including unipolar depression, bipolar depression, and mania
anaclitic depression	psychological state among infants separated from their mother characterized by unresponsive apathy, listlessness, weight loss, increased susceptibility to illness; it is thought to be the earliest state related to depression
anger turned inward	in psychodynamic theories, the hypothesized cause of depressive disorders
attributions in learned helplessness	in human helplessness, causal explanations of uncontrollable events thought to influence reactions to these events

global-specific	explanation in terms of a pervasive (global) versus a circumscribed (specific) factor
internal-external	explanation in terms of oneself (internal) or other people/circumstances (external)
stable-unstable	explanation in terms of a recurring (stable) or transient (unstable) factor
automatic thoughts	according to Beck, discrete, negative statements told to oneself quickly and habitually that produce and maintain depression
Beck Depression Inventory (BDI)	self-report questionnaire developed by Aaron T. Beck that measures the prevalence and severity of twenty-one common depressive symptoms
biogenic amines	neurochemicals involved in neural transmission in the medial forebrain bundle and periventricular system
breakdown	process in which a neurochemical is chemically broken down and rendered inactive
catecholamine hypothesis	biological theory of depression proposing that depression results from decreased availability of norepinephrine, a biogenic amine
childhood depression	depressive disorder among children, once thought to be rare, currently thought to be much more common
chronic hypomanic disorder	chronic low-level form of mania
cognitive therapy for depression	approach to therapy developed by Beck that attempts to change the thoughts and justifications of depressed patients (see Chapter 5, "Essential Terms")
cognitive triad	according to Beck, negative thoughts about the self, ongoing experience, and the future that produce depression
depressed mood	sad, blue, miserable feelings
depressive disorder	disorder characterized by a depressed mood, a negative view of oneself and the future, diminished motivation, loss of pleasure, and sleep and eating disturbances
bipolar depression	depression alternating with mania; manic-depression
unipolar depression	depression without mania
depressive personality	personality style characterized by excessive dependence on others for self-esteem and difficulty tolerating frustration; thought to predispose individuals to depressive disorders
dysthymia	chronic depression
electroconvulsive shock therapy (ECT)	therapy for depression in which an electric current is passed through the brain of the patient
endogenous depression	depressive disorder marked by psychomotor retardation, severe symptoms, lack of reaction to environmental events during depression, loss of interest in life, somatic symptoms; thought to arise from disordered biology (cf. exogenous depression)

episodic depression	depressive disorder of less than two years' duration, marked by clear onset
errors in logic	according to Beck, erroneous reasoning that produces depression
arbitrary inference	drawing a conclusion in absence of evidence
magnification/minimization	evaluations that magnify bad events and minimize good events
overgeneralization	drawing conclusions on the basis of a single fact
personalization	taking responsibility for bad events in the world
selective abstraction	focusing on insignificant details and ignoring important features
exogenous depression	depressive disorder marked by less severe symptoms, reaction to environmental events during depression; thought to be precipitated by a life stressor (cf. endogenous depression)
learned helplessness	phenomenon in which organisms exposed to uncontrollable events display subsequent cognitive, motivational, and affective deficits; proposed as a model of depression
lithium	drug used to treat bipolar depression and mania
mania	excessive elation, expansiveness, irritability, talkativeness, inflated self-esteem, and flight of ideas
manipulation	motive for a suicide attempt: desire to manipulate other people
MAO inhibitors	drugs that block breakdown of norepinephrine; used to treat depression
medial forebrain bundle (MFB)	brain structure involved in reward; thought to be involved in depression
normal depression	sad mood occasionally experienced by most people in the course of everyday life
periventricular system (PVS)	brain structure involved in punishment
premenstrual depression (late luteal phase dysphoric disorder)	controversial diagnostic category, in which depressive symptoms among women occur just prior to menstruation
psychomotor retardation	symptom of severe depression, wherein physical movement—walking and talking—is markedly slowed
reattribution training	therapy technique for depression in which the patient is encouraged not to blame him- or herself irrationally for bad events
reserpine	sedative given to patients with high blood pressure that can cause depression as a side effect presumably because it depletes norepinephrine
reuptake	process in which a neuron that has secreted a neurochemical reabsorbs it
seasonal affective disorder (SAD)	form of bipolar depression in which depressive episodes are triggered by short days (with little sunlight)

somatic therapy for depression	biological treatment of depression: ECT, MAO inhibitors, tricyclics, dream deprivation
suicide	· killing of oneself
altruistic suicide	suicide required by society
anomic suicide	suicide precipitated by a shattering break in an individual's relationship to society
egoistic suicide	suicide by an individual with too few ties to fellow humans
surcease	motive for suicide: desire to see an end to problems
tricyclics	drugs used to treat depression that block the reuptake of norepinephrine

SAMPLE EXAM

1. The most common psychological disorder is
   a. phobia.
   b. schizophrenia.
   c. psychosomatic disorder.
   d. depression.
2. Bipolar depression is the same as
   a. manic-depression.
   b. chronic depression.
   c. episodic depression.
   d. anaclitic depression.
3. Normal depression differs from clinical depression in
   a. the number of symptoms.
   b. the severity of symptoms.
   c. the frequency of symptoms.
   d. the duration of symptoms.
   e. both *a* and *c*.
   f. both *b* and *d*.
   g. *a, b, c,* and *d*.
4. The most widespread symptom of depression is
   a. sadness.
   b. negative view of future.
   c. sleep disturbance.
   d. suicidal thoughts.
5. The Beck Depression Inventory is used to
   a. diagnose depression.
   b. measure severity of depressive symptoms.
   c. recommend treatment.
   d. assess illogical thinking.
6. A depressed person sees herself as
   a. negative.
   b. ambivalent.
   c. positive.
   d. variable.
7. Research suggests that depressives
   a. may see the world more accurately than individuals who are not depressed.
   b. may see the world as accurately as individuals who are not depressed.
   c. may see the world less accurately than individuals who are not depressed.
   d. none of the above.
8. How do depressed people respond to success?
   a. They increase their expectations of future success.
   b. They decrease their expectations of future success.
   c. They do not change their expectations of future success.
   d. None of the above.
9. Psychomotor retardation refers to
   a. a form of mental retardation.
   b. an aspect of the emergency reaction.
   c. a slowing down of movement.
   d. a symptom of anxiety.
10. Depressed individuals show all of the following except
    a. sleep disturbance.
    b. decreased appetite.
    c. loss of sexual desire.
    d. indifference to body.

11. The endogenous-exogenous distinction is hoped to correspond to
    a. severe versus mild depressive disorders.
    b. unipolar versus bipolar depressive disorders.
    c. biological versus psychological depressive disorders.
    d. chronic versus episodic depressive disorders.

12. Endogenous is to exogenous as
    a. up is to down.
    b. former is to latter.
    c. right is to wrong.
    d. in is to out.

13. Which of the following depressive symptoms are more common in endogenous depression than in exogenous depression?
    a. psychomotor retardation
    b. sadness
    c. sleep disturbance
    d. reaction to environmental events

14. The endogenous-exogenous distinction is
    a. supported by research.
    b. contradicted by research.
    c. both supported and contradicted by research.
    d. neither supported nor contradicted by research.

15. Studies over time suggest that during the twentieth century, the prevalence of depression has
    a. decreased over time.
    b. stayed much the same.
    c. increased over time.
    d. fluctuated.

16. Which one of the following statements is true?
    a. Women are more likely to be depressed than men.
    b. Men are more likely to be depressed than women.
    c. Women and men are equally likely to be depressed.
    d. Sex differences in depression have changed over the years.

17. DSM-III-R regards premenstrual depression as
    a. firmly established.
    b. needing more study.
    c. nonexistent.

18. Depression is to anaclitic depression as
    a. up is to down.
    b. inside is to outside.

    c. abnormal is to normal.
    d. parent is to infant.

19. Which of the following are true?
    a. Prevalence of depression does not differ markedly across different social classes.
    b. Prevalence of depression does not differ markedly across different races.
    c. Prevalence of depression differs across different social classes.
    d. Prevalence of depression differs across different races.

20. All of the following increase the chances of depression except
    a. early childhood loss.
    b. absence of an intimate relationship.
    c. recent loss.
    d. serious religious commitment.

21. Among most inpatients depressions get better within
    a. one month.
    b. three months.
    c. six months.
    d. one year.

22. After experiencing a depressive episode, one's chances of doing so again within the next ten years are
    a. 90 percent.
    b. 50 percent.
    c. 33 percent.
    d. 10 percent.

23. Chronic depression develops in what percent of people experiencing a depressive episode?
    a. 90
    b. 30
    c. 33
    d. 10

24. Biological accounts of depression focus on the
    a. brain.
    b. heart.
    c. immune system.
    d. spleen.

25. The MFB is to the PVS as
    a. dark is to light.
    b. reward is to punishment.
    c. inside is to outside.
    d. behaviorism is to cognitive theory.

26. According to the biological model, depression is
    a. a thought disorder caused by too much dopamine.

b. a motivational disorder caused by too little norepinephrine.

c. a behavioral disorder caused by too much epinephrine.

d. an emotional disorder caused by too little serotonin.

27. Of the biogenic amines, which is thought to be involved in depression?
a. norepinephrine
b. epinephrine
c. dopamine
d. serotonin
e. histamine

28. Norepinephrine can be inactivated by
a. sublimation.
b. reuptake.
c. breakdown.
d. tolerance.

29. Depression is treated with all of the following drugs except
a. thorazine.
b. imipramine.
c. tricyclics.
d. MAO inhibitors.

30. Tricyclics are to MAO inhibitors as
a. salt is to pepper.
b. reuptake is to breakdown.
c. thorazine is to valium.
d. inside is to outside.

31. All of the following support the biomedical account of depression except
a. effectiveness of drug therapies.
b. depression is sometimes a side effect of medication.
c. early loss predisposes an individual to depression.
d. depression is sometimes a product of hormonal changes.

32. Electroconvulsive shock therapy for severe depression is
a. highly effective.
b. somewhat effective.
c. ineffective.
d. somewhat effective, but only for men.

33. The reason ECT works
a. has been pinpointed by researchers.
b. has not been pinpointed by researchers.
c. is of no interest to researchers.
d. none of the above.

34. The psychodynamic account of depression emphasizes all of the following except
a. fixation at the anal stage.

b. anger turned inward.
c. excessive dependence.
d. helplessness.

35. Freud sought to understand depression by explaining the difference between
a. id and superego.
b. sexuality and aggression.
c. mourning and melancholia.
d. sadness and grief.

36. According to Freud, the depressed individual is actually angry at
a. someone who is loved.
b. someone who is hated.
c. the self.
d. someone who is not known.

37. Suppose you were told that you would be introduced to someone with a depressive personality. You would expect this individual to be
a. charming.
b. oblivious.
c. depressed.
d. independent.

38. Negative thoughts are to Beck as what is to Seligman?
a. happiness
b. hopelessness
c. helplessness
d. helpfulness

39. According to Beck, the depressed individual has a negative view of all of the following except the
a. self.
b. past.
c. present.
d. future.

40. All of the following are errors of logic described by Beck except
a. arbitrary inference.
b. selective abstraction.
c. personalization.
d. depersonalization.

41. A depressed person says that she is a bad mother because her baby occasionally cries. What error in logic is she making?
a. arbitrary inference
b. selective abstraction
c. personalization
d. depersonalization

42. A depressed person says that he is responsible for the national debt. What error in logic is he making?
a. arbitrary inference
b. selective abstraction

c. personalization
d. depersonalization

43. A depressed person says that she is a bad person because her mother died. What error in logic is she making?
a. arbitrary inference
b. selective abstraction
c. personalization
d. depersonalization

44. All of the following are targets for cognitive therapy for depression except
a. anger turned inward.
b. automatic thoughts.
c. attributions.
d. assumptions.

45. Compared to drug therapy for depression, cognitive therapy
a. takes longer.
b. has less relapse.
c. is as effective.
d. *a* and *b*.
e. *a* and *c*.
f. *b* and *c*.
g. all of the above.

46. Learned helplessness was first discovered among
a. mice.
b. rats.
c. dogs.
d. monkeys.
e. people.

47. Learned helplessness deficits result from
a. unpredictable events.
b. uncontrollable events.
c. undesirable events.
d. unknown events.

48. Helplessness deficits include all of the following except
a. motivational deficits.
b. learning deficits.
c. emotional deficits.
d. unconscious deficits.

49. Learned helplessness in people involves
a. expectations.
b. appraisals.
c. attributions.
d. beliefs.

50. All of the following are dimensions along which helplessness theory describes attributions except
a. internal versus external.
b. controllable versus uncontrollable.
c. stable versus unstable.
d. global versus specific.

51. Suppose you cannot work the crossword puzzle in the newspaper this morning. According to helplessness theory, the most depressing causal attribution for your failure is
a. "I didn't have my coffee."
b. "The light is bad."
c. "I'm stupid."
d. "Crossword puzzles are stupid."

52. In the above example, the least depressing causal attribution is
a. "I'm stupid."
b. "I didn't have enough time this morning."
c. "Crossword puzzles are difficult."
d. "I'm not good at the puzzles in this paper."

53. The parallel between learned helplessness and depression is evident in all of the following except
a. passivity.
b. cognitive deficits.
c. anger turned inward.
d. norepinephrine depletion.

54. Learned helplessness can be prevented by
a. immunization.
b. stress.
c. relaxation.
d. none of the above.

55. The attributional reformulation as an explanation of depression has been investigated in studies of
a. children.
b. adults.
c. both.
d. neither.

56. Pessimistic explanatory style is a _____ of(for) depression.
a. necessary and sufficient cause
b. consequence
c. symptom
d. risk factor

57. Recent research suggests that in the course of successful cognitive therapy for depression, explanatory style
a. changes for the better.
b. stays the same.
c. changes for the worse.

58. Which one of the following is *not* a weakness of the cognitive approach to depression?
a. It is based on research.
b. It does not explain all forms of depression.

c. It does not explain why somatic therapies for depression are successful.

d. It is controversial.

59. The best account of depression is that proposed by the
   a. biomedical model.
   b. psychodynamic model.
   c. cognitive model.
   d. none of the above.

60. Mania that occurs without depression is
   a. nonexistent.
   b. rare.
   c. frequent.
   d. always the case.

61. Symptoms of mania include all of the following except
   a. a euphoric mood.
   b. racing thoughts.
   c. insomnia.
   d. attribution of bad events to internal, stable, and global causes.

62. Bipolar depression
   a. is more frequent among men than among women.
   b. is more frequent among women than among men.
   c. is equally frequent among men and women.
   d. has seen a change in sex differences over the years.

63. In bipolar depression, the first episode of mania occurs in
   a. childhood.
   b. adolescence.
   c. early adulthood.
   d. middle age.

64. What is the current thinking about genetic and bipolar disorder?
   a. There is no genetic predisposition.
   b. There is a genetic predisposition.
   c. Research results are contradictory.

65. The preferred treatment of bipolar depression is
   a. flooding.
   b. assertiveness training.
   c. lithium.
   d. MAO inhibitors.

66. Seasonal affective disorder is a form of
   a. unipolar depression.
   b. bipolar depression.
   c. mania.
   d. any of the above.

67. Most suicides are preceded by
   a. anxiety disorders.
   b. affective disorders.
   c. schizophrenic disorders.
   d. somatoform disorders.

68. Who does not belong?
   a. Cleopatra
   b. Marilyn Monroe
   c. Sid Vicious
   d. Ronald Reagan

69. Which one of the following is *not* a myth about suicide?
   a. Individuals who talk about killing themselves do not kill themselves.
   b. Individuals who are suicidal will always be suicidal.
   c. Individuals who attempt suicide may be rational.
   d. Women succeed at suicide less frequently than men.

70. Vulnerability to suicide is influenced by
   a. race.
   b. age.
   c. nationality.
   d. all of the above.

71. Suicide is on the rise particularly among
   a. teenage males.
   b. teenage females.
   c. males in their twenties.
   d. females in their twenties.
   e. males and females in their thirties.

72. Suppose an individual attempted suicide because he wished to benefit his community. His motive is
   a. anomic.
   b. egoistic.
   c. altruistic.
   d. none of the above.

73. Suicide attempts motivated by surcease are
   a. more frequent than those motivated by manipulation.
   b. as frequent as those motivated by manipulation.
   c. less frequent than those motivated by manipulation.
   d. the same as those motivated by manipulation.

74. Factors that predict suicide attempts include
   a. intent.
   b. hopelessness.
   c. anger.
   d. all of the above.

75. Suicide notes are usually
    a. grandiose.
    b. mundane.
    c. creative.
    d. none of the above.

Answer Key for Sample Exam

1. d   (p. 307)
2. a   (p. 308)
3. g   (p. 308)
4. a   (p. 309)
5. b   (p. 314)
6. a   (p. 310)
7. a   (p. 310)
8. c   (p. 313)
9. c   (p. 313)
10. d   (p. 315)
11. c   (p. 316)
12. d   (p. 316)
13. a, c (p. 316)
14. c   (p. 316)
15. c   (p. 317)
16. a   (p. 319)
17. b   (p. 320)
18. d   (p. 320)
19. a, b (p. 321)
20. d   (p. 322)
21. c   (p. 323)
22. b   (p. 324)
23. d   (p. 324)
24. a   (p. 325)
25. b   (p. 326)
26. b   (p. 325)
27. a, d (p. 326)
28. b, c (p. 327)
29. a   (p. 327)
30. b   (p. 327)
31. c   (p. 329)
32. a   (p. 328)
33. b   (p. 329)
34. a   (p. 329)
35. c   (p. 330)
36. a   (p. 330)
37. a   (p. 331)
38. c   (p. 332)
39. b   (p. 332)
40. d   (p. 333)
41. b   (p. 333)
42. c   (p. 334)
43. a   (p. 333)
44. a   (p. 334)
45. g   (p. 334)
46. c   (p. 337)
47. b   (p. 338)
48. d   (p. 337)
49. a, c (p. 338)
50. b   (p. 339)
51. c   (p. 339)
52. b   (p. 339)
53. c   (p. 342)
54. a   (p. 344)
55. c   (p. 340)
56. d   (p. 345)
57. a   (p. 344)
58. a   (p. 346)
59. d   (p. 347)
60. b   (p. 348)
61. d   (p. 349)
62. c   (p. 350)
63. c   (p. 350)
64. b   (p. 352)
65. c   (p. 353)
66. b   (p. 354)
67. b   (p. 355)
68. d   (p. 356)
69. c, d (p. 356)
70. d   (p. 358)
71. c   (p. 359)
72. c   (p. 360)
73. a   (p. 360)
74. a, b (p. 361)
75. b   (p. 361)

SELF-TEST

1. _____ is the most widespread psychological disorder and is _____.

2. The two types of depressive disorders are _____ depression and _____ depression.

3. Depression is widely regarded as a disorder of _____, but it also has characteristic _____, _____, and _____ symptoms.

4. Depressed people have a _____ view of the self, experience, and the future.

5. Research surprisingly suggests that depressed individuals may see reality more _____ than nondepressed individuals.

6. Depressed people tend not to _____ voluntary responses; extremely depressed people may show _____.

7. Common in depression is loss of _____.

8. _____ depression is thought to be precipitated by a life stressor, while _____ depression is thought not to be.

9. Women are _____ vulnerable to depression than men.

10. The earliest psychological state that may be related to depression is _____ depression.

11. Until recently, it was thought that childhood depression was _____ .

12. Research shows that depressed individuals are more likely to have experienced early _____ than nondepressed individuals.

13. Brown and Harris identified four factors that help make an individual invulnerable to depression: first, whether the individual has an _____ relationship; second, whether the individual has a _____ away from home; third, whether the individual has fewer than _____ still at home; and fourth, whether the individual has a serious _____ commitment.

14. Among outpatients, the average depressive episode lasts about _____ months, and among inpatients, the average depressive episode lasts about _____ months.

15. Once a depressive episode has occurred, one of two patterns may develop. In about _____ percent of cases, depression will not recur. In about _____ percent of cases, depression will recur.

16. The biomedical model of depression proposes that the neurotransmitter _____ is involved.

17. Tricyclics affect the _____ of norepinephrine, while MAO inhibitors affect its _____ .

18. About _____ percent of depressed patients improve with antidepressant medication.

19. Electroconvulsive shock therapy is _____ for severe depression. When it is administered to only one-half of the brain, it is _____ .

20. The psychodynamic model of depression proposes that it results from _____ turned inward.

21. According to Freud, depressives _____ lost love objects.

22. The depressive personality is one in which a person is inordinately dependent on other people for _____ .

23. Beck proposes two cognitive mechanisms for depression: the _____ and _____ .

24. When a depressed individual draws a conclusion when there is little evidence, this is _____ .

25. Focusing on one insignificant detail while ignoring more important features is _____ .

26. A global conclusion based on a single fact is _____ .

27. Gross errors of evaluation resulting from attention to an unimportant bad event are examples of _____ .

28. Incorrectly taking responsibility for bad events is _____ .

29. Cognitive therapy for depression is directed at the _____ of the depressive. It has four major techniques: first, detection of _____; second, _____ testing; third, _____ training; and fourth, changing _____.

30. Research suggests that cognitive therapy for depression may be _____ effective as drug therapy.

31. Learned helplessness theory proposes that depression results from the expectation that _____ and _____ will be independent.

32. Learned helplessness involves _____, _____, and _____ deficits.

33. Uncontrollable bad events are thought to produce depression when they are attributed to _____, _____, and _____ causes.

34. According to learned helplessness theory, self-esteem loss in depression results from _____ attributions for bad events.

35. Explanatory style can be changed by _____.

36. Problems of the cognitive model of depression are several. First, it is not clear _____ is modeled. Second, it does not account for the _____ symptoms of depression.

37. The best model of depression seems to be _____.

38. Bipolar depressives alternate between _____ and _____.

39. The thoughts of a manic individual are _____.

40. Bipolar depression is _____ among women as it is among men.

41. The cause of bipolar depression is _____.

42. The treatment of choice for bipolar depression is _____; however, this treatment has serious _____.

43. The most disastrous consequence of depression is _____.

44. Approximately _____ percent of suicidal patients are depressed.

45. Women are _____ likely than men to attempt suicide, but _____ likely to succeed.

46. Suicide _____ with age.

47. Modern thinkers propose two fundamental motives for suicide: _____ and _____.

48. Most suicide notes are _____.

Answer Key for Self-Test

1. Depression; on the rise
2. unipolar; bipolar
3. mood; thought; motivational; physical
4. negative
5. accurately
6. initiate; psychomotor retardation

7. appetite
8. Exogenous; endogenous
9. more
10. anaclitic
11. rare
12. losses
13. intimate; job; three children; religious
14. three; six
15. 50; 50
16. norepinephrine
17. reuptake; breakdown
18. 70
19. effective; unilateral
20. anger
21. incorporate
22. self-esteem
23. cognitive triad; errors in logic
24. arbitrary inference
25. selective abstraction
26. overgeneralization
27. magnification
28. personalization

29. thoughts; automatic thoughts; reality; reattribution; alternatives; depressogenic assumptions
30. as
31. responses; outcomes
32. cognitive; motivational; emotional
33. internal; stable; global
34. internal
35. cognitive therapy
36. what kind of depression; somatic
37. none
38. mania; depression
39. grandiose
40. as common
41. partly genetic
42. lithium; side effects
43. suicide
44. 80
45. more; less
46. increases
47. surcease; manipulation
48. mundane

TYING IT TOGETHER

Depression is one of the better-understood disorders largely because research employing a variety of strategies has converged in the understanding it has provided (Chapter 6). Depression is a disorder that exists on many levels: somatic (Chapter 3), emotional (Chapter 4), behavioral (Chapter 5), cognitive (Chapter 5), and experiential (Chapter 4). Individuals may become depressed because they have other disorders, such as schizophrenia (Chapter 12) and brain damage (Chapter 17). Traditionally, depression has been regarded as a disorder of mood (i.e., emotion), and this may have blinded investigators to the important role of other factors. However, depression is now being approached from a variety of directions, and successful therapies exist where none did before (Chapter 19).

One of the newest perspectives on depression is the cognitive model (Chapter 5). Research using laboratory models (Chapter 6) has shown depression to be as much a thought disorder as a mood disorder, and cognitive therapies for depression (Chapter 19) may be as effective as drug therapies.

Childhood depression illustrates the difficulties in conceiving and diagnosing disorders among children (Chapter 16). Developmental differences may alter the manifestation of depressive symptoms across the life-span, or at least the ease with which diagnosticians can recognize them. Indeed, psychodynamic theorists feel that children cannot be depressed because they lack a fully developed superego. Contemporary opinion is slowly embracing the notion that children can be depressed, but this is still a controversial idea. Behind this changing perspective is the increased use of behavioral assessment (Chapter 7). Some children act like depressed adults. Does it not make sense to view them as depressed, whether or not they verbalize sad and hopeless feelings?

Depression is one of the few fatal psychopathologies. Suicide attempts are frequently preceded by depressive symptoms, particularly hopelessness regarding the future (Chapter 5). The legal system must grapple with suicide and how to regard it (Chapter 18). Should intervention be undertaken if a suicidal individual is depressed (and, therefore, not thinking correctly)? Should intervention not be undertaken if a suicidal individual is not depressed? Are "suicidal" life styles like the Type A behavior pattern (Chapter 10) or alcohol abuse (Chapter 14) the province of the court?

FURTHER READINGS

Abramson, L. Y., Seligman, M. E. P., & Teasdale, J. D. (1978). Learned helplessness in humans: Critique and reformulation. *Journal of Abnormal Psychology, 87,* 49–74.

Burns, D. D. (1980). *Feeling good: The new mood therapy.* New York: Morrow.

Durkheim, E. (1951). *Suicide.* New York: Macmillan.

Egeland, J. A., et al. (1987). Bipolar affective disorders linked to DNA markers on chromosome 11. *Nature, 325,* 783–787.

Freud, S. (1976). Mourning and melancholia. In J. Strachey (Ed. and Trans.), *The standard edition of the complete psychological works of Sigmund Freud* (Vol. 14, pp. 243–258). New York: Norton. (Original work published 1917)

Kleinman, A., & Good, B. (1985). *Culture and depression: Studies in the anthropology and cross-cultural psychiatry of affect and disorder.* Berkeley, CA: University of California Press.

McKnew, D. H., Jr., Cytryn, L., & Yahraes, H. C., Jr. (1983). *Why isn't Johnny crying?* New York: Norton.

Peterson, C., & Seligman, M. E. P. (1984). Causal explanations as a risk factor for depression: Theory and evidence. *Psychological Review, 91,* 347–374.

Rado, S. (1929). The problem of melancholia. *International Journal of Psychoanalysis, 9,* 420–438.

Rosenthal, N. E., et al. (1986). Seasonal affective disorder in children and adolescence. *American Journal of Psychiatry, 143,* 356–368.

Rutter, M., Izard, C. E., & Read, P. R. (1986). *Depression in young people: Developmental and clinical perspectives.* New York: Guilford.

Seligman, M. E. P. (1975). *Helplessness: On depression, development, and death.* San Francisco: Freeman.

Shneidman, E. (1967). *Essays in self-destruction.* New York: Science House.

TERM-PAPER TOPICS

1. Why are women more likely to be depressed than men? Review the possible explanations, and evaluate them in light of existing evidence.

2. What biological processes seem to be involved in bipolar depression? How does lithium affect these processes?

3. Post-partum depression is a depressive episode occurring to some women after childbirth. Is post-partum depression a special type of depression, or does it conform to what is known about other types of depression?

4. The learned helplessness theory of depression is controversial. What issues are involved? How may they be resolved?

5. Uncontrollable events may precede a number of disorders: phobias, peptic ulcer, sudden death, depression, and so on. It is obvious that uncontrollability is harmful, but what determines exactly how it is harmful? In other words, why does a given person become fearful rather than depressed following an uncontrollable event?

6. Discuss recent research into treatment of seasonal affective disorder. How solidly established is this supposed disorder?

EXERCISES

Exercise One—Depression and Uncontrollability

The purpose of this exercise is to demonstrate the basic premise of the learned helplessness model of depression: uncontrollable events result in feelings of helplessness and depression.

Talk to men and women who have just

ended a serious romance. Ask them how much control they perceived over the end of the romance. Ask them how helpless and depressed they felt about the breakup. According to learned helplessness theory, the less control perceived by an individual over an important event like a breakup, the more depressed that person will be in response to it.

Hill, C. T., Rubin, Z., & Peplau, L. A. (1976). Breakups before marriage: The end of 103 affairs. *Journal of Social Issues, 32,* 147–168.

Seligman, M. E. P. (1975). *Helplessness: On depression, development, and death.* San Francisco: Freeman.

Weiss, R. S. (1976). The emotional impact of marital separation. *Journal of Social Issues, 32,* 135–145.

Exercise Two—Depression and Logical Errors

In this exercise, you will evaluate the hypothesis by Aaron Beck that depressed individuals make logical errors in their interpretation of events involving themselves.

Among your friends identify sad and happy individuals. (You may want to gauge their feelings by administering the questionnaire in Exercise Five of Chapter 5). Ask each individual to specify three bad events that occurred to him or her during the past year. Then ask the person to specify the major cause for each event and to provide evidence for believing the suggested cause to be the one.

According to Beck, the sad people should be likely to justify their suggested causes in illogical ways: by irrelevant evidence, by exaggerated evidence, by out-of-context evidence, and so on. Is this the case?

Beck, A. T. (1967). *Depression: Clinical, experimental, and theoretical aspects.* New York: Harper & Row.

Exercise Three—Learned Helplessness

In this exercise, you will perform a learned helplessness experiment.

The learned helplessness phenomenon is striking: following experience with uncontrollable events, individuals have trouble learning to control events that indeed are controllable. You can demonstrate this easily. Obtain twenty 3" × 5" index cards. On ten of them, write five letters (two vowels and three consonants) in a random order. Make sure that these letters do not spell a word regardless of how they are rearranged. On another ten, write five letters (two vowels and three consonants) in a random order that do spell a word when rearranged in the right order. Ask some individuals to try to solve these anagram problems. Give them thirty seconds per card. First, show them the ten cards with no answers. Do not let on that there really are no solutions. Then, show then the ten cards with answers. How many of the solvable anagrams do these individuals answer correctly? Compare this to the performance of other individuals who attempt to solve only the second set of problems—the solvable ones.

Hiroto, D. S., & Seligman, M. E. P. (1975). Generality of learned helplessness in man. *Journal of Personality and Social Psychology, 31,* 311–327.

The Schizophrenias

CHAPTER OVERVIEW

Chapter 12 is concerned with schizophrenia, a set of disorders entailing sweeping disturbances in thought, behavior, and mood. Its substantive criteria include a gross impairment in reality testing and the simultaneous disturbance of several psychological processes. The major types of schizophrenia are paranoid (characterized by delusions of persecution or grandeur), disorganized (characterized by silliness and incoherence), catatonic (characterized by enormously excited or strikingly frozen motor behavior), residual (absence of prominent symptoms but persistent peculiarities), and undifferentiated (not classifiable as one of the other types).

Theories of schizophrenia variously emphasize genetic, biochemical, familial, and societal determinants. Twin studies, adoption studies, family studies, and at-risk studies converge in their support for a genetic component to schizophrenia. Current biological theorizing suggests two independent clusters of schizophrenic symptoms, the first tied to excess dopamine and the second to abnormal brain structure. But biological factors do not make up the entire picture. Other investigations suggest that disordered communication within schizophrenic families may partly cause the disorder. It also has been suggested that schizophrenia is a sane reaction to an insane world—a withdrawal from a situation that is otherwise impossible.

Until the 1950s, treatment of schizophrenia was largely custodial. When neuroleptic drugs were introduced, they profoundly changed treatment. Thought to operate through the blocking of dopamine, these drugs decrease Type I schizophrenic symptoms and have made it possible for many individuals to leave mental hospitals. However, these drugs have severe side effects, and they are not the complete answer to the treatment of schizophrenia.

ESSENTIAL TERMS

adoption studies of schizophrenia	technique for studying the etiology of schizophrenia, in which the prevalence of schizophrenia among children of schizophrenics who are adopted by nonschizophrenics is assessed
affect	emotion
antihistamine	synthetic drug that benefits individuals with asthma or allergies and that exerts a tranquilizing effect
at-risk studies of schizophrenia	technique for studying the etiology of schizophrenia, in which the prevalence of schizophrenia among children at risk for the disorder because of various factors is assessed

catatonic schizophrenia	schizophrenia characterized by motor behavior that is either enormously excited or strikingly frozen
clang association	association produced by rhyme of words
cognitive filter	mechanism of attention that sorts out stimuli to determine which will be admitted to attention and which will not, thought to be disrupted in schizophrenia
communication deviance	inability of parent to establish and maintain a shared arena of attention with child
concealment of meaning	characteristic of communication in schizophrenic families in which individuals hide information when it is clear that it exists
concordant twins	both members of a set of twins have the same disorder (*see* chapter 3, "Essential Terms")
corpus striatum	brain area of high dopamine concentration
co-twin	in twin studies of schizophrenia, the twin examined for the presence or absence of schizophrenia after identification of the index case
delusion	false belief resisting all argument, sustained in the face of all contrary evidence
delusion of control	common schizophrenic delusion that one's thought or behavior is being controlled from without
delusion of grandeur	common schizophrenic delusion that one is especially important
delusion of persecution	common schizophrenic delusion that individuals, groups, or the government have malevolent intentions and are out to "get" the individual
delusion of reference	common schizophrenic delusion involving ideas of reference
dementia praecox	term coined by Emil Kraepelin in 1896 to describe schizophrenia, literally meaning early or premature deterioration
denial of meaning	characteristic of communication in schizophrenogenic families in which individuals deny the reality of meanings and events, consciously or unconsciously
discordant twins	one member of a set of twins has a disorder and the other member does not (*see* Chapter 3, "Essential Terms")
disorganized (hebephrenic) schizophrenia	schizophrenia characterized by apparent silliness and incoherence
divided self	R. D. Laing's description of the schizophrenic self operating on two levels: the silent self, vulnerable and afraid to emerge, and the smokescreen self, disguised to conceal and protect the silent self
dizygotic twins (fraternal twins; DZ twins)	twins developed from two different eggs
dopamine hypothesis	explanation of schizophrenia that proposes that the disorder results from too much dopamine in the brain (*see* Chapter 3, "Essential Terms")

double-bind	characteristic of communication in schizophrenogenic families in which individuals are given mutually exclusive messages, which can neither be satisfied nor avoided
expressed emotion	style of expressing emotions within a family
extra-pyramidal effects	Parkinson-like symptoms resulting from prolonged use of major tranquilizers
family studies of schizophrenia	technique for studying the etiology of schizophrenia, in which the prevalence of schizophrenia within families is assessed
hallucination	false sensory perception with a compelling sense of reality, occurring in the absence of stimuli that ordinarily provoke such a perception
idea of reference	belief that one is especially noticed by others (*see* Chapter 15, "Essential Terms")
index case (proband)	in twin studies of schizophrenia, the twin first seen at psychiatric clinic
injection of meaning	characteristic of communication in schizophrenogenic families in which the clear meaning of another's message is denied and another meaning substituted
milieu therapy	therapy technique in which the patient is provided with training in social communication, work, and recreation (cf. moral treatment—*see* Chapter 2, "Essential Terms")
monozygotic twins (identical twins; MX twins)	twins developed from a single egg
mystification	characteristic of communication in schizophrenogenic families in which the individual is encouraged to doubt feelings, perceptions, and experiences
neuroleptic	drug used to treat schizophrenia; major tranquilizer; psychotropic agent; e.g., phenothiazine
neurotransmitter	chemical responsible for communication between neurons (*see* Chapter 11, "Essential Terms")
overinclusive thinking	characteristic of schizophrenic thinking: tendency to form concepts from both relevant and irrelevant information
paranoid schizophrenia	schizophrenia characterized by systematized delusions of persecution and/or grandeur
Parkinson's disease	neurological disease characterized by stiffness of the arms and legs, flat facial expression, and tremors, thought to result from too little dopamine in the brain
phenothiazine	neuroleptic that blocks brain receptors for dopamine
schizophrenia	disorder of thinking from which flows troubled behavior and troubled mood
acute schizophrenia	schizophrenia marked by a rapid and sudden onset of very florid symptoms
chronic schizophrenia	schizophrenia marked by a prolonged history of withdrawal

residual schizophrenia	schizophrenia without prominent symptoms, marked by persistent peculiarities
Type I schizophrenia	schizophrenia characterized by positive symptoms (e.g., hallucinations and delusions)
Type II schizophrenia	schizophrenia characterized by negative symptoms (e.g., poverty of speech and flat affect)
schizophrenogenic family	family that fosters the emergence of schizophrenia in family members
substantia nigra	bundle of nerves connecting the brain stem to the corpus striatum
superphrenic	individual who is both related to schizophrenic(s) and recognizably outstanding in politics, science, or the arts
tardive dyskinesia	neurological disorder involving sucking, lip smacking, and tongue movements resulting from prolonged use of major tranquilizers
therapeutic community	therapy technique in which patients live and work under guidance
twin studies of schizophrenia	technique for studying the etiology of schizophrenia, in which concordance and discordance of schizophrenia between monozygotic twins versus dizygotic twins are assessed
undifferentiated schizophrenia	schizophrenia not able to be classified as catatonic, disorganized, residual, or paranoid

SAMPLE EXAM

1. Schizophrenia involves
   a. thought.
   b. behavior.
   c. mood.
   d. all of the above.
2. Which one of the following is *not* a myth about schizophrenia?
   a. Schizophrenics are dangerous.
   b. Schizophrenics have split personalities.
   c. Schizophrenia is a lifelong disorder.
   d. Schizophrenia only exists in technological cultures.
3. Kraepelin described schizophrenia as
   a. general paresis.
   b. lycanthropy.
   c. dementia praecox.
   d. senility.
4. The term *schizophrenia* was coined by
   a. Galen.
   b. Kraepelin.
   c. Linnaeus.
   d. Bleuler.
5. Both Kraepelin and Bleuler adhered to the
   a. biomedical model.
   b. psychodynamic model.
   c. behavioral model.
   d. cognitive model.
   e. existential model.
6. Meyer adhered to the
   a. biomedical model.
   b. psychodynamic model.
   c. behavioral model.
   d. cognitive model.
   e. existential model.
7. All of the following are people who are at risk for schizophrenia except
   a. a person under forty-five years of age.
   b. a male.
   c. an urban resident.
   d. a member of the lower class.
8. The substantive criteria for a DSM-III-R diagnosis of schizophrenia include
   a. impairment in reality testing.

b.   excessive anxiety.
c.   hallucinations.
d.   delusions.

9. Delusion is to hallucination as
    a.   pea is to pod.
    b.   belief is to perception.
    c.   avoidance is to escape.
    d.   complex is to simple.

10. All of these are types of schizophrenia
    except
    a.   catatonic.
    b.   hebephrenic.
    c.   psychotic.
    d.   paranoid.

11. A schizophrenic patient acts silly. What
    type of schizophrenia is suggested?
    a.   paranoid
    b.   disorganized
    c.   catatonic
    d.   undifferentiated
    e.   residual

12. A schizophrenic patient acts suspicious.
    What type of schizophrenia is suggested?
    a.   paranoid
    b.   disorganized
    c.   catatonic
    d.   undifferentiated
    e.   residual

13. A schizophrenic patient does not move.
    What type of schizophrenia is suggested?
    a.   paranoid
    b.   disorganized
    c.   catatonic
    d.   undifferentiated
    e.   residual

14. A schizophrenic patient is difficult to as-
    sign to a category. What type of
    schizophrenia is suggested?
    a.   paranoid
    b.   disorganized
    c.   catatonic
    d.   undifferentiated
    e.   residual

15. A schizophrenic patient shows no
    prominent symptoms, just persistent and
    distressing behavior. What type of
    schizophrenia is suggested?
    a.   paranoid
    b.   disorganized
    c.   catatonic
    d.   undifferentiated
    e.   residual

16. What about schizophrenic thought is
    disordered?
    a.   content
    b.   process
    c.   both content and process
    d.   neither content nor process

17. It is thought that a schizophrenic's atten-
    tion is abnormal in that
    a.   too many stimuli are let in.
    b.   too few stimuli are let in.

18. Overinclusive thinking among
    schizophrenics is similar to which type of
    logical error described by Beck among
    depressives?
    a.   personalization
    b.   minimization
    c.   selective abstraction
    d.   arbitrary inference

19. Which of these statements is true?
    a.   Schizophrenics ignore common asso-
         ciations to words and attend to the
         context in which words are used.
    b.   Schizophrenics attend to common
         associations to words and ignore the
         context in which words are used.

20. A schizophrenic patient believes that
    people on television are speaking to him.
    What kind of delusion is this?
    a.   delusion of grandeur
    b.   delusion of control
    c.   delusion of persecution
    d.   delusion of reference

21. A schizophrenic patient believes that his
    doctor is manipulating his thoughts.
    What kind of delusion is this?
    a.   delusion of grandeur
    b.   delusion of control
    c.   delusion of persecution
    d.   delusion of reference

22. A schizophrenic patient believes that he
    is directly in line for the British crown.
    What kind of delusion is this?
    a.   delusion of grandeur
    b.   delusion of control
    c.   delusion of persecution
    d.   delusion of reference

23. A schizophrenic patient believes that the
    CIA is spying on him. What kind of delu-
    sion is this?
    a.   delusion of grandeur
    b.   delusion of control
    c.   delusion of persecution
    d.   delusion of reference

24. Delusions may result from the schizophrenic's attempt to make sense of his experience. This process is
    a. different in kind from that maintaining the beliefs of normal individuals.
    b. different in degree from that maintaining the beliefs of normal individuals.
    c. the same as that maintaining the beliefs of normal individuals.

25. Schizophrenic affect is all of the following except
    a. nonexistent.
    b. inappropriate.
    c. ambivalent.
    d. seemingly flat.

26. According to Laing's concept of the divided self,
    a. schizophrenic communication is gibberish.
    b. schizophrenic communication is literal.
    c. schizophrenic communication is a disguise.
    d. none of the above.

27. Acute schizophrenia is distinguished from chronic schizophrenia on the basis of all of the following except
    a. suddenness of onset.
    b. number of episodes.
    c. precipitating incident.
    d. presence of hallucinations.

28. Type I schizophrenia is characterized by all these except
    a. delusions.
    b. flat affect.
    c. hallucinations.
    d. thought disorder.

29. Type II schizophrenia is characterized by all these except
    a. delusions.
    b. flat affect.
    c. poverty of speech.
    d. social withdrawal.

30. Neuroleptics affect
    a. positive symptoms.
    b. negative symptoms.
    c. both.
    d. neither.

31. Twin studies indicate that
    a. schizophrenia is caused by genes.
    b. schizophrenia is caused by the environment.

c. both *a* and *b*.
d. neither *a* nor *b*.

32. Family studies of schizophrenia indicate that one's chances of being schizophrenic are greatest if one has
    a. a schizophrenic cousin.
    b. a schizophrenic sibling.
    c. a schizophrenic parent.
    d. two schizophrenic parents.

33. Adoption studies of schizophrenia suggest that
    a. schizophrenia is caused by genes.
    b. schizophrenia is caused by the environment.
    c. both *a* and *b*.
    d. neither *a* nor *b*.

34. Which of these statements is true?
    a. Identical twins are more likely to be diagnosed schizophrenic than fraternal twins.
    b. Fraternal twins are more likely to be diagnosed schizophrenic than non-twin siblings.
    c. Identical twins are less likely to be diagnosed schizophrenic than fraternal twins.
    d. Fraternal twins are less likely to be diagnosed schizophrenic than non-twin siblings.
    e. Identical twins are as likely to be diagnosed schizophrenic than fraternal twins.
    f. Fraternal twins are as likely to be diagnosed schizophrenic than non-twin siblings.

35. What is a superphrenic?
    a. a chronic schizophrenic
    b. a creative relative of a schizophrenic
    c. an alien schizophrenic
    d. a long-lived schizophrenic

36. The neurotransmitter thought to be involved in schizophrenia is
    a. norepinephrine.
    b. dopamine.
    c. serotonin.
    d. thorazine.

37. Evidence for the dopamine hypothesis comes from investigations of
    a. neuroleptics.
    b. Parkinson's disease.
    c. amphetamine-induced psychosis.
    d. all of the above.

38. What happens when someone with schizophrenia is given amphetamine?
    a. Schizophrenic symptoms increase.
    b. Schizophrenic symptoms stay unchanged.
    c. Schizophrenic symptoms decrease.

39. What happens when someone with schizophrenia is given anti-Parkinson medicine?
    a. Schizophrenic symptoms increase.
    b. Schizophrenic symptoms stay unchanged.
    c. Schizophrenic symptoms decrease.

40. What happens when someone with Parkinson's disease is given amphetamine?
    a. Parkinson symptoms increase.
    b. Parkinson symptoms stay unchanged.
    c. Parkinson symptoms decrease.

41. What happens when someone with schizophrenia is given neuroleptics for a long time?
    a. Parkinson symptoms increase.
    b. Parkinson symptoms stay unchanged.
    c. Parkinson symptoms decrease.

42. Amphetamine psychosis results from
    a. too much dopamine.
    b. not enough dopamine.

43. Neuroleptics
    a. block dopamine receptors.
    b. open dopamine receptors.

44. Parents who are critical and over-involved with their children are high in
    a. communication deviance.
    b. expressed emotion.
    c. psychopathy.
    d. Type I deviance.
    e. Type II deviance.

45. Parental failure to establish a shared area of attention is _____ deviance.
    a. attentional
    b. communication
    c. expressed
    d. Type I
    e. Type II

46. Communication within schizophrenogenic families is characterized by all of the following except
    a. mystification.
    b. double-bind.
    c. denial of meaning.
    d. injection of meaning.

47. Suppose that one family member encourages another family member to

doubt his perceptions of a situation. This is an example of
    a. mystification.
    b. double-bind.
    c. denial of meaning.
    d. injection of meaning.

48. Suppose that one family member tells another family member to do something and then yells at him for not having a mind of his own. This is an example of
    a. mystification.
    b. double-bind.
    c. denial of meaning.
    d. injection of meaning.

49. Suppose that one family member throws a brick through a window, and then tells another family member that the window is not broken. This is an example of
    a. mystification.
    b. double-bind.
    c. denial of meaning.
    d. injection of meaning.

50. Suppose that one family member calls the police to complain about another family member and then tells that family member that he was just trying to be helpful. This is an example of
    a. mystification.
    b. double-bind.
    c. denial of meaning.
    d. injection of meaning.

51. Type I schizophrenia is linked to
    a. brain function.
    b. brain structure.
    c. both.
    d. neither.

52. Type II schizophrenia is linked to
    a. brain function.
    b. brain structure.
    c. both.
    d. neither.

53. Schizophrenia seems to be overrepresented among the lower class. Research suggests that the reason for this is that
    a. lower-class individuals are more apt to become schizophrenic than middle-class individuals.
    b. schizophrenic individuals are more apt to move from the middle class to the lower class than non-schizophrenic individuals.
    c. both *a* and *b*.
    d. neither *a* nor *b*.

54. According to Laing, schizophrenia is
    a. a learned behavior.
    b. a social role.
    c. withdrawal from an insane world.
    d. a mental illness.
55. Which does not belong?
    a. antihistamine
    b. neuroleptic
    c. amphetamine
    d. major tranquilizer
56. The neuroleptics alleviate
    a. guilt.
    b. depression.
    c. thought disorder.
    d. all of the above.
57. All of the following are side effects of
    the neuroleptics except
    a. extra-pyramidal effects.
    b. tardive dyskinesia.
    c. diarrhea.
    d. drowsiness.
58. Which statement is true?
    a. Neuroleptics cure schizophrenia.
    b. Neuroleptics alleviate some
       schizophrenic symptoms.
    c. Neuroleptics cure psychological
       problems among schizophrenics.
    d. all of the above.

Answer Key for Sample Exam

1.	d	(p. 364)	30.	a	(p. 383)
2.	d	(p. 365)	31.	c	(p. 385)
3.	c	(p. 366)	32.	d	(p. 387)
4.	d	(p. 365)	33.	c	(p. 388)
5.	a	(p. 366)	34.	e, f	(p. 387)
6.	c	(p. 366)	35.	b	(p. 391)
7.	b	(p. 369)	36.	b	(p. 392)
8.	a	(p. 368)	37.	d	(p. 393)
9.	b	(p. 368)	38.	a	(p. 392)
10.	c	(p. 370)	39.	a	(p. 393)
11.	b	(p. 370)	40.	c	(p. 393)
12.	a	(p. 370)	41.	a	(p. 392)
13.	c	(p. 371)	42.	a	(p. 393)
14.	d	(p. 372)	43.	a	(p. 395)
15.	e	(p. 372)	44.	b	(p. 396)
16.	c	(p. 373)	45.	b	(p. 396)
17.	a	(p. 375)	46.	b	(p. 397)
18.	d	(p. 375)	47.	a	(p. 396)
19.	b	(p. 377)	48.	b	(p. 397)
20.	d	(p. 377)	49.	c	(p. 397)
21.	b	(p. 377)	50.	d	(p. 397)
22.	a	(p. 377)	51.	a	(p. 395)
23.	c	(p. 377)	52.	b	(p. 395)
24.	c	(p. 379)	53.	c	(p. 398)
25.	a	(p. 380)	54.	c	(p. 399)
26.	c	(p. 382)	55.	c	(p. 401)
27.	d	(p. 382)	56.	c	(p. 402)
28.	b	(p. 383)	57.	c	(p. 402)
29.	a	(p. 383)	58.	b	(p. 402)

SELF-TEST

1. Schizophrenia is a disorder of _____, but it also involves disturbances in _____ and _____.

2. There are numerous myths about schizophrenia. In truth, schizophrenics are not _____; they do not have _____; and they are not necessarily schizophrenic for _____.

3. To describe what is now called schizophrenia, Kraepelin introduced the term _____, which means _____.

4. Kracpelin felt that schizophrenia was _____; in contrast, Meyer felt that schizophrenia was _____.

5. Schizophrenia occurs mainly among individuals who are under _____ years of age.

6. The two substantive criteria for schizophrenia are _____ and _____.

7. Delusions are false _____.

8. Hallucinations are false _____.

9. In _____ schizophrenia, the individual has systematic delusions about persecution.

10. In _____ schizophrenia, the individual is silly and incoherent.

11. In _____ schizophrenia, the motor behavior of the individual is enormously excited or strikingly frozen.

12. Schizophrenia that is not able to be classified as paranoid, disorganized, residual, or catatonic is _____ schizophrenia.

13. In _____ schizophrenia, there is an absence of prominent symptoms.

14. _____ difficulties may provide a fertile soil for hallucination.

15. The most common schizophrenic hallucinations are _____.

16. Schizophrenics' difficulties with attention seem to involve a _____ of the cognitive filter.

17. Schizophrenic thinking is _____ inclusive.

18. A belief that television newscasters are speaking to one is an _____.

19. Common schizophrenic delusions are delusions of _____, _____, _____, and _____.

20. Research suggests that delusions are a "normal" consequence of abnormal _____.

21. Schizophrenic affect often is either _____ or _____.

22. According to Laing, schizophrenics have a _____.

23. _____ schizophrenia involves positive symptoms like hallucinations and delusions, and _____ schizophrenia involves negative symptoms like flat affect and poverty of speech.

24. At least five factors may cause schizophrenia: _____, _____, _____, _____, and _____.

25. Twin studies suggest that schizophrenia has a _____ component; so, too, do _____ studies, _____ studies, and _____ studies.

26. Compared to the general population, the prevalence of schizophrenia among twins is _____.

27. Research suggests that the neurotransmitter _____ may be involved in schizophrenia. Specifically, it is thought that too _____ of this neurotransmitter may cause schizophrenia. There are several lines of evidence for this hypothesis. First, the neuroleptics _____ the availability of this neurotransmitter. Second, prolonged use of the neuroleptics may result in symptoms like those of _____, which seems to involve too _____ of this neurotransmitter. Third, amphetamine psychosis, which is indistinguishable from schizophrenia, involves too _____ of this neurotransmitter.

28. _____ families may encourage schizophrenia among their members through _____ communication.

29. Thought disorders may be influenced by _____ of meaning, _____ of meaning, and _____ of meaning.

30. The dopamine hypothesis applies particularly to _____.

31. Abnormal brain structure may be at the base of _____.

32. Schizophrenia is overrepresented among the _____ class.

33. Laing argues that schizophrenia is a _____ reaction to an insane world.

34. The drugs used to treat schizophrenia are called _____; two of the most common are _____ and _____.

35. The neuroleptics reduce _____, but they do not reduce _____.

36. Two of the serious side effects of neuroleptics are _____ and _____.

37. The neuroleptics have greatly _____ the number of institutionalized schizophrenics. However, many of these patients are _____.

38. Two factors seem to dictate schizophrenic relapse: the _____ of the home and _____ the patient spends there.

39. The full treatment of schizophrenia may someday involve _____ or _____.

Answer Key for Self-Test

1. thought; mood; behavior
2. dangerous; split personalities; life
3. *dementia praecox*; early deterioration
4. biological; environmental
5. forty-five
6. gross impairment of reality testing; disturbance of several psychological processes
7. beliefs
8. perceptions
9. paranoid
10. disorganized
11. catatonic
12. undifferentiated
13. residual
14. Perceptual
15. auditory
16. breakdown
17. over
18. idea of reference
19. grandeur; control; persecution; reference
20. perceptions
21. flat; inappropriate
22. divided self
23. Type I; Type II
24. genetics; biochemistry; abnormal brain structure; family; society
25. genetic; adoption; family; at-risk
26. equal
27. dopamine; much; decrease; Parkinson's disease; little; much
28. Schizophrenogenic; disordered
29. injection; concealment; denial
30. Type I
31. Type II
32. lower
33. sane
34. neuroleptics; haloperidol; chlorpromaxine
35. positive symptoms; negative symptoms
36. extra-pyramidal effects; tardive dyskinesia
37. reduced; readmitted
38. emotional quality; how much time
39. milieu therapies; therapeutic communities

TYING IT TOGETHER

Schizophrenia is one of the "best" examples of abnormality since all of the elements that count toward a judgment of abnormality may be present in this disorder: suffering, maladaptiveness, irrationality, unpredictability, vividness, observer discomfort, and violation of standards (Chapter 1). Descriptions of schizophrenic-like disorders are found throughout history and across cultures (Chapter 2). When the legal system becomes involved with abnormal psychology (Chapter 18), it is often out of concern for schizophrenic individuals.

Schizophrenia is also one of the most complex disorders. Various explanations have been offered, representing most of the major approaches to abnormality (Chapters 3–5). Most explanations have been at least partly supported by a variety of research strategies (Chapter 6). Schizophrenia seems to have biological components—genetic inheritance, neurotransmitter imbalance, and abnormal brain structure (Chapter 3). The twin studies used to investigate the causes of schizophrenia are elegant, and the dopamine hypothesis has received converging support from a variety of sources, including laboratory models and experiments (Chapter 6). But schizophrenia also has psychological and social components. It may result from disordered patterns of communication within families. It is overrepresented among the lower class. Schizophrenia responds well to milieu therapy (Chapter 19), the modern equivalent of humane treatment (Chapter 2).

Granted the complexity of schizophrenia, perhaps it is not surprising that its diagnosis (Chapter 7) and treatment (Chapter 19) remain problematic. Some have expressed the opinion that schizophrenia is a myth, a label used to rationalize both inadvertent and willful persecution of powerless individuals who may be "marching to their own drummer." The relationship of schizophrenia to creativity is consistent with this interpretation, but the suffering and maladjustment of individuals with schizophrenic symptoms should not be forgotten.

FURTHER READINGS

Bateson, G., Jackson, D. D., Haley, J., & Weakland, J. (1956). Toward a theory of schizophrenia. *Behavioral Science, 1,* 251–264.

Bernheim, K. F., & Lewine, R. R. J. (1979). *Schizophrenia: Symptoms, causes, and treatments.* New York: Norton.

Fox, J. G. (1970). *Gone is shadows' child.* Plainfield, NJ: Logos International.

Gottesman, I., & Shields, J. (1972). *Schizophrenia and genetics: A twin study vantage point.* New York: Academic Press.

Greenberg, J. (1964). *I never promised you a rose garden.* New York: Signet.

Laing, R. D. (1965). *The divided self: An existential study in sanity and madness.* Baltimore: Pelican.

Laing, R. D., & Esterson, A. (1971). *Sanity, madness, and the family: Families of schizophrenics* (2nd ed.). New York: Basic Books.

Lidz, T., Fleck, S., & Cornelison, A. (1965). *Schizophrenia and the family.* New York: International Universities Press.

Murphy, H. B. M. (1978). Cultural influences on incidence, course, and treatment response. In L. C. Wynne, R. L. Cromwell, & S. Matthysse (Eds.), *The nature of schizophrenia: New approaches to research and treatment* (pp. 586–594). New York: Wiley.

Sarbin, T. R., & Mancuso, J. C. (1980). *Schizophrenia: Medical diagnosis or moral verdict.* New York: Pergamon.

Seidman, L. J. (1983). Schizophrenia and brain dysfunction: An integration of research neurodiagnostic findings. *Psychological Bulletin, 94,* 195–238.

Vonnegut, M. (1975). *The Eden express.* New York: Praeger.

Yalom, I. E., & Elkin, G. (1974). *Every day gets a little closer: A twice told therapy.* New York: Basic Books.

TERM-PAPER TOPICS

1. Evaluate R. D. Laing's claims about schizophrenia in *The Divided Self* with research investigating the long-term consequences of schizophrenia. Is Laing mostly right or mostly wrong? Take a stand and defend it.

2. The side effects of neuroleptics cause more distress than schizophrenia. Evaluate this claim, touching on both short-term and long-term side effects.

3. If schizophrenia has a genetic component, just what is it? In other words, what specifically is inherited that may bring about schizophrenia?

4. Describe the research investigating children at high risk for schizophrenia who did not develop the disorder. What are the implications of this research for theories about the cause of schizophrenia?

5. What are the implications of the distinction between Type I and Type II schizophrenia? Describe a future edition of DSM that takes this distinction into account.

6. Evaluate the controversy surrounding the plight of the homeless mentally ill, some large number of whom are schizophrenic, in light of what you know about the causes and treatments of schizophrenia.

EXERCISES

Exercise One—Beliefs about Schizophrenia

This exercise allows you to see the variability of beliefs about schizophrenia.

Talk to a number of individuals about schizophrenia. Ask them questions like

1. What is schizophrenia?
2. What are the symptoms of schizophrenia?
3. Do schizophrenics have split personalities?
4. Are schizophrenics dangerous?
5. What are the causes of schizophrenia?
6. Who is at risk for schizophrenia?
7. What are the treatments of schizophrenia?
8. Is schizophrenia incurable?
9. Do you know anyone who has had schizophrenia?

Also, repeat these questions for "nervous breakdown," which many people use in place of "schizophrenia."

What is the range of beliefs? Are there differences between beliefs about schizophrenia and beliefs about nervous breakdowns? Which beliefs are consistent with what is known about schizophrenia? Which are inconsistent?

Bernheim, K. F., & Lewins, R. R. J. (1979). *Schizophrenia: Symptoms, causes, treatments.* New York: Norton.

Seeman, W. V. (1982). *Living and working with schizophrenia.* Toronto: University of Toronto Press.

Exercise Two—Chronic Patients

The purpose of this exercise is to gain first-hand knowledge of how chronic patients are treated in a mental hospital.

Arrange a tour for your class at a local psychiatric hospital. Ask to be told about the chronic wards. Who stays on them? What are their diagnoses? Prognoses? What kinds of therapy are they given? What are their lives like?

Exercise Three—Work on a Chronic Ward

The purpose of this exercise is to gain experience in the care of chronic psychiatric patients.

Volunteer to work as an aide in a chronic ward of a local psychiatric hospital. Use your work as an opportunity to examine your beliefs about how people with psychological problems should be treated.

CHAPTER 13

Sexual Behavior, Dysfunction, and Disorder

CHAPTER OVERVIEW

This chapter describes three types of sexual problems; sexual dysfunction, paraphilias, and transsexuality. To introduce these problems, the chapter discusses human sexual behavior and how it has been studied scientifically. The pioneering research by Kinsey and by Masters and Johnson is emphasized.

Sexual dysfunctions are problems involving the sexual response; all are "inabilities" and may affect arousal, performance, and/or orgasm. In many cases, sexual dysfunctions have psychological causes, of which anxiety is thought to be the most common. Masters and Johnson have pioneered direct sexual therapy to treat dysfunctions, and it seems highly successful.

Paraphilias are sexual object choices that interfere with affectionate erotic relationships between two human beings. These include fetishes (in which sexual arousal only occurs in conjunction with an inanimate object), sadism (in which sexual arousal only occurs when pain is inflicted on another), and masochism (in which sexual arousal only occurs when pain is inflicted on the self). Paraphilias occur overwhelmingly among men. The psychodynamic and behavioral accounts of paraphilias are described, and it is suggested that the behavioral account is more complete. Behavioral treatments, which are somewhat successful, are discussed.

Homosexuality is covered in this chapter, and the point is made that only homosexuality that is uncomfortable to the person—ego-dystonic homosexuality—is considered a disorder.

Finally, the chapter ends with the topic of transsexuality. A transsexual is a man who feels like a woman trapped in a man's body, or a woman who feels like a man trapped in a woman's body. Transsexuality is rare, and it causes are little understood. At the present time, the only treatment for transsexuality is a sex-change operation, a controversial procedure.

ESSENTIAL TERMS

androgen-insensitivity syndrome	hormonal problem in which fetus lacks receptors for the hormone androgen
bisexuality	sexual activity with both men and women
bypassing	focusing on fantasy during sexual activity and not on one's partner
cathexis	in psychoanalytic theory, the charging of a neutral object with psychical energy, either positive or negative

counterbypassing	sexual therapy technique that broadens awareness during sexual activity by encouraging partners to talk about negative feelings
covert sensitization	treatment for paraphilias in which imagined sexual stimuli are followed by aversive stimuli
direct sexual therapy	therapy for sexual dysfunction developed by Masters and Johnson in which patients are not treated individually but as couples who receive instruction while explicitly practicing sexual behavior under the systematic guidance of a therapist
erectile dysfunction	sexual dysfunction characterized by a recurrent inability to have or maintain an erection for intercourse
primary erectile dysfunction	erectile dysfunction in which an erection sufficient for intercourse has never been achieved
secondary erectile dysfunction	erectile dysfunction in which the ability to have an erection sufficient for intercourse has been lost
exhibitionism	sexual dysfunction involving the exposure of genitals to unwitting and usually unwilling strangers
fetish	sexual object choice that is inanimate
gender identity	one's awareness of being male or female
gender role	public expression of gender identity; what an individual does and says to indicate that he is a man or she is a woman
homosexuality	sexual activity between individuals of the same sex
ego-dystonic homosexuality	sustained pattern of homosexuality that is a source of distress to the individual and is accompanied by a desire to acquire or increase heterosexual activity
ego-syntonic homosexuality	sustained pattern of homosexuality that is neither a source of distress nor something the individual desires to change
masochism	sexual dysfunction in which an individual becomes sexually aroused by having suffering or humiliation inflicted on him or her
masturbation	stimulation of one's own genitals
orgasmic dysfunction	sexual dysfunction characterized by a recurrent inability to have an orgasm
primary orgasmic dysfunction	orgasmic dysfunction in which orgasm has never occurred
secondary orgasmic dysfunction	orgasmic dysfunction in which the ability to have an orgasm has been lost
paraphilia	sexual dysfunction characterized by sexual arousal to the unusual or bizarre; e.g., fetish
pedophilia	sexual dysfunction involving sexual relations with children below the age at which they can reasonably be expected to give mature consent
premature ejaculation	recurrent inability to exert any control over ejaculation

pseudo-hermaphrodite	individual with female chromosomes, hormonally masculinized as a fetus, born with ambiguous-looking genitals
retarded ejaculation	recurrent difficulty in ejaculating during sexual intercourse
sadism	sexual dysfunction in which an individual becomes sexually aroused by inflicting physical and psychological suffering or humiliation
sensate focus	direct sexual therapy technique that attempts to decrease anxiety during intercourse
sexual dysfunction	disorder involving sexuality: arousal, performance, orgasm
sexual object choice	types of persons, parts of the body, and situations that are the subject of one's sexual fantasies
sexual unresponsiveness	sexual dysfunction characterized by lack of sexual desire and impairment of physical excitement in appropriate situations
transsexualism	sexual dysfunction involving the belief that one is a woman trapped in the body of a man, or a man trapped in the body of a woman
transvestism	sexual dysfunction in which a man persistently dresses in women's clothes in order to achieve sexual arousal
voyeurism	sexual dysfunction involving the observation of a naked body, disrobing, or the sexual activity of an unsuspecting victim

SAMPLE EXAM

1. The first major contribution to the scientific study of sexual behavior was by
   a. Galen.
   b. Freud.
   c. Kinsey.
   d. Masters and Johnson.

2. The research technique employed by Kinsey was
   a. clinical case history.
   b. experimental study.
   c. correlational study.
   d. experiment of nature.
   e. laboratory model.

3. Surveys of sexual behavior are probably
   a. nonrandom assignment.
   b. subject bias.
   c. experimenter bias.
   d. all of the above.

4. The research technique employed by Masters and Johnson was
   a. clinical case history.
   b. experimental study.
   c. correlational study.
   d. experiment of nature.
   e. laboratory model.

5. The sexual response consists of these phases:
   a. excitement to arousal to orgasm.
   b. arousal to excitement to orgasm.
   c. orgasm to arousal to excitement.
   d. arousal to orgasm to excitement.

6. *Refractory* means
   a. responsive.
   b. retarded.
   c. premature.
   d. unresponsive.

7. Orgasm by men and orgasm by women
   a. are experienced differently.
   b. are experienced similarly.

8. Sexual dysfunction occurs in which stage of sexual response?
   a. desire
   b. excitement
   c. orgasm
   d. all of the above

9. Sexual unresponsiveness is a problem with
   a. desire.
   b. excitement.
   c. orgasm.
   d. all of the above.

10. Impotence is the same as
    a. frigidity.
    b. premature ejaculation.
    c. low sperm count.
    d. erectile dysfunction.

11. A man who has never had an erection is suffering from
    a. primary erectile dysfunction.
    b. secondary erectile dysfunction.
    c. situation specific dysfunction.
    d. all of the above.

12. Focus on fantasy during sexual activity, as opposed to focus on one's partner, is called
    a. anhedonia.
    b. bypassing.
    c. fetishing.
    d. paraphilia.

13. A woman who has lost the ability to have an orgasm is suffering from
    a. primary orgasmic dysfunction.
    b. secondary orgasmic dysfunction.
    c. situation specific dysfunction.
    d. all of the above.

14. Retarded ejaculation is a problem with
    a. arousal.
    b. excitement.
    c. orgasm.
    d. all of the above.

15. Most sexual dysfunction has
    a. physical causes.
    b. psychological causes.
    c. physical and psychological causes.
    d. it is not known at the present time.

16. Direct sexual therapy fails to benefit
    a. 10 percent of clients.
    b. 25 percent of clients.
    c. 50 percent of clients.
    d. 75 percent of clients.
    e. 95 percent of clients.

17. Masters and Johnson usually treat
    a. only males.
    b. only females.
    c. only partners.
    d. it depends.

18. The premise of sensate focus is that
    a. depression leads to sexual dysfunction.
    b. anxiety leads to sexual dysfunction.
    c. boredom leads to sexual dysfunction.
    d. arousal leads to sexual dysfunction.

19. Counterbypassing is a _____ technique.
    a. diagnostic
    b. sexual therapy
    c. statistical
    d. transsexual
    e. transvestite

20. The proportion of males who masturbate is
    a. 10 percent.
    b. 33 percent.
    c. 50 percent.
    d. 95 percent.

21. The proportion of females who masturbate is
    a. 10 percent.
    b. 33 percent.
    c. 50 percent.
    d. 95 percent.

22. The frequency of premarital intercourse within a culture is influenced by
    a. the prevalence of venereal disease.
    b. the availability of birth control.
    c. social stratification.
    d. all of the above.

23. Homosexuality in our culture is
    a. more common among men than among women.
    b. more common among women than among men.
    c. equally common among men and women.
    d. none of the above.

24. All of these are paraphilias except
    a. fetish.
    b. sadism.
    c. masochism.
    d. transsexualism.

25. Fetishes are
    a. more common among men than among women.
    b. more common among women than among men.
    c. equally common among men and women.
    d. none of the above.

26. A fetish is usually acquired during
    a. infancy.
    b. childhood.
    c. puberty.
    d. early adulthood.
    e. middle age.

27. A man who dresses in women's clothing in order to achieve sexual arousal is a
    a. homosexual.
    b. bisexual.
    c. transsexual.
    d. transvestite.

28. Sadism is to masochism as
    a. east is to west.
    b. reward is to punishment.
    c. giving is to receiving.
    d. in is to out.

29. Sadism takes its name from
    a. a French marquis.
    b. Sadie Hawkins.
    c. John Cougar.
    d. Larry Flynt.

30. Masochism takes its name from
    a. Bonnie Raitt.
    b. a German novelist.
    c. an Arctic explorer.
    d. Abraham Maslow.

31. Which of these statements is true?
    a. Sadism is more common among men than women, and masochism is more common among women than men.
    b. Sadism is more common among women than men, and masochism is more common among men than women.
    c. Sadism and masochism both are more common among men than women.
    d. Sadism and masochism both are more common among women than men.

32. Rape seems best described as an instance of
    a. sexual dysfunction.
    b. paraphilia.
    c. crime.
    d. none of the above.

33. Exhibitionism is to voyeurism as
    a. stimulus is to response.
    b. in is to out.
    c. reward is to punishment.
    d. presence is to absence.

34. Pedophilia involves
    a. feet.
    b. shoes.
    c. children.
    d. birds.

35. Exhibitionism is
    a. more common among men than among women.
    b. more common among women than among men.
    c. equally common among men and women.
    d. none of the above.

36. Voyeurism is
    a. more common among men than among women.
    b. more common among women than among men.
    c. equally common among men and women.
    d. none of the above.

37. Pedophilia is
    a. more common among men than among women.
    b. more common among women than among men.
    c. equally common among men and women.
    d. none of the above.

38. Suppose you were told that you were to meet someone who is an exhibitionist. You would expect him to be
    a. loud.
    b. insecure.
    c. unmarried.
    d. over fifty years of age.

39. The most heavily punished sexual crime is
    a. voyeurism.
    b. transsexualism.
    c. agoraphobia.
    d. pedophilia.

40. Suppose you were told that you would meet someone who is a child molester. You would expect him to be
    a. crude.
    b. religious.
    c. liberal.
    d. none of the above.

41. The psychoanalytic account of paraphilia emphasizes
    a. cathexis.
    b. catharsis.
    c. sublimation.
    d. fixation at the oral stage.

42. The behavioral account of paraphilia emphasizes
    a. Pavlovian conditioning.
    b. operant conditioning.
    c. modeling.
    d. all of the above.

43. The behavioral account of paraphilia does a good job explaining
    a. acquisition.
    b. persistence.
    c. both acquisition and persistence.
    d. neither acquisition nor persistence.

44. The most successful treatment of the paraphilias seems to be
    a. insight therapy.
    b. covert sensitization.
    c. drug therapy.
    d. all of the above.

45. Homosexuality is considered a disorder when it is
    a. frequent.
    b. ego-syntonic.
    c. ego-dystonic.
    d. illegal.

46. Dissatisfaction with one's homosexuality may arise from
    a. the homosexual's desire to have children.
    b. societal attitudes toward homosexuality.
    c. rejection by the homosexual's family.
    d. all of the above.

47. The Ames-Ellis theory of homosexuality proposes that homosexuality is caused by events during
    a. pregnancy.
    b. infancy.
    c. childhood.
    d. early adolescence.
    e. late adolescence.

48. Homosexuality may be changed through
    a. psychoanalysis.
    b. behavior therapy.
    c. drug therapy.
    d. none of the above.

49. Transsexuality seems to originate in
    a. the womb.
    b. childhood.
    c. adolescence.
    d. early adulthood.

50. Most transsexuals are
    a. homosexuals.
    b. bisexuals.
    c. transvestites.
    d. none of the above.

51. The most effective treatment of transsexuality is that associated with the
    a. biomedical model.
    b. psychodynamic model.
    c. behavioral model.
    d. cognitive model.
    e. existential model.

Answer Key for Sample Exam

1.	c	(p. 412)	27.	d	(p. 429)
2.	c	(p. 412)	28.	c	(p. 430)
3.	a, b	(p. 412)	29.	a	(p. 431)
4.	b	(p. 413)	30.	b	(p. 431)
5.	b	(p. 414)	31.	c	(p. 431)
6.	d	(p. 415)	32.	c	(p. 432)
7.	b	(p. 415)	33.	a	(p. 434)
8.	d	(p. 415)	34.	c	(p. 435)
9.	a	(p. 416)	35.	a	(p. 433)
10.	d	(p. 417)	36.	a	(p. 434)
11.	a	(p. 417)	37.	a	(p. 435)
12.	b	(p. 418)	38.	b	(p. 433)
13.	b	(p. 418)	39.	d	(p. 435)
14.	c	(p. 419)	40.	b	(p. 435)
15.	b	(p. 419)	41.	a	(p. 436)
16.	b	(p. 422)	42.	a	(p. 437)
17.	c	(p. 422)	43.	c	(p. 437)
18.	b	(p. 423)	44.	b	(p. 438)
19.	b	(p. 424)	45.	c	(p. 439)
20.	d	(p. 425)	46.	d	(p. 441)
21.	c	(p. 425)	47.	a	(p. 442)
22.	d	(p. 425)	48.	b	(p. 442)
23.	a	(p. 426)	49.	a, b	(p. 446)
24.	d	(p. 428)	50.	d	(p. 445)
25.	a	(p. 429)	51.	a	(p. 448)
26.	b	(p. 429)			

SELF-TEST

1. Sexual problems include _____ , _____ , and _____ .

2. Kinsey made the first major contribution to the scientific understanding of human sexuality with an _____ procedure, in which he asked questions about _____ .

3. Masters and Johnson studied human sexuality with an _____ procedure, in which they studied the _____ of sex.

4. The sexual response consists of three phases: _____, _____, and _____; dysfunctions can occur in _____ phases.

5. Sexual response in men and women is _____.

6. Lack of sexual desire is called _____.

7. A recurrent inability to have or maintain an erection is _____.

8. Orgasmic dysfunction in men includes _____ ejaculation and _____ ejaculation.

9. The majority of cases of sexual dysfunction are caused by _____ factors.

10. To treat sexual dysfunction, Masters and Johnson developed _____.

11. The major strategy of direct sexual therapy is _____, which attempts to reduce _____.

12. Direct sexual therapy usually involves the treatment of _____.

13. Masters and Johnson report that only _____ percent of patients fail to improve with direct sexual therapy.

14. Men are _____ likely than women to masturbate; about _____ percent of men do so.

15. Societal attitudes toward premarital intercourse have become _____ over the years.

16. About _____ percent of men and _____ percent of women have had some homosexual activity.

17. Only _____ homosexuality is considered a psychological disorder; _____ homosexuality is not considered a disorder.

18. Individuals who are neither exclusively heterosexual nor exclusively homosexual are called _____.

19. One type of paraphilia in which a person is sexually aroused by a nonliving object is called a _____; it is a disorder of sexual _____.

20. There are three major types of paraphilias: those that involve _____; those that involve _____ and _____; and those that involve _____.

21. _____ is when a man dresses in the clothes of a woman in order to achieve sexual arousal.

22. In _____, sexual arousal results from the infliction of suffering or humiliation on another; in _____, sexual arousal results from receiving suffering or humiliation from another.

23. Individuals who expose their genitals to unwitting strangers are _____ ; those who observe the sexual activity of others are _____ ; and those who have sex with children are _____ .

24. Paraphilias occur almost exclusively among _____ .

25. The psychodynamic model explains the paraphilias in terms of _____ .

26. The behavioral model explains the paraphilias in terms of _____ .

27. Behavioral therapy for the paraphilias includes _____ and _____ .

28. One's dissatisfaction with his homosexuality may have several sources. First, he may wish to have _____ . Second, _____ may disapprove. Third, his _____ may also disapprove.

29. Traditional psychotherapy is _____ in changing homosexual orientation.

30. A transsexual is a man who feels like a _____ , or a woman who feels like a _____ .

31. An individual with ambiguous-looking genitals is a _____ .

32. At present, the only treatment for transsexuality is a _____ .

33. The cause of transsexuality is _____ .

Answer Key for Self-Test

1. sexual dysfunctions; paraphilias; transsexuality.
2. interview; sexual practices
3. experimental; physiology
4. desire; physical excitement; orgasm; all
5. similar
6. sexual unresponsiveness
7. erectile dysfunction
8. premature; retarded
9. psychological
10. direct sexual therapy
11. sensate focus; anxiety
12. couples
13. 25
14. more; 95
15. more
16. 33; 20
17. ego-dystonic; ego-syntonic
18. bisexuals
19. fetish; object choice
20. inanimate objects; suffering; humiliation; nonconsenting partners
21. Transvestism
22. sadism; masochism
23. exhibitionists; voyeurs; pedophiles

24. men
25. cathexis
26. Pavlovian conditioning
27. covert sensitization; reconditioning
28. children; society; family
29. ineffective
30. woman; man
31. pseudo-hermaphrodite
32. sex-change operation
33. unknown

TYING IT TOGETHER

Although Freud was greatly concerned with sexuality, the psychodynamic model (Chapter 4) is not the model of choice with which to explain sexual dysfunctions. Most sexual disorders do not appear to have physical causes, although a sound knowledge of neurology (Chapter 17) is needed to make this differential diagnosis. Instead, the behavioral model (Chapter 5) has proven most useful in conceiving and treating these disorders, which often involve anxiety (cf. Chapters 8 and 9). Direct sexual therapy, as pioneered by Masters and Johnson, uses behavioral techniques to teach couples more satisfying ways of relating to each other sexually (Chapter 19). Like other behavioral techniques, these were developed through laboratory experimentation (Chapter 6) and careful behavioral and physiological assessment (Chapter 7).

Psychoanalytic theory is more helpful in explaining paraphilias, although again, the behavioral model seems viable. The behavioral approach leaves unanswered the questions of why only men have fetishes and why mostly men are sadists and masochists. Perhaps cultural and historical factors (Chapter 2) explain this puzzling sex difference, but the possible role of biology should not be overlooked.

No theory gives a good account of transsexuality. Although this disorder can be treated with a sex-change operation, the results are not always satisfactory. Since transsexuality importantly involves beliefs, perhaps the cognitive model (Chapter 5) may someday prove useful in explaining this rare phenomenon. Changing societal conceptions of masculinity and femininity may mitigate the distress experienced by the transsexual.

That homosexuality is no longer considered a psychological disorder underscores the changing nature of abnormality (Chapter 2). As observer discomfort is reduced, so too is the tendency to judge a given life-style as abnormal (Chapter 1).

FURTHER READINGS

Bayer, R. (1987). *Homosexuality and American psychiatry*. Princeton, NJ: Princeton University Press.

Boswell, J. (1980). *Christianity, social tolerance, and homosexuality*. Chicago: University of Chicago Press.

Garfinkel, H. (1967). Passing and the managed achievement of sex status in an intersexed person. In *Studies in ethnomethodology*. Englewood Cliffs, NJ: Prentice-Hall.

Kinsey, A., Pomeroy, W., & Martin, C. (1948). *Sexual behavior in the human male*. Philadelphia: Saunders.

Kinsey, A., Pomeroy, W., Martin, C., & Gebhard, P. (1953). *Sexual behavior in the hu-man female*. Philadelphia: Saunders.

Masters, W. H., & Johnson, V. E. (1966). *Human sexual response*. Boston: Little, Brown.

Money, J., & Erhardt, A. A. (1972). *Man and woman/boy and girl*. Baltimore: Johns Hopkins.

Stoller, R. J. (1985). *Observing the erotic imagination*. New Haven, CT: Yale University Press.

Vance, E. B., & Wagner, N. N. (1976). Written descriptions of orgasm: A study of sex differences. *Archives of Sexual Behavior, 5,* 87–98.

TERM-PAPER TOPICS

1. The research procedures of Alfred Kinsey have been criticized. So, too, have the procedures of William Masters and Virginia Johnson. Granted their purposes, how else might these studies have been completed?

2. Masters and Johnson have been credited with dispelling false beliefs about sexuality that originated in the theories of Freud. What were these beliefs? How did research suggest them to be incorrect?

3. Explain and evaluate the ethical issues raised by direct sexual therapy as developed by Masters and Johnson.

4. Why do men have fetishes? Conversely, why don't women? What does this difference suggest about the causes of other sex differences in the prevalence of disorders?

5. How has the AIDS epidemic changed sexual behavior among homosexuals? Among heterosexuals?

EXERCISES

Exercise One—Attitudes toward Homosexuality

In this exercise, you will ascertain attitudes toward homosexuality.

Talk to a variety of people you know about homosexuality. Ask them these questions:

1. What is homosexuality?
2. How many people are homosexuals?
3. What causes homosexuality?
4. Are homosexuals crazy?
5. Are homosexuals ill?
6. Are homosexuals immoral?
7. Should one's homosexual orientation be changed?
8. Can one's homosexual orientation be changed?
9. Do you know any homosexuals?

You can expect a variety of opinions, and you can expect them to be strongly held. Anticipate the possibility that some people will not wish to speak to you at all about homosexuality, and respect their right not to do so.

Use this exercise as an opportunity to examine your own attitudes toward homosexuality. What are they? Why is homosexuality such an emotionally charged subject?

Bell, A., & Weinberg, M. (1978). *Homosexualities*. New York: Simon & Schuster.

Exercise Two—Perceptions of Sexual Practices

The purpose of this exercise is to demonstrate the discrepancies between the actual prevalence of certain sexual practices and people's perceptions of their prevalence.

Read through Kinsey's books and obtain his estimated figures for the prevalence of various sexual practices: homosexuality, masturbation, premarital intercourse, extramarital intercourse, and so on. Then ask people of your acquaintance to estimate these figures. Are they accurate or inaccurate? Do men and women make different estimates? Show them the actual estimates, and assess their reactions.

You will probably find considerable discrepancies between what people think and what they do. How do you explain these discrepancies?

Kinsey, A., Pomeroy, W., & Martin, C. (1948). *Sexual behavior in the human male.* Philadelphia: Saunders.

Kinsey, A., Pomeroy, W., Martin, C., & Gebhard, P. (1953). *Sexual behavior in the human female.* Philadelphia: Saunders.

Exercise Three—Erotic Fantasies

The purpose of this exercise is to gain an appreciation of the range of individuals, objects, situations, and occurrences that may be sexually arousing.

Talk to individuals you know well about the content of their erotic fantasies. How varied are these? Do they have much to do with these individuals' actual sexual practices? Do men and women report different fantasies?

What is your conclusion about "normal" and "abnormal" sexual fantasies?

Exercise Four—Knowledge Concerning AIDS

The purpose of this exercise is to understand what people do and do not understand about AIDS.

Talk to individuals you know well about their beliefs concerning AIDS. Do they understand common ways this disease is transmitted? Do they know what safe sex means? Do they believe that the population as a whole knows what they do about AIDS?

Psychoactive Substance Use Disorders

CHAPTER OVERVIEW

Chapter 14 concerns itself with psychoactive drug abuse, which many consider the nation's major health problem. Although people abuse a variety of different drugs, all abused drugs share several properties: (a) their initial effect is pleasurable; (b) their continued effect is tolerance; and (c) their cessation is characterized by withdrawal. These temporal patterns can be explained by the opponent-process model of addiction.

Psychoactive drugs mimic the action of naturally produced compounds in one's brain that produce pleasure. For instance, endorphins are compounds that mitigate pain when released by the brain during times of pain and stress; narcotics like morphine and heroin are chemically similar to endorphins.

Early research attempts to find a personal-ity style predisposing drug abuse focused on the oral-dependent personality, but they met with little success. More recently, links between antisocial personality in adolescence and drug abuse in adulthood have been established.

The bulk of the chapter describes several types of drugs—alcohol, narcotics, stimulants like cocaine and amphetamine, hallucinogens like marijuana, PCP, and LSD, and tobacco—in terms of their effects on the person, their physiological mechanism, the medical and social complications they create, and current modes of treatment. In general, treatment for substance abuse disorders is difficult. Many strategies seem to have short-term success, but relapse of the treated individual remains common.

ESSENTIAL TERMS

addictive drug	substance that first produces pleasure and later tolerance, associated with withdrawal when use ceases
affective pleasure	pleasant emotional state that accompanies use of addictive drugs
affective tolerance	loss of addictive drug's affective pleasure with continued use
affective withdrawal	dysphoric emotional state following sudden cessation of addictive drug
alcohol	psychoactive drug contained in fermented and distilled beverages

Alcoholics Anonymous	self-help group for recovering alcoholics
amphetamine	psychoactive drug that stimulates and energizes; a stimulant
cocaine	psychoactive drug in the coca plant; a stimulant
crack	potent and inexpensive form of cocaine; a stimulant
delirium tremens	severe alcohol withdrawal symptoms, including disorientation, seizures, and hallucinations
endorphin	endogenous opioid
endorphin compensation hypothesis	theory that people drink alcohol to increase endogenous opioid activity
flashback	episode resembling drug intoxication months or even years after drug use is discontinued
hallucinogen	psychoactive drug that produces large perceptual changes; e.g., LSD
hashish	resin from the tops of cannabis plants; a hallucinogen
heroin	psychoactive drug transformed from morphine; a narcotic
LSD	lysergic acid diethylamide; extremely potent hallucinogen
marijuana	cannabis plant; a hallucinogen
methadone	long-lasting synthetic narcotic used in substitution therapy for addicts
morphine	psychoactive drug extracted from opium; a narcotic
narcotic	psychoactive drug that reduces pain without producing loss of consciousness
nicotine	active ingredient in tobacco
opium	psychoactive drug in the opium poppy; a narcotic
opponent-process model of addiction	theory that addictive drugs activate both a pleasurable process (Process A) and a negative process (Process B) that oppose each other in effects
oral-dependent personality	immature and dependent style of behaving once thought to predispose drug abuse
PCP	phencylidine; psychoactive drug developed as an anesthetic that produces hallucinations and confusion; a hallucinogen
stimulant	psychoactive drug that increases alertness and decreases fatigue; e.g., cocaine, amphetamine
tension reduction hypothesis	theory that people drink alcohol to reduce tension
tobacco	dried leaves of tobacco plant
THC	tetrahydrocannabinol; active ingredient in marijuana

SAMPLE EXAM

1. Substance abuse creates _____ problems.
   a. emotional
   b. financial
   c. health
   d. social
   e. all of the above

2. When drugs are legalized, use
   a. decreases.
   b. stays the same.
   c. increases.
   d. not known.

3. An addictive drug is one that leads to
   a. pleasure.
   b. tolerance.
   c. withdrawal.
   d. all of the above.
   e. none of the above.

4. According to the opponent-process model of addiction, addictive drugs initially activate
   a. Process A.
   b. Process B.
   c. Process C.
   d. craving.
   e. tolerance.

5. The _____ grows with repeated drug use.
   a. Process A
   b. Process B
   c. Process C
   d. pleasure
   e. sensitivity

6. Cues associated with drug use may elicit
   a. pleasure.
   b. tolerance.
   c. craving.

7. Which of these drugs affects neurotransmitters in the brains?
   a. alcohol
   b. cocaine
   c. narcotics
   d. tobacco
   e. all of the above
   f. none of the above

8. The endogenous analogues to narcotic substances are called
   a. endorphins.
   b. killer cells.
   c. methadone.
   d. neurotransmitters.

9. Research shows the oral-dependent personality _____ associated with drug use, and the antisocial personality _____ associated.
   a. to be; to be
   b. to be; not to be
   c. not to be; to be
   d. not to be; not to be

10. Compared to the children of nonalcoholic parents, the children of alcoholic parents are _____ as likely to abuse alcohol.
   a. half
   b. just
   c. twice
   d. four times
   e. ten times

11. According to the tension reduction theory of alcohol abuse, people drink _____ stress.
   a. before
   b. during
   c. after
   d. a and b
   e. b and c

12. According to the endorphin compensation hypothesis of alcohol use, people drink _____ stress.
   a. before
   b. during
   c. after
   d. a and b
   e. b and c

13. Alcohol and narcotics resemble each other with respect to
   a. behavioral effects.
   b. cross-tolerance.
   c. pharmacological effects.
   d. response to opiate blockers.
   e. all of the above.

14. Alcohol abuse costs the United States more than _____ dollars every year in terms of lost productivity, health care, and legal costs.
   a. ten million
   b. one hundred million
   c. one billion
   d. ten billion
   e. one hundred billion

15. Alcohol can be described as a
    a. depressant.
    b. hallucinogen.
    c. stimulant.
    d. none of the above.
    e. all of the above.

16. Alcohol withdrawal can be relieved by
    a. alcohol.
    b. strong coffee.
    c. exercise.
    d. cold showers.

17. The major concern of alcohol rehabilitation programs is
    a. anxiety.
    b. depression.
    c. relapse.
    d. schizophrenia.
    e. withdrawal.

18. Which of these drugs is made from opium?
    a. heroin
    b. morphine
    c. methadone
    d. all of the above

19. Narcotics reduce one's
    a. consciousness.
    b. health.
    c. pain.
    d. tolerance.

20. Intravenous drug users are at increased risk for
    a. AIDS.
    b. hepatitis.
    c. both.
    d. neither.

21. In substitution therapy for heroin, _____ is prescribed to the addict.
    a. methadone
    b. naloxone
    c. morphine
    d. opium

22. Compared to heroin, methadone has a _____ pharmacological effect.
    a. shorter
    b. longer
    c. similar
    d. painful

23. Crack is a form of cocaine that is particularly
    a. inexpensive.
    b. potent.
    c. both.
    d. neither.

24. Stimulants work by blocking the reuptake of
    a. dopamine.
    b. endorphins.
    c. norepinephrine.
    d. a and c.
    e. b and c.

25. Symptoms of withdrawal from cocaine are chiefly
    a. behavioral.
    b. emotional.
    c. physical.
    d. a and b.
    e. a and c.

26. In recent years, cocaine use has
    a. decreased.
    b. stayed the same.
    c. increased.
    d. not known.

27. Treatments developed so far for cocaine dependence are
    a. ineffective.
    b. promising.
    c. effective.

28. When first described, LSD was thought to provide insight into
    a. anxiety disorders.
    b. depression.
    c. mania.
    d. schizophrenia.

29. THC is the active ingredient in
    a. cocaine.
    b. LSD.
    c. marijuana.
    d. PCP.

30. The original use of marijuana in the United States was
    a. medicinal.
    b. recreational.
    c. religious.
    d. all of the above.
    e. none of the above.

31. Marijuana has _____ half-life.
    a. a short
    b. a long
    c. no

32. Medical complications of marijuana use include all of the following except
    a. low sperm count.
    b. impaired menstrual cycles.
    c. lung cancer.
    d. fetal abnormalities.
    e. all of these are possible complications.

33. Tobacco taxes in the United States pro-
    duce about _____ dollars per year in
    taxes.
    a. one million
    b. ten million
    c. one billion
    d. five billion
    e. eight billion

34. The active ingredient in tobacco is
    a. endorphin.
    b. nicotine.
    c. PCP.
    d. tar.
    e. THC.

35. Tobacco use shows
    a. withdrawal.
    b. tolerance.
    c. both.
    d. neither.

36. Which of these is not a major conse-
    quence of smoking?
    a. cancer
    b. coronary heart disease
    c. chronic obstructive pulmonary
       disease
    d. all of these are major consequences
    e. none of these are major
       consequences

37. Which of these techniques is effective in
    the long-run for treating smoking?
    a. nicotine gum
    b. rapid smoking
    c. hypnosis
    d. all of the above
    e. none of the above

Answer Key for Sample Exam

1.	e	(p. 450)	20.	c	(p. 473)
2.	c	(p. 451)	21.	a	(p. 474)
3.	d	(p. 458)	22.	b	(p. 474)
4.	a	(p. 458)	23.	c	(p. 476)
5.	b	(p. 458)	24.	d	(p. 476)
6.	c	(p. 460)	25.	d	(p. 477)
7.	e	(p. 450)	26.	c	(p. 478)
8.	a	(p. 456)	27.	a	(p. 478)
9.	c	(p. 454)	28.	d	(p. 479)
10.	d	(p. 455)	29.	c	(p. 480)
11.	d	(p. 463)	30.	e	(p. 480)
12.	c	(p. 464)	31.	b	(p. 480)
13.	e	(p. 465)	32.	e	(p. 481)
14.	e	(p. 466)	33.	e	(p. 482)
15.	a	(p. 467)	34.	b	(p. 482)
16.	a	(p. 467)	35.	c	(p. 483)
17.	c	(p. 468)	36.	d	(p. 484)
18.	a, b	(p. 472)	37.	e	(p. 484)
19.	c	(p. 472)			

SELF-TEST

1. _____ is the leading health problem in the United States today.

2. Alcohol dependence decreases one's average life expectancy by _____ years.

3. Drug characteristics that determine abuse include the obvious factor of _____ as well
   as whether the drug is _____.

4. Addictive drugs share in common the characteristics of affective _____, _____,
   and _____.

5. The _____ proposes that addictive drugs activate two affective processes.

6. According to the opponent-process model of addiction, _____ corresponds to the
   dose and duration of the drug, and is followed and opposed by _____, which grows
   in strength with _____.

7. Reminders of drugs may elicit _____.

8. Endogenous morphine, also called _____, is chemically similar to _____.

9. Research shows that the _____ personality does not predispose drug use, although the _____ personality does.

10. _____ may have a genetic predisposition.

11. The most commonly used psychoactive substance is _____.

12. According to the tension reduction hypothesis, people should drink _____ stressful situations.

13. According to the endorphin compensation hypothesis, people should drink _____ stressful situations.

14. There are a number of parallels between the long-term effects of alcohol and those of _____.

15. Alcohol _____ central nervous system activity.

16. The severe form of alcohol withdrawal is called _____.

17. The best-known self-help group for alcoholism is _____.

18. The original source of narcotics was the _____.

19. The most frequently abused narcotic is _____.

20. Reasons for initially using narcotics _____ reasons for continuing to use them.

21. There are _____ medical complications associated with narcotic use and withdrawal.

22. The social consequences of narcotics are _____.

23. The two major treatments for opiate dependence are _____ and _____.

24. Two examples of stimulants are _____ and _____.

25. The exception to declining drug use in recent years is _____.

26. Stimulants work by blocking the reuptake of _____.

27. Withdrawal from stimulants resembles _____.

28. There are _____ effective treatments for cocaine dependence.

29. _____ cause perceptual changes and hallucinations.

30. The most potent hallucinogens include _____ and _____, whereas the least potent is _____.

31. The active ingredient in marijuana is _____.

32. Marijuana appears not to have a Process B because of the _____ of Process A.

33. Episodes that resemble intoxication that occur months after the discontinuation of drug use are _____.

34. Tobacco was first used by _____.

35. The addicting ingredient in tobacco is _____.

36. About _____ people die prematurely every year in the United States from smoking.

37. Smoking is medically harmful mainly because it leads to _____, _____, and _____.

38. Among those who quit smoking, as many as _____ resume within one year.

39. Alcohol may contribute to the spread of the AIDS epidemic by _____ and _____.

Answer Key for Self-Test

1. Substance abuse
2. twelve
3. availability; addictive
4. pleasure; tolerance; withdrawal
5. opponent-process model of addiction
6. Process A; Process B; repeated drug use
7. conditioned craving
8. endorphin; narcotics
9. oral-dependent; antisocial
10. Alcoholism
11. alcohol
12. before or during
13. after
14. narcotics
15. depresses
16. delirium tremens
17. Alcoholics Anonymous
18. poppy
19. heroin
20. may differ from
21. few
22. profound
23. substitution; abstinence
24. cocaine; amphetamine
25. cocaine
26. monoamines (like dopamine and norepinephrine)
27. depression
28. no known
29. Hallucinogens
30. PCP; LSD; marijuana
31. THC
32. long duration
33. flashbacks
34. Native Americans
35. nicotine
36. 350,000
37. coronary heart disease; cancer; chronic obstructive pulmonary disease
38. 75%
39. increasing high-risk behavior; impairing immunity

TYING IT TOGETHER

Chapter 2 makes the important point that abnormality must be placed within its cultural and historical context. This idea is important in understanding disorders of substance abuse. Not too long ago, all drug use was regarded as drug abuse, but in the 1960s and 1970s America became very much a drug-using society. Now the pendulum is swinging back, although tobacco and alcohol remain billion-dollar industries. Illicit drug use in some segments of our society is distressingly high. News stories about sports and politics are as apt to mention drug abuse as not. Drug treatment and rehabilitation are not as successful as desired (Chapter 19).

Drug abuse involves the body in important ways, and an understanding of drug effects must be based on an understanding of brain structure and function (Chapter 17). Nevertheless, the biomedical model (Chapter 3) is not the full answer to drug disorders. The recommendation by existential psychologists (Chapter 4) that our actions reflect willful choice must be incorporated into our explanations and treatments of drug abuse. And so must the fact that the behaviors associated with drug abuse reflect the prevailing rewards and punishments in one's environment, as well as people's beliefs about drugs (Chapter 5).

Other disorders may give rise to drug abuse, as individuals attempt to self-medicate. For instance, the lower rate of depression among men than women (Chapter 11) may reflect the greater rate of substance abuse found among men, who may be trading one problem (depression) for another (drug abuse). The fear and anxiety disorders (Chapter 8) may also lead to drug abuse as people attempt to allay their feelings of trepidation.

At the same time, drug abuse may lead to other disorders. Nicotine and alcohol may exacerbate psychosomatic disorders like peptic ulcers and hypertension (Chapter 10) and such neurological disorders as amnesia (Chapter 17). Sexual dysfunctions (Chapter 13) may result from drug abuse, as may depression (Chapter 11) and a host of neurological problems (Chapter 17). Drug abuse weakens the body's immune system overall (Chapter 10), putting the abuser at risk for the spectrum of infectious diseases.

Prolonged use of stimulants like amphetamines and cocaine may result in hallucinations, delusions, and other schizophrenic-like symptoms (Chapter 12). Indeed, information about drug-induced psychoses has helped in the development of theories about the role of neurotransmitters in schizophrenia (Chapter 3).

FURTHER READINGS

Beecher, E. M. (1972). *Licit and illicit drugs.* Mount Vernon, NY: Consumers Union.

Bernstein, D. A., & Glasgow, R. E. (1979). Smoking. In O. F. Pomerleau & J. P. Brady (Eds.), *Behavioral medicine: Theory and practice.* Baltimore: Williams & Wilkins.

Desmond, E. W. (1987). Out in the open: Changing attributes and new research give fresh hope to alcoholics. *Time,* November 30, pp. 80–90.

Marlatt, G. A. (1983). The controlled-drinking controversy: A commentary. *American Psychologist, 38,* 1097–1110.

Vaillant, G. E. (1983). *The natural history of alcoholism.* Cambridge, MA: Harvard University Press.

Zimberg, S., Wallace, J., & Blume, S. B. (Eds.) (1985). *Practical approaches to alcoholism psychotherapy* (2nd ed.). New York: Plenum.

TERM-PAPER TOPICS

1. Survey recent evidence that alcoholism has a genetic predisposition. What possible mechanisms for this predisposition have been suggested? What are the treatment implications of this evidence? What, if anything, do they say about the role of individual responsibility in drug abuse?

2. Why are some drugs legal and other drugs illegal? Trace the history of drug legislation in this country. How does it reflect political considerations?

3. Compare and contrast the United States and England with regard to treatment of narcotics addicts. Which approach seems preferable?

4. What patterns in drug use and drug abuse seem likely to continue into the future? Be sure to take into account the AIDS epidemic. Describe patterns of drug use and drug abuse in the year 2050.

EXERCISES

Exercise One—Psychoactive Drugs and Opponent Processes

In this exercise, you will investigate some of the behavioral effects of two common psychoactive drugs: caffeine and chocolate. Can you detect the operation of Process A and Process B hypothesized by the opponent-process model of addiction?

If it does not offend you to do so, and if it is not medically inadvisable, use yourself as a subject in this drug study. While you may not think of caffeine and chocolate as psychoactive drugs, they satisfy all the criteria specified in the text. Drink three cups of strong coffee (not instant) within twenty minutes. Or eat three large chocolate bars in the same amount of time.

Pay attention to how your respond to these rather large does of drugs. What happens to your attention? Your energy level? Your mood? Your physical coordination? As time passes, what sorts of changes do you experience? Do you crave more coffee or chocolate?

If you are an "experienced" drug user, compare your experiences with someone who is not. Or vice versa. Does the opponent-process model describe the differences between the two of you?

Note: *Do not make yourself ill with this exercise!* Some people have an inordinate capacity for coffee or chocolate, probably because of habituation. But if you are a teetotaler, so to speak, do not get carried away.

Exercise Two—Alcoholics Anonymous

The purpose of this exercise is to learn about Alcoholics Anonymous firsthand.

Contact a local AA group and arrange a classroom presentation by some of the members. Ask them to tell their stories, and to explain how AA helps them not to drink.

Bill W. (1976). *Alcoholics Anonymous: The story of how many thousands of men and women have recovered from alcoholism* (3rd ed.). New York: Alcoholics Anonymous World Services.

Exercise Three—On Any Given Sunday: Drugs and Sports

You will use the knowledge you have gained from the text to evaluate statements made in the sports pages about drug use and drug abuse.

Read your local sports pages, *Sports Illustrated,* or the *Sporting News.* Chances are that there will be a number of claims and counter-claims about drugs. Based on what you have learned, which claims make sense? Which claims make no sense? Why do some professional athletes use drugs? How may they be encouraged to stop using drugs? Is drug abuse by celebrities more prevalent than drug abuse by the general population? Numbers aside, how is it different?

CHAPTER 15

Personality Disorders

CHAPTER OVERVIEW

Personality disorders are pervasive and inflexible ways of behaving that result in social and/or occupational maladjustment. This chapter discusses the various personality disorders described in DSM-III-R.

The best understood of these disorders is the antisocial personality disorder. Also termed *psychopathy* or *sociopathy*, this disorder is characterized by a rapacious attitude toward others manifested in lying, stealing, cheating, and worse. Antisocial personality is not the same thing as criminality, but it may involve considerable criminal activity. Research suggests that sociopaths are physiologically underaroused and deficient at avoidance learning. This may account for their failure to learn from mistakes. There may be a genetic basis to this underarousal.

The other personality disorders are not as well understood, and controversy exists over whether individuals indeed have the pervasive traits assumed by their descriptions: (a) paranoid personality disorder (characterized by inordinate suspicion and distrust); (b) histrionic personality disorder (marked by overdramatic emotional displays); (c) narcissistic personality disorder (characterized by outlandish sense of self-importance); (d) avoidant personality disorder (distinguished by social withdrawal combining hypersensitivity to rejection and desire for acceptance); (e) dependent personality disorder (characterized by excessive reliance on others to make important decisions for the self); (f) obsessive-compulsive personality disorder (marked by inappropriate preoccupation with details); (g) passive-aggressive personality disorder (characterized by indirect resistance to social and occupational demands); (h) schizoid personality disorder (marked by deficiency in the ability to form social relationships); (i) schizotypal personality disorder (characterized by odd behavior); and (j) borderline personality disorder (distinguished by unstable relationships, moods, and behaviors).

ESSENTIAL TERMS

antisocial personality disorder (sociopathy; psychopathy)	personality disorder characterized by a rapacious attitude toward others: chronic insensitivity and indifference to the rights of others marked by lying, stealing, and/or cheating
avoidant personality disorder	personality disorder characterized by turning away: social withdrawal combining hypersensitivity to rejection with a desire for acceptance and affection
borderline personality disorder	personality disorder characterized by instability in a variety of areas: interpersonal relationships, behavior, mood, and/or self-image

criminal	individual apprehended and convicted of a crime; not necessarily the same as an antisocial personality
dependent personality disorder	personality disorder in which an individual habitually allows others to make major decisions, to initiate important actions, and to assume responsibility for significant areas of his or her life
depersonalization	sense of estrangement from the self and the environment
electroencephalogram (EEG)	psychophysiological assessment device that measures electrical activity of the brain
histrionic personality disorder	personality disorder characterized by a long history of calling attention to oneself and of emotional displays in response to insignificant events
idea of reference	belief that one is especially noticed by others
machoism	term for histrionic personality disorder among males
moral insanity	nineteenth-century term for antisocial personality disorder, thought then to be a disorder of will
narcissistic personality disorder	personality disorder in which an individual has an outlandish sense of self-importance, shown by self-absorption, self-aggrandizing fantasies, and exhibitionistic needs for constant admiration
obsessive-compulsive personality disorder	personality disorder in which the individual consistently and pervasively strives for perfection
paranoid personality disorder	personality disorder in which an individual is always suspicious of others' motives
passive-aggressive personality disorder	personality disorder characterized by resistance to social and occupational performance demands in the form of procrastination, dawdling, stubbornness, inefficiency, and forgetfulness
personality disorder	mental disorder in which an individual's traits are inflexible and a source of social and occupational maladjustment
schizoid personality disorder	personality disorder characterized by habitual inability to form social relationships, reflected in an absence of desire for social involvements, indifference to praise and criticism, insensitivity to feelings of others, and/or lack of social skill
schizotypal personality disorder	personality disorder involving long-standing oddities in thinking, perceiving, communicating, and behaving
trait	habitual and characteristic tendency to perceive and respond to the environment
XYY syndrome	chromosomal disorder in which a male has an extra male (Y) chromosome, thought to predispose criminal behavior, although the mechanism is not clear

SAMPLE EXAM

1. Which of these does not belong?
   a. paranoid personality disorder
   b. antisocial personality disorder
   c. sociopathy
   d. psychopathy
   e. moral insanity

2. Antisocial personality disorders involve all of the following except
   a. unconventionality.
   b. observer discomfort.
   c. suffering.
   d. irrationality.

3. Which of these statements is true?
   a. Criminal behavior is a necessary condition for antisocial personality disorder.
   b. Criminal behavior is a sufficient condition for antisocial personality disorder.
   c. Antisocial personality disorder is a necessary condition for criminal behavior.
   d. Antisocial personality disorder is a sufficient condition for criminal behavior.
   e. None of the above.

4. Individuals with personality disorders
   a. are different in degree from individuals without personality disorders.
   b. are different in kind from individuals without personality disorders.
   c. are essentially the same as individuals without personality disorders.

5. A diagnosis of antisocial personality disorder is based on all of the following criteria except
   a. antisocial behavior.
   b. long-standing pattern.
   c. origin in early adulthood.
   d. manifestation in a variety of domains.

6. Sociopaths seem to lack
   a. motives for crimes.
   b. guilt over crimes.
   c. concern for others.
   d. all of the above.

7. Suppose you were told that you were to meet someone for lunch who had an antisocial personality disorder. You would expect this individual to be
   a. a male.
   b. married.

   c. emotionally shallow.
   d. all of the above.

8. Current thought on the origins of sociopathy emphasizes all of the following except
   a. parental absence.
   b. learning deficits.
   c. genetics.
   d. underarousal.

9. Which of these statements is true?
   a. Punishment for juvenile offenses leads to later offenses.
   b. Moderate punishment for juvenile offenses leads to later offenses.
   c. Severe punishment for juvenile offenses leads to later offenses.
   d. None of the above.

10. Psychopaths seem to have difficulty with
    a. Pavlovian conditioning.
    b. operant conditioning.
    c. escape responding.
    d. avoidance responding.

11. Underlying the learning deficits of psychopaths may be
    a. overarousal.
    b. underarousal.
    c. low intelligence.
    d. depression.

12. Suppose you were told that a psychopath had just moved next door. You would be *least* wary of
    a. burglary.
    b. forgery.
    c. assault.
    d. con games.

13. Sociopaths seem to be sensitive to
    a. physical punishment.
    b. tangible punishment.
    c. social punishment.
    d. none of the above.

14. Twin studies indicate that
    a. criminality is not genetic.
    b. criminality is partly genetic.
    c. criminality is totally genetic.
    d. the relationship between criminality and genetics is unclear.

15. Adoption studies indicate that
    a. criminality is not genetic.
    b. criminality is partly genetic.
    c. criminality is totally genetic.
    d. the relationship between criminality and genetics is unclear.

16. The XYY chromosome pattern has been hypothesized to be
    a. linked with violence among men.
    b. linked with violence among women.
    c. linked with violence among men and women.
    d. linked with violence among transsexuals.

17. Research shows that individuals with the XYY chromosome pattern are convicted of
    a. more violent crimes than other individuals.
    b. more nonviolent crimes than other individuals.
    c. as many crimes as other individuals.
    d. fewer crimes than other individuals.

18. Abnormal EEG patterns among psychopaths are consistent with the
    a. biomedical model.
    b. psychodynamic model.
    c. behavioral model.
    d. cognitive model.
    e. existential model.

19. Suppose you met someone who was inordinately distrustful and suspicious. If this individual had a personality disorder, it would be
    a. paranoid personality disorder.
    b. schizoid personality disorder.
    c. schizotypal personality disorder.
    d. histrionic personality disorder.

20. Suppose you met someone who was inordinately emotional and dramatic. If this individual had a personality disorder, it would be
    a. paranoid personality disorder.
    b. schizoid personality disorder.
    c. schizotypal personality disorder.
    d. histrionic personality disorder.

21. Suppose you met someone who was inordinately preoccupied with the self. If this individual had a personality disorder, it would be
    a. narcissistic personality disorder.
    b. avoidant personality disorder.
    c. dependent personality disorder.
    d. obsessive-compulsive personality disorder.

22. Suppose you met someone who was inordinately sensitive to rejection. If this individual had a personality disorder, it would be
    a. narcissistic personality disorder.
    b. avoidant personality disorder.
    c. dependent personality disorder.
    d. obsessive-compulsive personality disorder.

23. Suppose you met someone who was inordinately unable to assume responsibility. If this individual had a personality disorder, it would be
    a. narcissistic personality disorder.
    b. avoidant personality disorder.
    c. dependent personality disorder.
    d. obsessive-compulsive personality disorder.

24. Suppose you met someone who was inordinately preoccupied with trivial details. If this individual had a personality disorder, it would be
    a. narcissistic personality disorder.
    b. avoidant personality disorder.
    c. dependent personality disorder.
    d. obsessive-compulsive personality disorder.

25. Passive-aggressiveness may be expressed by all of the following except
    a. violence.
    b. procrastination.
    c. stubbornness.
    d. forgetfulness.

26. Suppose you met someone who was inordinately strange. If this individual had a personality disorder, it would be
    a. paranoid personality disorder.
    b. schizoid personality disorder.
    c. schizotypal personality disorder.
    d. histrionic personality disorder.

27. Suppose you met someone who was inordinately estranged from other people. If this individual had a personality disorder, it would be
    a. paranoid personality disorder.
    b. schizoid personality disorder.
    c. schizotypal personality disorder.
    d. histrionic personality disorder.

28. You expect that someone with a borderline personality disorder would be
    a. unstable.
    b. weird.
    c. emotionally flat.
    d. withdrawn.

29. Self-theorists trace borderline personality disorder to difficulties experienced during
    a. infancy.
    b. childhood.
    c. early adolescence.
    d. late adolescence.
    e. adulthood.

30. Personality disorders are controversial because
    a. they assume the existence of stable and pervasive traits.
    b. they are difficult to treat.
    c. they are genetically based.
    d. all of the above.

SELF-TEST

1. When an individual's _____ ways of perceiving and thinking are _____ and a source of _____, the person has a personality disorder.

2. The best known personality disorder is the _____ personality disorder, also known as _____ or _____.

3. Antisocial personality disorders are marked by _____ toward others.

4. _____ are not necessarily individuals with antisocial personality disorders.

5. DSM-III-R criteria for antisocial personality disorder are threefold. First, the antisocial behavior must be _____; second, it must be evident before age _____; and third, it must be evident in at least _____ classes of behavior.

6. The criminal activities of psychopathic individuals do not _____.

7. Psychopathic individuals seem not to experience _____ as do other individuals.

8. Research shows that antisocial personality disorder is associated with a _____ childhood.

9. _____ punishment may dissuade a juvenile from future criminal activities.

10. Psychopaths are deficient at _____ learning, presumably because they are chronically _____.

11. Twin studies show that criminality may be _____, but the role of the _____ should be underscored.

12. Adoption studies show that criminality may be _____.

13. Men with the _____ chromosome pattern have been thought to be prone to _____ crimes. Research suggests that this hypothesis is _____.

14. Sociopaths show abnormal _____ patterns, implying _____ immaturity.

15. Individuals who are chronically suspicious and distrustful may have a _____ personality disorder.

16. Individuals who habitually draw attention to themselves through inappropriate emotional displays may have a _____ personality disorder.

17. An outlandish sense of _____ is the hallmark of a narcissistic personality disorder.

18. Individuals with an avoidant personality disorder combine _____ to rejection with a desire for _____.

19. When a person habitually allows others to make the important decisions, this person may have a _____ personality disorder.

20. An inappropriate preoccupation with insignificant details characterizes the _____ personality disorder.

21. Indirect resistance to social and occupational performance demands suggests the presence of a _____ personality disorder.

22. If an individual has a deficiency in the ability to form _____, he or she may have a schizoid personality disorder.

23. An individual who has a long history of odd behavior may have a personality disorder, which is thought to predispose _____.

24. Markedly unstable individuals may be those with _____ personality disorders.

25. The entire idea of personality disorders may be criticized by doubting the assumption that people have pervasive _____.

26. Diagnostic reliability for the personality disorders is typically _____, except for _____ personality disorders.

Answer Key for Self-Test

1. characteristic; inflexible; maladjustment
2. antisocial; psychopathy; sociopathy
3. indifference
4. Criminals
5. long-standing; fifteen; four
6. make sense
7. emotions
8. difficult
9. Moderate
10. avoidance; underaroused
11. inherited; environment
12. inherited
13. XYY; violent; false
14. EEG; brain
15. paranoid
16. histrionic
17. self-importance
18. hypersensitivity; acceptance
19. dependent

20. obsessive-compulsive
21. passive-aggressive
22. relationships
23. schizotypal; schizophrenia
24. borderline
25. traits
26. poor; antisocial

TYING IT TOGETHER

According to Chapter 1, the identification of abnormality involves a social judgment. This is nowhere better illustrated than in the case of personality disorders, which involves not simply disrupted "personality" but also disrupted relationships with other people. In one way or another, each personality disorder results in discomfort among observers (see Chapter 1). Treatments for personality disorders that do not take into account their inherently social nature are apt not to be successful (Chapter 19).

The best understood personality disorder—the antisocial personality—seems to be brought about by abnormally low levels of anxiety (see Chapters 8 and 9), resulting in deficiencies in avoidance learning (Chapter 5). Perhaps the capacity to experience fear and anxiety (Chapter 8) is necessary for the superego to develop (Chapter 4). Various research strategies have converged to provide our understanding of the antisocial personality (Chapter 6), and its explanation partakes of the several models of abnormality (Chapters 3–5).

Doubts have been raised about the existence of the other personality disorders. These disorders assume the existence of pervasive and stable traits, but research does not strongly support such an assumption. Contemporary personality psychology is increasingly attentive to the situational determinants of behavior. Thus, "personality" may be better described by the behavioral model (Chapter 4), and cross-situational regularities in behavior may be less common than has been presumed. Accordingly, diagnosis of personality disorders (Chapter 7) is not perfectly reliable or valid.

It has often been assumed that personality disorders predispose more serious psychopathologies when stress is encountered. Thus, individuals with obsessive-compulsive personality disorders are thought to be at risk for obsessive-compulsive disorders (Chapter 9), those with dependent personality disorders are thought to be at risk for depression (Chapter 11), those with schizotypal disorders are thought to be at risk for schizophrenia (Chapter 12), and so on. Research has not consistently supported this assumption, perhaps because of the aforementioned difficulties in diagnosing personality disorders.

The borderline personality disorder has an interesting history. Diagnostic schemes prior to DSM-III held that an individual was either neurotic (Chapter 8) or psychotic (Chapter 12). However, the line between the two is fuzzy, and individuals with both neurotic and psychotic manifestations had to be classified somewhere. Hence, the borderline-personality-disorder category was proposed for individuals who fall at the "border" of neurosis and psychosis. You will remember, however, that this disorder no longer has this meaning. At the present, it refers to individuals with markedly unstable lives.

FURTHER READINGS

Jarvik, L. F., Klodin, V., & Matsuyama, S. S. (1973). Human aggression and extra Y chromosome: Fact or fantasy? *American Psychologist, 28,* 674–682.

Kaplan, M. (1983). A woman's view of DSM-III. *American Psychologist, 38,* 786–792.

Loehlin, J. C., & Nichols, R. C. (1976). *Heredity, environment, and personality: A study of 850 sets of twins.* Austin: University of Texas.

Mailer, N. (1979). *The executioner's song.* Boston: Little Brown.

Millon, R. (1981). *Disorders of personality: DSM-III, Axis II.* New York: Wiley.

Wilson, J. Q., & Herrnstein, R. J. (1985). *Crime and human nature.* Cambridge, MA: Harvard University Press.

TERM-PAPER TOPICS

1. In the past, psychologists have proposed that personality disorders set the stage for more serious disorders. What is the evidence for this idea?

2. Evaluate the research linking the XYY chromosome disorder to violence. What is your conclusion about genetics and criminality?

3. What alternative interpretation of the personality disorders is suggested by social learning theory?

4. Describe several additional personality disorders that fit the general definition and seem prevalent in our society. Speculate on their causes.

EXERCISES

Exercise One—Famous Personalities: Disordered or Not?

The purpose of this exercise is to demonstrate the difficulties involved in describing a person's life style in terms of a personality disorder.

Many celebrities seem eccentric. Some celebrities seem to have a personality disorder: a rigid and inflexible way of acting that results in problems for themselves and others. On the other hand, there are alternative ways of interpreting what these people are doing that does not mention personality disorders.

Read a biographical account of an eccentric celebrity. Does the person about whom you have read seem to have a personality disorder? Is there a better way to interpret his or her exaggerated and inflexible behavior? Possible biographies include:

Brodie, F. M. (1981). *Richard Nixon: The shaping of his character.* New York: Norton.

Devaney, J. (1982). *Blood and guts: The true story of General George S. Patton, USA.* New York: Messner.

Hanna, D. (1976). *"Come up and see me sometime": An uncensored biography of Mae West.* New York: Belmont.

Ludwig, E. (1940). *Three portraits: Hitler, Mussolini, Stalin.* New York: AMS Press.

Mailer, N. (1981). *Marilyn.* New York: Grosset & Dunlap.

Stock, N. (1982). *The life of Ezra Pound: An expanded edition.* Berkeley, CA: North Point Press.

Wells, R. (1977). *Vince Lombardi: His life and times.* Canoga Park, CA: Major Books.

Wicker, T. (1969). *JFK and LBJ.* Baltimore: Penguin.

Woodward, B. (1984). *Wired: The short life and fast times of John Belushi.* New York: Pocket Books.

Note: One cannot meaningfully diagnose an individual just from a biography; the best that one can do is to describe the public self presented there. What a celebrity is "really like" remains unknown.

Millon, T. (1981). *Disorders of personality: DSM-III, Axis.* New York: Wiley.

Exercise Two—Incorrigible Criminals

In this exercise, you will learn from a direct source about chronic criminals and their actions.

Arrange a classroom lecture by a local parole officer, judge, or attorney about incorrigible criminals. Does it make sense to describe some of these criminals as psychopaths? Is any form of punishment or rehabilitation effective?

Exercise Three—The Variability of Personality

The purpose of this exercise is to demonstrate that an individual's "personality" is not static.

Repeat the first part of Exercise One from Chapter 7. That is, ask a group of five or six people who know each other well to describe each member of the group in terms of striking personality traits.

Is there considerable variability in the way a given person is described? What are the implications for diagnosing personality disorders?

Mischel, W. (1968). *Personality and assessment.* New York: Wiley.

CHAPTER 16

Childhood Disorders and Mental Retardation

CHAPTER OVERVIEW

This chapter is concerned with problems suffered by children and adolescents. These problems are more difficult to understand than those of adults since they occur in the context of development and may be situationally specific and transient. Five major types are distinguished: disruptive behavior disorders, emotional disorders, habit and eating disorders, developmental disorders, and gender identity disorders. These are described in terms of its manifestation, presumed cause, and preferred treatment.

Behavioral disorders involve either aggression, rule breaking, and/or inappropriate attention. Boys are more likely to have these problems, which appear to have genetic and environmental causes. Treatment for the behavioral disorders is not well developed.

Emotional disorders are those in which fear, anxiety, and shyness predominate, and include childhood phobias. They seem similar to anxiety disorders among adults, and behavioral therapies may be promising in their treatment. Habit disorders involve habitual physical behaviors, such as enuresis, stuttering, anorexia nervosa, bulimia, and obesity. In most cases, therapy with behavioral techniques can be helpful. Intellectual disorders are instances of mental retardation, which result either from genetic and environmental influences or from injury and disease. Developmental disorders range from specific learning disabilities to mental retardation to autism.

(Gender identity disorders are discussed in Chapter 13.)

ESSENTIAL TERMS

amniocentesis	*in utero* technique for detecting Down's syndrome
anorexia nervosa	habit disorder characterized by substantial loss of body weight and deliberate restriction of calorie intake
attention-deficit hyperactivity disorder	childhood disorder marked by inpulsivity, inattention, and hyperactivity
autism	pervasive developmental disorder characterized by a child's failure to develop the ability to respond to others
bulimia	habit disorder characterized by alternate gorging with food, and then purging of that food by vomiting, or using laxatives or diuretics
conduct disorder	disorder characterized by aggression and rule breaking

cultural-familial retardation	retardation caused by genetic and environmental influences as opposed to pathological physical conditions
delayed auditory feedback	therapy technique for treatment of stuttering in which the stutterer's speech is played back through earphones with a one-second delay
developmental disorder	childhood disorder involving enormous developmental tardiness (specific developmental disorder) or gross developmental failure (pervasive developmental disorder)
disruptive behavior disorder	general class of childhood disorders encompassing attention-deficit hyperactivity disorders, conduct disorders, and oppositional defiant disorders
Down's syndrome	mental retardation caused by chromosomal abnormality and accompanied by almond-shaped and slanted eyes and numerous physical anomalies
echolalia	tendency to repeat or echo immediately or after a brief period precisely what one has just heard
emotional disorder	childhood disorder in which symptoms of fear, anxiety, inhibition, shyness, and overattachment predominate
enuresis	involuntary voiding of urine at least twice a month for children between five and six, and once a month for those who are older
habit disorder	childhood disorder with a habitual physical component; e.g., stuttering
hyperactivity	gross overactivity of motor behavior accompanied by developmentally inappropriate inattention and impulses
mainstreaming	educational strategy of educating mentally retarded children with other schoolchildren
mental retardation	subaverage intellectual functioning accompanied by deficient adaptive behavior and manifested before age eighteen
obesity	excess body fat
oppositional defiant disorder	childhood disorder in which a child is negative, hostile, and defiant
phenylketonuria	mental retardation caused by a metabolic disorder in which phenylalanine cannot be digested, resulting in irreversible brain damage
pronominal reversal	tendency to use "I" where "you" is meant, and vice versa
Ritalin	brand name of methylphenidate, an amphetamine used to treat hyperactivity
school phobia	common childhood phobia characterized by refusal to attend school
separation anxiety disorder	childhood disorder centering around fear of separation from parents
serotonin	neural transmitter that is involved in perception and memory, thought to be abnormal in autistic children

shadowing   therapy technique for treatment of stuttering in which the therapist reads from a book while the stutterer repeats the words after they are heard

stuttering   habit disorder involving disturbed speech rhythm, often in pronouncing initial consonants in certain words

syllable-times speech   therapy technique for treatment of stuttering in which stutterers are required to speak in time to a metronome

SAMPLE EXAM

1. It is perhaps more difficult to understand the disorders of children than those of adults for all the following reasons except that
   a. children's problems are often situationally specific.
   b. children's problems are not serious.
   c. children's problems arise in the course of development.
   d. children often cannot communicate a problem directly through language.

2. If a child's problem involves habitual physical symptoms, she has
   a. a disruptive behavior disorder.
   b. an emotional disorder.
   c. a habit disorder.
   d. a developmental disorder.

3. If a child's problem involves mental retardation, he has
   a. a disruptive behavior disorder.
   b. an emotional disorder.
   c. a habit disorder.
   d. a developmental disorder.

4. If a child's problem involves shyness and fear, he has
   a. a disruptive behavior disorder.
   b. an emotional disorder.
   c. a habit disorder.
   d. a developmental disorder.

5. If a child's problem involves hyperactivity, he has
   a. a disruptive behavior disorder.
   b. an emotional disorder.
   c. a habit disorder.
   d. a developmental disorder.

6. If a child's problem involves the failure to learn language, she has
   a. a disruptive behavior disorder.
   b. an emotional disorder.
   c. a habit disorder.
   d. a developmental disorder.

7. All of these are risk factors for delinquency except
   a. a large family.
   b. school difficulties.
   c. being middle class.
   d. parental criminality.

8. The most effective treatments for conduct disorders are those suggested by the
   a. biomedical model.
   b. psychodynamic model.
   c. behavioral model.
   d. cognitive model.

9. Hyperactivity involves which of the following symptoms?
   a. short attention span
   b. impulsive actions
   c. inability to hold still
   d. all of the above

10. Among the successful treatments for some hyperactive children are
    a. tranquilizers.
    b. antidepressants.
    c. stimulants.
    d. depressants.

11. Behavioral techniques for treating hyperactivity are based on
    a. Pavlovian conditioning.
    b. operant conditioning.
    c. modeling.
    d. all of the above.

12. Childhood emotional disorders correspond to which adult disorders?
    a. anxiety disorders
    b. affective disorders
    c. schizophrenic disorders
    d. none of the above

13. The most common childhood emotional disorder is
    a. conduct disorder.
    b. hyperactivity.
    c. phobia.
    d. separation anxiety.

14. Separation anxiety is often triggered by
    a. change.
    b. hormones.
    c. parental divorce.
    d. trauma.

15. Childhood fears include all of the following except
    a. animal phobia.
    b. agoraphobia.
    c. school phobia.
    d. fear of the dark.

16. The childhood emotional disorder that is easiest to treat is
    a. conduct disorder.
    b. hyperactivity.
    c. phobia.
    d. separation anxiety.

17. Which does not belong?
    a. autism
    b. enuresis
    c. stuttering
    d. anorexia

18. The cause of enuresis is compatible with the
    a. biomedical model.
    b. psychodynamic model.
    c. behavioral model.
    d. cognitive model.
    e. existential model.

19. The most successful treatment for enuresis is that based on the
    a. biomedical model.
    b. psychodynamic model.
    c. behavioral model.
    d. cognitive model.
    e. existential model.

20. Someone who stutters would be expected to have particular difficulty saying
    a. "Please pass the potatoes."
    b. "I ironed out the idiotic ideas."
    c. "He had to have help."
    d. "Eat the edible eggplant."

21. All of the following are treatments for stuttering except
    a. shadowing.
    b. desensitization.
    c. delayed auditory feedback.
    d. syllable-timed speech.

22. Anorexia nervosa most obviously involves
    a. weight loss.
    b. depression.
    c. anxiety.
    d. thought disorder.

23. In what percent of cases does anorexia result in death?
    a. 1 percent
    b. 5 percent
    c. 20 percent
    d. 33 percent

24. The cause of anorexia may be
    a. faulty communication within the family.
    b. hormonal.
    c. sexual.
    d. all of the above.

25. Bulimia usually involves
    a. binges.
    b. purges.
    c. both.
    d. neither.

26. Bulimia frequently co-occurs with
    a. alcoholism.
    b. depression.
    c. mania.
    d. schizophrenia.

27. A strict definition of obesity (i.e., weight is greater than 20 percent of the median weight of children the same height) results in an estimate of how many obese children in the United States?
    a. 1 to 2 million
    b. 3 to 4 million
    c. 5 to 8 million
    d. 9 to 12 million

28. Obesity results from
    a. biological factors.
    b. behavioral factors.
    c. both biological factors and behavioral factors.

29. Most individuals who are retarded fall into which category?
    a. mild mental retardation
    b. moderate mental retardation
    c. severe mental retardation
    d. profound mental retardation

30. Cultural-familial retardation is the result of
    a. genetic influences.
    b. environmental influences.
    c. injury influences.
    d. illness influences.

31. Which of these educational strategies has been most effective for training mentally retarded children?
    a. segregating them
    b. mainstreaming them
    c. both *a* and *b*
    d. neither *a* nor *b*

32. Down's syndrome arises because of
    a. faulty learning.
    b. metabolic abnormality.
    c. neurotransmitter insufficiency.
    d. chromosomal abnormality.

33. Phenylketonuria arises because of
    a. faulty learning.
    b. metabolic abnormality.
    c. neurotransmitter insufficiency.
    d. chromosomal abnormality.

34. The difference between specific developmental disorders and pervasive developmental disorders involves
    a. slow development versus no development.
    b. early onset versus late onset.
    c. environmental causes versus biological causes.
    d. emotional problem versus behavioral problem.

35. Reading difficulties are more common among
    a. boys than girls.
    b. children who developed language late than children who developed language early.
    c. children with family members who have reading difficulties than children with family members who do not have reading difficulties.
    d. *a* and *b*.
    e. *a* and *c*.
    f. *b* and *c*.
    g. all of the above.

36. Which is a pervasive developmental disorder?
    a. autism
    b. anorexia
    c. stuttering
    d. hyperactivity

37. All of these are symptoms of autism except
    a. echolalia.
    b. failure to respond to others.
    c. mental retardation.
    d. insistence on sameness.

38. Autism occurs more frequently among
    a. boys than girls.
    b. lower-class children than upper-class children.
    c. both *a* and *b*.
    d. neither *a* nor *b*.

39. Current ideas about the causes of autism are compatible with the
    a. biomedical model.

    b. psychodynamic model.
    c. behavioral model.
    d. cognitive model.
    e. existential model.

40. The neurotransmitter thought to be involved in autism is
    a. dopamine.
    b. norepinephrine.
    c. serotonin.
    d. chlorpromazine.

41. Current treatments of autism are derived from the
    a. biomedical model.
    b. psychodynamic model.
    c. behavioral model.
    d. cognitive model.
    e. existential model.

42. The prognosis for autistic children appears
    a. good.
    b. modest.
    c. bad.
    d. unknown.

43. The best prognostic indicator for childhood autism is
    a. age of onset.
    b. IQ.
    c. echolalia.
    d. parental concern.

Answer Key for Sample Exam

1.	b	(p. 520)		23.	c	(p. 536)
2.	c	(p. 521)		24.	d	(p. 538)
3.	d	(p. 521)		25.	c	(p. 538)
4.	b	(p. 521)		26.	b	(p. 539)
5.	a	(p. 521)		27.	c	(p. 540)
6.	e	(p. 521)		28.	c	(p. 540)
7.	c	(p. 525)		29.	a	(p. 542)
8.	c	(p. 526)		30.	a, b	(p. 544)
9.	d	(p. 527)		31.	d	(p. 546)
10.	c	(p. 529)		32.	d	(p. 543)
11.	b	(p. 529)		33.	b	(p. 544)
12.	a	(p. 530)		34.	a	(p. 547)
13.	d	(p. 531)		35.	g	(p. 546)
14.	d	(p. 531)		36.	a	(p. 547)
15.	b	(p. 533)		37.	c	(p. 551)
16.	c	(p. 532)		38.	a	(p. 553)
17.	a	(p. 534)		39.	a	(p. 553)
18.	a	(p. 534)		40.	c	(p. 554)
19.	c	(p. 535)		41.	c	(p. 555)
20.	a	(p. 535)		42.	b	(p. 556)
21.	b	(p. 536)		43.	b	(p. 556)
22.	a	(p. 536)				

SELF-TEST

1. Children's problems are more difficult to understand than those of adults because they occur in the context of _____; also, children often cannot _____ a problem directly through _____.

2. To be considered a disorder, a child's problem must be _____, and it must _____ the child or others.

3. Children's disorders fall into these general categories: _____, _____, _____, _____, and _____.

4. The disruptive behavior disorders of children are divided into _____ disorders, _____ disorders, and _____ disorders.

5. Conduct disorders are _____ likely among boys than girls.

6. Children with conduct disorders tend to come from _____ social environments.

7. Children who show conduct disturbance also have problems in maintaining _____.

8. Historically, treatment of conduct disorders has been largely _____; at the present, treatments derived from _____ seem promising.

9. Disorders of attention are often accompanied by _____.

10. Hyperactive children sometimes show improvement when treated with _____ drugs.

11. When feelings of inferiority, social withdrawal, shyness, fear, and overattachment predominate, a child may have an _____ disorder.

12. Childhood fears are surprisingly _____.

13. Habit disorders have a habitual physical component. Among these disorders are _____, _____, _____, _____, and _____.

14. Enuresis may be successfully treated with _____ techniques.

15. Three techniques for the treatment of stuttering are _____, _____, and _____.

16. Anorexia is characterized by substantial loss of _____ and the deliberate _____.

17. Anorexia nervosa is _____ likely among girls than boys.

18. Death may occur in _____ of cases of anorexia nervosa.

19. The cause of anorexia is _____.

20. The most common form of mental retardation is _____, which results from _____ and _____ influences; less common is mental retardation resulting from _____ and _____.

21. The educational strategy of placing mentally retarded children in regular classrooms is called _____ .

22. Mental retardation associated with an extra chromosome is _____ .

23. Mental retardation associated with an inability to metabolize phenylalanine is _____ or _____ .

24. Developmental disorders fall into two types. The first, _____ developmental disorders, involves developmental lags. The second, _____ developmental disorders, involves developmental failures.

25. In autism, the child's ability to _____ fails to develop.

26. Autistic language is characterized by _____ and _____ .

27. Autistic children insist on _____ .

28. The cause of autism is _____ .

29. The best predictor of prognosis for autistic children is _____ .

Answer Key for Self-Test

1. development; communicate; language
2. persistent; impair
3. disruptive behavior; emotional; habit; developmental; and gender identity
4. conduct; oppositional; attention-defect hyperactivity
5. more
6. unpleasant
7. attention
8. unsuccessful; social learning theory
9. hyperactivity
10. stimulant
11. emotional
12. common
13. enuresis; stuttering; anorexia nervosa; bulimia; obesity
14. behavioral
15. delayed auditory feedback; shadowing; syllable-timed speech
16. body weight; restriction of calories
17. more
18. 20
19. unknown
20. cultural-familial retardation; genetic; environmental; illness; injury
21. mainstreaming
22. Down's syndrome
23. phenylketonuria; PKU
24. specific; pervasive
25. respond to others
26. echolalia; pronominal reversal
27. sameness
28. probably biological
29. IQ

TYING IT TOGETHER

Childhood disorders fit uneasily with the rest of the disorders described in the textbook since they occur in the context of development. One of the truisms of developmental psychology is that little is invariant. Child development is well described by family resemblances (Chapter 1), and when its fuzzy concepts are coupled with those inherent in abnormal psychology, the result can be confusing. At the present time, psychologists concerned with childhood disorders are split on the issue of how to approach them. Should they be explained by generalizing "downward" from what is known about disorders in adults? Or does the field need its own psychology, based on a developmental model rather than on one of the prevailing adult models (Chapters 3–5)?

The answer probably is both. Some childhood disorders are profitably viewed as similar to adult disorders. Childhood fears, for instance, seem analogous to the adult phobias (Chapter 8), and childhood depression overlaps considerably with adult depression (Chapter 11). On the other hand, other childhood disorders are uniquely problems of children. The developmental disorders, for instance, must be approached in their own respect and not as variations of adult disorders. Autism seems to be a "new" disorder, and it is in particular poorly understood. Attempts to assimilate it within the psychodynamic (Chapter 4) or behavioral (Chapter 5) models have not been successful.

The adult disorders described in the other chapters frequently have their origin in childhood: emotional disorders (Chapters 8 and 9), depression (Chapter 11), paraphilias (Chapter 13), transsexuality (Chapter 13), drug abuse (Chapter 14), personality disorders (Chapter 15), and schizophrenia (Chapter 12). Increased research and theoretical attention may clarify not only disorders of childhood but also disorders that partly originate there.

The ethical and legal issues that arise when abnormality comes to the attention of the court (Chapter 18) are compounded when children are involved. Parents have traditionally been accorded "rights" that may thwart their children. On the other hand, the line between intervention and interference is fuzzy, and caution is needed when the legal system becomes concerned with children.

FURTHER READINGS

Axline, V. M. (1964). *Dibs: In search of self; Personality development in play therapy.* Boston: Houghton Mifflin.

Benton, A., & Pearl, D. (1978). *Dyslexia: An appraisal of current knowledge.* New York: Oxford University.

Bettelheim, B. (1967). *The empty fortress: Infantile autism and the birth of the self.* New York: Free Press.

Boskind-White, M., & White, W. C. (1983). *Bulimarexia: The binge/purge cycle.* New York: Norton.

Bruch, H. (1978). *The golden cage.* Cambridge, MA: Harvard University Press.

Edgerton, R. B. (1979). *Mental retardation.* Cambridge, MA: Harvard University Press.

Feingold, B. F. (1974). *Why your child is hyperactive.* New York: Random House.

Halmi, K. A. (1978). Anorexia nervosa: Recent investigations. *Annual Review of Medicine, 29,* 137–148.

Pyle, R. L., Mitchell, J. E., & Eckert, E. D. (1981). Bulimia: A report of 34 cases. *Journal of Clinical Psychiatry, 42,* 60–64.

Russell, G. (1979). Bulimia nervosa: An ominous variant of anorexia nervosa. *Psychological Medicine, 9,* 429–448.

TERM-PAPER TOPICS

1. What is hyperactivity? Is it on the increase? If so, why? If not, then why do some think so?

2. Why are boys more apt to be retarded than girls? What does this suggest about sex differences in other disorders?

3. Compare and contrast childhood fears and adult phobias. What do your comparisons and contrasts suggest about the causes of phobias?

4. Evaluate the evidence linking childhood conduct disorder to adult antisocial personality disorder.

5. Summarize the evidence that autism is a biological phenomenon. In light of what is not known, what kinds of biological treatments might someday be possible?

EXERCISES

Exercise One—Childhood Disorders

In this exercise you will learn firsthand about common psychological disorders of children.

Arrange a classroom lecture by an elementary school teacher or counselor about common psychological disorders of childhood—hyperactivity, learning disability, depression, phobia, and so on. How are these manifest? How do they disrupt the child at school? How are they treated?

Exercise Two—Local Educational Practices

In this exercise, you will learn how your local school district approaches the education of children with intellectual, emotional, and physical difficulties.

Arrange a classroom lecture by a member of your local school board about the district's philosophies toward mainstreaming children with intellectual, emotional, and/or physical problems. What are the goals? What are the difficulties in achieving them? What changes would your lecturer like to see made?

Exercise Three—Work in a Classroom

You will gain firsthand experience in the care of children in this exercise.

Volunteer to work as a teacher's aide at a local elementary school or child-care center. Ask to be placed in a classroom with difficult children. Use this experience as an opportunity to examine your beliefs about such children and how they should be treated.

CHAPTER 17

Disorders of the Nervous System and Psychopathology

CHAPTER OVERVIEW

This chapter describes disorders of the nervous system: so-called organic syndromes that have a clear basis in pathology of the structure or function of the nervous system. The chapter presents several basic principles describing how the brain and nervous system work, because they help explain how neurological disorders are manifested in behavior, how they can be diagnosed, and how they might be treated.

The brain is organized biochemically, spatially, laterally, and hierarchically. Neurological disorders can result from disruption of any of these modes of organization. Neurological function is achieved by a balance between inhibition and excitation of neurons. Again, disorders can involve problems with either process. Redundancy exists in the nervous system, allowing in many cases recovery from illness or injury. However, some areas of the brain are more vulnerable to damage than others, and these are where pathology is most likely to originate.

With these principles stated, the varieties and causes of nervous system disorders are described. Diagnosis is the strong point of neurology, and there exist techniques and devices that allow strong inferences about the exact nature of neurological dysfunction. Four disorders are described in detail: disorders of language (aphasias), disorders of reading (dyslexias), disorders of memory (amnesic syndromes), and dementia (e.g., Alzheimer's disease).

The chapter concludes with a discussion of how neurological disorders are treated, and with a caution about expecting too much—or too little—from a neurological approach to disorders.

ESSENTIAL TERMS

AIDS dementia	dementia caused directly by AIDS virus
Alzheimer's disease	common type of dementia often involving amnesia and/or language disorder
amnesic syndrome	disorder of memory
amyotrophic lateral sclerosis (ALS)	movement disorder of unknown origin; also called "Lou Gehrig's disease"
anterograde amnesia	loss of memory for events since onset of amnesia
aphasia	disorder of language

aura	unusual sensations or feelings that foreshadow an epileptic seizure
Babinski sign	foot reflex normally shown only by infants
Broca's area	part of the brain involved in speech, specifically, syntax (grammar)
CAT scan (computer-assisted tomography)	device for taking three-dimensional X-ray pictures of the brain
consolidation block theory	theory of the amnesic syndrome that proposes the basic deficit to be in the formation (consolidation) of new long-term memories
corpus callosum	connection between the brain's hemispheres
deep dyslexia	reading difficulty characterized by semantic difficulty
dementia	progressive loss of variety of higher mental functions
dyslexia	reading disorder
EEG (electroencephalogram)	assessment device for measuring electrical activity of the brain
epilepsy	disorder marked by excessive activity of the nervous system (seizures)
explicit memory	memory that requires one to consciously recollect past experiences (cf. implicit memory)
frontal lobes	part of the brain thought to be involved in planning and executing action
functional syndrome	abnormality caused by abnormal experience through the operation of normal brain mechanisms (cf. organic syndrome)
glia cells	supportive tissue in the brain
gray matter	areas where nerve cell bodies are concentrated
hippocampus	part of the brain thought to be involved in amnesia
implicit memory	memory that requires one to perform tasks, not consciously recollect events (cf. explicit memory)
Korsakoff's syndrome	common type of amnesia resulting from alcoholism
left-sided neglect	neurological syndrome caused by damage to the right parietal area of the brain and resulting in neglect of functions that involve the left side of the body (dressing, writing, reading, and so on)
localization of function	doctrine that particular mental functions are to be found in specific parts of the brain
MRI (magnetic resonance imaging)	technique for forming images on the brain by measuring spinning of hydrogen atoms
negative symptom	symptom characterized by loss or deficiency (cf. positive symptom)
neuron	basic unit of the nervous system

neurotransmitter	chemical released by one neuron to communicate with another neuron
organic syndrome	abnormality caused by known pathology of the nervous system (cf. functional syndrome)
Parkinson's disease	movement disorder caused by degeneration of neurons leading to a depletion of dopamine in the brain
partial consolidation deficit theory	theory of the amnesic syndrome that proposes the basic deficit to be incomplete store and retrieval of memories
perseveration	difficulty in making transitions between one action and the next
PET scan (positron emission tomography)	device for assessing activity in different brain regions by measuring positron emission
phonological dyslexia	difficulty reading by sound
Pick's disease	dementia caused by damage to frontal lobes
positive symptom	symptom characterized by increased behavior or nervous system activity (cf. negative symptom)
projection areas	parts of the brain that receive sensory inputs
rCBF (regional cerebral blood flow)	technique for measuring blood flow within different regions of the brain
retrieval failure theory	theory of the amnesic syndrome that suggests the basic deficit to be in retrieval of memories
retrograde amnesia	loss of memory for events prior to onset of amnesia
SPECT scan (single photon emission computerized tomography)	device for assessing activity in different brain regions by measuring photon emission
split-brain syndrome	result of surgical procedure that severs connections between the brain's hemispheres, resulting in what can be described as "two consciousnesses in one head"
left hemisphere	cerebral hemisphere that is better at analysis
right hemisphere	cerebral hemisphere that is better at synthesis
surface dyslexia	reading difficulty characterized by problems with words that violate standard pronunciation
synapse	gap separating one neuron from another, into which neurotransmitters are secreted
Wernicke's area	part of the brain that accomplishes perception of speech
white matter	areas where axons are concentrated into tracts

SAMPLE EXAM

1. The difference between organic and functional syndromes lies in
   a. etiology.
   b. diagnosis.
   c. prognosis.
   d. all of the above.
   e. none of the above.

2. Pathologies studied by psychologists _____ overlap with those studied by

neurologists.
a. do not
b. partly
c. completely

3. The gap between two neurons is the
a. synapse.
b. dead pool.
c. interneuronal space.
d. glia.
e. corpus callosum.

4. Neurotransmitters _____ neurons.
a. excite
b. inhibit
c. both
d. neither

5. Multiple sclerosis is a disorder of
a. synapses.
b. glia cells.
c. the corpus callosum.
d. the limbic system.

6. Redundancy in the brain is achieved by
a. alternate pathways.
b. duplication of hemispheres.
c. excess neurons.
d. all of the above.
e. none of the above.

7. Different areas of the brain
a. have the same vulnerability.
b. differ in vulnerability.
c. differ in vulnerability, but it depends on the individual.

8. What does it mean to say that the brain is biochemically organized?
a. higher levels of the brain build on lower levels of the brain
b. neurons that produce the same neurotransmitters tend to be located close to one another
c. neurons close to one another are likely to perform the same function
d. the brain is differentiated on a left-right basis

9. Parkinson's disease is associated with
a. too little dopamine.
b. too much dopamine.
c. too little norepinephrine.
d. too much norepinephrine.

10. The cause of amyotrophic lateral sclerosis (ALS) is
a. excess neurotransmitter.
b. aluminum toxicity.
c. chromosomal abnormality.
d. unknown.

11. What does it mean to say that the brain is spatially organized?

a. higher levels of the brain build on lower levels of the brain
b. neurons that produce the same neurotransmitters tend to be located close to one another
c. neurons close to one another are likely to perform the same function
d. the brain is differentiated on a left-right basis

12. Pioneering research by Broca gave support to the position of
a. empiricism.
b. evolution.
c. localization.
d. psychoanalysis.
e. rationalism.

13. Nerve cell bodies are concentrated into
a. antimatter.
b. gray matter.
c. white matter.
d. nothing matters.
e. smatterings of ignorance.

14. Motor functions are to sensory functions as
a. front is to back.
b. top is to bottom.
c. left is to right.
d. inside is to outside.

15. Planning is localized in the _____ of the brain.
a. back
b. bottom
c. front
d. top

16. What does it mean to say that the brain is laterally (horizontally) organized?
a. higher levels of the brain build on lower levels of the brain
b. neurons that produce the same neurotransmitters tend to be located close to one another
c. neurons close to one another are likely to perform the same function
d. the brain is differentiated on a left-right basis

17. If an individual has an injury on the right side of the brain, the idea of contralateral projection would imply that
a. she would show impairment on the right side of her body.
b. she would show impairment on the left side of her body.
c. she would show impairment on both sides of her body.
d. none of the above.

18. Research with split brains suggests that the
    a. right hemisphere is involved in synthesis.
    b. left hemisphere is involved in synthesis.
    c. right hemisphere is involved in analysis.
    d. left hemisphere is involved in analysis.

19. Language disorders are apt to occur when there is
    a. right-hemisphere damage.
    b. left-hemisphere damage.

20. What does it mean to say that the brain is hierarchically (vertically) organized?
    a. higher levels of the brain build on lower levels of the brain
    b. neurons that produce the same neurotransmitters tend to be located close to one another
    c. neurons close to one another are likely to perform the same function
    d. the brain is differentiated on a left-right basis

21. According to John Hughlings Jackson, higher levels of the brain
    a. appear later in evolution.
    b. appear later in development.
    c. are more vulnerable to injury or illness.
    d. all of the above.
    e. none of the above.

22. A disorder of language is
    a. aphasia.
    b. apraxia.
    c. dyslexia.

23. A disorder of movement is
    a. aphasia.
    b. apraxia.
    c. dyslexia.

24. A disorder of reading is
    a. aphasia.
    b. apraxia.
    c. dyslexia.

25. Which of these devices or techniques records the brain's electrical activity?
    a. CAT scan
    b. EEG
    c. MRI
    d. PET scan
    e. rCBF

26. Which of these devices or techniques takes a three-dimensional X-ray of the brain?
    a. CAT scan
    b. EEG
    c. MRI
    d. PET scan
    e. rCBF

27. Which of these devices or techniques measures the movement of hydrogen atoms in the brain?
    a. CAT scan
    b. EEG
    c. MRI
    d. PET scan
    e. rCBF

28. Which of these devices or techniques assesses the brain's blood flow?
    a. CAT scan
    b. EEG
    c. MRI
    d. PET scan
    e. rCBF

29. Which of these devices or techniques estimates the brain's metabolic activity?
    a. CAT scan
    b. EEG
    c. MRI
    d. PET scan
    e. rCBF

30. Broca's area is to Wernicke's area as
    a. expressive aphasia is to receptive aphasia.
    b. receptive aphasia is to expressive aphasia.
    c. expressive aphasia is to conduction aphasia.
    d. conduction aphasia is to expressive aphasia.

31. Broca's aphasia is now regarded as a problem with
    a. grammar.
    b. phonology.
    c. pragmatics.
    d. semantics.
    e. syntax.

32. Which of these is a common route in reading, from print to meaning?
    a. conversion to sound and then to meaning
    b. direct conversion to meaning
    c. both
    d. neither

33. In _____ dyslexia, there is a problem with reading by sound.
    a. deep
    b. phonological
    c. surface

d. all of the above
e. none of the above

34. _____ memory is affected in the amnesic syndrome.
a. Primary
b. Secondary
c. both
d. neither

35. Chronic alcoholism leads to
a. Alzheimer's disease.
b. Babinski's sign.
c. Down's syndrome.
d. Korsakoff's syndrome.
e. Parkinson's disease.

36. _____ to the hippocampus produces the amnesic syndrome.
a. Bilateral damage
b. Unilateral damage
c. a or b

37. The _____ theory of amnesia has trouble explaining retrograde amnesia.
a. consolidation block
b. retrieval failure
c. partial consolidation deficit
d. all have trouble
e. none have trouble

38. _____ memory refers to memory that does not involve conscious recollection.
a. Explicit
b. Implicit
c. both
d. neither

39. Alzheimer's disease produces
a. delirium.
b. dementia.
c. dissociation.
d. all of the above.
e. none of the above.

40. Research suggests that _____ may be involved in Alzheimer's disease.
a. biochemical deficits
b. chromosomal abnormalities
c. excess aluminum
d. malformed neurons
e. none of the above

41. Neurology is at its best when _____ disorders.
a. diagnosing
b. treating
c. both
d. neither

Answer Key for Sample Exam

1.	a	(p. 558)	22.	a	(p. 575)
2.	b	(p. 558)	23.	b	(p. 559)
3.	a	(p. 560)	24.	c	(p. 579)
4.	c	(p. 560)	25.	b	(p. 572)
5.	b	(p. 561)	26.	a	(p. 573)
6.	d	(p. 571)	27.	c	(p. 573)
7.	b	(p. 570)	28.	e	(p. 574)
8.	b	(p. 562)	29.	d	(p. 574)
9.	a	(p. 562)	30.	a	(p. 576)
10.	d	(p. 562)	31.	e	(p. 578)
11.	c	(p. 562)	32.	c	(p. 580)
12.	c	(p. 576)	33.	b	(p. 580)
13.	b	(p. 562)	34.	b	(p. 582)
14.	a	(p. 564)	35.	d	(p. 583)
15.	c	(p. 564)	36.	a	(p. 585)
16.	d	(p. 567)	37.	d	(p. 587)
17.	b	(p. 567)	38.	b	(p. 587)
18.	a, d	(p. 567)	39.	b	(p. 590)
19.	b	(p. 567)	40.	a, b, c, d	
20.	a	(p. 568)		(p. 591)	
21.	d	(p. 568)	41.	a	(p. 595)

SELF-TEST

1. _____ syndromes are caused by known pathology of the nervous system, whereas _____ syndromes are not. The line between the two is often _____ .

2. _____ and _____ work with organic syndromes, and _____ and _____ work with clinical syndromes.

3. A loss of language is called _____ .

4. The basic unit of the nervous system is the _____ ; these units communicate with each other by means of _____ .

5. Besides neurons, the nervous system is also composed of_____ cells.

6. The brain is organized in several ways. That neurons with similar biochemical properties are located together is_____ organization. That neurons close to each other perform the same function is_____ organization. That the brain is organized on a left-right basis is_____ organization. And that higher levels of the brain build on lower levels is_____ organization.

7. Redundancy in the nervous system is accomplished by_____ than necessary, _____ to accomplish the same end, and the same functions in_____.

8. Neurons cannot be_____, but they can_____ if damaged.

9. Parkinson's disease is associated with a depletion of_____.

10. The left half of the brain controls the_____ of the body, and the right half of the brain control the_____ of the body.

11. Severing the connections between the two brains results in a_____.

12. The left brain appears to be involved in tasks requiring_____, and the right brain appears to be involved in tasks requiring_____.

13. Lower levels of the brain appear_____ in evolution and_____ in development. Also, they are_____ vulnerable to injury or illness.

14. People with damage to their frontal lobes often show difficulty making transitions from one action to another. This is called_____.

15. Damage to the nervous system can express itself in both_____ and_____ symptoms.

16. Epilepsy is caused by_____ of the nervous system, which leads to_____.

17. Among the devices that aid neurological diagnosis are the_____ (which records the brain's electrical activity), the_____ (which takes a three-dimensional X-ray of the brain),_____ (which detects magnetic activity of atoms in the brain),_____ (which assesses blood flow to different parts of the brain), and the_____ (which measures brain metabolic activity.

18. The classical view of Broca's aphasia regards it as a disorder of language_____, but the current view sees it as a problem of_____.

19. Difficulty in reading is called_____.

20. Reading involves two pathways,_____ and_____.

21. Developmental dyslexia in some cases resembles_____ dyslexia.

22. According to William James, memory had_____ and_____ components.

23. _____ results from chronic alcoholism.

24. The_____ is involved in the amnesic syndromes.

25. The full amnesic syndrome is produced by _____ damage to the hippocampus.

26. Damage to the skull can produce a transient amnesic syndrome, but usually only when _____ has been lost.

27. None of the theories of amnesia that posit a single process can explain _____ .

28. The progressive loss of higher mental functions is _____, and its most common cause is _____ .

29. Two theories of Alzheimer's disease are currently entertained, one pointing to excess _____ and the other to _____ abnormalities.

30. Dementia resulting from damage to the frontal lobes is called _____ .

31. The strength of neurology is _____; its weakness is _____ .

32. Psychologists should rely neither _____ nor _____ on the neurological approach in explaining and treating psychopathologies.

Answer Key for Self-Test

1. Organic; functional; fuzzy
2. Neurologists; neuropsychologists; psychiatrists; clinical psychologists
3. aphasia
4. neuron; neurotransmitter
5. glia
6. biochemical; spatial; lateral; hierarchical
7. more neurons; alternate pathways; both hemispheres
8. replaced; recover
9. dopamine
10. right; left
11. split brain
12. analysis; synthesis
13. earlier; earlier; less
14. perseveration
15. positive; negative
16. excessive activity; seizures
17. EEG; CAT scan; MRI; rCBF; PET scan
18. expression; syntax
19. dyslexia
20. sound; sight
21. phonological
22. primary; secondary
23. Korsakoff's syndrome
24. limbic system
25. bilateral
26. consciousness
27. retrograde amnesia
28. dementia; Alzheimer's disease
29. aluminum; chromosomal
30. Pick's disease
31. diagnosis; treatment
32. too much; too little

TYING IT TOGETHER

This chapter describes disorders that are compatible with the biomedical model (Chapter 3), yet even the neurological disorders have fuzzy boundaries (Chapter 1) influenced by cultural values and practices. In an illiterate society, reading difficulty is not a problem at all.

Neurological diagnosis is more sophisticated than typical psychological assessment (Chapter 7), probably because it is based on well-understood neurological principles derived from many years of research (Chapter 6).

Will all the psychopathologies someday be the province of neurology? The answer here is no, because the role of experience is undeniable in many of these disorders, including fears and phobias (Chapter 8), hysteria (Chapter 9), depression (Chapter 11), and so on. Indeed, recent work in health psychology (Chapter 10) implies that even physical illness reflects psychological factors.

Nonetheless, an understanding of neurology is necessary for a full understanding of any psychopathology, because all phenomena of behavior has some basis in the nervous system. This idea is well illustrated for psychosomatic disorders (Chapter 10), schizophrenia (Chapter 12), and drug abuse (Chapter 14).

Treatment for neurological disorders is not as advanced as diagnosis. In part this reflects lack of knowledge, but also it reflects the fact that neurons cannot be replaced if destroyed. The psychological therapies, particularly those based on the environmental model (Chapter 5), prove useful in helping patients with neurological damage to overcome their problems (Chapter 19), just as eyeglasses help people cope with vision problems.

FURTHER READINGS

Allport, S. (1986). *Explorers of the black box.* New York: Norton.

Gardner, H. (1976). *The shattered mind.* New York: Vintage.

Gazzaniga, M. S. (1988). *Mind matters: How the mind and brain interact to create our conscious lives.* Boston: Houghton Mifflin.

Goldstein, K. (1939). *The organism.* New York: American Book Company.

Lenneberg, E. H. (1967). *Biological foundations of language.* New York: Wiley.

Lezak, M. D. (1976). *Neuropsychological assessment.* New York: Oxford.

Luria, A. (1970). The functional organization of the brain. *Scientific American, 222,* 66–78.

Ornstein, R., & Thompson, R. F. (1984). *The amazing brain.* Boston: Houghton Mifflin.

Sacks, O. (1985). *The man who mistook his wife for a hat and other clinical tales.* New York: Summit.

TERM-PAPER TOPICS

1. An understanding of brain laterality is critical for understanding neurological disorders. Some theorists believe that lateralization is also important in schizophrenia and other psychopathologies. Review the evidence for this claim. What is your conclusion.

2. Freud was originally trained as a neurologist. In what ways is psychoanalysis still a neurological approach, although phrased in psychological language?

3. Injury or illness involving the hormonal systems of the body can result in a variety of abnormalities of thought, mood, and disorder. Survey these abnormalities. Which glands are most vulnerable to injury or illness?

4. What is the evidence pro and con for the possibility that autism is a neurological disease?

5. How does language development depend on development of the brain and nervous system? Explain this relationship, particularly in terms of its effect on disorders of language.

6. What might the future hold for the treatment of neurological disorders?

EXERCISES

Exercise One—Rehabilitation Medicine

The purpose of this exercise is to learn first-hand about rehabilitation medicine.

Volunteer to work as an aide at your local hospital. Ask to work on a rehabilitation ward, where patients have had strokes, amputations, or other occurrences that necessitate adjustment to some loss of function.

Above and beyond their obvious losses, what have the patients lost? How are they affected psychologically? How do the rehabilitation counselors, nurses, and physicians attempt to help patients? How must patients help themselves?

Exercise Two—Alzheimer's Disease

In this exercise, you will learn about the characteristics and progression of Alzheimer's disease.

Talk to individuals with family members who have Alzheimer's disease. When was their condition first apparent? What progression was shown? Under what circumstances does the family member seem to do well? When does he or she do particularly poorly?

Gruetzner, H. (1988). *Alzheimer's: A caregiver's guide and sourcebook.* New York: Wiley.

Exercise Three—Neuropsychological Testing

The purpose of this exercise is to learn more about neuropsychological testing.

Arrange a classroom lecture by a neuropsychologist who can explain the Halsted-Reitan battery (a set of tests for determining the nature and extent of neurological damage). Ask the neuropsychologist to present several examples of the "detective work" involved in neuropsychological diagnosis. In each case, how has the diagnosis aided rehabilitation?

Golden, C. J. (1981). *Diagnosis and rehabilitation in clinical neuropsychology* (2nd ed.). Springfield, IL: Thomas.

Exercise Four—Brain-Imaging Techniques

CAT scans, PET scans, and other high-tech marvels for glimpsing at the structure and function of the nervous system are increasingly used, but few individuals are familiar with them. In this exercise, you will gain some familiarity with these assessment devices.

Arrange a tour of a local hospital that has one or more of these devices. Ask to see them, and to have someone explain to your class how they work and the uses to which they are put.

Sochurek, H. (1987). Medicine's new vision. *National Geographic, 171*(2), 2–41.

The Law and Politics of Abnormality

CHAPTER OVERVIEW

Chapter 18 looks at abnormality from a legal and political perspective. First, what criteria are used to justify involuntary commitment? Among those described are impaired judgment, need for treatment, inability to care for oneself, grave disability, and dangerousness. It is sometimes difficult to assess these and to argue that they are valid grounds for involuntary commitment. Second, what rights are enjoyed by a mental patient? Third, what standard of proof should be required in commitment procedures: preponderance of evidence, clear and convincing proof, or beyond a reasonable doubt? Fourth, does involuntary commitment provide the right to be treated?

Fifth, how has the insanity plea been used to excuse an individual from the consequences of criminal acts? Different rules have been employed by courts in defining the grounds for an insanity plea: the "right-wrong" test, the "product of mental disease" test, and the "appreciate and conform" test. Sixth, the topic of incompetence to stand trial is briefly discussed.

The chapter goes on to discuss social and state abuse of abnormal psychology. Psychiatric hospitalization may be used to persecute an individual who does not have a disorder. Society stigmatizes ordinary people who have sought psychiatric help.

ESSENTIAL TERMS

appreciate and conform	criterion for an insanity plea: does an individual as the result of mental disturbance lack the capacity to appreciate criminality of conduct or to conform his or her conduct to requirements of law?; American Law Institute (ALI) Rule
competence to stand trial	capacity to understand legal proceedings and/or to assist in one's own defense
criminal commitment	coerced psychiatric hospitalization of people who have acted harmfully but are not legally responsible because they lack a "guilty mind"
criminal insanity	psychological distress coupled with a record of past violence and expectation of future violence
due process of law	legal privileges afforded anyone whose liberty is threatened by state action

grave disability	inability to provide for one's own personal needs for food, clothing, and shelter
guilty but mentally ill	new verdict that has replaced "not guilty by reason of insanity" verdict in some states; results in commitment to a mental institution rather than a prison
insanity plea	legal defense of individuals thought not to be responsible for wrongdoing because of whole or partial irrationality when the crime took place
involuntary commitment	process whereby the state hospitalizes people for their own good, even over their protest
mens rea	guilty mind, not present if an insanity plea is justified
product of mental disorder	criterion of an insanity plea: was the unlawful act produced by mental disorder?; Durham rule
psychological disability	ill-defined precondition for involuntary commitment involving impaired judgment, need for treatment, behavioral disability, and dangerousness to self and/or others
right to treatment	right of an involuntarily committed individual to be treated after commitment
right-wrong test	criterion of insanity plea: did the individual know what was done, and did the individual know it was wrong?; M'Naghten rule
standard of proof	criteria that legal evidence must meet to be used to restrict a person's freedom, among them preponderance of evidence, beyond a reasonable doubt, and clear and convincing proof

SAMPLE EXAM

1. The problem in defining grounds for involuntary commitment is parallel to
   a. the nature-nurture issue.
   b. the problem in defining abnormality.
   c. the difficulty in isolating causes of abnormality.
   d. the problem in treating autism.

2. Required in all states for involuntary commitment is
   a. psychological disability.
   b. impaired judgment.
   c. need for treatment.
   d. danger to self or others.

3. Incarcerating an individual because he is predicted to be dangerous in the future is at odds with
   a. common sense.
   b. Western legal tradition.
   c. research findings.
   d. the biomedical model.

4. In Operation Baxtrom, what proportion

of the "criminally insane" acted violently within four years of release?
   a. 3 percent
   b. 10 percent
   c. 50 percent
   d. 97 percent

5. What is the "thank you" test?
   a. Individuals who are not grateful should be hospitalized.
   b. Individuals who are grateful should be hospitalized.
   c. Individuals who will not work for thanks alone should not be clinical psychologists.
   d. Individuals who would be grateful after recovery should be hospitalized.

6. All of these are included in due process except the right to
   a. challenge witnesses.
   b. refuse psychological tests.
   c. legal counsel.
   d. trial by jury.

7. All of these are standards of proof except
   a. statistical significance.
   b. preponderance of evidence.
   c. beyond a reasonable doubt.
   d. clear and convincing proof.

8. The most stringent standard of proof is
   a. statistical significance.
   b. preponderance of evidence.
   c. beyond a reasonable doubt.
   d. clear and convincing proof.

9. According to the Supreme Court, the minimum standard of proof for involuntary commitment should be
   a. statistical significance.
   b. preponderance of evidence.
   c. beyond a reasonable doubt.
   d. clear and convincing proof.

10. Someone unable to adequately care for himself or herself has _____ disability.
   a. behavioral
   b. grave
   c. lethal
   d. psychological

11. "Right to treatment" includes all these except
   a. individual treatment plan.
   b. attempt to cure.
   c. rationale for attempt to cure.
   d. cure.

12. Patients are best off when given _____-based treatment.
   a. community
   b. home
   c. hospital
   d. no difference

13. Thomas Szasz is opposed to
   a. voluntary commitment.
   b. involuntary commitment.
   c. criminal commitment.
   d. all commitment.

14. In what proportion of homicide cases is the insanity defense used?
   a. less than 1 percent
   b. 3 percent
   c. 25 percent
   d. 50 percent

15. The insanity plea is based on the notion of
   a. free will.
   b. due process.
   c. overdetermined behavior.
   d. clear and convincing proof.

16. What is the "right-wrong" test?
   a. Did the individual do something wrong?
   b. Did the individual know later that what he did was wrong?
   c. Did the individual know at the time that what he was doing was wrong?
   d. All of the above.

17. What is the "product of mental disease" test?
   a. Did the individual do something wrong?
   b. Did the individual know at the time that what he was doing was wrong?
   c. Did the individual suffer from mental disease at the time he did something wrong?
   d. Did the individual's wrong act result from mental disease?

18. Why was the "product of mental disease test" withdrawn?
   a. reliance on expert testimony by psychiatrists
   b. difficulty in defining mental disease
   c. both *a* and *b*
   d. neither *a* nor *b*

19. What is the "appreciate and conform" test?
   a. Did the individual do something wrong?
   b. Did the individual appreciate at the time that he did something wrong?
   c. Did the individual have the ability at the time to conform to the law?
   d. Did the individual cooperate after arrest?

20. Which test for the insanity plea is currently used?
   a. right-wrong test
   b. appreciate and conform test
   c. product of mental disease test
   d. all of the above
   e. none of the above

21. The text calls the "guilty but mentally ill" verdict
   a. contradictory.
   b. progressive.
   c. reactionary.
   d. unnecessary.

22. A defendant found incompetent to stand trial is
   a. more common than a defendant acquitted because of the insanity plea.
   b. as common as a defendant acquitted because of the insanity plea.
   c. less common than a defendant acquitted because of the insanity plea.

23. Incompetent to stand trial means that the defendant
    a. was mentally ill when the crime of which he was accused was committed.
    b. is mentally ill at the time of the trial.
    c. cannot understand the proceedings of the trial.
    d. cannot assist in her own defense.

24. A person who will never be competent to stand trial
    a. can be held indefinitely.
    b. cannot be held indefinitely.

25. Potentials for abuse in the diagnosis of mental illness arise from all these except
    a. political motives.
    b. problems in defining abnormality.
    c. changing criteria for abnormality.
    d. due process.

26. Individuals committed involuntarily for political reasons probably have which elements of abnormality?
    a. observer discomfort
    b. unconventionality
    c. irrationality
    d. none of the above

27. Abuse of the mentally ill by the state and abuse of the mentally ill by society are similar in that
    a. both occur in the Soviet Union but not in the United States.
    b. both are motivated by fear.
    c. both are rare.
    d. all of the above.

Answer Key for Sample Exam

1.	b (p. 604)	15.	a (p. 618)
2.	a (p. 605)	16.	c (p. 621)
3.	b, c (p. 606)	17.	d (p. 622)
4.	a (p. 608)	18.	c (p. 622)
5.	d (p. 608)	19.	b, c (p. 623)
6.	b (p. 610)	20.	b (p. 622)
7.	a (p. 611)	21.	a (p. 624)
8.	c (p. 611)	22.	a (p. 624)
9.	d (p. 612)	23.	c, d (p. 624)
10.	b (p. 609)	24.	b (p. 625)
11.	d (p. 613)	25.	d (p. 626)
12.	a (p. 615)	26.	a, b (p. 628)
13.	b (p. 616)	27.	b (p. 630)
14.	a (p. 618)		

SELF-TEST

1. The process by which the state hospitalizes people for their own good over their protest is _____.

2. For involuntary commitment, all states require that the individual be suffering from a _____, but this is poorly defined.

3. Among the incapacitating conditions required for involuntary commitment are _____, _____, _____, and _____.

4. It is extremely difficult to predict _____.

5. The rights and privileges accorded to citizens by the law are collectively termed _____. This may be violated in cases of involuntary commitment.

6. Three standards of proof, in increasing stringency, are _____, _____, and _____.

7. If individuals are committed involuntarily, they also have the right to _____.

8. One of the major consequences of guaranteeing greater rights to mental patients is that these patients have increasingly been _____.

9. The legal defense that claims a defendant not to have a "guilty mind" is the _____.

10. The insanity defense claims that the defendant was irrational_____ .

11. The insanity defense is invoked in_____ percent of homicide cases that come to trial.

12. Historically, there have been three views of the insanity defense. First, the M'Naghten rule asks if the defendant knew_____ from_____; second, the Durham rule asks if the crime was produced by_____; and third, the ALI rule asks if the defendant appreciated the_____ of his or her conduct or lacked the ability to _____ to the requirements of the law.

13. Much more common than the insanity defense is the defendant's_____.

14. Until recently, there was_____ on how long people could be held until judged competent to stand trial.

15. Political abuse of abnormal psychology capitalizes on whether people possess a_____ to abnormal people; also important are_____ conceptions of abnormality and the enormous_____ given to psychiatrists and psychologists by the state.

16. State abuse of abnormal psychology is probably underlied by_____ .

17. Society_____ ordinary people who have sought mental health care.

Answer Key for Self-Test

1. involuntary commitment
2. psychological disability
3. impaired judgment; need for treatment; dangerousness; grave disability
4. dangerousness
5. due process
6. preponderance of evidence; clear and convincing proof; beyond a reasonable doubt
7. treatment
8. released
9. insanity plea
10. at the time of the crime
11. fewer than 1
12. right; wrong; mental disease; wrongfulness; conform
13. incompetence to stand trial
14. no limit
15. family resemblance; changing; power
16. fear
17. stigmatizes

TYING IT TOGETHER

Central to the law is the assumption of free will and individual responsibility. As you have seen, only the existential approach addresses this notion (Chapter 4). The other models of abnormality embrace an assumption of determinism and hence are at odds with the basis of our country's legal system. Nevertheless, law and psychology come into frequent contact with each other concerning matters of involuntary commitment, competence to stand trial, the insanity plea, and so on. A more insidious interaction also occurs: the abuse of abnormal psychology by the state and by society. Witch-hunts are not necessarily phenomena of the past (Chapter 2). This chapter details the attempts by law and psychology to meld the assumptions of the respective disciplines, since their interaction is inevitable. Law, like the field of abnormal psychology, evolves. As you read this chapter, important changes in the legal procedures detailed may be occurring.

The law can deal more satisfactorily with some instances of abnormality than with others. "Willful" abnormality seems to defy both legal and psychological intervention. Lifestyles that involve psychosomatic illness (Chapter 10), suicide attempts (Chapter 11), drug abuse (Chapter 14), and antisocial activities (Chapter 15) are similar, but they are regarded differently by the law. A historical view (Chapter 2) partly explains this inconsistency, but it does not suggest how to resolve it.

Chapter 18 observes that legal, political, and social abuse may inadvertently result from the fuzzy nature of abnormality. That is, the family resemblance idea helps explain the lack of precision associated with the identification, explanation, and treatment of abnormality. It is unfortunate that most people are not accustomed to thinking in terms of family resemblances. The legal system in particular is at odds with such a formulation. Perhaps if abnormality and its fuzzy nature were better understood, both inadvertent and intentional abuses occasioned by observer discomfort (Chapter 1) would be decreased.

FURTHER READINGS

Coleman, L. (1984). *The reign of error: Psychiatry, authority, and law.* Boston: Beacon.

Fireside, H. (1979). *Soviet psychoprisons.* New York: Norton.

Goffman, E. (1961). *Asylums: Essays on the social situation of mental patients and other inmates.* Garden City, NY: Anchor.

Insanity defense: Under fire. (1981, April 20). *U.S. News & World Report*, p. 11.

Kesey, K. (1962). *One flew over the cuckoo's nest.* New York: New American Library.

Mathews, T., & Cook, W. J. (1976, March 1). Patty's defense. *Newsweek*, pp. 20–24.

Medvedev, Z. A., & Medvedev, R. A. (1979). *A question of madness.* New York: Norton.

Szasz, T. S. (1961). *The myth of mental illness.* New York: Harper & Row.

Szasz, T. S. (1970). *The manufacture of madness: A comparative study of the Inquisition and the Mental Health Movement.* New York: Dell.

TERM-PAPER TOPICS

1. What are current opinions within psychology and within society at large about the insanity plea? Do you think changes may be made in response to these opinions?

2. Chapter 18 describes several ways in which the legal system comes into contact with abnormality. What other ways may occur in the years to come?

3. In recent years, the rights of research subjects have been articulated, and legislation has been enacted to protect them. Describe this legislation. Describe its effect on psychological research. Has this been good or bad?

4. The federal government awards millions of dollars in research grants to psychologists. What political and ethical issues are raised by this relationship? Is there reason for alarm?

5. How frequently are individuals involuntarily committed to mental hospitals for political reasons? How can such cases be recognized?

EXERCISES

Exercise One—Beliefs about the Insanity Plea

Talk to a number of individuals of your acquaintance about the insanity plea. Ask them these questions:

1. What are the grounds for pleading insanity?
2. How are these grounds established?
3. How frequently is the insanity plea made?
4. With what success is the insanity plea made?
5. Is the insanity plea necessary?
6. Can a person be both guilty and insane?
7. What changes in the insanity plea may be made?

Which beliefs are consistent with what is known about abnormality? Which are inconsistent? What is your attitude toward the insanity plea?

Bromberg, W. (1979). *The uses of psychiatry in the law: A clinical view of forensic psychiatry.* Westport, CT: Quorum Books.

Exercise Two—Commitment

The purpose of this exercise is to learn about commitment procedures in your community.

Arrange a panel discussion for your class in which a lawyer, judge, psychiatrist, and psychologist explain how individuals are involuntarily committed in your town. What safeguards are present? How frequently do commitments occur? Do you agree with local procedures?

Exercise Three—Persecution and Abnormality

In this exercise, you will learn about abuses of psychology by the state.

Arrange a classroom lecture by someone from Amnesty International. Ask this person to speak in particular about persecution in the guise of psychological treatment. What examples of such persecution are provided? What is the evidence that this persecution has occurred? In what countries is such persecution most likely? What can be done to prevent these abuses of psychology?

CHAPTER 19

A Consumer's Guide to Psychological Treatment

CHAPTER OVERVIEW

The final chapter of the textbook synthesizes much of the previous material by presenting a guide to choosing a form of psychotherapy. There are a number of factors common to all successful psychotherapy: client characteristics such as free choice, hope, and appropriate expectations, therapist characteristics such as warmth, empathy, and genuineness, and a good working relationship between the client and the therapist. There are things to be wary of in a therapist as well.

Methods of psychotherapy may be either global or specific. Prominent approaches to therapy are based on the various models of abnormality: biomedical, psychoanalytic, behavioral, cognitive, and existential. The bulk of the chapter describes which specific therapy seems best indicated for which specific disorder.

Community psychology attempts to prevent and contain disorders. As such, it is an important adjunct to traditional therapy, which is undertaken only after a problem has developed.

ESSENTIAL TERMS

Alcoholics Anonymous (AA)	group for treatment of alcoholism that stresses self-help, group support, and hope
aversion therapy	behavior therapy technique in which an undesired behavior is eliminated by pairing it with aversive consequences
behavior therapy	therapy based on the learning approach
biological therapy	specific therapy that attempts to resolve problems by physiological intervention; e.g., electroconvulsive shock
child-care	safe and healthy environment for preschool children whose parents work
cognitive restructuring	specific therapy that attempts to illuminate irrational thoughts, to make clear their irrational basis, and thereby to change them
cognitive therapy	therapy developed by Aaron T. Beck which attempts to change thoughts and justifications of depressed or anxious patients (*see* Chapters 5 and 11, "Essential Terms")

common treatment factors	factors that determine the success of a therapy above and beyond the specific techniques and orientations of the therapist
community psychology	approach to psychological problems that attempts to prevent and contain them
consciousness raising group	variant of the self-help group composed of individuals with similar political and/or intellectual beliefs who together explore "personal" problems
containment service	community psychology program that attempts to limit the consequences of psychological crises
contingency contracting	behavior therapy technique in which desired behavior is increased and undesired behavior is decreased by drawing up a contract that stipulates rewards and punishments for relevant behaviors
contingency management	behavior therapy technique in which frequency of behavior is changed by altering consequences of behavior
controlled drinking	goal of some treatments for alcohol abuse: not abstinence but restricted intake
covert sensitization	behavior therapy technique in which aversion to unwanted behavior is induced by pairing that behavior with vividly imagined aversive consequences
crises treatment	short-term psychotherapy for psychological crises in which the therapist is extremely active, helping the client focus on problems, providing support, and devising solutions
day hospital (or night hospital)	part-time hospital intended to serve as a transition from full-time hospitalization to discharge and as a treatment center for those who were never hospitalized
dereflection	existential therapy technique in which client's attention is turned from symptoms to what may be done for him- or herself and others in the absence of preoccupation with symptoms (*see* Chapter 4, "Essential Terms")
dream analysis	psychoanalytic technique in which the latent meaning of a dream's manifest content is interpreted to reveal unconscious conflicts
electroconvulsive shock therapy	therapy for depression in which an electric current is passed through the brain of the patient (*see* Chapter 11, "Essential Terms")
empathy	characteristic of a successful therapist: the ability to understand experiences and feelings and to explain their meaning to the client during psychotherapy
existential therapy	global therapy based on existential psychology in which the client is encouraged to take responsibility for his or her problems
flooding	behavior therapy technique in which anxiety is extinguished by exposing the client to actual fear-producing situations (*see* Chapters 5 and 8, "Essential Terms")
free association	technique of psychoanalytic therapy in which the client relaxes and says whatever comes to mind

genuineness	characteristic of a successful therapist: the ability to avoid communicating in a phony or defensive manner
Gestalt therapy	global therapy developed by Fritz Perls in which the client is encouraged to live in the "here and now" (*see* Chapter 4, "Essential Terms")
global therapy	therapy that attempts to resolve psychological problems by changing the underlying personality problems (cr. specific therapy)
halfway house	domicile with only paraprofessionals in residence, intended as a transition between hospital and community; community lodge
hot-line	twenty-four hour phone service for people who are undergoing deep distress
implosion	variant of flooding in which the client imagines fearful scenes
incompatible behavior	behavior therapy technique in which undesired behavior is eliminated by training the person to engage in behavior that makes undesired behavior difficult to perform; e.g., systematic desensitization
insight therapy	global therapy that encourages personal insight into sources of psychological problems
job training and retraining	community psychology program for training the unemployed in skills necessary to find and keep jobs
lithium	drug used to treat bipolar depression and mania (*see* Chapter 11, "Essential Terms")
MAO inhibitor	drug used to treat depression; it blocks the breakdown of norepinephrine (*see* Chapter 11, "Essential Terms")
marriage and family counselor	therapist who treats relationship problems that arise within the family
methadone maintenance	biological therapy for heroin addiction in which methadone is substituted for heroin (*see* Chapter 14, "Essential Terms")
modeling	behavior therapy technique in which the client is exposed to desired behavior modeled by another person (*see* Chapter 8, "Essential Terms")
Operation Headstart	community psychology program for preschool children that intends to encourage development of cognitive and intellectual skills necessary for school
paradoxical intention	existential therapy technique in which the client is encouraged to indulge and exaggerate symptoms (*see* Chapter 4, "Essential Terms")
placebo effect	positive treatment outcome resulting from administration of placebo (*see* Chapter 6, "Essential Terms")
psychiatric attendant	paraprofessional who works exclusively in psychiatric hospitals; psychiatric aide
psychiatric nurse	nurse specializing in the care of hospitalized psychiatric patients

psychiatric social worker	social worker who has completed a two-year postgraduate program in individual and group social-work techniques, including extensive training in interviewing and treatment
psychiatrist	physician who has completed three-year residency in mental-health facility
psychoanalysis	global therapy based on psychoanalytic theory that attempts to make unconscious impulses conscious so that an acceptable means of satisfying them can be found
psychoanalyst	therapist, usually a psychiatrist, with training in psychoanalysis
psychological therapy	systematic series of interactions between a trained therapist who has been authorized by society to minister to psychological problems and one or more clients who are troubled, or troubling others, because of such problems; the goal of psychological therapy is to produce cognitive, emotional, and behavioral changes that will alleviate the problems
psychologist	individual with advanced graduate training in clinical, counseling, or school psychology who offers psychological assessment and therapeutic services
clinical psychologist	psychologist who works mainly with psychological difficulties
consulting psychologist	psychologist who works with psychological difficulties and vocational problems
school psychologist	psychologist who works with academic difficulties, mainly among children
rational-emotive therapy	therapy founded by Albert Ellis that attempts to change the irrational beliefs of an individual (*see* Chapter 5, "Essential Terms")
residential treatment center	approach to treatment of distressed individuals in the community or special residences, without hospitalization
Role Induction Interview	brief interview prior to therapy in which expectations of clients about treatment are molded
self-help group	community of former patients who have banded together to help each other
skills therapist	therapist with special training in work-related, recreational, and/or artistic techniques
specific therapy	therapy that attempts to resolve psychological problems without changing underlying personality problems (cf. global therapy)
stimulus control	behavior therapy technique in which the likelihood of a behavior is increased by magnifying stimuli that promote that behavior and eliminating stimuli that undercut it
Synanon	self-help live-in community for treatment of narcotic addiction

systematic desensitization	behavior therapy technique in which stimuli that elicit fear are paired with relaxation or other pleasant experiences (*see* Chapters 5 and 8, "Essential Terms")
therapeutic alliance	relationship between client and therapist characterized by shared sense of goals of treatment and how they can best be achieved
time out	behavior therapy technique in which undesired behavior is eliminated by removing the client to a "neutral" environment when that behavior is manifested
TOPS (Take Off Pounds Sensibly)	group for the treatment of obesity that provides information and social support
transference	in psychoanalysis, transfer by clients of emotions, conflicts, and expectations from diverse sources on to their therapist (*see* Chapter 4, "Essential Terms")
tricyclic	drug used to treat depression that blocks reuptake of norepinephrine (*see* Chapter 11, "Essential Terms")
warmth	characteristic of a successful therapist: the ability to communicate deep and genuine caring to the client
Weight Watchers	group for the treatment of obesity; it provides information and social support

SAMPLE EXAM

1. What percent of Americans will see a psychotherapist at some point in their lives?
   a. 1
   b. 10
   c. 20
   d. 33
   3. 50

2. Which one of the following has a Ph.D degree?
   a. psychologist
   b. psychiatrist
   c. psychiatric social worker
   d. psychiatric nurse

3. Which one of the following has medical training?
   a. psychologist
   b. psychiatrist
   c. psychiatric social worker
   d. psychiatric nurse

4. Which one of the following works almost exclusively in a hospital?
   a. psychologist
   b. psychiatrist
   c. psychiatric social worker
   d. psychiatric nurse

5. Common treatment factors include all of the following but
   a. choice by the client.
   b. training of the therapist.
   c. expectations of the client.
   d. personal qualities of the therapist.

6. The purpose of the Role Induction Interview is to
   a. mold client expectations about treatment.
   b. make a diagnosis.
   c. ascertain a prognosis.
   d. all of the above.

7. Which of the following is(are) not characteristics of placebo effects?
   a. probably shams
   b. possibly mediated by endorphins
   c. often powerful
   d. well understood

8. All of the following are characteristics of the successful therapist except
   a. empathy.
   b. warmth.
   c. genuineness.
   d. experience.

9. Therapeutic alliance refers to shared
   a. goals.
   b. personality characteristics.
   c. problems.
   d. rationales.

10. A client should be wary of all these except
    a. an obnoxious therapist.
    b. a friendly therapist.
    c. sexual exploitation by therapist.
    d. a suspiciously expensive therapist.
    e. lack of treatment goals.

11. The most effective therapies are those associated with the
    a. biomedical model.
    b. psychodynamic model.
    c. behavioral model.
    d. cognitive model.
    e. none of the above.

12. All of the following are ways to assess the effectiveness of psychotherapy except
    a. termination of treatment.
    b. personal satisfaction.
    c. personality change.
    d. target behavior change.

13. Does any federal body monitor and regulate psychotherapies?
    a. yes
    b. no

14. Which of these therapies is a specific therapy?
    a. psychoanalysis
    b. cognitive therapy
    c. electroconvulsive shock therapy
    d. all of the above

15. Insight therapies are mainly associated with the
    a. biomedical model.
    b. psychodynamic model.
    c. behavioral model.
    d. cognitive model.
    e. existential model.
    f. none of the above.

16. All of these are behavioral therapies except
    a. systematic desensitization.
    b. flooding.
    c. lithium.
    d. time out.

17. All of these are behavior therapy techniques except
    a. stimulus control.
    b. behavioral contrast.
    c. covert sensitization.
    d. time out.

18. Which one of the following is most similar to cognitive therapy?
    a. rational-emotive therapy
    b. Rolfing
    c. psychoanalysis
    d. Gestalt therapy

19. If you had a problem with fear, you would choose a therapy associated with the
    a. biomedical model.
    b. psychodynamic model.
    c. behavioral model.
    d. cognitive model.
    e. none of the above.

20. If you had a problem with anxiety, you would choose a therapy associated with the
    a. biomedical model.
    b. psychodynamic model.
    c. behavioral model.
    d. cognitive model.
    e. none of the above.

21. If you had a problem with obsessions, you would choose a therapy based on the
    a. biomedical model.
    b. psychodynamic model.
    c. behavioral model.
    d. cognitive model.
    e. none of the above.

22. If you had a problem with compulsions, you would choose a therapy based on the
    a. biomedical model.
    b. psychodynamic model.
    c. behavioral model.
    d. cognitive model.
    e. none of the above.

23. If you had a problem with depression, you would choose a therapy derived from the
    a. biomedical model.
    b. psychodynamic model.
    c. behavioral model.
    d. cognitive model.
    e. none of the above.

24. If you had a problem with bipolar depression, you would choose a therapist who advocated the
    a. biomedical model.
    b. psychodynamic model.
    c. behavioral model.
    d. cognitive model.
    e. none of the above.

25. Which model gives rise to a therapy for sexual dysfunction that is as successful as

direct sexual therapy as used by Masters and Johnson?
a. biomedical model
b. psychodynamic model
c. behavioral model
d. cognitive model
e. existential model
f. none of the above

26. For which of these problems is the least successful treatment available?
a. phobia
b. addiction
c. depression
d. sexual dysfunction

27. The problem with treating smoking is
a. initial stopping.
b. relapse.
c. both.
d. neither.

28. About _____ of smokers who quit start again within the following year.
a. 10%
b. 25%
c. 50%
d. 75%
e. 90%

29. Treatment of heroin addiction with methadone maintenance is an example of the
a. biomedical model.
b. psychodynamic model.
c. behavioral model.
d. cognitive model.
e. none of the above.

30. Synanon is to AA as what is to alcohol?
a. narcotics
b. obesity
c. agoraphobia
d. schizophrenia

31. The problem with obesity is
a. losing weight.
b. maintaining weight loss.
c. both *a* and *b*.
d. neither *a* nor *b*.

32. Anorexia appears best treated with techniques derived from the
a. biomedical model.
b. psychodynamic model.
c. behavioral model.
d. cognitive model.
e. none of the above.

33. Bulimia appears best treated with techniques derived from the
a. biomedical model.
b. psychodynamic model.

c. behavioral model.
d. cognitive model.
e. none of the above.

34. The quickest treatments for schizophrenia are associated with the
a. biomedical model.
b. psychodynamic model.
c. behavioral model.
d. cognitive model.
e. existential model.
f. none of the above.

35. The text concludes that _____ treatment is needed for schizophrenia.
a. biological
b. psychological
c. both
d. neither

36. Self-exploration is best accomplished through therapy based on the
a. biomedical model.
b. psychodynamic model.
c. behavioral model.
d. cognitive model.
e. existential model.
f. none of the above.

37. The purpose of community psychology is captured by
a. "Don't fire until you see the whites of their eyes."
b. "A stitch in time saves nine."
c. "I love you for your pink Cadillac."
d. "Nice guys finish last."

38. All of the following are examples of community psychology except
a. child-care.
b. Operation Headstart.
c. Watergate.
d. job retraining.

39. Hot-lines are most similar to
a. crisis treatment.
b. psychoanalysis.
c. logotherapy.
d. Gestalt therapy.

40. The first hot-line was established for
a. child abuse.
b. drug overdose.
c. spouse abuse.
d. suicide.

41. All of these are examples of containment except
a. hot-lines.
b. crisis treatment.
c. Operation Headstart.
d. shelters for battered women.

42. Which one of the following does not belong?
    a. ostracism
    b. day hospital
    c. night hospital
    d. halfway house

43. Which one of the following does not belong?
    a. AA
    b. CR group
    c. N.Y. Yankees
    d. TOPS

Answer Key for Sample Exam

1. c (p. 633)	4. d (p. 635)	7. a, d (p. 640)
2. a (p. 635)	5. b (p. 638)	8. d (p. 641)
3. b (p. 635)	6. a (p. 639)	9. a (p. 643)

7. a, d (p. 640)   26. b (p. 659)
8. d (p. 641)   27. b (p. 659)
9. a (p. 643)   28. d (p. 659)
10. b (p. 645)   29. a (p. 661)
11. e (p. 646)   30. a (p. 662)
12. a (p. 647)   31. b (p. 662)
13. b (p. 648)   32. c, d (p. 663)
14. c (p. 648)   33. c, d (p. 664)
15. b, e (p. 648)   34. a (p. 664)
16. c (p. 650)   35. c (p. 665)
17. b (p. 650)   36. b, e (p. 666)
18. a (p. 651)   37. b (p. 667)
19. c (p. 656)   38. c (p. 668)
20. c (p. 656)   39. a (p. 670)
21. e (p. 657)   40. d (p. 670)
22. c (p. 657)   41. c (p. 669)
23. a, b, d (p. 657)   42. a (p. 673)
24. a (p. 659)   43. c (p. 674)
25. f (p. 659)

SELF-TEST

1. The goal of psychological therapy is to produce _____, _____, and _____ changes that will alleviate psychological problems.

2. Clinical psychologists usually have a _____ degree, while psychiatrists have a _____ degree.

3. Successful psychotherapy depends on the establishment of a good _____.

4. Common treatment factors include the _____ of the client, his or her _____ and _____, the _____ of the therapist, and the _____ between the client and the therapist.

5. To shape client expectations about psychotherapy, some therapists conduct a _____.

6. Positive treatment outcomes resulting from inert interventions are _____.

7. Good therapists, regardless of orientation, tend to have personal qualities of _____, _____, and _____.

8. Therapist _____ is not clearly related to effectiveness.

9. Therapists should be avoided who seem _____, _____, and _____.

10. Therapists should freely _____ and _____.

11. Among the criteria with which to assess successful psychotherapy are _____, _____, and _____.

12. At the present time, the federal government _____ regulate psychotherapies.

13. _____ therapies do not attempt to alter personality, while _____ therapies do attempt to do so, usually through _____ .

14. The two classes of specific therapies are _____ therapies and _____ therapies.

15. Drugs and electroconvulsive shock are examples of _____ therapies.

16. Systematic desensitization, flooding, and modeling are _____ techniques.

17. Rational-emotive therapy is an example of _____ therapy and is similar to the therapy for depression developed by _____ .

18. Global therapies are mainly those based on the _____ model or the _____ model.

19. Free association is a technique of _____ .

20. Paradoxical intention and dereflection are used in _____ therapy.

21. For fears and phobias, the treatment of choice is based on the _____ model.

22. For compulsions, the treatment of choice is based on the _____ model.

23. The treatment of choice for bipolar depression is _____ ; for unipolar depression, there are _____ successful treatments.

24. For sexual dysfunctions, one would probably seek out _____ .

25. Treatment of the addictions seems to require a _____ approach.

26. The quickest treatment for schizophrenia is _____ , but long-term treatment may entail _____ as well.

27. Global therapies are best for achieving the goals of _____ and changing the _____ .

28. Community psychology attempts to _____ and _____ psychological problems. Child-care and job training are examples of _____ , while "hot-lines" and crisis treatment are examples of _____ .

29. Alternatives to the traditional mental hospital have recently been developed and include _____ hospitals, _____ houses, _____ treatment centers, and _____ groups.

Answer Key for Self-Test

1. cognitive; emotional; behavioral
2. Ph.D.; M.D.
3. therapeutic alliance
4. free choice; hopes; expectations; personal qualities; match
5. Role Induction Interview
6. placebo effects
7. empathy; warmth; genuineness
8. experience
9. obnoxious; sexually exploitative; expensive
10. answer questions; set treatment goals

11. personal satisfaction; personality change; impact of treatment on target behaviors
12. does not
13. Specific; global; insight
14. biological; psychological
15. biological
16. behavioral
17. cognitive; Beck
18. psychodynamic; existential
19. psychoanalysis
20. existential
21. behavioral
22. behavioral
23. lithium; several
24. direct sexual therapy
25. broad-spectrum
26. neuroleptics; milieu therapy
27. self-exploration; self
28. prevent; contain; prevention; containment
29. day (night); halfway; residential; self-help

TYING IT TOGETHER

The textbook has described the field of psychopathology. How is abnormality defined (Chapter 1)? What has been its history (Chapter 2)? How is it explained (Chapters 3–5)? How is it investigated (Chapter 6) and assessed (Chapter 7)? What are the major types of abnormality (Chapters 8–17)? And what is the legal and political context of abnormality (Chapter 18)?

It is appropriate that the textbook ends with a discussion of how abnormality is treated. Abnormal psychology has always been concerned with how best to alleviate the suffering of individuals who have psychological problems, and the creation of effective treatment is the bottom line of the field. To this end, explanation, research, and diagnosis are undertaken. It is necessary and often useful to distinguish among types of abnormality. None of these is a pure type; rather, each is defined by a family resemblance. Abnormality involves disorders ar a variety of levels—biological, emotional, behavioral, and cognitive—and any given therapy is directed at the level thought to be disordered. This last chapter presents state-of-the-art knowledge about which therapy is best for which problem. It is based on the information presented in the rest of the textbook.

FURTHER READINGS

Bloch, S. (1982). *What is psychotherapy?* New York: Oxford University Press.

Frank, J. D. (1974). *Persuasion and healing: A comparative study of psychotherapy.* Rev. ed. New York: Schocken.

Garfield, S. L. (1981). Psychotherapy: A 40-year appraisal. *American Psychologist, 36,* 174–183.

Garfield, S. L., & Bergin, A. E. (1986). *Handbook of psychotherapy and behavior change.* 3rd ed. New York: Wiley.

TERM-PAPER TOPICS

1. Only recently have well-managed investigations of therapy effectiveness been conducted. What difficulties had to be solved before these investigations could be done? What difficulties remain?

2. Compare and contrast the specific training of the various mental-health professionals. What conclusions do you draw on the basis of your results about how best to choose a psychotherapist?

3. In recent years, many mental patients have been discharged into the community. What effect has this had on the former patients? What effect has this had on the community?

EXERCISES

Exercise One—Repackaging Chapter 19

The purpose of this exercise is to organize the treatment recommendations made in Chapter 19 in a different format.

Recast the text material from Chapter 19 in the form of a *Consumer Reports* article. Use tables and ratings similar to those in *Consumer Reports*. Is this a better way to present these ideas, or not?

Exercise Two—Treatment Referrals

In this exercise, you will practice making therapy referrals for different types of psychological problems.

Based on what you have learned, make an educated suggestion about the form of therapy indicated for the following individuals:

1. a six-year old girl has trouble learning how to read
2. a middle-aged man drinks a case of beer every evening
3. your mother is deathly afraid of German shepherds
4. a teenage girl has stopped eating anything except tuna fish
5. a thirty-year-old man barricades himself at home and claims that the CIA is persecuting him
6. a college student attempts suicide
7. your father is found wandering the streets, not knowing who he is
8. your elderly neighbor suddenly loses his ability to speak
9. your sister, who is twenty years old, washes her hands 250 times per day
10. your spouse reports no satisfaction from sexual intercourse

Compare your referral suggestions to those of your classmates.

Exercise Three—Different Psychotherapies

The purpose of this exercise is to compare and contrast psychotherapy as practiced by different professionals.

Arrange a panel discussion for your class by several different mental-health practitioners: clinical psychologist, counseling psychologist, psychiatrist, psychiatric social workers, and so on. Ask them to address what is common to their therapy approaches and what is different. What conclusions about therapy do your reach?